Cyril Burt
Psychologist

CYRIL BURT
Psychologist

L. S. HEARNSHAW

Vintage Books

A DIVISION OF RANDOM HOUSE

NEW YORK

First Vintage Books Edition, April 1981

Copyright © 1979 by L.S. Hearnshaw

All rights reserved under International and Pan-American Copyright
Conventions. Published in the United States by Random House, Inc.,
New York, and simultaneously in Canada by Random House of
Canada Limited, Toronto. Originally published by Cornell
University Press, Ithaca, in 1979.

Library of Congress Cataloging in Publication Data
Hearnshaw, Leslie Spencer.
Cyril Burt, psychologist.
Reprint of the ed. published by Cornell University Press, Ithaca.
Bibliography: p.
Includes indexes.
1. Burt, Cyril Lodowic, 1883-1971. 2. Psychologists—England
—Biography. I. Burt, Cyril Lodowic, Sir, 1883-1971. II. Title.
[BF109.B88H4 1981]   150'.92'4   80-6131
ISBN 0-394-74689-9

Manufactured in the United States of America

Contents

Preface   vii

1. Background and Education   1
2. Influences Shaping Burt's Psychology   16
3. Liverpool and the London County Council   25
4. Innate General Cognitive Ability   46
5. The Subnormal and the Gifted   72
6. Applied Psychology   87
7. Developments in English Education   111
8. University College, London   128
9. Factors of the Mind   154
10. Years of Retirement   182
11. Subsidiary Interests   211
12. Posthumous Controversies   227
13. The Man   262
14. The Psychologist   292

Appendixes

1. List of Publications by Cyril Burt   321
2. Theses Presented by Burt's Students   339
3. The Burt Archives   348
4. General Bibliography   353

Index of Names   361
Index of Topics   366

Preface

I must begin by recounting the origins of this book. A few days after Cyril Burt's death at the age of 88 on 10 October 1971, I received a telephone call from London asking me if I would deliver the address at the Memorial Service in his honour which had been arranged for the afternoon of October 21st in St Mary's Church, Primrose Hill. I was a little surprised at this request as I had not myself been a pupil or a colleague of Burt, and my contacts with him had been mainly official, as a fellow examiner and committee member, and I had only once visited him at his flat in Elsworthy Road. My only qualification for undertaking the task was as an historian of British psychology, who had written favourably about his work and influence. However, I agreed to accept the assignment, and the Memorial Address that I delivered on that occasion was subsequently published in the *Bulletin* of the British Psychological Society. After the service I met and talked to Cyril Burt's sister, Dr Marion Burt, and a month later I received a letter from her asking me if I would write a full-length biography of her brother. I replied that owing to University and other commitments it would be impossible for me to get down to this immediately, but that I should be interested in undertaking it, provided that the work could be spread over some years. This was agreed, and Dr Marion Burt generously provided me with a grant of £300 to cover incidental expenses.

Concurrently with these negotiations I also received an invitation from the Secretary of the British Academy, of which Burt had been a Fellow, to write a 6,000 word memoir for the 1972 volume of their *Proceedings*, which was due to appear in October 1972. I accepted this invitation also, and sent my obituary memoir to the Secretary on 15 August 1972. At this time my assessment of Burt and his work was almost wholly favourable. My own standpoint in psychology was, and indeed still is, broadly in accord with his. I knew from my contacts with Burt as examiner and committee member that he could be difficult and prickly in business matters, but I regarded this as the justifiable prerogative of a great man in his dealings with lesser mortals. When approached for information I had always found him, as others did, too, exceedingly generous in his response. It never occurred to me to suspect his integrity. I must admit, however, that at that time, although I had read most of Burt's pre-1940 writings, I was familiar with only a fraction of his huge post-war output of articles.

It took me some years to read through the corpus of Burt's writings and the large collection of correspondence, memoranda, diaries, lecture notes and other material handed over to me by Dr Marion Burt and by Cyril Burt's secretary-housekeeper, Miss G. Archer. I could not commence the task of writing until after I had retired from my chair at the University of Liverpool in September 1975, and returned from an extended trip to Australia and New Zealand the following year. By that time attitudes to Burt and his work had changed dramatically. Kamin's *Science and Politics of I.Q.* had been published in October 1974, and shortly after I had started the actual writing of my own book in September 1976, Oliver Gillie's *Sunday Times* article unleashed a flood of denigration over Burt's reputation. Burt's work had become problematic, and his integrity a matter of doubt. Though it did not seem to me that Gillie had convincingly proved his charge of fraud, the problems he pointed to were undoubtedly genuine problems, which could not be dismissed outright, and these, together with the anomalies noted by Kamin, and confirmed by Jensen, rendered my task both unexpectedly different, and far more difficult than I had anticipated when I undertook it.

All this involved me in a good deal of extra research, particularly in the Greater London and University College Record Offices, and the University of London Library, and a further detailed analysis of Burt's own diaries and papers. Moreover it had obviously become embarrassing to be dependent on Burt's sister for financial support. I wrote to her in November 1976 informing her that a good deal of extra work was going to be needed, and that it was desirable that the expenses involved should be covered by an entirely independent source. I was grateful, therefore, when the Research Awards Advisory Committee of the Leverhulme Trust Fund informed me in March 1977 that they had awarded me one of their Emeritus Fellowships to cover the additional expenses needed for the extended investigations now required.

Gradually, as evidence accumulated from a variety of sources, I became convinced that the charges against Burt were, in their essentials, valid, and the problem became that of explaining how a man of Burt's eminence and exceptional gifts could have succumbed in this way. The problem became, in fact, a medico-psychological one. I am not so rash as to suppose that I have by any means cleared up all the mysteries raised by Burt's work. I hope, however, that I have succeeded in establishing the main outlines of the solutions, and that my verdicts will seem both soundly based and fair. I have tried to pay tribute to Burt's many achievements and many positive qualities without disguising his culpable shortcomings.

A book of this kind, which has been written for the general reader as well as for psychologists, and which is restricted in length, cannot go into abstruse technicalities. However, it has been impossible to discuss Burt's work without employing a number of technical terms, and the general reader who finds some of these unfamiliar may be referred to *The Penguin Dictionary of Psychology* (J. Drever) or the Fontana/Collins *Encyclopedia of Psychology* (H. J. Eysenck, W. J. Arnold and R. Meili). Burt's publications covered very wide ground, and often manifested a high level of mathematical, as well as psychological and philosophical expertise— so much so that it would be difficult for any one commentator to cover every aspect of them adequately. To the experts my treatment of technical issues will at times seem too brief and too perfunctory: I make no apology for this. My intention has been to provide a balanced sketch of the whole of Burt's life and work, leaving the discussion of highly technical detailed matters to the learned journals and the experts— if indeed these matters are still of current interest; for I believe that Burt's work is by now mainly a concern for historians.

I could not have carried out the task of writing Burt's biography without a great deal of help from others. In particular I have had the full cooperation of his sister, the late Dr Marion Burt, and his housekeeper-secretary, Miss Gretl Archer, to whom Sir Cyril bequeathed the bulk of his estate. They made available to me the large volume of correspondence, diaries, memoranda and other personal papers which have now been lodged in the Archives of the University of Liverpool. They have answered my queries, and commented constructively on some of the draft chapters I submitted to them. At the same time they never interfered, nor made any attempt to influence my judgments. At the beginning of April 1978 I felt that I could no longer honourably refrain from telling Dr Marion Burt the gist of my conclusions regarding her brother's later work. (She had up till then only seen drafts of my first and third chapters.) I had been reluctant to do this earlier, while my investigations were still in progress, as she was over 85 years of age, and had an enormous admiration for her brother. When Dr Gillie's article appeared in the *Sunday Times* Dr Marion Burt regarded it 'as a storm in a tea-cup', and remained 'convinced of

Cyril's integrity' (Letter, 18 November 1976). It was painful for
me to have to inform her that the evidence had finally forced me to
accept the accusations. Her response, I thought, was rather remarkable. She simply said that if I was to substantiate the charges I should
need much more space than the 100,000 words originally agreed
with the publishers. When I informed her that I had been granted
permission to extend the length of the book she replied, 'I am
delighted to know that you have been granted more space for the
biography' (Letter, 15 April 1978). This was my last letter from
Dr Marion Burt. I had arranged to visit Malvern and talk with her
the following month, but she died suddenly at the age of 87 on 14
May 1978. In my contacts and correspondence with her I acquired
a great respect for her shrewd intelligence and common sense. She
was for me a living exemplar of something of real quality in the
Burt family.

I am particularly grateful to those friends and former colleagues
who have read and commented on several of my draft chapters: Dr
Charlotte Banks, formerly of University College, London; Dr
C. B. Frisby and Mr D. F. Vincent, formerly of the National Institute
of Industrial Psychology; Professor D. W. Harding, formerly of
Bedford College, London; Dr S. Barton Hall, formerly Director of
the sub-department of Psychological Medicine in the University of
Liverpool; and Professor Alec Rodger, formerly of Birkbeck
College, London. I have made a number of changes in my text as
a result of their comments; but I have not always agreed with their
criticisms, and I alone am responsible for the text as published.

I must also thank the Archivists of the Greater London Record
Office, the British Psychological Society, the British Broadcasting
Corporation, and University College, London, Records Office, and
the Librarian of the Department of Education and Science, for their
help, and for the trouble they took to unearth material relating to
Burt.

I am grateful to numerous people who have given me permission to
quote from their letters. At the same time I must apologise to a number
of correspondents with whom I was unable to get in touch, and whom
I have quoted without permission. In no cases were their letters
marked 'Confidential'. I have to thank a large number of individuals
for writing to me, talking to me, or providing me with copies of their
correspondence with, or other material relating to, Burt. These
include: Professor R. J. Audley (University College, London); Professor L. B. Birch (McGill University); Professor P. L. Broadhurst
(University of Birmingham); Professor R. B. Cattell (University
of Hawaii); Professor A. D. B. and Dr Ann Clarke (University of
Hull); Professor J. Cohen (University of Manchester); Dr Agnes

Crawford (University of Liverpool); Professor G. C. Drew (University College, London); Professor H. J. Eysenck (Institute of Psychiatry, London); Professor H. E. Field (Canterbury University, New Zealand); Dr Fraser Roberts, F.R.S. (Guy's Hospital Genetic Centre); Mr L. J. Gue (Deputy Secretary, University College, London); Professor A. R. Jensen (University of California, Berkeley); Dr A. R. Jonckheere (University College, London); Professor C. E. M. Hansel (University College, Swansea); Mrs E. Harper (née Flugel); Professor R. Hinchcliffe (Institute of Laryngology and Otology, London); Professor Liam Hudson (Brunel University); Professor L. J. Kamin (Princeton University); Miss Gertrude Keir (University College, London); Mr M. McAskie (University of Hull); Professor D. W. McElwain (University of Queensland); Dr J. B. Parry (formerly of the War Office); the late Professor T. H. Pear (University of Manchester); Miss Margaret Proctor (Principal Educational Psychologist, Inner London Education Authority); Mrs Winifred Raphael (formerly of the National Institute of Industrial Psychology, London); Mr R. Rawles (University College, London); Mr R. S. Reid (Association of Educational Psychologists); Professor R. W. Russell (Vice-Chancellor, Flinders University, Adelaide); the late Dr R. R. Rusk (formerly of Glasgow); Mr V. Serebriakoff (President of Mensa); Dr J. Shields (Genetics Section, Institute of Psychiatry, London); Dr W. Stephenson (Columbia, Missouri); Professor A. Summerfield (Birkbeck College, London); Dr R. H. Thouless (University of Cambridge); Professor J. Tizard (Institute of Education, London) and Professor P. E. Vernon (University of Alberta).

I am grateful to Miss Pamela Yeomans of the Faculty of Arts office, University of Liverpool, for re-typing parts of my own typescript, and to my successor, Professor D. B. Bromley, for permitting me the continued use of the facilities of my old department. Finally I must thank my wife, Dr Gwenneth Hearnshaw, for her critical reading of the whole of my text, for many improvements of wording, and for her meticulous proof reading.

To all those former students and colleagues of Cyril Burt, who admired his intellectual powers and appreciated his help, I must apologise for any pain that parts of my biography may occasion. I, too, at one time had an unqualified admiration for Burt, and have no wish simply to disparage him. As an historian my only concern has been to ascertain and to state the truth to the best of my ability.

25 July 1978
L. S. Hearnshaw
Department of Psychology,
The University of Liverpool

CHAPTER ONE

Background and Education

Today, in the last half of the twentieth century, psychology has become an established profession. Academic departments of psychology are thronged with students, posts for psychologists are advertised almost daily in the press, and many young people are drawn towards careers in psychology. In the first decade of the century, however, the position was very different. There were no psychological jobs, apart from a few academic lectureships, and the number of students in the few universities where psychology was taught was insignificant. In the change that has taken place over three quarters of a century Cyril Burt, as far as Great Britain is concerned, led the way. He was the first person who was primarily a psychologist, the first to function as a psychologist outside the walls of a university. His psychological predecessors had been philosophers, medical men, educationists, biologists—men like Spencer, Bain, Darwin, Ward, Stout, McDougall and C. S. Myers—and even freelances like Galton. Burt was the first Britisher to devote his life simply and solely to psychology, who was paid for being a psychologist, and who never practised in any other field. As a pioneer his position is incontestable.

At the beginning of the century it required unusual circumstances to turn a young man towards such a doubtful and precarious career as psychology. What was it in Cyril Burt's make-up and background that steered him in this direction?

There had been a tradition of professional activity stretching over several generations in the Burt family, which came from the West Country on the borders of Somerset and Dorset. There are records of land near Montacute being granted to a Burt in Tudor days, and over six generations there were surgeons, ministers and teachers in the family. Burt's grandfather, George Edward Burt, who ran a chemist's shop first in Westminster, and then, after an unsuccessful venture in Canada, in Dulwich, had six children, five of whom emigrated to the United States, Australia or Canada, a descendant of the Canadian Burts becoming Professor of Electrochemistry in the University of Toronto. Grandfather Burt, though not markedly successful in worldly terms, had a lively and cultivated mind. His one extravagance was books, and his grandson, who took after him, was much influenced by his visits to the grandpaternal home in Feltham. His wife, Cyril's grandmother, was a Barrow, and claimed to be descended from Newton's mathematical tutor at Cambridge. The fourth of their six children, Cyril Cecil Barrow Burt, the only one remaining permanently in England, followed an old family tradition and took up a medical career. His early years were difficult ones. Born in 1857 he did not obtain his M.R.C.S. until 1887, and his L.R.C.P. until 1890. Long before he had qualified he had married in 1880 Martha Evans from Monmouth, of part Welsh descent, and Cyril Lodowic (a Saxon name), born on 3 March 1883, was the first of two children, his sister, Marion, being born eight years later, in 1891. To support his family Burt senior kept a chemist's shop, leaving his wife in charge when he was away in hospital. The Burts also took in student lodgers. On qualifying, he became an assistant house surgeon and obstetrical assistant at Westminster Hospital.

The Burts lived in London until 1892, and the young Cyril (who to distinguish him from his father was generally called Loddie at home) went first to a Board School near St James's Park, the family home being in a now much altered street named Petty France, once the quarter of French wool merchants, and the site of Milton's home from 1652 to 1660. The background of history and tradition which formed the setting throughout Burt's life in his formative years was, no doubt, to have an important influence on his cast of mind. By 1890 life in London was beginning to affect Dr Burt's health. A spell in Jersey, where Cyril went to a dame's school and picked up a smattering of French, failed to effect a cure, and in 1892 Dr Burt decided to leave London for a rural practice at Snitterfield, some five miles from Stratford-upon-Avon.[1] There, in a small village of a few hundred inhabitants, set in the midst of a beautiful, historic countryside, remote and isolated (as the Trevelyans who owned the Manor refused to allow the railway to run through their property), the Burt family resided for twenty-seven years. The practice, which Dr Burt ran single-handed, was never a prosperous one. Dr Burt's predecessor, who had been at Snitterfield for forty years, was keener on hunting than on medicine, and the practice had been neglected. In 1894 Dr Burt earned only £206 in fees, and to run a practice and a large house (which now houses a firm of four medical practitioners) together with a three-acre garden, he had to employ a domestic servant and a gardener-groom, and keep a horse and trap. Though the practice soon improved and

1. Dr Burt actively commenced practising in Snitterfield in October 1893, having held a stop-gap practice in Warwick for over a year.

extended to neighbouring villages, including Claverdon, where the Galtons lived, Dr Burt was too dedicated a doctor to press for fees from impoverished villagers who needed medical attention. So money was always tight, and financial stringency was to worry Cyril throughout his educational career, which was made possible only by his own success in winning scholarships. His later interest in opportunities for gifted children was a natural outcome of his own scholastic career.

From 1892 to 1895 Cyril went to King's School, Warwick, an ancient foundation dating back to the time of Edward the Confessor. He did well there, winning many prizes, and finally gaining a scholarship to Christ's Hospital, then still located in the City of London. The preparatory school regime was a strenuous one, for Snitterfield was six miles from Warwick, and the journey was difficult. Rising before seven, by candle light in the winter, Cyril would leave home in a dog-cart at 7.45 a.m. and rendezvous at a cross-roads two miles away with a farmer who was driving his own son to the same school. The return journey was made by train to Claverdon, followed by a one and a half mile walk and a lift in a baker's cart back to Snitterfield. There was still homework to be done for the next day, and Cyril was never physically robust. Hence the decision to send him away to boarding school when he was twelve years old rather than letting him stay on at the King's School.

Christ's Hospital, where Burt was a pupil from 1895 to 1902, brought a total change of scene and a return to his birthplace, London. For this famous school, founded by Edward VI in 1553 as a home for orphans and other needy children, was then set in the heart of the City. Many well-known men, including the authors Coleridge, Lamb and Leigh Hunt, had been pupils there, and the school had built up a reputation for scholarship both on the classical and mathematical sides. In a family with such a long medical tradition it would have been natural if the young Cyril had also turned to science as a preparation for medicine. But Dr Burt was a wise and cultured man, who while perhaps he hoped that his son would follow in his footsteps never brought pressure to bear. There was a rich background of interests in the home—literary, scientific, religious and artistic—and Dr Burt himself, though a devotee of the great Thomas Huxley, was a firm believer in the value of a classical education. So to the classical side Cyril went.

His tastes were already intensely intellectual and partly because throughout his life he suffered from extreme shortsightedness he had no talent for sports and a dislike for gymnastics. In spite of this his school days were enjoyable. The tough regime, which started with before-breakfast preparation at 7 a.m. and finished with evening preparation lasting until 8.15 p.m., seemed to suit him. He was a lively youngster with a very quick mind, and 'Little Bertie', as he was inevitably called, was quite a favourite and made some good friends. Several of his contemporaries became eminent: Sir Cyril Fox, Director of the National Museum of Wales, Sir John Forsdyke, Director of the British Museum, and Sir John Beazley, Professor of Classical Archaeology at Oxford. Burt himself, though never in quite the top flight scholastically, in the last two years became a member of the select and coveted group of 'Grecians'. 'I have at last obtained what I have worked for for nearly six years with many disappointments. I am a Grecian', he writes exultantly to his parents in 1900.

His interests were perhaps always too wide for him to excel in classics as such. He read extensively in literature, politics, economics, history, religion and philosophy, including some first incursions into psychology. He was, and indeed remained throughout his life, an avid note-taker, and summaries of the books he read, and the sermons he heard, were meticulously accumulated. Among the summaries was a précis of James Ward's long and famous article on Psychology in the *Encyclopaedia Britannica*, made when Burt was fifteen years old. But classics was the mainstay of his school work and pretty intensive. 'So far this term,' he writes in one letter home, 'we have finished VIII Iliad, IX book of Vergil, the II book of Thucydides, Juvenal's X Satire, sampled Cicero's De Oratore, and are engaged on Sophocles' Electra and Demosthenes' Orations. In addition we do several Greek and Latin proses a week, and Latin hexameters and Greek iambics (about 20 lines of each composition a week). Our composition usually consists of a piece of Addison, or Scott, and for verse Shakespeare or Tennyson. Very often we have to do it without any dictionaries or help at all.' If Burt in later life was a master of lucid English, the explanation no doubt lies in the classical training he received. His schooldays were valuable, too, in providing him with an intimate knowledge of London, which served him in good stead in his later professional life. In his spare time he wandered round the City, visited museums, galleries, and churches, sometimes with an aunt or his grandfather. He claimed years after that it was no problem for him to drop his later-acquired Oxford veneer, and mix and talk with the Cockney inhabitants of London. He probably got more from London than he would have got from Horsham, where Christ's Hospital moved in 1902, the year in which Burt left. But he did go down in 1897 to the laying of the foundation stone of the new school by the Prince of Wales, and his account of the day in a letter home is a good example of his descriptive gifts and powers of observation even at the comparatively young age of fourteen.

We started for Horsham at 9.45 from London Bridge and arrived at the special station about half past ten. We stopped at a platform lately tarred and strewn with sand, which was erected a little distance on the other side of Horsham. The little town we saw as we passed was decorated for the occasion. The band played as we marched [sic] through a hole in the hedge and along a newly made road of big flints carelessly thrown along the way and bordered by an edge of curb stones placed at each side. When we arrived at the site of the new buildings we dispersed over the grounds. The view from here is very pretty, but it did not excel the beauty of the autumn-tinted plants and trees on the Downs which we saw from the train. At 12.15 we took our places in the larger of the two marquees, where we listened for the greater part of half an hour to some music played by the school band, and while they rested we looked around us and gazed at the tent wherein all were assembled who wished to see the ceremony. In front was a stage erected in the centre of which were two large stones, the lower of these was a plain solid block, the other—the foundation stone—which was suspended from the roof was engraved with a suitable inscription. This stone, when we first entered, was turned round slowly by two workmen so that all could read the writing. Afterwards, however, it was placed in position and the masons went away. Then there appeared on the platform various persons of the order of Freemasons, and also the Lord Mayor and Lady, these latter, however, were without any badge that might indicate their rank except a kind of locket or medal which shone as if it were diamonds and was worn by 'His Worship'. Among others that appeared on the platform was the Head Master in his gown, ties and white gloves (these latter were worn by most of the officials). All these people appeared to be impatient for the arrival of the Prince for they kept going off the stage, then coming back again conversing amongst themselves. Presently, when the time for the laying the foundation of our new school was drawing near, we were suddenly roused by the rumble of the wheels of distant carriages and by the claps of the people, and soon we could see through the opening in the tent the carriage pass attended by Huzzars. A few minutes later the dignitaries of the order came on the stage in procession, the Grand Master—The Prince of Wales—the Grand Sword Bearer—the Grand Secretary, Treasurer, and the Grand Chaplain (who looked like some ruffled, stage-plotting villain, perhaps some wicked magician), the Bishop of Colchester or Chichester—I forget which. Amongst others were three Masters of the Lodges bearing two golden ewers, and one vessel which they are to call a cornucopia. The Prince advanced to the left of the platform where were standing a few persons whom I had not previously noticed dressed like private gentlemen. . . . After plenty of 'bowing and scraping' on the part of the functionaries, and a little stiff inclination on the part of the two persons who were about to take the principal part in the ceremony the man in the shabby overcoat fumbled about first for his spectacles and case, which he first of all dropped on the floor, and then for a few pieces of dirty paper (N.B. I am not sure about the dirt), folded up to about two square inches and placed in a pocket in his green-hued coat—this he unfolded and proceeded to read. His attitude was peculiar in the extreme. The papers (three in number) looked like two half sheets and one whole sheet of notepaper fastened together by a paper fastener, these he held in his two hands, in his right he also held his spectacle case while in his left was his walking stick which during the reading of the address pointed straight at the heart of the Prince. The man-of-the-shabby-overcoat (who looked extremely like the Duke of Cambridge as to the whiskers) proceeded to mumble out in a very husky voice that which was scrawled on bits of paper. He commenced with 'Yer rile Highness' and then went on to say that 'Yer rile Highness', as he called the Prince, had been sent by his Mother to lay the Foundation Stone of the school of which he was President, and then he grumbled out a lot of rubbish, bowed and folded up his papers almost as small as before, and handed them to the Prince, who all this time had been standing like a wax figure. His Royal Highness then read his reply, which was written on more respectable papers which he had been holding in his hands. This done the papers were handed to the other man—I mean the shabby old chap. When all these rites and ceremonies were over we marched, or rather attempted to march, to what used to be the dairy rooms of the Aylesbury Company, which had been white-washed and scrubbed, and had to do *in lieu* (as the novels say) of dining rooms. Our dinner consisted of cold meat, 'piccolili', and bread rolls, and a little pat of butter and some cheese; 'liquid food' was ginger-beer in tumblers and red glass jugs. After this we marched again to the temporary station and embarked for our homeward journey.[2]

Throughout his life Burt retained these acute powers of obser-

2. Burt, C. L. Letter to his parents, 25 October 1897.

vation, and vivid description, and together with his eye for the idiosyncrasies of character, they served him well in his clinical work.

His schooldays culminated in a scholarship to Jesus College, Oxford, where his Welsh ancestry on his mother's side no doubt recommended him. He chose this in preference to a less valuable exhibition to St John's College, Cambridge, which he was also offered, and it is interesting to speculate what difference it would have made to his psychological future had he gone to Cambridge and come under the influence of Rivers and Myers, instead of Oxford and McDougall.

It is important to remember that while he was at school and university Burt's holidays and vacations were spent mainly at his home at Snitterfield. For over twenty years this isolated rural village was the stable centre of his life. Society at Snitterfield, like that of most villages, was highly stratified. There were the Trevelyans, who owned the estate, the Lowsons, another land-owning family, and Lady Eva Dugdale, sister of the Earl of Warwick. The bulk of the agricultural labouring population was extremely poor. Agriculture at the end of the nineteenth century was in a depressed condition, and agricultural wages averaged less then £1 a week, extras in kind included. A few professional people, tenant farmers, and tradesmen constituted a middle group. So Burt's social life was restricted, and he was thrown back a great deal on himself, occupying himself with reading, music, painting, walking, botanising, cycling and pony riding, carrying out simple scientific experiments in the garden shed, and entertaining his much younger sister with theatrical shows and games. Not that Burt held himself aloof from village activities. He became treasurer of the Snitterfield Choral Society; he took organ lessons, and occasionally played the organ in church; he participated in village theatricals and was an active member of the Band of Hope. On one theatrical outing he and his village companions visited the home of the popular novelist, Marie Corelli, in Stratford and put on a show dressed up as Elizabethan mummers.

As the village physician, Dr Burt of course had entrée to all sections of society, and during school holidays the young Cyril would often accompany his father on his rounds, and occasionally assist in the sick room. In this way he came into contact with eminent neighbours, such as Sir George Otto Trevelyan (a member of several of Gladstone's cabinets, and better known as the biographer of his uncle Macaulay, and father of the historian, G. M. Trevelyan), and the Galtons of nearby Claverdon. Dr Burt was a frequent visitor to Claverdon, and an admirer in particular of

Francis Galton, who from time to time came to stay with his brother and sister. It was while accompanying Dr Burt on his rounds that Cyril first came into contact with Francis Galton—a contact that was a major influence in shaping his career. The closest friends of the Burts, however, were the village schoolmaster's children, the Harpers. The two boys were some years younger than Cyril, but intelligent, and eventually they did well as teacher and railway engineer. Cyril spent much time walking and arguing with them. The girls in the family were younger, but Cyril made friends with other village maidens, and there are diary records of kisses and hand-holdings with a Rosie and a Connie, and a resolute determination that these affairs should go no further! Nevertheless, in spite of these village activities and friendships Burt stood inevitably somewhat apart. Though not in any way stand-offish, he had been away to school and received an intensive education which marked him off from those around him. He became, and remained, an inwardly self-sufficient person, never dependent on others or on the social life around him. Though for over half a century his working life was spent in London, he never became wholly a Londoner or a participant in the social life of the capital. The twenty formative years at Snitterfield could not be erased—not even by Oxford, where he matriculated in October 1902.

In 1902 nearly a quarter of a century had passed since the reforms of 1878 which were gradually to turn Oxford into a forward-looking university. But changes were slow, and Professor Percy Gardiner, writing in 1903, voiced the view that 'Oxford is before all things conservative'.[3] It was still essentially a teaching university. There were no postgraduate degrees apart from the higher doctorates, and few postgraduate students. The aim of an Oxford education was to turn out educated gentlemen rather than experts or specialists. A generation earlier Matthew Arnold[4] had compared Oxford unfavourably with German universities, and not a great deal had altered since then. The classical 'Greats' course, or Literae Humaniores, was still the most prestigious degree course—a four-year course, consisting of five terms of classical language and literature, and seven terms of ancient history and philosophy, logic, ethics and modern philosophy—a course which by its breadth stretched the mind, but, according to Percy Gardiner, encouraged 'superficiality and onesidedness', and discouraged research and advanced study. This was the course to which Cyril Burt found himself committed. He had hoped to switch to science in preparation for a medical career, and in the vacation preceding his arrival at

3. Gardiner, Percy. *Oxford at the Crossroads*, 1903.
4. Arnold, Matthew. *Schools and Universities on the Continent*, 1868.

Oxford had mugged up some chemistry and biology. But the college authorities would not allow it. He had been awarded a scholarship in classics, and classics he must study. In his second term at Oxford he was still talking of changing to science before or after taking 'Greats', adding 'By the way, if I specialised medically, I should perhaps find lunacy most interesting. I should feel at home in an asylum, too.' But the switch never took place.

The college which Burt entered, Jesus College, was a small college. In the first decade of the century its undergraduate numbers did not exceed one hundred, of whom only half actually resided in college. Founded in 1571 by Queen Elizabeth I, it had had from the beginning a strong Welsh connection. A proportion of its scholarships was confined to Welshmen, and in the 1900s about half its undergraduates were Welsh. In such a small community every undergraduate knew his fellow undergraduates, and games and social activity were the passport to popularity. It was not perhaps an ideal environment for an intellectual, somewhat introspective young man, who disliked all forms of sport and the rowdier sort of sociability. Burt did not greatly appreciate some aspects of college life; in fact, the irresponsible and somewhat loutish behaviour of some of his fellow undergraduates disgusted him. But the Principal, Professor (later Sir) John Rhys, the eminent Celtic scholar, kept a reasonably firm grip on the college, and was an excellent head, who took a personal interest in every undergraduate. Thus the tone of the college was basically sound, and Burt soon found a small group of kindred spirits. So his Oxford life was enjoyable as well as intellectually stimulating. Sixty-five years later one of his Oxford friends, K. L. Kenrick, after reading a popular article of Burt's, wrote to him:

It took me back to October 4th 1902 when I arrived at Coll. Jesu. Oxon. without knowing a single soul in college, or university, or city. There was a knock on the door, and you appeared. 'My name's Burt. What's yours? Come and have a cup of coffee.' I came and we started to talk, and didn't stop till 2 a.m. We talked on all possible topics under the sun or moon—except one, which unless I am much misinformed is the chief topic of conversation among undergraduates everywhere. A day or two later Lacey joined us, and we became the three unarmed musketeers, and we kept on talking for four years. We didn't even know of the existence of another sex except our mothers and sisters. What a lovely monastic life it was, wasn't it? Not one of us had any money. We had to watch every copper . . . I think they were happy days. I remember you used to spend many days at the

Radcliffe Camera, 10 a.m. to 10 p.m. without food or drink,
reading Shakespeare and everything about him instead of doing
your Lit.Hum. . . . I remember also the notes you kept of every
book you read, in neat, tiny handwriting, headed 'Progress to
Perfection'. I also remember the shrine of the Venus of Milo
which you established in a window with a crimson velvet back-
cloth.

Burt's qualities were appreciated by those who got to know him
well, and indeed he is described by one of them as 'a loveable
character'.

Certainly he was ambitious. He was constantly making good
resolutions, many of them exaggeratedly high-flown, only to
lament, sometimes a week or so later, that they had been broken.
He drove himself at times excessively hard, working twelve, or
even fourteen hours a day, only to fall into a slack mood when he
could not concentrate at all. He writes of 'my intermittent apathy
and inertness, my anxiety for work and uprightness, and yet
perpetual failure, daydreaming, affections, temporary insanity'.
Finance was a constant worry. His college scholarship was worth
£80 a year. In addition he had a £50 exhibition from the Grocers
Company (his mother's family had had a grocery business in
Monmouth). He received further financial assistance from a generous London merchant, Mr H. W. Thomson, a governor of Christ's
Hospital, as a result of an earlier chance meeting on London Bridge.
Mr Thomson noticed a small boy in a blue coat standing on the
bridge, watching river traffic. Questioned as to whether he liked
his school, the small boy, Cyril Burt, answered with enthusiasm.
The gentleman went away leaving a coin in his hand. Finding it to
be a sovereign, Burt went after him and said, 'Sir, you must have
made a mistake. You meant it to be a shilling.' He had not made a
mistake, but was so taken with Burt that he kept in touch with him,
and took him with a friend in his yacht one vacation round the Isle
of Wight. Later he was to supplement Burt's inadequate scholarships. 'It would be a pity if small and wearing economies were to
interfere with your work, so I enclose a cheque for £25', he wrote
early in 1903, and throughout Burt's Oxford career he was prepared
to help. Dr Burt, of course, did what he could, and in 1904, on the
occasion of Cyril's twenty-first birthday, sent him £100. But the
unremunerative practice prevented him from providing substantial,
regular supplementation of his son's scholarships.

Perhaps equally trying were the restrictions of the classical
curriculum itself. Burt had already acquired very broad interests in
both the arts and the sciences, but the first part of the course, known

as Moderations, was narrowly confined to classical languages and texts, covering ground that had already been pretty intensively covered at school. The second part, Literae Humaniores, had a wider scope, particularly on the philosophical side, and an optional area within philosophy was psychology. The prevailing mode of thought in Oxford philosophy at the turn of the century was a form of idealism derived from Hegel. F. H. Bradley was the leading figure in Oxford philosophy, and the writings of T. H. Green, who had died in 1882, were still very influential. Both were unsympathetic to empirical psychology, and Oxford psychology was then a very obscure backwater trickle. Four years before Burt matriculated, a Readership in Mental Philosophy (as it was called) had been established by a wealthy electrical engineer, Dr Henry Wilde. A devoted follower of John Locke, he required that the Reader should study the mind as Locke had studied it, non-experimentally. The first holder of the post, G. F. Stout (1898–1903), had no desire to experiment, and analytical psychology of a philosophical kind had become accepted as an elective subject in the final honours school of Literae Humaniores. Stout's successor, William McDougall, appointed in 1904, was less amenable. He had no intention of shunning the laboratory, and arranged to have experimental facilities, in spite of Dr Wilde's disapproval, in Professor Gotch's physiological department. There he collected around him a small group of voluntary students, William Brown, J. C. Flugel, May Smith, and Cyril Burt. This little group, all the members of which later became distinguished psychologists, and their inspiring and dynamic leader, were a crucial factor in Burt's development and in his decision to take up psychology. Not that Burt neglected the more orthodox subjects in his curriculum. In particular he was deeply interested in, and permanently influenced by, his philosophical training, especially by William Ross's lectures on Aristotle, and by Cook Wilson's and H. W. B. Joseph's lectures on logic. Joseph's *Introduction to Logic* which appeared during his final year (1906), and which returned largely to Aristotelian sources, played an important part in shaping Burt's views on reasoning, and in providing a structure for his factorial scheme. He later stated his belief that a training in philosophy was the best foundation for a psychologist.[5] Throughout his life he retained a lively interest in philosophical developments, though not always a sympathetic one towards trends he disliked. But it was his introduction to psychology that was decisive to his career, and the excitement of participating in McDougall's work. At times he was

5. Burt, C. L. Autobiography in Murchison, C. (ed.) *A History of Psychology in Autobiography*, Vol. IV, 1952, p. 59.

McDougall's only student, and would spend the whole day at work and in discussion with him. McDougall's experiments on hypnosis and suggestibility were of special interest to him. And then McDougall, aware of his interest in Galton, set him a project to do with the standardisation of the psychological tests being used for the anthropometric survey sponsored by the British Association. This involved meeting Karl Pearson, whose Robert Boyle lecture on Eugenics he had already heard, correspondence with and further meeting with Galton, and in his final year his first contacts with Spearman, who had recently returned from Germany. Thus the foundations for Burt's later work were already being laid while he was still a student at Oxford.

But even to Burt, the worker, Oxford was not solely work. He attended societies, listened to speakers, and occasionally gave papers himself. His interests in theology and in music found ample scope. He heard famous men, like Lord Rosebery, whom he considered the finest orator he had ever heard, and scholars like Andrew Lang. The text of Burt's own paper on G. K. Chesterton delivered to the Delian Society in 1905 is still extant. With these distractions and the (from an examination point of view) irrelevancy of psychology, it is hardly surprising that his second class in Honour Moderations was followed in the summer of 1907 by a second class in Literae Humaniores. He had spread himself too widely to secure Firsts: but he did well. He had a long viva, which suggests that he was in the running for an alpha mark, and in the following year he was awarded the John Locke Scholarship in Mental Philosophy, founded like the Readership in 1898 by Henry Wilde, and held since by a series of distinguished men. The fact that the scholarship is not awarded in years when no candidate sufficiently meritorious applies is evidence that Burt's final placing was well above average. It was this scholarship that enabled him to advance his psychological training in Germany at the University of Würzburg. But before he did that he spent another year at Oxford, taking a Teachers' Diploma under M. W. Keatinge's direction, and doing his practical work at Clifton College, which he found a very agreeable place. So but for the John Locke he might well have become a schoolmaster! Nevertheless, this year was also valuable preparation for Burt's subsequent career in educational psychology, giving a wider knowledge of schools and the educational system. Then came the award of the John Locke, which opened up the opportunity of further training in psychology.

Where was this training to be obtained? Obviously, in Germany; for Germany, since 1879, when Wundt established the world's first psychological laboratory in Leipzig, was the undisputed leader in this new science, and remained so up to the outbreak of war. But Germany had numerous universities, and several excellent psychology departments. Which should Burt choose? No doubt after discussions with McDougall, who had himself been trained at Göttingen and knew Germany well, the choice fell on the University of Würzburg, where under Oswald Külpe the psychology department had gained the reputation of breaking free of the restrictions of Wundtian orthodoxy into exciting new fields of enquiry. In the decade before the Great War a succession of young British psychologists, H. J. Watt, J. C. Flugel, C. W. Valentine, T. H. Pear, and Cyril Burt were to acquire their psychological polish in Würzburg.[6]

So in the summer of 1908 Cyril Burt arrived in Würzburg. He was only there a few months, and unlike Watt he carried out no research. What he did was to acquire a good working knowledge of the German language, of which he already had more than a smattering, to soak himself in the latest developments of German psychology, and to absorb the stimulating cosmopolitan atmosphere of a German university town in the early part of the century. He obtained lodgings in Bandersacherstrasse with Frau Präsidialsecretarswitwe Frank. 'My landlady,' he writes in a letter home, 'is wonderfully kind. She has given me a better room, formerly occupied by a German student, and given me twice as much to eat, and fruit in-between-times, mending my waistcoat, and irons my trousers. And has meals with me, so that we can chatter.' He soon acquired strict German habits of work, studying for ten hours a day, often on Sunday as well. 'I have learned a wonderful lot of psychology here, far more than I ever dreamt of doing,' he writes in a letter to his sister, and he soon found that in some areas British psychology was extremely backward, for example, in educational psychology, where he soon came under Meumann's influence. He was deeply impressed by the facilities available for research in German universities, not only in Würzburg, but in other neighbouring universities (Frankfurt, Heidelberg) which he visited. Professor Külpe himself was extremely friendly. 'We went to an evening meal at Külpe's the other day. It was wonderful . . . Külpe is a delightfully clever and homely man.' 'He is great on the psychology of aesthetics', Burt writes in another letter to his sister. And the experience of being in such cosmopolitan company he found delightful. Visitors from other countries frequently came to Würzburg, men like Michotte from Louvain, who was already establishing a reputation in psychology. And he got an invitation

6. Hearnshaw, L. S. British Psychologists at the University of Würzburg at the Beginning of the Century. In Kuhn, O. *Grossbritannien und Deutschland*, 1974.

from Michotte to call in at Louvain on his way home. But the prime influence was naturally Külpe himself and the group of research assistants working on the psychology of the higher thought processes. This work was of formative importance to Burt, and contributed to his later work on tests of intelligence, as did the work of Meumann, Bobertag, and Chotzen, with which he also became familiar. But Burt by no means confined himself to the psychology of intellectual processes. He soaked himself in as much psychology as possible. He heard distinguished figures like von Frey on the sense organs, and K. Bühler on the psychophysiology of education; he became acquainted with Gestalt psychology and with psychoanalysis; and he went to the International Congress of Philosophy at Heidelberg at the end of August.

Hard work, and novel intellectual excitement, however, did not prevent some leisure-time relaxation, and Burt learned in particular to appreciate the glories of Würzburg architecture, and the beauties of the surrounding Bavarian countryside. 'The district,' he writes, 'is simply enchanting, with its vine-covered hills and attractive villages', and he gives vivid descriptions of cathedral services. 'Yesterday a wonderful service in the cathedral, flags, banners, bands, swords, uniforms, decorations, monks, friars, priests in purple, bishops' mitres, croziers *ad lib.* to celebrate St Peter's day', and, he adds, 'In the evening we go to a café and drink *bier* (quite a respectable proceeding and patronised by the local clergy and by *most* respectable families— including the younger girls).'

There was one further important consequence of the Würzburg visit for Burt— the cementing of his Oxford friendship with J. C. Flugel, and the establishment of his friendship with C. W. Valentine, both of whom were at Würzburg with him, and both of whom were to remain close and lifelong friends. In comparison with Burt, Flugel was something of a dilettante. He came from a wealthy family of German origin which had settled in Yorkshire, and he could afford to enjoy himself without taking life too seriously. Nevertheless he was a very able, original and amusing man, whose contributions to psychoanalysis, of which he became a devoted follower, experimental psychology and the history of psychology were of a high quality. C. W. Valentine, who eventually became Professor of Education in the University of Birmingham, was an essentially English character, who perhaps did not get much out of his German experience, apart from an interest in experimental aesthetics. But his rugged commonsense proved a useful corrective to Burt's more speculative and theoretical turn of mind. Both Flugel and Valentine were to play a large part in Burt's life.

In September 1908 Burt returned to England, and the following month he took up his first teaching post at the University of Liverpool. Largely as a result of his own ability and his own efforts, with moral, but only minimal financial support from his father, he had obtained a first-rate education, which, though biased towards the humanities, was broad and deep. This he supplemented with what he had acquired from a cultivated home, and from his own avid scientific curiosity. So, though he did not possess any formal qualifications in psychology, he was not badly equipped for his time to commence a career in the subject.

CHAPTER TWO

Influences Shaping Burt's Psychology

Cyril Burt received his university education and commenced his career as a psychologist in the first decade of the twentieth century, a decade which was one of the most momentous in the history of psychology, and, indeed, in human thought in general. In almost every branch of human knowledge revolutionary new developments were taking place, and Burt's alert mind was stimulated and shaped by many of these exciting contemporary events.

In 1908, when Burt completed his formal education and took up his first psychological post, psychology was rapidly expanding. As a scientific discipline it was about a generation old. Wundt's laboratory in Leipzig had been followed by further laboratories in Germany, the United States, Great Britain and France; by new journals; and by the setting up of learned societies such as the American Psychological Association in 1892, and the British Psychological Society in 1901. The dawn of the twentieth century saw psychology breaking out into new territory with the publication of Freud's *Interpretation of Dreams* (1900), William James's *Varieties of Religious Experience* (1902), Pavlov's early papers on conditioned reflexes (1903), Spearman's first paper on factor analysis (1904), Binet's intelligence scale (1905), and, in the allied field of neurophysiology, Sherrington's *Integrative Action of the Nervous System* (1906). The Würzburg psychologists and the Gestalt psychologists in Germany, the behaviourists in the United States, and the Hormic movement of McDougall in Great Britain had already emerged, or were just about to emerge, on to the psychological scene. Although among the general public, including much of the learned world, there was still much misunderstanding of, and indeed prejudice against, psychology, it was beginning to achieve some recognition among progressive thinkers. In his Presidential Address to the British Association for the Advancement of Science at York in the summer of 1906 the biologist, Sir Ray Lankester, then Director of the Natural History Museum, said 'I have given a special heading to this subject [psychology] because its emergence as a definite line of experimental research seems to me one of the most important features of the progress of science in the past quarter of a century.' For psychologists the decade in which Burt was fortunate enough to commence his serious study of the subject was perhaps the most exciting decade since the death of Aristotle.

In Great Britain, however, the situation with regard to psychology was in some respects an ambivalent one. On the one hand, the foundations of a scientific psychology, in empirical philosophy and evolutionary biology, were to a considerable extent British; but, on the other hand, the opposing forces, both philosophical and institutional, exerted a stronger inhibiting influence on the development of a scientific psychology than they did in either Germany or America. British universities, dominated by Oxford and Cambridge, were exceptionally conservative institutions. Their curricula were rigid and restricted, and in the sciences they had been slow in establishing laboratory facilities. Even in physics the Cavendish laboratory in Cambridge and the Clarendon laboratory in Oxford were not founded until the 1870s; and, as for London, Karl Pearson could lament, just before the close of the century, that there did not exist a physical laboratory worthy of the capital. The position in Germany and the United States was very different, and psychology was much more readily accepted into the academic fold.

But in addition to their conservatism there were influences directly hostile to psychology within British universities. Psychology was still generally regarded as a branch of philosophy rather than accepted as a science, and the idealistic mood which dominated British philosophy from the 1880s, until undermined by G. E. Moore and Bertrand Russell in the early 1900s, was openly antagonistic to psychology. T. H. Green, the Oxford philosopher, in asserting that 'the consciousness through which alone nature exists for us is neither natural nor a result of nature',[1] had clearly ruled out altogether the very possibility of a scientific psychology—and Green had a very wide following.

Because of these resistances British psychology at the beginning of the century was institutionally extremely weak. Two small laboratories had been set up in 1897, at University College, London, and in the University of Cambridge. In the previous year a lectureship in comparative psychology had been established at Aberdeen. Scotland, indeed, was more friendly to psychology than England, and laboratories followed at Edinburgh in 1906, and Glasgow in 1907. In Oxford, as we have seen, the terrain was particularly hostile. The Reader in Mental Philosophy, appointed under the terms of Dr Wilde's bequest in 1898, was specifically instructed to study the human mind non-experimentally, and it

1. Green, T. H. *Prolegomena to Ethics*, 1883, Bk I, ch. ii.

needed the forthright William McDougall to breach this requirement. Not until after the Second World War had the resistances to psychology in Oxford sufficiently broken down to allow psychology to become recognised as a degree subject in its own right.

In spite of these institutional blockages, however, British psychology was by no means stagnant. James Ward (1843–1925) and G. F. Stout (1860–1944) were both powerful theoretical psychologists, and their work was to provide the foundations for most British psychology for more than a generation. Ward's famous article on Psychology in the Ninth Edition of the *Encyclopaedia Britannica* (1885) constituted a rejection of associationism, which had dominated British psychology from the time of Locke in the seventeenth century to the time of Bain in the late nineteenth. The focal point of mind, according to Ward, lay in the unitary subjective activity of attention. It was the continuity of attention, not the laws of association, that accounted for what he called 'the presentational continuum', the immediate data of consciousness. Ward's article, it is worth noting, was Burt's first introduction to psychology, while he was still a schoolboy, and his Oxford teacher, McDougall, regarded his own work as 'an endeavour to carry to its logical conclusion that critical rejection of the mosaic psychology which had been a main theme of the psychological writing of James Ward' and others.[2] So Ward must be accounted an important influence in the formation of Burt's views.

Like Ward, Stout, who was still at Oxford when Burt entered the University, was in revolt against associationism, which he considered had failed to do justice to the unity and continuity of psychic life. In its place Stout postulated a process of 'noetic synthesis' involving the apprehension of 'wholes' round the 'central idea of a topic'. Broadly speaking, the power of noetic synthesis corresponds to the concept of intelligence. But even more important than cognition in Stout's psychology was conation. Fundamentally the unity of mind was a unity of interest, a conative rather than a merely cognitive unity. Mind, in other words, was active, not passively receptive, as it had been conceived in the older associationism. It was this doctrine, set out in Stout's *Analytical Psychology* (1896) and his *Manual of Psychology* (1st edn 1898; 5th edn 1938) and widely accepted in Britain, that was largely responsible for the cool reception by British psychologists of Pavlovian and behaviouristic ideas before the Second World War, and, on the other hand, their receptiveness to both Gestalt psychology and psychoanalysis.

The other major influence in British psychology at the beginning

2. McDougall, W. *An Outline of Psychology*, 1923, p. x.

of the century was Darwinian biology. Darwin himself, as the recent publication of his 'Notebooks on Man'[3] has demonstrated, was fully conscious of the psychological implications of his evolutionary theory. Man, even if in some respects unique, was still a product of the natural kingdom; his mind had evolved as well as his bodily organism. Psychology, in its foundations, was therefore a biological science; mental characteristics were subject to the universal laws of variation and inheritance; and mind was involved in the process of adaptation and in the struggle for existence. The intricacies of instinctive behaviour, the peculiarities of emotional expression, and the development of the higher qualities of intelligence found for the first time a plausible explanation in Darwinian theory.

The influence of Darwin on the development of psychology was far-reaching. The way had already been prepared by Herbert Spencer's *Principles of Psychology* (1855), which took an evolutionary standpoint, and by the developmental neurology of Hughlings Jackson. Before the end of the century evolutionary doctrine had opened the way for the rise of comparative psychology, and the work of men like Romanes (1848–1894) and Lloyd Morgan (1852–1931); it had inspired the scientific study of child development beginning, in this country, with Sully (1843–1923); and above all it formed the basis of Francis Galton's (1822–1911) work on individual differences and heredity, which was the source of most of Cyril Burt's psychological enquiries. For Burt, in spite of his period of education in Germany, was first and foremost a British psychologist, and his outlook was influenced primarily by the main currents of British psychology that have been outlined above.

Burt, however, was not merely a psychologist, nor influenced only by developments within psychology itself. His interests were wide, and from his university days onward up to the end of his life he read extensively and kept abreast of knowledge in many fields, including the physical and biological sciences. His outlook in psychology was indeed in no small measure shaped by the advances in physics and biology that marked the early years of the century. In physics the quantum theory of Planck (1900), the statistical mechanics of Willard Gibbs (1901) and Einstein's special theory of relativity (1905) had undermined and transformed the classical Newtonian theories which had dominated the nineteenth century. Burt was one of the first psychologists to grasp the implications of the new physics for psychology. He saw that the cruder forms of

3. Gruber, Howard E. *Darwin on Man*, 1974.

mechanistic determinism were not a scientific requirement, and later he came to regard the new physical outlook as a support for his own statistical work on the factorial structure of the mind.

Burt was similarly among the first to appreciate the genetical developments that ushered in twentieth-century biology. Genetics had been the Achilles heel of the original Darwinian theory. Darwin himself had arrived at no satisfactory explanation of the mechanism of inheritance, and the statistical approach of his cousin, Francis Galton, though producing some evidence for the importance of heredity in plants, animals, and human beings, failed to explain the underlying processes. These processes in broad outline had, of course, been discovered some decades earlier by Mendel, but his work languished in obscurity until suddenly in April 1900 the Dutch botanist De Vries simultaneously rediscovered the Mendelian 3:1 ratio in a crossing experiment and lighted upon Mendel's original paper of 1866. As the century opened the modern science of genetics was reborn. Weismann, whose book *Essays upon heredity and kindred biological problems* was translated into English in 1889, had prepared the way by suggesting that chromosomes were the carriers of the hereditary material, and by insisting on the asymmetric relationship of what he called the germ and the soma (the germ influences the soma, but the soma cannot retroactively influence the germ) — a view that was to have a marked influence on the outlook of later geneticists.

Mendel's rediscovered work soon became known to, though it was some time before it became generally accepted by, British scientists. In May 1900 William Bateson in a paper to the Royal Horticultural Society used Mendel's laws to interpret his own experiments on hybridisation, and in doing so gave rise to one of the most acrimonious disputes in the history of British science. For the followers of Galton's statistical or (as it was termed) biometrical approach to heredity regarded the Mendelian doctrine of discontinuity as directly opposed to their own ideas of continuous variation, which they considered established by the binomial distribution of most biological variables. The bitter arguments which resulted between Karl Pearson, the leader of the biometricians, and William Bateson did at least bring to the focus of public attention the whole question of heredity, and the forming of the Eugenics Society in 1907 to further the eugenic views which Galton had been propounding for over twenty years, was an index of the public interest aroused, particularly with regard to the social implications of genetics. The Pearson-Bateson controversy was, of course, ultimately shown to be misguided. R. A. Fisher, in a famous paper of

1918[4] which even at that date was regarded as too controversial to be accepted by the Royal Society of London, demonstrated that Mendelism could be reconciled with the continuous distribution of the biometricians, given that a character was simultaneously affected by numerous Mendelian factors. This had, in fact, been shown much earlier by the Cambridge statistician, Udny Yule, in a neglected paper of 1902.[5] But it was not until the 1920s and the work of Morgan in America and Goldschmitt in Germany on 'genes' (as Morgan named the Mendelian factors) that Mendelian genetics was fully accepted by biologists. It is a remarkable tribute to Burt that, although in a sense a protégé of Galton, Pearson and the biometric school, he was among the first adherents of the Mendelian viewpoint in Britain.[6] Throughout his life he was not only a convinced Mendelian, but also an upholder of the Weismannian doctrine of asymmetry, which, indeed, seemed to find support in the later discoveries of the molecular biologists. What is certain is that the genetical developments of the early part of the century which so excited the scientific community during Burt's most formative years, were deeply and permanently to colour his views on psychology, and, in particular, his views on intelligence.

Towards another development of the period Burt was much less well informed, and probably much less sympathetic. This was the growth of sociology, and of the related discipline of anthropology. The developments in sociology were mainly European and American. The major works of European sociology by Durkheim, Weber and Pareto appeared between 1893 and 1916 contemporaneously with the revolutionary changes in physics and biology already mentioned, but there is no indication that Burt was familiar with, or interested in, their writings,[7] and towards American work he always felt a certain antipathy. Indeed, in spite of his gift for languages, and his travels abroad, there was always a streak of insularity about Burt. There was something alien about sociology; and as for British sociology it was at that time almost non-existent. The only chair of sociology in the British Isles was the chair founded

4. Fisher, R. A. The correlation between relatives on the supposition of Mendelian inheritance. *Trans. Roy. Soc. Edin.*, *52*, 1918, 399–433.

5. Yule, G. Udny. Mendel's laws and their probable relations to inter-racial heredity. *New Phytologist*, *I*, 1902, 193–207, 222–40. See also Pearson, E. S. Some reflexions on continuity in the development of mathematical statistics, 1885–1920. In Pearson, E. S. and Kendall, M. G. *Studies in the History of Statistics and Probability*, 1970.

6. Burt, C. L. The inheritance of mental characters. *Eugen. Rev., IV*, 1912, 1–33.

7. There is one brief, formal reference to Durkheim in *The Young Delinquent*, 1925.

in 1907 at the London School of Economics and held by L. T. Hobhouse until his death in 1929. Until recently there were no chairs of sociology at either Oxford or Cambridge, and until the 1950s there was some excuse for even well-educated Englishmen being almost wholly blind to all but the superficialities of the sociological dimension of human nature. The general ignorance of British psychologists of the sociological investigations being carried out elsewhere was illustrated in *The Study of Society*, a symposium edited by F. C. Bartlett and M. Ginsberg in 1939. Ginsberg himself, who succeeded Hobhouse in the London chair, was the only member of the group to show any appreciation of the work of continental sociologists, and Burt significantly did not attend the Cambridge meeting of the symposium at all. At no stage of his career does he give any indication of having any acquaintance with, or interest in, the sociological literature. In the list of books he read there is almost nothing that can be described as sociological, in spite of the wide nature of his tastes. This lacuna shows itself clearly in his few contributions to social psychology, in the chapters on 'How the Mind works in Society' in *How the Mind Works* (1933), and in his Hobhouse lecture (1953) on 'Contributions of Psychology to Social Problems'.

Perhaps more strange was his neglect of anthropology, because British anthropology was a good deal more highly developed than British sociology, and particularly in Cambridge where Burt worked for a brief period, the links between psychology and anthropology were strong. Moreover Burt's Oxford teacher, McDougall, was himself something of an anthropologist; he had been a member of the famous Cambridge Anthropological Expedition to the Torres Straits in 1899, and had followed this up with field work in Borneo. None of this, however, seems to have brushed off on Burt, and subsequently he showed no particular interest either in the work of Malinowski, Radcliffe Brown and their followers in Great Britain or the work of American anthropologists. The absence in Burt's intellectual equipment of a sociological component— an absence which was by no means made up by his experiences in social settlements and slum areas, or his familiarity with the data of social surveys— was, after his retirement, to involve him in controversies with the growing sociological school of educationists and child psychologists. While the sociologists often displayed a prejudice against, or an incomprehension of, the genetical side of development, Burt showed an equal incomprehension of the sociological outlook, an incomprehension that goes back to the early stages of his career. Hence the arguments that arose, though often protracted, proved singularly inconclusive.

This gap in Burt's equipment was partly compensated, but not of course filled, by his surprising and increasing expertise in statistics—surprising because his education had been a classical one, and he received very little formal mathematical training after the age of sixteen. In spite of this he became a competent mathematician, and a leading figure in the field of mathematical psychology. His interest in Galton, and later in Galton's follower, Karl Pearson, had, however, early apprised him of the relevance of statistics to psychological enquiry, and from his Oxford days onwards he worked intensively to acquire not only a knowledge of statistics, but an understanding of their mathematical foundations. His education coincided with a blossoming of statistical methodology. Building on Galton's work on correlation Pearson had introduced, between 1893 and 1907, numerous technical improvements and extensions (e.g. multiple correlation, biserial correlation, etc.) and had introduced additional tests, such as the much-used χ^2 for goodness of fit. In these productive years Pearson and his school had provided psychologists with many of the basic tools they were to use in their rapidly expanding science. Burt was one of the first to grasp the importance of these developments in statistics.

Of all the influences which impinged on Burt in the early days of his career the two most important were the inspiration of his early contacts with Galton, and the encouragement of his teacher, William McDougall, for whom he always retained strong feelings of respect.

It was a stroke of fortune that Snitterfield should have been located only a few miles from the Galtons' Claverdon home and that Burt's father should have been their family physician, thus bringing the young Cyril into direct contact with the aged Francis Galton. Galton, of course, was not primarily or merely a psychologist; but nevertheless his contributions to psychology, though brilliantly suggestive rather than systematic, were of seminal importance. The essence of his contribution was firstly to focus on what he called 'talent and character' as the central themes of psychology (as opposed to the ideas and the feelings of traditional British psychology); secondly to stress the role of individual differences, which had either been overlooked or minimised by earlier psychologists; and thirdly to forge the first primitive tools, psychometric and statistical, to deal with the new areas he was opening up. 'Until the phenomena of any branch of knowledge,' he asserted, 'have been submitted to measurement and number, it cannot assume the status and dignity of a science. . . . They [statistics] are the only tools by which an opening can be cut through the formidable thicket of difficulties that bar the path of those who pursue the science of man.'[8] As a result of his own quantitative studies, and possibly to some extent his own prejudices, he was convinced that both talent and character were largely inherited. The influence of Galton on Burt was undoubtedly a decisive one, and later in life Burt was to describe his own work at University College, London, as aimed at preserving and developing the Galtonian tradition. Both in its viewpoint and in its methodology it was essentially Galtonian.

McDougall's influence was rather different. Burt got from him, above all, advice and encouragement, but he never followed closely in McDougall's footsteps either in physiological or social psychology. Certain McDougallian features became incorporated into Burt's own views, for example, McDougall's hierarchical scheme of character structure (instincts, sentiments, and master sentiment); his belief, following Galton, that human personality was compounded of character and intellect; and McDougall's animistic dualism, expounded in *Body and Mind* (1911), was certainly one of the sources of Burt's own very similar standpoint. It was perhaps this last aspect of McDougall's work that made the deepest impression on Burt, for he was later to write 'In other countries when psychology changed from a branch of philosophy to an experimental science, it adopted the general materialistic basis that had become so popular among scientists towards the close of the nineteenth century. The fact that this did not happen in Britain is due primarily to McDougall.'[9]

In his early days, therefore, Burt came under the influence of two powerful personalities. All the same it is still amazing that his life's goals were formulated with such clarity and such assurance even before he had completed his university training. He seemed almost from the start to know precisely what he wanted to do—to make a study of individual psychology and the individual differences between men—and to this he stuck tenaciously from the time of his first substantial piece of psychological research under McDougall's supervision almost to the day of his death.

8. Galton, F. Psychometric experiments. *Brain, II*, 1879, 149–62; and *Natural Inheritance*, 1889, p. 62.

9. Burt, C. L. Unpublished letter, 1964.

CHAPTER THREE

Liverpool and the London County Council

I

At its meeting on 1 June 1908, the Faculty of Science of the University of Liverpool unanimously recommended that Mr Cyril L. Burt, Scholar of Jesus College, Oxford, and John Locke Scholar of the University of Oxford, be elected Assistant Lecturer in Physiology, and Lecturer in Experimental Psychology for three years from 1 October 1908, at a salary of £150 per annum. Shortly after hearing of his appointment Burt went off to spend the summer in Würzburg, returning to England in September and briefly visiting his parents at Snitterfield before proceeding to take up his new post. He was to remain in Liverpool for nearly five years, and in several ways this was a decisive period in his development. His research interests became more clearly formulated; his early papers brought him to the notice of psychologists; he gained a first-hand experience of social problems and social conditions; and, above all, his close personal contact with Sherrington permanently influenced his psychological outlook.

Sherrington indeed was the driving force behind the establishment of courses in Psychology in the University of Liverpool. Already Fellow of the Royal Society, Sherrington had been appointed to the Holt Chair of Physiology in 1895, and by the turn of the century had gained an international reputation for his work on the physiology of the nervous system. In 1904 he was to deliver his Silliman lectures at Yale University which were published two years later as *The Integrative Action of the Nervous System* (1906), one of the great classics of physiology. Sherrington, however, was more than a brilliant experimenter; he was a man of broad culture and wide interests, a poet, an historian of science and a philosopher. He had a synthetic grasp of the problems with which he was dealing, and never forgot that mammalian organisms, equipped with brains and nervous systems that could be dissected by the physiologist, also possessed minds, which needed equally to be studied. His own researches on the nervous system merged into problems of an essentially psychological nature, perceptual, emotional, and volitional. Hence his encouragement of psychology—an encouragement that lasted throughout his long life.

Sherrington's first moves in the establishment of psychology in the University of Liverpool date back to 1899, only four years after his appointment. In that year he introduced lectures in elementary psychophysiology for science and education students, the lectures being illustrated by experiments. The following session an Advanced Psychology course was added, designed for candidates for the Final B.Sc. degree, and again practical classes were included in the syllabus. In 1902 a young American psychologist, R. S. Woodworth, was appointed to the staff, and he was followed by W. G. Smith, who was later to set up the Edinburgh department, and H. J. Watt, who moved on to Glasgow. Burt was the fourth psychologist to work in Sherrington's department, and his stay was the longest.

Burt's tasks were to take over all the teaching of psychology to medical, education, science and social science students, including most of the practical classes; to assist Sherrington with some of his experimental work; and to continue with the researches on intelligence which he had commenced in Oxford under McDougall. He was fortunate to find in Liverpool a number of stimulating and helpful colleagues, such as Professor Campagnac, the recently appointed Professor of Education, and the philosophers, MacCunn and Mair, who were, for philosophers, unusually friendly to psychology. The number of students taking courses in psychology was quite considerable. Burt estimated that he had to teach some fifty medicals, a dozen or so from the social science department, a few philosophy students, as well as a large group of some sixty education students. Finally there were up to half a dozen taking the full B.Sc. Psychology course, and soon a small number of postgraduates were attracted to psychology. Burt's work was centred in the physiology department, the main practical classes taking place in its laboratory when the physiologists did not need it. The modest annual grant for apparatus of £20 was increased in the 1912–13 session owing to the growing number of students taking psychology. Burt's lectures covered the sense organs with great thoroughness (it was an area of psychology in which he always showed an interest) and went on to include topics such as intelligence, the inheritance of ability, sex differences, hypnosis and Freudian psychoanalysis. His practical classes were often exciting, and included such things as hypnosis and the detection of mock criminals in realistically staged situations. Among the students these demonstrations became affectionately known as 'Burt's music hall turns'.

In 1905 the Committee of the Anthropological Section of the British Association—a committee which originally had Francis Galton as its chairman—drew up a scheme for a comprehensive survey of the population of Great Britain. A special sub-committee under McDougall was set up to consider the gathering of psychological measurements, and McDougall recruited his students, C. L. Burt, J. C. Flugel, and H. B. English, to assist him in constructing and standardising suitable tests. In 1907 the Board of Education added its weight to the project, recommending the 'anthropometric observation of children in schools', and this considerably facilitated the obtaining of permission to test school children, first in Oxford, and then in Liverpool and elsewhere. At this time progressive opinion was seriously concerned about the level of national intelligence, its place in national decay, and the possible influence of genetic factors in bringing this about. In 1906 David Heron, one of Karl Pearson's co-workers, had published evidence that the birth rate differed widely with social class, and that the least intelligent sections of the population were reproducing far more rapidly than the most intelligent.[1] So the investigations being carried out by McDougall and his team were backed by a good deal of support.

Burt's own research was primarily focused on the problem of finding the most suitable kinds of test for assessing intelligence, and, in particular, on determining whether tests involving higher and more complex mental functions might not show a closer connection with general intelligence than was shown by simpler mental functions such as sensory discrimination and motor reactions. He also proposed to verify the mathematical methods of analysis which Spearman had devised a few years earlier. Burt's findings were published in a long article in the *British Journal of Psychology* in 1909,[2] an article which might have been even longer had not the editor, James Ward, insisted in the elimination of the detailed statistical tables. Burt's findings confirmed the view that the more complex and novel tests correlated best with general intelligence and with teachers' assessments of intelligence. He also confirmed Spearman's finding of a general tendency to hierarchical order in correlation matrices, but noted that there was a discernible, though small, tendency for subordinate groups of allied tests to correlate among themselves. He agreed with Spearman that 'the main significance of this hierarchy of experimental performance is . . . that we are led to infer that all the functions of the human mind, the simplest and most complicated alike, are probably

1. Heron, D. *The Relation of Fertility in Man to Social Status*, 1906.
2. Burt, C. L. Experimental tests of general intelligence. *Brit. J. Psychol.*, III, 1909, 94–177.

processes within a single system'. In other words the investigation gave support to Spearman's general factor of intelligence. The difference in performance between pupils in elementary schools, and those in an exclusive private preparatory school, was noted, and as practice did not improve performance, it was suggested that the differences were innate.

This work continued in Liverpool. In his second published paper[3] Burt went on to describe tests of a higher and more complex order than those previously used. Deriving inspiration partly from his Oxford training in logic, and partly from Meumann's work with which he had become familiar in Germany, Burt devised a number of new reasoning tests, including complex analogies, syllogisms, sentence formation and the reconstruction of dissected pictures. The tests were administered in various Liverpool secondary schools to both boys and girls. Test of logical inference and 'apperception' (i.e. involving complex synthetic activity) gave the highest correlations with general intelligence, and were least vitiated by sex, social class and other differences.

Burt's next move was to employ these newly devised tools in the elucidation of two particular questions; firstly, what were the mental differences between the sexes? and secondly, what was the role of inheritance in determining mental characteristics? In his study of sex differences[4] he had the assistance of a Wallasey schoolteacher, R. C. Moore, who later became Director of Education for Hull. Together they tested a sample of Wallasey children for a wide range of capabilities, perception, motor processes, association, reasoning, and also emotional dispositions (using a variety of methods, including the psychogalvanic reflex, which had been discovered by Féré in 1888, but had not been widely used at the time Burt adopted it). The conclusion Burt and Moore reached, that 'with few exceptions innate sex differences in mental constitution are astonishingly small—far smaller than common belief and common practice would lead us to expect', was at the time a striking one. Only a few years earlier Havelock Ellis in *Man and Woman*,[5] reviewing all the available evidence on sex differences, came to unflattering conclusions as to female capacity for abstract thought. Burt's findings were, therefore, a significant step on the road to the recognition of sex equality. His experimental investigations into

3. Burt, C. L. Experimental tests of higher mental processes and their relation to general intelligence. *J. Exp. Ped., I*, 1911, 93–112.

4. Burt, C. L. and Moore, R. C. The mental differences between the sexes. *J. Exp. Ped., I*, 1912, 273–84, 355–88.

5. Ellis, Havelock. *Man and Woman*, 4th edn 1904, pp. 209–14.

differences in emotional characteristics were also of a pioneering nature and marked the beginning of his long interest in this topic.

The second question—inheritance—was to play an even more central role throughout Burt's life. In his first contribution to the subject, his article 'The Inheritance of Mental Characters',[6] he already shows his theoretical mastery and extensive knowledge of the biological as well as psychological literature. For a young man still in his twenties it is in many respects an impressive piece of work, but more for its theoretical grasp than for its empirical findings. Burt's own data were relatively slight, consisting of a small-scale experiment in two Oxford schools, and some unfinished surveys in Liverpool. Largely on the basis of these he is prepared to assert that 'among individuals mental capacities are inherited. Of this the evidence is conclusive'. Many years later in his Eugenics Society paper on 'Intelligence and Fertility'[7] Burt quoted correlations between the intelligence of parents and children, between siblings, and between the intelligence of children, social class and family size, based on this Liverpool work without ever previously having reported the full data. When questioned about this by Professor L. S. Penrose he wrote:

The investigations to which you refer were carried out in 1909–11. . . . They formed part of a joint research organised from the University Social Settlement. Fred Marquis, the Warden [now Lord Woolton, but he was a lecturer in Social Science and an ardent Socialist in those days], collected the occupational, economic and social data. Moore, a teacher working under me for a Ph.D., did most of the tests in the schools. I did most of the testing on the adults. The bulk of the testing was done on 255 pupils, aged 11–12, at three main schools—65 at a school in a somewhat superior neighbourhood, 130 at a medium school (Moore's), and 60 at a poor school near the docks. The intelligence of the parents was assessed primarily on the basis of their actual jobs, checked by personal interviews; about a fifth were also tested to standardise the impressionistic assessments. And the correlations you cite were calculated by just lumping all three groups together. The general plan of the research was based on investigations reported by Pearson and Heron. The chief innovation was the introduction of group and individual tests which really formed the main topic of my own investigation. The genetic studies (if I can call them that) were incidental.[8]

6. Burt, C. L. *Eugen. Rev., IV*, 1912, 1–33.
7. Burt, C. L. *Occasional Papers on Eugenics, 2.* Eugenics Society, 1946.
8. Burt, C. L. Letter to Professor L. S. Penrose, 5 February 1962.

Inadequate reporting and incautious conclusions mark this first incursion of Burt into the genetic field. We have here, right at the beginning of his career, the seeds of later troubles. The rough and impressionistic methods, too, would not stand scrutiny now, though in their day they were an advance on those previously employed, by Pearson for example in his studies of mental inheritance.[9]

The final section of the article dealt with the mental characters of races, both 'savage races' as they were still then commonly termed, and European races. Burt's conclusion on 'savages', after reviewing the findings of British and American researches, is interesting. 'The superiority of modern civilised man is not due to hereditary powers and capacities.' Burt was not a 'racist', and never at any time expressed 'racist' opinions, except to suggest on the basis of test results that there might perhaps be a certain intellectual superiority among Jews. When it came to European races Burt thought that the persistence of group characteristics after emigration did suggest some slight innate tendencies, and that these slight tendencies might be decisive in determining 'the destiny of nations'. However, his final conclusion was, 'In the case of the individual we found the influence of heredity large and indisputable; in the case of the race, small and controversial.'[10]

Burt's Liverpool years were arduous but enjoyable. Work sometimes took up to as many as fifteen hours a day. In addition to his research, and reading for his regular classes, he undertook a good deal of extra-mural lecturing, some of it as far afield as Barrow. He spoke at meetings of the British Association and the British Psychological Society, and he played a prominent part in the L.C.C. Conference of Teachers in 1912 and 1913. In Liverpool there was a lot going on at the Settlement (see below) and at the University. The University staff was then small and fairly close-knit. So there were dinners with the Sherringtons; with the philosopher Mac-Cunn, at whose house he first met the distinguished Manchester philosopher, Samuel Alexander; with the historian Ramsay Muir and others. There were concerts, theatres, croquet and chess; and, in the vacations, trips to the Isle of Man, and abroad to Switzerland, Germany, France and Russia. Liverpool, too, gave more scope than Oxford to his fondness for feminine society. Though none of his liaisons at this period seem to have gone far, they were sufficiently strong to encourage him to take up dancing. Perhaps most important

9. Pearson, K. On the inheritance of mental and moral characteristics in man. *Biometrika, IV*, 1904, 131.

10. Burt, C. L. The inheritance of mental characters. *Eugen. Rev., IV*, 1912, 1–33.

for his future career was his residence in the University Settlement in Nile Street on the fringes of Liverpool's dockland. This Settlement had been established in 1906 'to assist in the provision of means of education and recreation for the people in the poorer districts of the south end of Liverpool, to inquire into the social conditions of the poor, and to consider the advance plans calculated to promote their welfare'.[11] Burt deliberately took up residence there to enable him to acquire a first-hand background knowledge of social conditions and it was here, in particular, that he first got interested in the problem of juvenile delinquency, and first saw the need for vocational guidance. The Settlement under the inspired leadership of Frederick Marquis attracted a brilliant group of young residents, which included V. H. Mottram, the physiologist, P. M. Roxby, the geographer, and Olaf Stapledon, philosopher and writer. Burt always regarded his years at the Settlement as one of his most valuable formative experiences, and from that time forward he was never unaware, as some critics unfairly allege, of the part played by social background in the shaping of personality and behaviour. In many ways Liverpool proved an ideal training ground for Burt, and, above all, there was his almost daily contact with Sherrington, one of the world's leading scientists, whose views on the nature of the organism permanently influenced Burt's outlook.

Burt's own reputation was by now firmly established, and when he applied for the post of Psychologist advertised by the London County Council in October 1912 he was warmly supported by Professors Sherrington and Campagnac from Liverpool, and Dr Spearman of University College, London. Spearman wrote, 'I can add that he is considered by most experts to be the most brilliant and promising of the younger generation of psychologists in the British Isles. In this opinion I concur. As regards his special qualifications for the post as detailed in the advertisement of the L.C.C. it is precisely in the examination of children that he has made his professional reputation.' Both Sherrington and Campagnac comment on the excellent personal relationships he had established with teachers and with children, and his 'admirable tact and discretion'. So in May 1913, when he had just turned 30 years of age, Burt left Liverpool to take up his new post in the wider scene of London, where nearly all the rest of his life was to be spent.

II

Burt arrived in London just before the outbreak of the First World War called a halt to more than a decade of educational expansion and

11. Liverpool University Settlement. Report, 1911–12.

reform. The establishment of the Board of Education in 1899 brought an end to the divisive control of public education, thus implementing one of the main recommendations of the Bryce Commission on Secondary Education which had reported in 1895. The Balfour Education Act of 1902 attempted to sort out the muddle of English education which had been so trenchantly exposed by Sidney Webb in his influential Fabian Tract of 1901.[12] The 1902 Act replaced the old School Boards, legally entitled to provide only elementary schooling, by Local Education Authorities, and empowered them to provide a whole range of schools—elementary, technical and secondary—with scholarships for those able enough to win them. London was originally excluded from the Act because of the complex problems of the relations between the county and the boroughs, but a London Education Act of 1903 resolved the issues, and the L.C.C. became the authority for all grades of education in London. The quality and standards of education in London and elsewhere were to be monitored by an enlarged inspectorate. The principal architect of the new Act was Robert Morant, who became Secretary of the Board of Education from 1902 to 1911. Morant was unashamedly élitist in his outlook, and had written of 'the need of voluntarily submitting the impulses of the many ignorant to the guidance and control of the few wise . . . and to the subordination of the individual (and therefore limited) notions to the wider and deeper knowledge of specialised experts in the science of national life and growth'.[13] This principle was incorporated into the Elementary School Code issued in 1904. 'It will be an important though subsidiary object of the School to discover individual children who show promise of exceptional capacity, and to develop their special gifts (so far as can be done without sacrificing the interests of the majority of the children) so that they may be qualified at the proper age to pass into secondary schools and be able to derive the maximum benefit from the education there offered them.' The majority of children must be educated to be 'efficient members of the class to which they belong'.[14]

The meritocratic principle was not, therefore, the brainchild of psychologists and intelligence testers; it was embedded in the foundations of the new scheme of secondary education which the 1902 Act established. The underprivileged, however, were not to be ignored in the new dispensation. The poor standard of health

12. Webb, Sidney. *The Education Muddle and the Way Out*, Fabian Tract No. 106, 1901.
13. Allen, B. M. *Sir Robert Morant*, 1934, pp. 125–6.
14. *Board of Education Report*, 1906, p. 127.

among the urban population was causing concern, and was the subject of a series of reports from an inter-departmental committee on Physical Deterioration in the years 1904 to 1906. Particular attention was paid to the results of malnutrition, largely as a result of Margaret Macmillan's work in Bradford, and a Bill introduced by the recently born Labour party successfully got through Parliament in 1906, permitting local authorities to provide school meals and set up voluntary care committees. It was followed in 1907 by an Act which obliged them to carry out the medical inspection of all children and to make provision for their health. 'The fundamental principle of the new Act', wrote Sir George Newman, who became Chief Medical Officer of the Board of Education, 'was the medical inspection and supervision of all children in the public elementary schools, and this with a view to adapting and modifying the system of education to the needs and capacities of the children, securing the early detection of unsuspected defects, checking incipient maladies at their onset, and furnishing the facts which would guide education authorities in relation to physical and mental development of children during school life.'[15] At the same time the mentally defective were the subject of a Royal Commission which was appointed in 1904, and reported in 1908. The Commission came to the conclusion that there were large numbers of mentally deficient persons in the community over whom insufficient care and control was exercised. In the great majority of cases such deficiency was the result of innate causes. In the Mental Deficiency Act of 1913 defectives were classified into four main groups: idiots, imbeciles, feeble-minded and moral defectives. Mentally defective children between the ages of 7 and 16 became the statutory responsibility of the education authorities.

By 1913, therefore, the year in which Burt arrived in London, the Local Education Authorities which the 1902 Act had set up had become responsible for a whole range of new educational and social provisions covering a broad spectrum of the community. They were confronted with challenging tasks, and it was to assist in coping with these tasks that the L.C.C., as the largest authority in the country, decided to appoint a psychologist. The appointment was to be concerned in the first place with the examination of pupils in elementary schools nominated for admission to schools for the mentally deficient. It was suspected that the medical officers hitherto responsible for this examination had been sending many pupils to special schools who were retarded rather than mentally deficient, and it was hoped that expensive mistakes could be avoided by means of psychological testing. So after some debate the Council

15. Board of Education. *Annual Report of the Chief Medical Officer*, 1910, p. 28.

finally agreed to appoint a psychologist rather than an additional medical officer. Thirty-eight applications were received in answer to the Council's advertisement of the post, and a short-list of six selected for interview. The short-list was an impressive one, including Dr Aveling (later Professor of Psychology at King's College, London), Dr William Brown (later Wilde Reader at Oxford), W. G. Sleight (Lecturer in Education at Graystoke Place Day Training College), S. H. Watkins (Lecturer in Education, University College, Cardiff), W. A. Winch (an inspector of schools with a Cambridge degree in Psychology) and Cyril Burt. Burt was the youngest of the short-listed candidates, but there is little doubt that, able as the others were, he was the best equipped for the particular job the Council had in mind. The post was a half-time post, carrying a salary of £300 per annum, for a trial period of three years, and the appointee was expected to fill in his remaining time with other assignments in teaching and research. The psychologist was attached to the inspectorate, not to the medical department. This had important advantages. The medicals were somewhat suspicious of the new arrival and although Dr Shrubsall, the medical officer primarily concerned with mental deficiency, was not unfriendly, the medical department as a whole disapproved of non-medical interference with what they regarded as a doctor's job. It took many years before the strained relations between psychologists and doctors were overcome, and Burt, in spite of his medical family background, remained throughout his life hostile to medical pretensions in the field of psychology. The inspectorate, on the other hand, provided a sympathetic environment together with important practical advantages such as a right of entry to schools and access to all records. The inspectors themselves were an able and progressive body of men, led by Dr C. W. Kimmins, the Chief Inspector, and Dr P. B. Ballard, both of whom possessed some training in psychology. Dominating the scene was the Chief Education Officer for London, Sir Robert Blair, a wholehearted supporter of Burt and his work.

To become sole psychologist (part-time) for all the school children of London, without any precedents to guide him as to how to go about his task, was a daunting assignment for a young man. But with astonishing rapidity and absence of bungling Burt came to terms with the problem, and mapped out a programme of work, which speedily began to produce results. In the first half-year of his appointment he planned to spend two days a week on testing children recommended for special schools and classes, another day a week on test construction, standardisation and administrative work, and the remaining time on outside duties and research.

Requests for assistance soon began to flow in from teachers, requests such as the following from a school in Bethnal Green: 'Thomas C. W. The above child is a pupil in this school. He is 7½ years old and has been submitted for special examination for m.d. school, but was referred back for 6 months. He is a continual nuisance in class and in my opinion not fit to be with normal children. He is not only mentally but morally deficient, and I should esteem it a favour if you could examine and report on him at your earliest opportunity.' In his report covering the first sixteen months of his appointment Burt was able to state, 'During the past year the psychologist has examined, personally or with the help of teachers, rather over 2000 children in the Council's schools. These children comprise in round figures, (1) about 400 subnormal children, (2) about 200 certified mental defectives, (3) about 1,400 normal children.'[16] It was an astounding achievement only made possible because Burt soon realised that if he was to achieve anything at all he had to subordinate purely academic to practical considerations. In an interesting letter to Dr Kimmins he explains his point of view.[17]

> I have come to realise in a very concrete way that a psychologist who is doing educational work is really starting a new and independent science. Educational psychology is not merely a branch of applied psychology. Medicine is not merely applied physiology. The medical investigator has been found, by practical exigencies, to build up an independent science of his own, of work not in the physiological laboratories, but in the hospital and by the bedside. Similarly the educational investigator cannot merely carry over the conclusions of academic psychology into the classroom. He has to work out almost every problem afresh, profiting by, but not simply relying on, his previous psychological training. He has to make short cuts to practical conclusions, which, for the time being, leave theory or pure science far behind. Education is thus not a simple field for the illustration and application of what is already known; it is, as you say, a great field for fresh research.

It must not be forgotten that, in spite of his later academic eminence, Burt was first and foremost a practical applied psychologist, and it was because his feet were firmly planted on the ground that his advice was so often highly regarded by those in positions of authority. It is equally worth pointing out that data collected with these practical considerations in mind, with 'short cuts' that left 'pure science far

16. L.C.C. *Report of the Council's Psychologist*, February 1915.
17. Burt, C. L. Letter to Dr Kimmins, 17 March 1914.

behind', did not always meet the more exacting requirements of subsequent research analysis. The vast bulk of Burt's data was collected fairly early in his professional career; a great deal of the analysis was undertaken from twenty to fifty years later.

Burt was London's official psychologist from his appointment in 1913 until his transfer to University College in 1932. Throughout this period he was engaged in routine clinical work, particularly with the subnormal and the delinquent. At first he had to rely on the help of teachers and care committee workers; later he could call on the assistance of staff from the National Institute of Industrial Psychology, to which he was for a time attached, and of an increasing band of research students. In the Council's service, too, were a number of experienced volunteers who were in a position to help. Burt put in several requests for paid assistants, but these requests were never granted, and throughout his period with the L.C.C. Burt had to rely on casual help only.

By the beginning of 1915, however, he was ready for new ventures. In January of that year he wrote to Dr Kimmins as follows:

I propose to begin systematically working through one or two districts in the county, visiting every school both ordinary and special. My chief object will be the examination of mentally defective candidates; but I propose, if possible, to include in my survey the following cognate problems,
 1. The distribution of backward children;
 2. The standardisation of scholastic and non-scholastic tests;
 3. The determination of average and extreme attainments.
I should be very glad to know if you have a preference or suggestions as to which district I should choose. If you have not, I should propose to commence with St Pancras, Holloway and Islington.[18]

The report of this investigation was published two years later as *The Distribution and Relation of Educational Abilities*, a report described by Sir Robert Blair in his Preface as 'a unique contribution to the scientific study of educational problems . . . the first of its kind in Europe or elsewhere'. It was divided into three sections. The first dealt with the distribution of educational ability among children in special schools for the mentally defective; the second with the distribution of educational ability among children in ordinary elementary schools; the third with the relation between abilities on different subjects in the school curriculum. 'Educational

18. Burt, C. L. Letter to Dr Kimmins, 9 January 1915.

I Cyril Burt: aged 2

II Cyril Burt: aged 4

III Family group: June 1893. Cyril Burt aged 10 years 3 months, Marion Burt aged 2 years 4 months

IV Park View, Snitterfield, Warwickshire: the Burts' home from 1893 to 1919 (photo by L. S. Hearnshaw, 1972)

V *Cyril and Marion Burt: 1900. Taken on Cyril Burt's becoming a Grecian at Christ's Hospital, and showing him wearing the school uniform*

VI Cyril Burt: 1906, having taken his B.A. at Oxford

variability', concludes Burt on the basis of these surveys, 'appears to be of much the same order as physical variability.' The educational system failed to push the brightest to the limits of their potentialities, and failed to make provision for the backward, whom Burt defined as 'children who, though not defective, are yet unable, about the middle of their school career, to do the work even of a class below their age'. Backwardness by two years or more accounted for nearly ten per cent of the school population, and could be attributed to the extent of about forty per cent to environmental causes and sixty per cent to innate causes. Medical treatment, smaller classes, and appeals to 'nobler emotional susceptibilities' (such as self-respect, craftsmanship, etc) could do something to improve the performance of the backward, even those whose backwardness was largely innate. The investigated borough contained over 30,000 elementary school children. Assuming that it was fairly representative Burt made 'a first and probably very inaccurate approximation' of the incidence of backwardness in London as a whole.

In the final part of the report Burt turned to the question of the relations between abilities in different subjects. Here he employed several standardised tests for scholastic attainment, and after subjecting the scores to analysis came to the conclusion that underlying educational achievement there was (i) a general educational ability, in which intelligence was an important, though not the only, component (memory, interest, and industry were also involved); (ii) specific factors—arithmetic, manual, linguistic, and a factor involved in composition. The existence of these special factors, some of which were strongly influenced by home circumstances, pointed to the desirability of 'cross-classifying', or streaming, for different school subjects.

Burt's next major report was his classic *Mental and Scholastic Tests*. First published by the L.C.C. in 1921, it was reprinted many times, and was used as a standard manual for the next thirty years by British educational psychologists. It contained two memoranda on Burt's revision and standardisation of the Binet-Simon scale, the first on the practical use of the method, and the second on the theoretical validity of the results, containing important sections on item.analysis, the distribution of intelligence, the mental ratio, the line of demarcation between normals and defectives, the relation between mental ability and educational attainments, the influence of sex and social status etc. The third memorandum introduced the famous and much-used series of scholastic tests for reading, spelling, arithmetic, writing, drawing, handwork and composition. *Mental and Scholastic Tests* was not only an invaluable practical manual for the psychologist and teacher, it also employed a number of technical procedures, such as item analysis, tetrachoric correlations, scaling from percentage scores and the application of partial regression equations, that were little known at the time among psychologists. It was particularly important, too, for the balanced approach which it advocated to testing. Tests were regarded as 'but the beginning, never the end, of the examination of the child. . . . The scientist may standardise the method; to apply that method and to appraise the results, demands the tact, the experience, the imaginative insight of the teacher born and trained'.[19] No merely mechanical application of tests was advocated; observation was as important as testing, and test scores themselves were 'the complex resultant of a thousand intermingling factors'. The work was remarkable for combining a humane breadth of outlook with a high level of technical competence and attention to detail, and it was justifiably regarded for many years as a standard work.

With his regional survey and this technical report behind him Burt could now concentrate on his clinical work, dealing first with the backward and subnormal, and then with 'the study of moral, disciplinary and temperamental difficulties', or, in other words, with the problems of delinquency. The delinquency material was published first in perhaps the most famous and widely read of all Burt's works, *The Young Delinquent* (1925). The material on backwardness was not collated until a good deal later, when it was published as *The Backward Child* (1937). The scheme adopted for studying and reporting on individual cases is set out in Burt's books, and summarised in Gertrude Keir's article on the history of child guidance.[20] It involved a comprehensive study of the educational, social, medical and psychological aspects of each case, and the assistance of teachers, care committee workers, medical officers, and sometimes of voluntary research assistants. Burt himself would often make home visits to check information. In the final appraisal of cases, however, it was his own clinical judgment on which Burt relied. Towards the end of his life he was to write, 'when reporting on a child referred to me as a potential delinquent or neurotic I should be quite at a loss to offer any trustworthy advice, if I confined myself solely to observing his behaviour or his verbal responses. . . . My aim has always been to gain some insight into his private thoughts and emotions, his ideas of what is pleasant or satisfying, or what is frightening and frustrating. I try to think

19. Burt, C. L. *Mental and Scholastic Tests*, 1921, Introductory Note.
20. Keir, Gertrude. A history of child guidance. *Brit. J. Educ. Psychol., XXII*, 1952. (This article was based on Burt and Keir's Memorandum to the Committee on Maladjusted Children.)

myself inside his skull, and imagine myself in his situation, seeing everything from his point of view.'[21] Everyone who observed Burt at work agrees that he was a highly skilled clinician, and that he made remarkably good rapport with children in particular. To assist him to do this Burt deliberately immersed himself in the social background from which his cases came. He resided for some years in the Settlement in Tavistock Place; he studied Booth's *London Life and Labour* in detail; and he explored the East End of London, putting up at times with East End families. A London schoolboy himself up to the age of nine, it was not too difficult for him to do this. 'I recommend every educational psychologist', he wrote later, 'to start by actually living with his cases and with their families.'[22] Burt's clinical work was not confined to school children coming to him through the education service. He was attached to a psychological clinic in Bedford Square, got interested in 'shell shock' cases, and on occasion treated more severe disorders. 'My young dementia praecox patient has gone home "cured" ', he wrote to his sister, '. . . she was certified as fit straight away for Bethlem, when she was sent to me. Will it be permanent?'[23] This wider clinical experience proved valuable when he delivered his Heath Clark lectures at the London School of Hygiene in 1933.[24]

If clinical work constituted the core of Burt's activities, other research interests were not neglected. He early got involved in the typography of children's reading books, and this led to a life-long interest in problems of typography generally, to the study of which he was to make a notable contribution. He concerned himself, indeed, with a whole variety of topics—the influence of loss of sleep on school work, the effects of home environment, and methods of teaching spelling, to mention but a few. And, of course, he was from the beginning, as a result of his Galtonian background, interested in twins. Quite soon after his appointment he informed Dr Kimmins of his interest in twins, and asked permission to collect data. His L.C.C. post afforded him an unusual opportunity to do so. It was not uncommon for working-class mothers to send one twin to a foster home or institution, and the L.C.C. kept records of addresses and details of both parents. This information was available to Burt, and to the Council's social workers. Burt accumulated this information, together with test results, in the course of his routine work over the years. Unfortunately he did not

21. Burt, C. L. The School Psychological Service. *J. & Newsletter, Assoc. Educ. Psychologists*. Unpublished memorandum sent to the editor. Burt Archives.
22. *Ibid.*
23. Burt, C. L. Letter to Dr Marion Burt, 13 April 1918.
24. Burt, C. L. *The Subnormal Mind*, 1935.

get around to analysing it until many years later, and by that time quantitative genetics had made large advances, whereas the original data had been collected fairly casually and without any clear-cut research design. This was to lead to serious difficulties later, and a good deal of criticism of Burt's 'adjusted' results.

Burt's activities, therefore, covered an astonishing range, and we must not forget that he was employed by the Council for only half his time, and that for four crucial years the nation was at war. Burt himself, because of his short-sight, was exempted from military service. But air raids brought London within the war zone, and Burt saw a school destroyed by bombs, where a dozen children were killed, and over fifty wounded, while gutters were running with blood. 'Nobody seems to mind danger a bit', he commented. And the war brought other involvements. In 1916 the British Association for the Advancement of Science set up, through its sub-section of Psychology, a Psychological War Research Committee. The Committee first met in January 1916 under Spearman's chairmanship. Burt was a member from the outset, and was secretary to two of the main sub-committees (medical and military). Most of the leading British psychologists of the day were associated with the enterprise. Among the topics investigated were tests of industrial fatigue, the efficiency of thrift posters, mental factors in alcoholism, rumour, the increase in juvenile crime, educational reconstruction, shell-shock, training in aerial observation, and the influences of the rum ration in the navy. Burt also personally studied the effects of air raids on children in a home for raid-shocked children started by Mrs Kimmins at Chailey in Sussex. The following year he was pressed to join the Ministry of Munitions as a statistician, where he was concerned with problems of equipment supply. 'Our aeroplane programme is some programme', he writes in a letter home, 'only at present it does not add up right. And Miss Pelling and I will have to spend nearly all to-morrow correcting the additions of the Air Board, before ever we can calculate how many machine guns we can order, and how many they will smash up monthly.'[25] Statistically it may not have been very high-level work, but it proved valuable practical experience. 'Most of all I valued the glimpses I was then able to obtain into the psychology of the supernormal adult.'[26] Winston Churchill was the then Minister of Munitions, and one of his comments on a memorandum of Burt's ran 'The art of statistical reporting is that of picking out plums. W.S.C.'

25. Burt, C. L. Letter to his parents, 13 April 1918.
26. Burt, C. L. Autobiography, p. 67. In Boring, E. G. *et al*. (eds) *History of Psychology in Autobiography, IV*, 1952.

In the year before the war the other half of Burt's time was spent at Cambridge, where he was invited by C. S. Myers to assist him in the new psychological laboratory. Burt visited Cambridge twice a week, on Thursdays and Saturdays, during term time. Among his senior pupils were F. C. Bartlett, who succeeded him as assistant, and later followed Myers as Director of the laboratory, and W. R. Muscio, an Australian, who became well known for his work on industrial psychology. Burt had a room in St John's College, and came in contact there with Udny Yule, the statistician, and W. H. R. Rivers, psychologist and anthropologist, and met the philosophers Bertrand Russell and C. D. Broad from nearby Trinity College.

The contact with C. S. Myers bore further fruit when in 1921 Myers was successful in establishing the National Institute of Industrial Psychology in London. Preliminary moves began when an organising committee, of which Burt was a member, was set up in 1919. A top priority of the Institute after its establishment was 'vocational research', and Burt was asked by the Executive Committee to prepare a report on the possibilities in this field. This Burt did, and as a result in 1922 he was offered a half-time post at the Insititute as senior investigator in charge of vocational research and guidance. Burt remained with the N.I.I.P. for two years, and during this period laid the foundations of the vocational guidance service, which was one of the Institute's main lines of work for fifty years. Burt had already carried out a brief informal study of vocational guidance as part of his L.C.C. duties. He now undertook a more systematic survey of the problem, carrying out a pilot investigation in a representative London borough, classifying on the one hand the jobs available for school leavers, and assessing on the other a sample of leavers themselves, who were to be followed up in their jobs for a period of two years. The investigation was carried out with the cooperation of the Industrial Fatigue Research Board and the assistance of four investigators. A report was published in 1926.[27] The investigation served as a model for several more ambitious vocational guidance studies carried out by the N.I.I.P. in the 1920s and 1930s by Burt's successors; it also set the pattern of the Institute's own vocational guidance services. The various tests devised by Burt in the course of this work were in use for many years by the N.I.I.P. Burt himself retained a connection with the Institute as a member of the Council and Technical

27. Burt, C. L., Smith, May et al. A Study in Vocational Guidance. Report No. 33. I.F.R.B.

Advisory Board, and of the editorial advisory panel of its journal *Occupational Psychology*.[28]

III

In October 1924 Burt resigned from his part-time post with the National Institute of Industrial Psychology to take up a new post as part-time Professor of Educational Psychology at the London Day Training College, to which he had been appointed in June of that year. The College became his headquarters from that time onwards until he transferred to the Chair of Psychology at University College in Gower Street in October 1932. His eight years at the London Day were in some respects the peak of Burt's career. He was at the height of his powers; he was in an environment that suited him admirably; his practical and his academic duties were nicely balanced. Burt continued to hold his L.C.C. post, merely transferring his clinic from the Victoria Embankment to the College premises in Southampton Row.

The London Day Training College, where Burt was to spend his happiest years, had been set up in 1902, following the general demand in the 1890s for training colleges without religious tests and having closer links with the universities. For its first thirty years the College was jointly administered by the London County Council and the University of London. The Principal of the College, who was also the University Professor of Education, was appointed by the University, and the College became recognised in 1910 as a School of the University. Burt's chair was the second chair to be founded, on a part-time basis while Burt occupied it, but becoming full-time when Professor Hamley succeeded him in 1932. The year Burt left, the College was wholly transferred to the University, renamed The Institute of Education and moved to new premises in the University precinct.

The atmosphere of the college was one in which Burt thrived. It was a smallish institution, where the staff were on intimate terms, and the student body was lively and accessible. The Principal, Sir Percy Nunn, was a man of considerable intellectual and moral power. A mathematician and physicist by training, he was highly sympathetic both to the philosophical and to the psychological aspects of education, and his book, *Education: its Data and First Principles*, first published in 1920, speedily became something of a classic. The lecturing staff were all able in their own spheres, and

28. Hearnshaw, L. S. Sir Cyril Burt and The N.I.I.P. *Occup. Psychol., XLVI*, 1972, 35–7.

as one ex-student was later to write, 'The chief thing that strikes one is our complete confidence in the staff as knowing their job, being capable of turning us into good teachers.'[29] There was a family feeling about the college, which expressed itself in vigorous corporate life, friendly social activities, dances, games and dramatic productions. Burt, though now in his forties, entered into this activity zestfully, particularly the dances. Indeed his relations with some of the women students became something of a talking point, and it was during his final years at the college that he eventually became engaged to one of them, Joyce Woods, whom he married in 1932.

But the most important feature of the college for Burt was the high status occupied by Psychology. Lectures in Psychology had been given before Burt's arrival, by the first Principal, Sir John Adams, and later by Sir Percy Nunn and the Vice-Principal, Miss Margaret Punnett. The groundwork had been laid, and what Burt did was to bring Psychology to life. 'The appointment of Professor Cyril Burt', writes the jubilee historian of the college, 'really established the place of educational psychology in the college. There was never a dull moment in "Squirrel Blurt's" lectures. Students were diverted by the application of intelligence tests, the introduction of actual case histories, or simple tests of coin spinning to test the reliability of the faculty of perception. Real "young deliquates", as the escorting porter termed them, attended Professor Burt in the College, and he occasionally brought one into the students' common room. Psychology was a live study; observations of children could be guided profitably, and there were shocks to be sustained in finding out one's own performance in intelligence tests. The students were attracted as well as amused.'[30] Burt was a popular figure among the students not only because of his witty showmanship, but because of his 'extreme clarity of thought', to quote another ex-student.[31]

Burt's qualities were particularly appreciated by the small band of research students that began to gather round him. Being a school of the University, the college could undertake postgraduate work, and from the middle 1920s there was a growing number of both M.A. and Ph.D. students. Among those who later became well known were R. B. Cattell, H. E. Field, A. G. Hughes, F. J. Schonell and C. S. Slocombe. Burt also had time to get on with the analysis and writing up of his own voluminous data. In the year

29. University of London Institute of Education. *Studies and Impressions, 1902–1952.*
30. *Ibid.*, pp. 72–3.
31. *Ibid.*, p. 45.

after he joined the college staff his *Young Delinquent* (1925) appeared, a book which had a far wider appeal than any of his earlier, more technical reports. He was no longer merely an expert, but a public figure. He was asked to broadcast, and by 1930 was giving a long series of radio talks on 'The Study of the Mind' and 'The Mind of the Child'. He was increasingly being consulted by the Board of Education, and during this period made major contributions to the Board's reports on psychological tests,[32] and on the mental development of children.[33] He was much involved in the initiation of child guidance in Great Britain, and was indeed invited, but declined, to become the Director of the first Child Guidance Clinic established in London in 1927.

At this peak period of his career there is no doubt that Burt was universally admired. He was a much-loved figure among students, and he was equally respected by the very able colleagues with whom he associated, and by the administrators and others with whom he came into contact in the course of his public activities. *The Young Delinquent* rapidly achieved an international reputation. Any suggestion that his work might be unsound, or his behaviour devious, would have been greeted with incredulity. In the intimacy of a close-knit society of able colleagues no doubtful conduct would have for long escaped detection. Burt may perhaps have been over-confident, and prone to play to the gallery, but there was no taint of duplicity. No fair assessment of Burt's work and personality is possible unless this phase of his career is given its due weight.

In March 1931, after he had been at the London Day Training College nearly seven years, Burt received a letter from the Provost of University College (Dr Allen Mawer) inviting him to apply for the Chair of Psychology shortly to be vacated by Professor Spearman. Burt was not the first psychologist to have been approached. Towards the end of 1930 Mr F. C. Bartlett of Cambridge was invited to apply: but he had no wish to leave Cambridge and turned the invitation down. Then an attempt was made to attract McDougall back from America. But he was then sixty years of age, and after some hesitation he decided that he was too old to up-root himself again. The third invitation went to Cyril Burt, and Burt was willing to let his name go forward. He was interviewed by a selection committee consisting of the Vice-Chancellor and Principal of the University of London, the Provost and three representatives of the Professorial Board of University College (Professor H. E. Butler, Latin; Professor C. A. Lovatt Evans, Physiology; and Professor J. Macmurray, Philosophy)

32. Board of Education. *Psychological Tests of Educable Capacity*, 1924.
33. Board of Education. *Report on the Primary School*, 1931.

together with three external experts (Mr F. C. Bartlett, Cambridge; Professor T. H. Pear, Manchester; and Professor G. F. Stout, St Andrews). The committee unanimously recommended Burt's appointment on the grounds of 'His distinguished contributions by research to the advancement of psychological science; his high reputation as a teacher; and his recognised eminence in his subject.'[34]

The appointment was announced on 19 June 1931, and it was originally intended that Burt should take up his post in August of that year. But difficulties arose in negotiations over his pension with the L.C.C., and these could not be resolved before the beginning of the session. In the event Burt was appointed as part-time acting head of the department for the session 1931–32. He took over Spearman's lecture courses, and the supervision of some postgraduate students, and was paid an honorarium of £200, but he continued in his post at the London Day Training College and his duties as L.C.C. psychologist until the end of August 1932. His full-time appointment at University College, London, dated from 1 September 1932. The L.C.C., however, forced to economise because of the economic depression, was unable to appoint another psychologist, and hoped that several psychologically trained school inspectors would be able to take over Burt's duties. No new psychologist was appointed to the Council's staff until after the Second World War, in 1949.

With his resignation from the Chair of Educational Psychology at the London Day Training College and from the post of Psychologist to the London County Council, an important phase of Burt's life came to an end: he left the field for the academy, and turned primarily from the collection to the analysis of data.

34. Report of Selection Committee for the Chair of Psychology. University College, Record Office, File 53.

CHAPTER FOUR

Innate General Cognitive Ability

I

Though in one sense Burt's appointment to the University College chair in 1932 marked a turning point in his career, its central thread remained unbroken. The central thread was the topic of intelligence—'innate, general, cognitive ability', as Burt defined it. His first publication in 1909,[1] and almost his final posthumous publication in 1972,[2] alike dealt with intelligence. Throughout his life intelligence was Burt's major preoccupation. As a disciple of Galton he conceived his task as 'the experimental determination of the mental character of individuals'. Individual psychology, according to Galton, had two facets, 'talent and character', or in more modern terminology, ability and personality. General ability, or intelligence, was, therefore, necessarily among its principal themes, and this was the theme on which Burt concentrated his efforts with remarkable persistence. He conceived his mission at University College as being to preserve the Galtonian tradition which had already been established there, and to uphold his department as a centre of individual or differential psychology. The college was a logical place for such an enterprise. Interest in empirical psychology went back to its founder, Bentham; Sully, Rivers and McDougall had established a laboratory with experimental facilities; Spearman, who was in charge of the department from 1907 to 1931, had focused its research on intelligence. Galton himself had been closely linked with the college. His disciple and biographer, Karl Pearson, held the chair of Applied Mathematics there for nearly fifty years (1885–1933), and in his will Galton bequeathed £45,000 to the College to establish a chair of Eugenics. Statistics, first under Karl Pearson, and then under R. A. Fisher, was a flourishing discipline. The environment was exactly right for Burt, and Burt's sympathy

1. Burt, C. L. Experimental tests of general intelligence. *Brit. J. Psychol., III*, 1909, 94–177.
2. Burt, C. L. The inheritance of general intelligence. *Amer. Psychol., XXVII*, 1972, 175–90.

with the traditions of the College, together with the reputation he had already acquired, made him a logical successor to Spearman.

Burt's work on intelligence goes back to 1906 when he was an Oxford undergraduate, and McDougall recruited him to cooperate in the British Association anthropometric project. It was an auspicious date. After some decades of debate and experiment, views on the nature of intelligence, and techniques for assessing intelligence, were beginning to crystallise. In 1904 Spearman,[3] after reviewing the chaotic history of the topic, put forward his 'two-factor' theory, proposed his law of 'the universal unity of the intellective function', and claimed to be able to measure 'general intelligence' objectively. The year 1905 saw the birth of intelligence testing as a practical applied discipline. In that year Meumann published the results of his tests on school children[4] and Binet and Simon launched their first intelligence scale, thus forging a usable tool from earlier experimental probes. Ten years previously in a famous paper on the psychology of individual differences[5] Binet and a former collaborator, Henri, had defined two major problems in the area, the study of how psychic processes vary from individual to individual, and the study of the relations between different psychic processes. Between 1895 and 1905 evidence of individual differences in all psychic processes had accumulated, and correlational methods had begun to be used to study their interrelations. The search for 'governing' psychic faculties, of which Binet had written, found an answer in Spearman's 'general intelligence', and in 1911 Stern proposed the I.Q. as a convenient index of this. The novelty of the 1900s was not in the concept of intelligence itself, but in its operational definition in terms of correlational techniques, and in the devising of practicable methods of measurement.

The concept, together with the term 'intelligence', had, of course, a much longer history. As Burt frequently pointed out, it goes back to Aristotle's 'voûs' and Cicero's 'intelligentia', and through the Scholastic philosophers of the Middle Ages it became incorporated into the languages of modern Europe. It soon began to acquire approximately its present connotation. As far back as the sixteenth century Richard Grafton, the chronicler, had spoken of 'an Englishman of good intelligence', and the eighteenth-century philosopher Thomas Reid wrote of 'intelligence, wisdom, and other mental

3. Spearman, C. E. General intelligence objectively determined and measured. *Amer. J. Psychol., XV*, 1904, 201–99.

4. Meumann, E. Intelligenzprüfungen an Kindern der Volkschule. *Expt. Pädogogik*, 1905.

5. Binet, A. and Henri, V. La Psychologie individuelle. *Ann. Psych., II*, 1895, 411–65.

qualities'.[6] Sir William Hamilton in 1846 had noted that the term
'intelligence' was 'loosely and variously employed in all our modern
languages'.[7] It was a strange quirk of Burt, who knew his history
pretty well, to insist, as he constantly did, that intelligence was
nevertheless 'a highly technical expression invented to denote a
highly technical abstraction',[8] and that it was hardly used before the
twentieth century. On the contrary, the idea was not a novel one
when psychologists began to lay their hands on it in the post-
Darwin period. The evolutionists had merely given the term a new
slant, Herbert Spencer conceiving intelligence as the supreme
function concerned with the adjustment of organisms to their
environment, and Galton as the most important of the ways in
which individuals differed hereditarily.

The popularity which the concept of intelligence suddenly
achieved in the first decade of the century was the result of various
converging influences in psychology, biology and statistics on the
one hand, and in society and social attitudes on the other. Psychologists had devised ways of measuring individual differences;
biologists had begun to unravel the basic laws of genetics; and
statisticians had created a battery of new methods for handling
complex, but imprecise, data. At the same time universal education
had become the rule in Western societies, and with it emerged new
problems of educability, educational selection and educational
backwardness, while the complexity of advancing technologies
generated problems of vocational placement. With this went a fear,
derived from fuller statistics and more thorough methods of
ascertainment, that the overfecundity of poor stock might lead to
a diminishing proportion of those capable of running an increasingly
intricate 'great society'. Many of these fears and attitudes found
expression in the Eugenics movement, fathered by Galton and
officially born with the founding of the Eugenics Society in 1907.
The period from 1907 to about 1930 was the heyday of Eugenics,
and by 1924 bibliographies of the subject were running to over five
hundred pages. Though the excesses of some eugenists brought the
movement into considerable discredit, the movement was not
without some scientific basis, and some of its proposals, such as
eugenic counselling, were sensible. This, then, was the background
when Burt commenced his work on intelligence. Burt was inevitably a child of his times, and his concept of 'innate, general,
cognitive ability' tuned in with the general mood.

6. Reid, T. *Essays on the Intellectual Powers of Man*, Essay vi, 1785.
7. Hamilton, W. *The Works of Thomas Reid*, Supplementary Dissertation, 1845.
8. Burt, C. L. The evidence for the concept of intelligence. *Brit. J. Educ. Psychol.*, XXV, 1955, 160.

II

Though this precise form of words was not used by Burt in his 1909 article on 'Experimental Tests of General Intelligence' the concept itself was clearly implied. In the address he gave at the end of that year to the Manchester Child Study Society intelligence was defined as 'all-round innate mental efficiency'. At the commencement of his investigation it was, he says, a convenient assumption; at its conclusion, although only forty-three subjects were tested with a dozen tests, he had 'no hesitation in assuming that such a capacity exists'.[9] In Appendix III of *Mental and Scholastic Tests* (1921) 'mental' has become 'cognitive' and the definition of intelligence runs 'innate, general, cognitive efficiency', or as he put it in his British Association address[10] 'general, inborn intellectual ability'. The final form of words 'innate, general, cognitive ability' occurs in his 1955 article, 'The Evidence for the Concept of Intelligence'.[11] Effectively he adhered consistently and stubbornly to this viewpoint throughout his career. It was for him almost an article of faith, which he was prepared to defend against all opposition, rather than a tentative hypothesis to be refuted, if possible, by empirical tests. It is hard not to feel that almost from the first Burt showed an excessive assurance in the finality and correctness of his conclusions. The evidence for the innateness of intelligence he regarded at a very early stage as 'conclusive'.[12] In 1923 he said, 'It is my personal conviction that the main outlines of our human nature are now approximately known, and that the whole territory of individual psychology has, by one worker or another, been completely covered in the large.'[13] Similarly, later in 1949 he was to claim that all the more important group factors of ability had been identified.[14]

Attacks upon the concept of innate general cognitive ability came from many quarters, and were directed at every item of Burt's definition. The concept of ability was attacked; the abstraction of the cognitive was attacked; the generality of intelligence was

9. Burt, C. L. The experimental study of general intelligence. *Child Study, IV*, 1911, 33–45, 77–100.

10. Burt, C. L. The Mental Differences between Individuals. Pres. Address Section J, *British Association for the Advancement of Science, Annual Report*, 1923.

11. Burt, C. L. *Brit. J. Educ. Psychol., XXV*, 1955, 158–77.

12. Burt, C. L. The inheritance of mental characters. *Eugen. Rev., IV*, 1912, 1–33.

13. Burt, C. L. The Mental Differences between Individuals. *Brit. Ass. Annual Report*, 1923.

14. Burt, C. L. The structure of the mind. *Brit. J. Educ. Psychol., XIX*, 1949, 100–11, 176–99.

attacked; and finally, and most fiercely of all, its innateness was hotly disputed. Underlying some of these attacks were not only legitimate scientific doubts about the evidence, but deep-seated philosophical differences as to the nature of scientific explanation and the relations of man and society.

The concept of ability, of course, implies at least relatively permanent potentialities or dispositions; in other words, a structured mind. Such potentialities or dispositions are a legacy of Aristotelian philosophy, and as such were antipathetic to the Galilean mode of thinking, which dominated the physical sciences and influenced psychology from the seventeenth century onwards. Hobbes was the first to insist that 'that which is really within us is only motion caused by the action of external objects',[15] and in our day the behaviourists have proclaimed a similar creed. Watson reduced abilities to habit systems which environmental changes could well alter; and later Skinner was to discard all internal structures, even habits. The attack on ability was brought to focus in 1954 by the Canadian psychologist, G. A. Ferguson, when he declared, 'the concept of intelligence, however it is framed, is no longer a useful scientific concept except as subsuming some defined set of clearly distinguishable abilities'.[16] An ability is simply 'what an individual can do', and he can do what he has learned to do. An ability, as measured by psychological tests, is performance 'at a crude limit of learning', and its role in subsequent learning is a matter of transfer. Such an analysis means in effect the discarding of ability in the traditional sense of the term, which implies a structured potentiality, and its replacement by a purely functional explanation.

The issue is, in fact, a metaphysical one. Does science demand functional explanations? Or is structure a permissible concept? The philosophers, or at least some of them, seem not averse to dispositional concepts and structures. Broad, Ryle and Popper, for example, among recent thinkers, all give dispositions their blessing.[17] So Burt's recognition of abilities cannot be summarily rejected, and it is certainly in accordance with the common sense recognition of a whole family of ability words. Burt had so little sympathy for reductionist theories, particularly behaviourism, and he had absorbed so thoroughly McDougall's teaching on 'mental structure' and 'the self', that he rarely thought it necessary explicitly

15. Hobbes, T. *Leviathan*, I, 6, 1651.

16. Ferguson, G. A. On learning and human ability. *Canad. J. Psychol., VIII*, 1954, 95–112.

17. Broad, C. L. *The Mind and its Place in Nature*, 1929, pp. 434ff.; Ryle, G. *The Concept of Mind*, 1949, ch. V; Popper, K. *Objective Knowledge*, 1972, pp. 71–2.

to defend the concept of ability as such.[18] It was throughout a presupposition of his whole approach to the psychology of the individual. He agreed with Stout that it was necessary to postulate 'permanent mental conditions lying outside consciousness, and yet playing an indispensable part in psychic process'.[19] The revival of structuralist modes of thinking in recent years[20] has provided support for this point of view.

The distinction between the cognitive and the orectic (or emotional and temperamental aspects of the mind) was equally a presupposition of Burt's thinking, and equally derived from his whole training in philosophy and psychology. This particular distinction is as old as Plato; and in any case Burt believed that the scientific approach is necessarily analytic, that science involves a hierarchy of propositions based on a hierarchy of abstract concepts. The critics, however, objected to his unreal abstraction of cognitive ability from the whole human being in his environment. Heim, for example, urged that 'intelligence . . . cannot be separated from other aspects of mental activity' and insisted on 'the necessity of studying intelligence as part of the total personality';[21] while another vocal critic, Brian Simon, complained that intelligence tests not only 'exclude, or attempt to exclude any emotional response', but 'isolate the individual from all social relations and any real life situation'.[22]

There are, of course, two distinct objections mixed up in these criticisms: firstly, the general objection to abstract concepts, and secondly the question as to whether the abstraction can be successful. On the first of these issues Burt was surely right. A scientific psychology must deal in abstractions; it must build up abstract conceptual models, which are then tested against reality. 'Every common term involves some degree of abstraction; but in science we have to break up what in daily life we treat as a single matter, and to consider by itself, or in abstraction, that which had not hitherto been specially noted and distinguished in the totality of some comparatively complete nature.'[23] So wrote the Oxford logician, H. W. B. Joseph, at whose feet Burt sat as an undergraduate. And this point of view he completely accepted. Moreover his

18. See, however, Burt, C. L. The Genetics of Intelligence, p. 20 in the Toronto Symposium On Intelligence, ed. W. B. Dockrell, 1970; and Burt, C. L. The Gifted Child, 1975, p. 56.

19. Stout, G. F. Analytical Psychology, vol. I, 1896, p. 21.

20. Piaget, J. Structuralism, 1971; Hearnshaw, L. S. Structuralism and intelligence. Internat. Rev. of Applied Psychol., XXIV, 1975, pp. 85–90.

21. Heim, A. The Appraisal of Intelligence, 1954, p. 1.

22. Simon, B. Intelligence Testing and the Comprehensive School, 1953, ch. ii.

23. Joseph, H. W. B. An Introduction to Logic, 2nd edn, 1916, p. 477.

critics are wrong in thinking that this implied either a neglect of the other facets of personality or of social environment. The clinician in his practical work naturally pieces together the information which his scientific abstractions have provided him with to form a composite judgment upon which to act. Burt made this clear when he wrote in the Preface to the second edition of *Mental and Scholastic Tests* (1947) 'Psychology is the science of the whole mind, not of its cognitive aspects only. . . . In my view the function of the school psychologist is to deal with every aspect of the child's personality and with all forms of training, moral and emotional, as well as intellectual.' And earlier he had stated on the question of environment, 'the psychologist must never be content to look at nothing but the mind before him. It is his task to extend his survey to the surrounding influences that are making the mind what it is; he must ascertain the current situations and the crucial problems which that mind is called upon to meet. To study a mind without knowing its *milieu* is to study fishes without seeing water.'[24] Burt cannot be accused in practice of an unduly abstract approach to the human individual. His critics have simply failed to read what he wrote.

Whether he in fact succeeded in measuring cognitive ability *per se* is, however, a different question. Burt claimed that 'the effects of the environment can be reduced to very small proportions by the careful selection of tests and systematic checking of results'.[25] He believed that by making adjustments and allowances for environmental disturbances (in ways which unfortunately he never precisely specified) 'reasonably accurate assessments can usually be obtained for innate general ability among children of school age'.[26] In the light of accumulating evidence during the 1960s of cultural and environmental influences not only on intelligence test scores, but on the growth of intelligence itself, these claims of Burt must be regarded with scepticism.[27] The practical difficulty of isolating the cognitive from other influences is not, however, an objection to its abstraction conceptually. The concept of 'cognitive ability' is in itself a defensible one.

Criticisms of Burt may more justifiably be directed at his failure to investigate cognition comparatively or experimentally. His approach was wholly psychometric, and the items he employed in his tests were derived from the general hypothesis that reasoning

24. Burt, C. L. The Mental Differences between Individuals. Pres. Address, Section J, *British Association for the Advancement of Science, Annual Report*, 1923.

25. Burt, C. L. Heredity and environment. *Bull. B. P. S., XXIV*, 1971, 12.

26. Burt, C. L. Quantitative genetics in psychology. *Brit. J. Math. Statist. Psychol., XXIV*, 1971, 1–21.

27. See Hunt, J. McV. *Intelligence and Experience*, 1961; and Vernon, P. E. *Intelligence and Cultural Environment*, 1969.

tests, involving complex synthetic activity, would give better measures of intelligence than simpler kinds of test. 'The essential element in all reasoning processes is, I suppose, the perception of relations', he stated;[28] and later he wrote, 'The method of test construction which I have found most effective is to construct a systematic scheme of possible problems, expressed to begin with in the notation of symbolic logic. In this way one can be sure of covering the entire ground; one can steadily add to the complexity of the test problems and the variety of the relations used; and one can be quite sure of the correctness of the answer intended.'[29] In other words his approach was an *a priori* one, influenced it is true by predecessors such as Meumann, and when his new tests correlated better with teachers' estimates of intelligence than did the earlier tests Burt seemed satisfied. He neither undertook a detailed analysis of the nature of intelligence in the manner of Spearman, nor empirical studies of the actual growth of intelligence in children in the manner of Piaget and Susan Isaacs. Piaget interestingly enough commenced his own investigations into the thinking of children when engaged on standardising Burt's reasoning tests for French pupils. He immediately came to the conclusion, however, that much more profitable than the statistical analysis of scores was the study of the children's mistakes; and this led him on to his profound researches into cognitive development. By comparison, the psychometric road which Burt persisted in following ran into relatively arid country.

III

If the concept of 'cognitive ability' is in itself an acceptable one, the question of its generality is more controversial, and this was a central feature of Burt's doctrine. Galton had adumbrated the distinction between general ability and specific abilities, but, as Burt pointed out,[30] at the beginning of the twentieth century there was still a good deal of discussion as to whether there was 'a single subjective activity', as Ward, for example, maintained, or, following the associationists, 'no discernible structure' and no unitary

28. Burt, C. L. Experimental tests of higher mental processes and their relation to general intelligence. *J. Exp. Ped., I,* 1911, 97.

29. Discussion Group on New British Intelligence Test, March 1960 (unpublished).

30. Burt, C. L. The evidence for the concept of intelligence. *Brit. J. Educ. Psychol., XXV,* 1955, 163.

activity. The method of factor analysis, first employed by Spearman in 1904, was an attempt to answer this question. Spearman believed that the observed correlations between test scores could be accounted for in terms of two 'factors', a general factor (g), and a set of specific factors (s). In his own words, 'All branches of intelligent activity have in common one fundamental function or group of functions.'[31] Though he hesitated to identify this function with intelligence as commonly understood, Spearman, nevertheless, termed his law 'the law of the universal unity of the intellective function', and he considered that it was somehow connected with the essence of intellectual activity. The debate about the existence and nature of Spearman's 'g' has extended right up to the present day. From the very start the necessity of 'g' was questioned, by Thomson and Brown in this country, and by Thorndike in the United States. Burt's first piece of research was specifically directed at testing Spearman's theory, and the outcome was to confirm Spearman's main conclusion of a universal general factor, though Burt also noted discernible, if small, group factors. From this support for a general factor Burt never deviated, though he was soon to accord more weight to group factors than Spearman was ever prepared to do, or than he himself had done in this first piece of work.

The general factor postulated by Spearman and Burt has been attacked from two sides; it has been attacked as unjustifiable on statistical grounds, and it has been attacked as a meaningless abstraction. The statistical attacks, apart from the early attacks by Thomson and Brown, came mainly from America. In 1938 Thurstone proposed seven primary abilities, and though he eventually admitted the possibility of a second-order general factor, this second-order factor appeared not to be unique. In 1963 Cattell, originally a pupil of Burt, split the general factor into fluid and crystallised intelligence. Finally Guilford in 1967 proposed a model of the intellect comprising no fewer than 120 factors without any general factor. On purely statistical grounds there is, indeed, no necessity for 'g'. Burt at times was prepared to admit that group factor solutions were 'nearly always possible',[32] but he maintained that on other grounds they were improbable. The concept of general ability, he believed, was ultimately derived not from statistical but from physiological and neurological considerations. 'The evidence of neurology,' he wrote,[33] 'suggests something very like general

31. Spearman, C. E. General intelligence objectively determined and measured. *Amer. J. Psychol.*, XV, 1904, 201–92.

32. Burt, C. L. In Butcher, H. J. (ed.) *Human Intelligence*, 1968, p. 70.

33. Burt, C. L. The evidence for the concept of intelligence. *loc. cit.*, 1955, 161.

ability', and Sherrington's account of the integrative action of the nervous system, he held, confirmed the unitary nature of the behaving organism, and its hierarchical structure. The positive and significant correlations between every form of cognitive activity merely provided statistical confirmation for a theory derived from other considerations. There must, Burt argued, as did Spearman before him, be some explanation of the almost universally positive correlations between all measures of human performance, and the postulation of a general factor of ability present in varying saturations in all performances was the most economical explanation. Even in Guilford's massive investigation[34] involving nearly 50,000 correlations fewer than five per cent were negative, and most of these not significantly so. Guilford's theory didn't really explain this, and the much earlier sampling theory propounded by Thomson, Burt argued, was not incompatible with the general factor hypothesis. In the unpublished second edition of Factors of the Mind Burt wrote, 'I rather fancy that the difference between Godfrey Thomson and myself is partly a matter of degree and partly a matter of alternative interpretation. If the brain were an undifferentiated mass of similar units, then I should argue that the very similarity of those units implied a general factor. The factor, of course, is not in itself another unit. It is merely a description of the pervasiveness of a certain quality.'[35] So finally it is on the evidence of brain functioning, not on statistics, that Burt bases his belief in a general factor. But statistics can assist in interpreting the nature of this factor (which need not, of course, be cognitive at all) by pointing to performances in which the general factor is markedly present, and these in fact turn out to be complex, high level, cognitive activities. So there is justification of talking of 'general cognitive ability'.

Is this concept, as other critics have asserted, a meaningless abstraction (Heim), a 'reification' (Stott), or a metaphysical entity (McLeish)?[36] It is certainly an abstract concept, not to be identified with any particular performance or manifestation of ability; but Burt has argued persuasively that such concepts are the stock-in-trade of all the sciences. To call it, as Stott does, a 'reification' is completely to misrepresent Burt's position, which he puts in Factors of the Mind[37] as follows: 'Our factors, therefore, are to be thought of in the first instance as lines or terms of reference only, not as

34. Guilford, J. P. and Hoepfner, R. The Analysis of Intelligence, 1971.

35. Burt, C. L. Factors of the Mind, 2nd edn (unpublished MS).

36. Heim, A. The Appraisal of Intelligence, 1954; McLeish, J. The Science of Behaviour, 1962.

37. Burt, C. L. Factors of the Mind, 1940, p. 18.

concrete psychological entities.' This is certainly not 'reification'. Nor is the concept meaningless or metaphysical. All directed human behaviour depends on information and information processing, and in the processing of information 'a nervous system acts to some extent as a single communication channel' (Broadbent),[38] or as Neisser puts it, in control systems 'the regress of control is not infinite: there is a highest or executive routine'[39]— a conclusion with which Newell and Simon,[40] approaching the matter from the angle of computer science and artificial intelligence, concur. According to them 'the assumption of scalable intelligence becomes tenable', and in so far as such measures become predictive over diverse environments they may be termed measures of general intelligence. It is also interesting to note that Burt, in his very first article on intelligence,[41] put forward 'the hypothesis that attention is the essential factor in intelligence'. This is a view that has come back into favour in recent years;[42] so it is not far-fetched to suggest that there is a good deal of plausibility, and a good deal of experimental support, for the doctrine of a general cognitive ability of a unitary character.

IV

Finally, and most controversially of all, Burt believed that intelligence was innate. In fact he went so far as to define intelligence as 'that part of the general cognitive factor which is attributable to the individual's genetic constitution',[43] though the I.Q. itself, as a raw measure of intelligence, was not wholly innate. 'With intelligence tests of the written group type,' Burt writes, 'only about 50 per cent of the individual variation is attributable to genetic differences; but with individual tests, carefully checked by reports of parents and school teachers, the proportion rises to about 75–80 per cent. However, all such estimates hold good only for the particular population, the particular trait, and the particular method with

38. Broadbent, D. E. *Perception and Communication*, 1958, p. 297.
39. Neisser, U. *Cognitive Psychology*, 1967, p. 296.
40. Newell, A. and Simon, H. A. *Human Problem Solving*, 1972, pp. 81–5.
41. Burt, C. L. Experimental tests of general intelligence. *Brit. J. Psychol., III*, 1909, 166.
42. Charlesworth, W. R. The role of surprise in cognitive development. In Elkind, D. and Flavell, J. H. *Studies in Cognitive Development*, 1969, pp. 257–314. Cunningham, M. *Intelligence: its Organization and Development*, 1972, ch. iv.
43. Burt, C. L. and Howard, M. The multifactorial theory of inheritance and its application to intelligence. *Brit. J. Statist. Psychol., IX*, 1956, 95–131.

which they were obtained. No single overall figure is possible.'[44] Nevertheless all Burt's estimates revolved around the figure given in the above quotation, rising to 88 per cent for adjusted assessments in the Burt and Howard paper.[45] These estimates of Burt have been hotly contested, and his evidence in support of them even dismissed as 'fraudulent'.

How did Burt come to these conclusions? Upon what evidence were they based? It must be admitted that he was easily persuaded. In 1912 he had already regarded his slender findings as 'conclusive'. By the time of his death they had become 'incontestable'.[46] It is illuminating to set out in formal, if slightly parodied, steps the argument for innateness as presented in Burt's 1909 article:[47]

1. Bishops are brighter than butchers (obviously).
2. The sons of bishops are better at dotting and other similar tests than the sons of butchers.
3. These tests correlate highly with intelligence as judged by teachers.
4. These tests do not depend on prior experience, and perform-ance does not improve with practice, or on retesting after 18 months: therefore, they must measure innate capacity.
5. The class differences cannot be accounted for by environmental deprivation, since the butchers could afford to pay 9d. per week in school fees.
6. Therefore, we may conclude that the superior proficiency and intelligence of the bishops' boys is inborn.

(Population: $N = 43$; 30 lower middle class; 13 upper class.)

Burt no doubt had an initial bias towards heredity, stemming from the intellectual climate in which he had been brought up. At no stage of his career did he display a shadow of doubt on what was very early a central article of his faith. According to Darwin all observable characteristics in living organisms displayed variation, and these variations were the resultant of both hereditary and environmental factors. Differences in innate constitution were the universal rule in nature. Galton had applied these basic ideas to human beings and to human abilities, and Burt had absorbed his teaching while still a schoolboy. He had, too, early in the century become familiar with the rediscovered findings of Mendel, and

44. Burt, C. L. art. Eugenics in *Chambers Encyclopedia*, 1961.
45. Burt, C. L. and Howard, M. *Loc. cit.*, 1956.
46. Burt, C. L. The inheritance of general intelligence. *Amer. Psychol.*, XXVII, 1972, 175–90.
47. Burt, C. L. Experimental tests of general intelligence. *Brit. J. Psychol.*, III, 1909, 94–177.

suggested their applicability to mental characteristics.[48] Fisher[49] was soon to show that discrete Mendelian factors were not incompatible with the continuous variation displayed by many human characters (height, for example, and intelligence). Burt was certainly familiar with Fisher's work by the 1930s, since he quotes Fisher's article in *The Backward Child*,[50] and later it became the basis of his quantitative estimates of the heritability of intelligence. These quantitative estimates led Burt to the conclusion that 'in a population of the particular type we have sampled, brought up in an environment of a certain definite and restricted character' assessed intelligence was to an overwhelming degree innate.[51]

Long before he had turned his attention to quantitative genetics Burt held that a number of converging lines of evidence pointed to this conclusion. He summarised these in his article 'Ability and Income',[52] and in his Eugenics Society lecture, 'Intelligence and Fertility',[53] broadly as follows: (i) Both mental deficiency and 'irremediable dullness' were demonstrably of genetic origin. (ii) Supernormal ability appears disproportionately common in members of certain families to an extent that cannot be accounted for by environment. (iii) The correlation between the tested intelligence of members of the same family is of the same order as the correlation between their heights and weights, and increases with the closeness of the family relationship. (iv) Dull children are found in the best of conditions, and bright children in the poorest, as Mendelian theory requires. (v) Improvements in environmental conditions lead to only very slight increases in I.Q. (vi) In uniform institutional environments the range of I.Q. is large, and the intelligence of the children still correlates with that of relatives with whom they have had no contact. (vii) The intelligence of identical twins is highly correlated even when they have been separated at an early age.

After his retirement Burt went on to support his position with the more powerful techniques of quantitative genetics. It is interesting to speculate what led him on to this. He was, as we have seen, already familiar in the 1930s with Fisher's pioneering article. Perhaps it was the publication of Mather's *Biometrical Genetics* in

48. Burt, C. L. The inheritance of mental characters. *Eugen. Rev.*, *IV*, 1912, 1–33.

49. Fisher, R. A. The correlation between relatives on the supposition of Mendelian inheritance. *Trans. Roy. Soc. Edin.*, *LII*, 1918, 399–433.

50. Burt, C. L. *The Backward Child*, 1937, p. 447.

51. Burt, C. L. and Howard, M. The multifactorial theory of inheritance and its application to intelligence. *Brit. J. Statist. Psychol.*, *IX*, 1956, 95–131.

52. Burt, C. L. *Brit. J. Educ. Psychol.*, *XIII*, 1943, 83–98.

53. Burt, C. L. Eugenics Society Occasional Papers, No. 2, 1946.

1949 that made him realise the potentialities of Fisherian methods, and perhaps the increasing attacks on his point of view by critics like Simon in the early 1950s prompted him to bring up new artillery.

Quantitative genetics is an extension of Mendelian genetics to continuously graded variables, and involves an analysis of total, or phenotypic, variance into its several components; firstly, into genotypic variance and environmental variance; secondly, a breakdown of the genotypic variance into additive variance (resulting from the combination of various genes at different loci), dominance variance (the effect of dominant genes), and interaction variance (the interaction between loci, known as the 'epistatic effect'); and finally a breakdown of the environmental variance into general (between individuals) and special (within individuals arising from incidental circumstances). Weight must also be given to genotype-environment interactions. Corrections to the formulae are required when mating is non-random, for example with inbred animal populations or with assortative mating in humans. Quantitative genetics has been successfully applied to a whole range of animal and plant characteristics (for example the milk yield of cattle, the body length of pigs, the fleece weight of sheep, the egg production of hens, the tail length of mice, the yield of maize and other grains), and in spite of the complexity of the genetic and environmental factors and their interactions the underlying theory has been substantially confirmed.[54]

Burt in applying the methods of quantitative genetics to human psychological characteristics went a step further. As Jensen[55] points out, Burt 'was undoubtedly the first psychologist to understand thoroughly, and to use, the important contributions of Fisher, Haldane and Mather in biometrical genetics. . . . In the theoretical aspects of the applications of quantitative genetics to psychological data Burt was outstandingly ahead of all others of his time'. In effecting this leap, however, Burt was making a large assumption, which went beyond the usual statistical assumptions upon which quantitative genetics rest, namely that human nature, which is certainly biological in its foundations, can be treated as though it were wholly biological, and thus equivalent to the nature of other species. The difficulty is that the environment for human beings is not merely physical, but cultural, not merely the here and now, but historical, and culture and history become internalised in a way that renders them no longer merely environmental. They become

54. Falconer, D. S. *Introduction to Quantitative Genetics*, 1975.

55. Jensen, A. R. Kinship correlations reported by Sir Cyril Burt. *Behavior Genetics*, IV, 1974, 1–28.

60 CYRIL BURT: PSYCHOLOGIST

constituent parts of the human organism, and the process of socialisation, taking place in the formative stages of childhood, moulds the developmental process in many of its psychologically most important aspects. Even Jinks and Fulker, in their review of biometrical genetical and other models and their discussion of correlated environments and genotype-environmental interactions, do not face up to this issue,[56] and Lewontin, who is highly critical of most studies on the genetics of human intelligence, still seems to think that 'no new original theory is required to apply the methods of quantitative genetics to human intelligence'.[57] This must be regarded as a dubious simplification. The significance of the influence of culture on intelligence has received a good deal of empirical support in recent years from the work of Hunt, Bruner, Cole et al., Labov, Luria and others[58] and it can be argued that Burt's model, borrowed from biometrics, was simply inappropriate to represent a human characteristic as culturally dependent as intelligence.

Burt would no doubt retort to this criticism by pointing out that the theoretical assumptions of the quantitative genetics model receive remarkable confirmation from the close fit of theoretical and observed correlations between the intelligence of relatives of various degrees of affinity. In the famous paper in which he first applied the multifactorial theory of inheritance to intelligence[59] he presents a table showing the close agreement between the theoretical and observed values, and concludes, therefore, that 'the validity of the multifactorial hypothesis seems fully confirmed'. In the same article he asserts that using 'carefully checked assessments of intelligence . . . about 12 per cent [of the variance] is apparently attributable to unreliability and to irrelevant environmental influences, and the rest to genetic constitution (including the effects of dominance and assortative mating)'. Burt was to repeat these conclusions with slight modifications and allegedly some additional material in several subsequent publications.[60]

56. Jinks, J. L. and Fulker, D. W. Comparison of the biometrical genetical, MAVA, and classical approaches to the analysis of human behaviour. *Psychol. Bull.*, LXIII, 1970, 311–49.

57. Lewontin, R. C. Genetic aspects of intelligence. *Annual Review of Genetics*, 1975, 387–403.

58. Hunt, J. McV. *Intelligence and Experience*, 1961; Bruner, J. S. *Towards a Theory of Instruction*, 1966; Vernon, P. E. *Intelligence and Cultural Environment*, 1969; Cole, M. *et al. The Cultural Context of Learning and Thinking*, 1971; Labov, W. *Language in the Inner City*, 1972; Luria, A. R. *Cognitive Development*, 1977.

59. Burt, C. L. and Howard, M. *Loc. cit.*, 1956.

60. Burt, C. L. The inheritance of mental ability. *Amer. Psychol.*, XIII, 1958, 1–15; The genetic determination of differences in intelligence. *Brit. J. Psychol.*, LVII, 1966, 137–53; The inheritance of general intelligence. *Amer. Psychol.*, XXVII, 1972, 175–90.

It is these supposed empirical confirmations by Burt that since his death have been called into question. The issues will be examined more fully in Chapter Twelve. What seems certain are: firstly, that the data which Burt used for his calculations were poor and unreliable; secondly, that he made a great many unexplained 'adjustments' and corrections to the raw scores of his tests; and thirdly, that he did this carelessly and inconsistently, with the result that, as Kamin has demonstrated,[61] the figures as they stand are quite improbable. It would seem that Burt, after having acquired a first-rate theoretical mastery of the field of quantitative genetics, was misguided enough to attempt to apply these highly sophisticated statistical techniques to scientifically almost worthless data, collected much earlier in his career, and that he did so with disastrous results. As one pair of critics put it, 'the most charitable comment one can make about Burt's studies is that they represent brilliant examples of how to violate every accepted canon of scientific research'.[62]

Why did Burt do this? We cannot be sure. But what is certain is that his views were coming increasingly under attack at the time, and he was clearly piqued by the criticism to which he was subjected. The creed to which he had devoted his life was being maligned; the causes he had supported coming under fire. The criticisms were, moreover, often quite obviously politically motivated, and Burt was being unjustly accused of aiming to assert 'the rightness of the existing order of things'. Burt was riled by these attacks. Though in some ways a traditionalist in his philosophical standpoint Burt was never a committed defender of the social establishment, and there is no indication either in his published or his unpublished writings that he wished to defend the 'existing order'.[63] Burt turned on his critics. He was an adept at showing up their muddles and misunderstandings, and he counterattacked by pointing out that most of their criticisms were academic. 'For the most part,' he said, 'the critics of the hereditarian view are content to rely on dogmatic affirmation and armchair argument. Few of them have attempted anything like systematic study of representative samples of children, based on quantitative scaling and up-to-date statistical techniques. The general style of defence seems to be: this, that, or the other condition in home or school *might* account for the apparent differences in ability quite as satisfactorily as the

61. Kamin, L. J. *The Science and Politics of I.Q.*, 1974.

62. Ginsberg, H. and Koslowski, B. Cognitive development. *Ann. Rev. Psychol.*, *XXVII*, 1976, 54.

63. Burt, C. L., and Howard, M. Heredity and intelligence: a reply. *Brit. J. Statist. Psychol.*, *X*, 1957, 33–63.

alleged genetic influence; therefore they *must* do so.'[64] There is some truth in this contention, though it certainly does not excuse Burt for using dubious statistics himself, nor exonerate him from the charge that he consistently underestimated the influence of the environment. He always believed that environmental influences on intelligence were comparatively slight, and that by careful selection of tests could be practically eliminated in assessing intelligence.[65] As far as the English school children with whom he was dealing were concerned, he held that their environmental background was 'comparatively uniform',[66] a statement which shows up his limited grasp both of the range and of the subtlety of environmental influences. True he considers these in some detail in both *The Young Delinquent* and *The Backward Child*, but when it comes to statistical analysis he was content to use very superficial assessments of environmental conditions, such as social class and occupational gradings, and impressionistic ratings of home conditions. He never made any detailed studies of the impact of environment such as those made by Fraser, Douglas or Wiseman, or more recently still in the National Child Development Study in Britain, or the Harvard Pre-School study in America. As Fraser says in her 1973 postscript, 'Until we know more about the specific effects on the child of the complex thing we call his environment, we are working in the dark.'[67] It is a legitimate criticism of Burt that he greatly underestimated this complexity, and, instead of calmly examining the issues raised by his critics, turned to polemics and dubious expedients.

Nevertheless Burt was almost certainly right in believing that a genetic factor is involved in intelligence. He may have overestimated its magnitude, his own empirical data may have been defective; and his criticisms of the environmentalists unsympathetic: still, all the same, intelligence may be partly innate. Nor is the question of the heritability of intelligence a meaningless question, as some critics have tried to make out. The charge of meaningless derives from a mistaken rejection of abstraction, upon which all scientific thought depends. Granted that heredity and environment always act together in practice, this does not imply that they cannot be singled out and independently assessed conceptually. The task may be difficult, but it is highly pertinent, and as applicable to human characters as to those of the animal kingdom, though the

64. Burt, C. L. Intelligence and heredity: some common misconceptions. *Irish J. Educ.*, *III*, 1969, 85.

65. Burt, C. L. Heredity and environment. *Bull. B. P. S.*, *XXIV*, 1971, 9–15.

66. Burt, C. L. *Irish J. Educ., loc. cit.*, 1969.

67. Fraser, E. *Home Environment and the School*, 3rd imp., 1973.

relevant models may be somewhat different. The extraordinary thing would be if there were *no* genetic component in intelligence, and if intelligence were unlike any other physical or psychological characteristic. If there is such a component, however, and if human beings differ in intelligence partly for genetic reasons, then it affects many issues, social, educational and vocational, and it is a fact which cannot be ignored. To this extent Burt was right; and there is enough evidence, leaving out his own studies altogether, to suggest that he was. How else, for example, can one account for the strange fact, more than once reported, that the offspring of inbred first-cousin marriages have significantly lower intelligence than the offspring of unrelated control marriages? Or for the lower I.Q.s of those with trisomy and other similar genetic defects?[68] Some genetic influence there almost certainly is: its magnitude perhaps can only be assessed when more adequate models have been developed, and far more research carried out on the complexity of cognitive development. Burt had a good cause to defend, but he made two major mistakes. He used doubtful means in the defence of his position: and in *defining* intelligence as '*innate* cognitive ability' he in effect begged the question. He should have restricted his definition to 'general cognitive ability', leaving the issue of its innateness and its degree to be determined empirically. Had he done this he would have avoided a good deal of trouble and criticism.

V

Two further features of Burt's views on intelligence came under almost equally vigorous attack—the approximate constancy of the I.Q., and the approximately normal distribution of intelligence in the population. His critics here as elsewhere often overstated their case, and misrepresented Burt's views. Burt never claimed, as some of them alleged, 'absolute constancy'.[69] In *Mental and Scholastic Tests*, where he first deals with this question, he only claims that I.Q.s are 'very nearly constant'.[70] He allows for the possibility of 'latent normality and latent deficiency'. There are some individuals 'whose imputed deficiency is apparently temporary only', and with subnormals there was often 'a perceptible drift towards diminution'. Burt's whole approach to development was in some ways a

68. Vandenberg, S. C. In Cancro, R. (ed.) *Intelligence: Genetic and Environmental Influences*, 1971.

69. Graham, C. Modern concepts of intelligence. *J. & Newsletter Assoc. Educ. Psych.*, 1970, 53–9.

70. Burt, C. L. *Mental and Scholastic Tests*, 1921, 2nd edn 1947, pp. 163–5.

sophisticated one, and he included an elaborate statistical appendix on 'Curves of Growth' in *The Backward Child* (1937). He states his views on constancy in definitive form in his posthumously published book, *The Gifted Child*.[71] Based on evidence from children aged 7–8 years, retested six years later at the ages of 13–14, he finds a correlation of 0·88 between I.Q.s at the two ages, which when corrected for unreliability rises to 0·93. Applying a difference formula this implies average I.Q. changes of ±4·5. Occasionally, under exceptional circumstances, Burt allows that changes in I.Q. may amount to 20 points or more. 'A few children,' he adds, 'prove to be late developers and make unexpected spurts; others develop precociously and then fail to fulfil their earlier promise; but such cases are far more infrequent than is commonly supposed.' The constancy, then, is not 'absolute', but does obtain in children of school age to a very high degree. Burt's corrected correlations are somewhat higher than those obtained by other investigators, as Vernon[72] pointed out. Nevertheless there is a good deal of support for a relative degree of constancy. Honzick,[73] surveying the results of four longitudinal studies, notes that correlations reach 0·80 by the age of 8, and it is only with infants and young children that constancy is much less marked. This agrees with Eysenck's conclusion that 'there is a satisfactory degree of constancy after the age of 8'.[74]

To this the critics give, broadly speaking, two types of answer. First, they say that intelligence tests are 'self-fulfilling'[75] in the sense that 'once the child has an I.Q. hung around his neck the teacher behaves accordingly'. There is insufficient evidence, however, to support the view that this is more than a very minor contributor towards constancy.[76] Second is the argument put forward by Hunt, namely that 'the I.Q. is not fixed at all unless the culture or the school fixes the programme of environmental encounters'.[77] In other words, such constancy as there is depends wholly upon social and institutional rigidities, not on any inherent property of intelligence. Now there is evidence that I.Q.s rise in favourable conditions

71. Burt, C. L. *The Gifted Child*, 1975, p. 43.

72. Vernon, P. E. *Secondary School Selection*, 1957, Appendix B.

73. Honzick, M. P. The Development of Intelligence. In Wolman, B. B. (ed.) *Handbook of General Psychology*, 1973.

74. Eysenck, H. J. *The Measurement of Intelligence*, 1973, p. 80.

75. Pidgeon, D. Modern concepts of intelligence. *J. & Newsletter Ass. Educ. Psychol., II*, 5, 1970, 39–52.

76. Jensen, A. R. *Educability and Group Differences*, 1973, ch. xiv.

77. Hunt, J. McV. Environment, Development and Scholastic Achievement. In Deutsch, M., Katz, I. and Jensen, A. R. (eds) *Social Class, Race and Psychological Development*, 1968, pp. 293–330.

and fall in adverse conditions, for example in Douglas's researches,[78] but Hunt's claim that I.Q. changes are *wholly* dependent on environmental encounters is not substantiated by the evidence. Indeed, the general failure of environmental and institutional enrichment programmes to produce really significant I.Q. changes undermines the force of the objection.[79]

Burt did not advocate constancy as a rigid and absolute dogma. He regarded a fairly high level of constancy as an empirically established fact under normal circumstances, and for the population of school children (not infants) with whom he was dealing. All the same there is no doubt that Burt oversimplified the issue and inclined too strongly towards constancy. Clarke, summarising the recent evidence, has argued that 'we have been dominated too long by notions of fixed characteristics, strong continuities and stability of the ordinal position of individuals. The more balanced view which modern data increasingly demand is of some stabilities, often attenuating over time, and some discontinuities and changes during human development.'[80]

Burt's view was an extreme one based on insufficient evidence, and it is comprehensible why it should have been so strongly attacked. To be stamped with an I.Q. which can never significantly change tends naturally to arouse strong emotional rejection. On the other hand the campaign against the normal distribution of intelligence arouses much less sympathy. Originally applied to the problem of errors of observation, and termed the 'curve of errors', the normal or Gaussian curve, as it is now usually called, was first applied to human measurement by a Belgian statistician, Quetelet, from whom it was borrowed by Galton. In his first book, *Hereditary Genius*,[81] Galton applied the law to mental characteristics, and proposed that human ability was distributed according to the 'law of deviation from the average'. And he produced rough evidence to support this proposal. In a later book, *Natural Inheritance*, he waxes lyrical about the law: 'I know of scarcely anything so apt to impress the imagination as the wonderful form of cosmic order expressed by the law of the frequency of error. The law would have been personified by the Greeks and deified, if they had known of it. It reigns with serenity . . . amidst the wildest confusion . . . whenever a large sample of chaotic elements are taken in hand and

78. Douglas, J. W. B. *The Home and the School*, 1964.

79. Jensen, A. R. *Educability and Group Differences*, 1973; Jencks, C. *Inequality*, 1972.

80. Clarke, A. D. B. Predicting human development: problems, evidence, implications. *Bull. Brit. Psychol. Soc., XXXI*, July 1978, 250–8.

81. Galton, F. *Hereditary Genius*, 1869, chs ii, iii.

marshalled in order of their magnitude, an unsuspected and most beautiful form of regularity proves to have been latent all along.'[82] Galton's follower, Karl Pearson, explored the mathematical properties of the normal curve, distinguishing various sub-types of distribution, and, most important, in 1900 formulating the χ^2 for goodness-of-fit, which made it possible to establish whether observational data significantly conformed to normality. Early in the century Pearson and his followers had applied the new statistic to a large mass of biological data.

This was the situation when Burt commenced his work as a psychologist, and he soon began applying the Pearsonian formulae to psychological measurements. He was not, of course, the first to do so. Spearman, Thorndike and William Brown had preceded him. At the L.C.C. Burt soon turned his attention to the distribution of educational abilities in a representative London borough. He plotted the number of children for each age in all the elementary schools of the district attaining each educational standard and demonstrated that 'the distribution approximates to the normal curve of error.'[83] But when backward and retarded children from special schools were included an asymmetry in the curve became apparent. Corrections, however, had to be made for the absence of brighter children in older age groups, and the raw numbers recalculated using standard deviation for each age as a unit. When this was done much of the apparent asymmetry vanished and the distribution approximated more closely to the normal curve.

Later Burt defended the normal distribution of intelligence in two articles,[84] in which he claimed that the distribution of intelligence was only 'approximately normal', and in fact conformed most closely to the moderately skewed Pearson Type IV curve, a variant of the perfectly normal distribution. He held that a 'consilience of inductions' supported this conclusion, and that whatever method of measurement was used (mental age scale, just noticeable differences of item difficulty, unit processes performed in a unit time) something like normality emerged.

It is difficult to understand why this conclusion should have aroused so much criticism, from Heim, Lewis, Richmond, Pidgeon and others. It seems eminently conformable to common sense observation. We generally recognise that extremes are rare, whether genius or severe subnormality, and average individuals abundant,

82. Galton, F. *Natural Inheritance*, 1889, p. 66.

83. Burt, C. L. *The Distribution and Relation of Educational Abilities*, 1917.

84. Burt, C. L. The distribution of intelligence. *Brit. J. Psychol.*, XLVIII, 1957, 161–75; Is intelligence distributed normally? *Brit. J. Statist. Psychol.*, XVI, 1963, 175–90.

and that this applies to most human attributes, including intelligence. Every teacher is familiar with this fact in his educational experience. Yet the critics assert that it is a 'gratuitous assumption'[85] or an 'artifact', depending on the way tests are constructed,[86] having no basis in reality. Sometimes, as with Heim, the objection to normality of distribution seems linked with a dislike of quantification as such; with other critics the basis of their objection seems less clear. In spite of Stevens's classic exposition of the principles of measurement in psychology a quarter of a century ago[87] all the critics seem to overlook the fact that measurement is always to some extent a conventional affair. 'The formal rules of mathematics,' Stevens points out, 'are arbitrary conventions' and he quotes Bell as saying that the mathematicians 'lay down the symbols and at the same time the rules according to which they must be combined'. The application of the normal curve to psychological data is a convenient convention, which accords fairly well both with commonsense observation and experimental evidence, and which enables useful calculations and predictions to be made. And this is the justification for its use. Were distributions markedly different from the normal (e.g. J-shaped, or U-shaped) tests of goodness-of-fit would soon reveal it, as they have revealed certain minor divergences.

VI

Perhaps all these objections stem from deeper causes. The topic of intelligence is of enormous sociological and educational significance. It is one of the main stumbling blocks in the way of egalitarian philosophies, and, therefore, arouses the ire of those with egalitarian sympathies. They would like to discredit the concept of intelligence itself, and every device and finding of the psychologist, attributing all observed psychological differences to iniquitous and remediable inequalities of circumstance. As one of the main protagonists of intelligence and intelligence testing, Burt was the target of much of their animosity. The educational aspects of the question will be considered later. Burt's statements on certain sociological questions will be examined here.

One of the first results of large-scale intelligence testing, such as that carried out by Burt in London between 1913 and 1924, was to

85. Heim, A. *The Appraisal of Intelligence*, 1954.
86. Richmond, W. K. Educational measurement: its scope and limitations. *Brit. J. Psychol.*, XLIV, 1953, 221–31.
87. Stevens, S. S. (ed.) *Handbook of Experimental Psychology*, 1951, ch. i.

demonstrate significant differences between social classes in average intelligence. Burt found a correlation of 0·32[88] which implied a moderate degree of relationship between social class and intelligence, but at the same time a great deal of overlap, and the presence of many able children in families of lower status, as well as dull ones in the upper classes. Burt's correlation was actually somewhat lower than that found in other studies. As Jensen observes, 'The substantial correlation averaging between 0·40 and 0·60 in various studies between indices of socio-economic status and phenotypic intelligence is one of the most constant and firmly established findings in psychological research.'[89] These findings can hardly be disputed; the question is, how are they to be interpreted? Are they, as Floud, Halsey and Martin, for example, assert, wholly the result of environmental inequalities?[90] Or are they, as Burt believed, based largely on genetic differences between the classes? 'I think we are bound to accept the view,' Burt wrote in answer to Floud, Halsey and Martin, 'that the differences in average intelligence exhibited by the different socio-economic classes in this country at the present time are mainly, though not perhaps entirely, the outcome of genetic differences.'[91] This issue is extremely difficult to resolve. Probably both sides were overdogmatic. The complexity of the genetic-environmental interactions in human populations is very great, and evidence can be produced to support both genetic and environmental influences in relation to social class. On purely genetic grounds Li has shown that genetic influences acting on their own will not sustain class differences, that 'the most important single phenomenon of the genetic model is that for any given class of parents their offspring will be scattered into various classes . . . only very strong social and environmental forces can perpetuate an artificial class; heredity does not. . . . Social forces are more conservative than hereditary ones.'[92] Class differences in intelligence can thus only be sustained if there is a certain degree of social mobility involving the upward movement of intelligent children, and the downward movement of the less intelligent. Burt accepted this, and in 1961[93] turned his attention to the relation between

88. Burt, C. L. Ability and income. *Brit. J. Educ. Psychol., XIII*, 1943, 83–98.

89. Jensen, A. R. *Educability and Group Differences*, 1973, p. 151.

90. Floud, J. E., Halsey, A. H. and Martin, J. M. *Social Class and Educational Opportunity*, 1956.

91. Burt, C. L. Class differences in intelligence. *Brit. J. Statist. Psychol., XII*, 1959, 15–33.

92. Li, C. C. In Cancro, R. (ed.) *Intelligence; Genetic and Environmental Influences*, 1971, p. 172.

93. Burt, C. L. Intelligence and social mobility. *Brit. J. Statist. Psychol., XIV*, 1961, 3–24.

intelligence and social mobility. The article he wrote raises a good many problems. In it Burt adjusts his earlier figures for social class and intelligence in various ways. The social classes are reduced from eight to six; weighted frequencies are substituted for the actual frequencies in each class; and the I.Q.s are rescaled to a mean of 100 and a standard deviation of 15. Burt then engages in various calculations. Assuming that the occupational distribution of intelligence has remained constant over a generation, and comparing the obtained distribution for the I.Q.s of parents and of children, he estimates that social mobility amounting to 22 per cent must have occurred to produce a steady state. His own small longitudinal investigation based on just over 200 average, and an unspecified number of gifted and backward, children resulted in a figure of 31 per cent mobility, which compares closely with the 29 per cent estimate of Glass.[94] In an analysis of the causal factors at work Burt concludes that intelligence is the most important factor, followed by motivation, home background and educational achievement. Although Burt admits 'the imperfect nature of the data' he was using, so many assumptions and adjustments were made in the course of his calculations that very little reliance can be placed on his conclusions.

Burt, of course, recognised in this article and elsewhere that social class did not depend solely on intelligence, and the multiplicity of causative factors was, he considered, the main explanation for the discrepancy between the distributions for intelligence and for incomes.[95] While intelligence, he believed, was approximately normally distributed, incomes were distributed in a J-shaped curve, with very few very high incomes, and a majority clustering near the bottom end. Nevertheless, because intelligence was the most important single factor in determining social class, and hence income, and because intelligence was predominantly genetic, Burt concluded that 'the wide inequality in personal income is largely, though not entirely, an indirect effect of the wide inequality in innate intelligence'. Subsequent and more thorough inquiries, such as those of Jencks[96] in America, suggest, however, that 'cognitive skills' bear very little relation to income. So Burt's conclusions must once again be accepted with reserve and considerable scepticism.

His findings as to the possible decline in the general level of the national intelligence were also based on somewhat tenuous reasoning. Though he hedged them round with reservations, he clearly

94. Glass, D. V. *Social Mobility in Britain*, 1954.
95. Burt, C. L. Ability and income. *Brit. J. Educ. Psychol., XIII*, 1943, 83–98.
96. Jencks, C. *Inequality*, 1972.

accepted them as probable. His evidence on this question was prepared for the Royal Commission on Population set up in 1944, and was incorporated in his Eugenics Society lecture in 1946[97] and in various other articles. For London he estimated a decline of about 1·5 points of I.Q. per generation, basing this partly on the differential birth-rate, and the effect of larger family sizes among the less intelligent sections of the population, and partly on direct Binet test measurements obtained on three separate occasions between 1913 and 1939. However, he admits that 'a wide margin of error must be allowed for imperfection in sampling, testing, and smoothing gradients', and that social changes made direct comparisons hazardous. He also admits that 'some kind of reversion, or regression effect may operate . . . which tends to keep the population mean rather more constant than the usual methods of computation would imply'. So there are plenty of reasons to doubt the firmness of Burt's final 'guess'.

There is a common feature in all Burt's incursions into the sociological field. They were all based on data gathered much earlier for quite different purposes (test standardisation, educational selection, vocational guidance). Some of the data, particularly those for parental intelligence, were so crude and unreliable that they could hardly be regarded as scientific. Yet Burt was prepared to use them subsequently as the basis for quite elaborate statistical analysis making adjustments, corrections, and a variety of assumptions. Though he usually included some proviso about unreliability, he neither supplied enough detail to enable others to assess the degree of unreliability nor did he hesitate to make use of the results as if they were at least fairly probable. His besetting weakness was to rely on statistical manipulations rather than empirical investigation, forgetting that poor data cannot yield sound conclusions. On the sociological side the critics had some grounds for their concern.

VII

Nevertheless the critics went too far in dismissing nearly everything Burt said about intelligence. Burt certainly replied to them in good measure. He seemed to relish controversy, and never missed an opportunity of giving back more than he got. His critics were often muddled, and sometimes unfair. Their own empirical evidence, when it existed, was often suspect, as Burt did not hesitate to point

97. Burt, C. L. *Intelligence and Fertility*. Eugenics Society Occasional Papers, No. 2, 1946.

out. Moreover their antipathy was often more than not ideological in origin.

The most serious criticism of Burt's work on intelligence was oddly enough one the critics did not often make—namely that it was so largely confined to the psychometric approach. If we have over the last half-century increased our understanding of the nature of intelligence, it has not been so much because of work in psychometrics, which has told us very little, but because of work in developmental psychology, in the pathological field (brain injuries, psychoses, senescence), in comparative psychology, particularly with primates, in experimental studies of thinking, and finally in the new field of artificial intelligence. In none of these fields did Burt make any significant contributions. Though in theory Burt admitted more than once the limited and provisional nature of the psychometric approach, in practice he made no such admission, and was prepared to back his psychometrically based conclusions with stubbornness and conviction, in spite of the fact that his original raw data were very imperfect.

Burt, however, was a powerful theorist. He was extremely erudite, and had an extensive knowledge, not only of psychology and its history, but of many developments in contemporary science, both physical and biological. He had an expert grasp of the principles of statistics, and, as an applied psychologist by training, a sound insight into practical problems and the practical usefulness of intelligence testing. The lacuna in his equipment was in the area of sociology. Hence his model of intelligence was based on philosophico-biological foundations, and provided little room for a sociological or cultural component. Nevertheless in spite of the limitation of his approach it had many sound features. The concept of 'general cognitive ability' has much to recommend it; and the hypothesis that this ability is to some extent innate is not without supporting evidence.

CHAPTER FIVE

The Subnormal and the Gifted

I

In the controversies that have arisen over Burt's work on intelligence, it is often forgotten that intelligence was only a single facet of his psychology. Burt was, on his own admission, essentially an individual psychologist, and as such concerned first and foremost with the total personality in its environmental setting, and only secondly with abstract qualities like intelligence. In studying the individual he had a double aim, at once scientific and practical. The practical aim was to assist individuals, especially children, to adjust to the demands of social life; the scientific aim to provide the necessary framework of concepts and battery of techniques to enable this to be done effectively.

For nineteen crucial years of his life, from 1913 to 1932, Burt was working as an applied psychologist. He was immersed in the vast job of coping with, and advising on, all the psychological problems of individual children and groups of children in the London area, and doing this virtually single-handed. He was not primarily a scientist, nor a research worker, but essentially a practitioner, realistic, shrewd, and quite prepared to rely on his hunches when hard knowledge was lacking. Nevertheless he insisted that the work of the psychologist must be based as far as possible on reliable knowledge, and on scientific techniques that provided the most precise possible information. He criticised psychiatry because 'it rests on no generally agreed or scientifically established theory of the structures and functions with which it deals'.[1] And in his own work he always had before him a clear-cut theoretical framework, which he endeavoured to improve by statistical analysis.

That framework found expression in the case-history schedule set out schematically in the first chapter of *The Young Delinquent*, and expounded in the first chapter of *The Subnormal Mind*. Burt's scheme was a synoptic one, embracing every aspect of the individual in his environment, and it has had a widespread influence throughout applied psychology in Great Britain. It is indeed remarkably

1. Burt, C. L. *The Subnormal Mind*, 1935, p. 326.

comprehensive, and Burt certainly cannot be accused of narrowness or one-sidedness. The psychologist must consider 'always the total situation, not the isolated personality'.[2] This means looking into social conditions, both material and cultural, and above all into family relationships. Because of the importance of heredity a full family history must be obtained. Then the individual himself must be examined both physically and psychologically. There must be an examination of all the various systems of the body, with particular attention to disturbances of the nervous and glandular systems, to vision and hearing, and to any ailments or defects which directly or indirectly might influence his mental state. The psychological examination itself involved two main areas, intellectual capacities and acquired skills on the one hand, and emotional and temperamental characteristics on the other. In each area the psychologist had to distinguish innate and acquired, general and specific traits. The most important traits were the general traits, general intelligence and general emotionality, then specific traits (specific abilities, 'sthenic' vs 'asthenic' temperaments), and finally acquired characters, such as skills, attainments, sentiments, interests and so on. In establishing his framework Burt relied a good deal on the results of factor analysis, and, on the temperamental side, on the hormic theory of his teacher, McDougall. The scheme had a commonsense validity which led to its wide acceptance.

In the collection of physical and social data Burt, of course, made use of the assistance of medical staff and social workers. But he always regarded the psychologist, in all normal cases, as the professional most competent to assess the case as a whole; for it was the psychologist who was concerned with the individual's inner directing powers and drives. The psychologist was uniquely equipped to assess these because of his mastery of psychological concepts and techniques. It was the new techniques at the disposal of the psychologist that made his assessments more than guesswork or the intuitions of unaided common sense. In particular in his assessment of abilities Burt made extensive use of psychological tests – tests for general ability, tests for special aptitudes, and tests of attainment, especially scholastic attainment. Burt, however, never relied exclusively on test scores. He always was prepared to 'adjust' test scores in the light of other information, for example from teachers; and he did not shrink from giving some weight to his own intuitions. He held that a psychologist ought to be a good observer, and to have the knack of probing intimate thoughts and feelings in the course of a few minutes.[3] He was himself an acute

2. Burt, C. L. *The Subnormal Mind*, 1935, p. 13.

3. *Ibid.*, p. 327.

observer of facial expressions and of gestures, and when it came to emotional traits he believed that the psychologist still had to rely largely on observation. He was sceptical as to the value of questionnaires, and he regarded the tests available to the psychologist in the area of personality (association tests, projective tests, and measures of psychosomatic function) as of somewhat limited usefulness. At bottom Burt was a clinician, who had imbibed clinical skills from his medical father at a very early age, and in the course of his experience developed them to a fine art. Observers of him at work are unanimous that he had a flair for establishing easy rapport with his 'cases', and remarkable powers of observation and clinical assessment.

As a working applied psychologist Burt necessarily had to focus these powers on certain problem areas; and the areas that concerned him especially were educational backwardness, juvenile delinquency, maladjustment of personality and, finally, exceptional giftedness.

II

The first task to which Burt devoted himself on his appointment as L.C.C. psychologist was the problem of educational backwardness. A prime reason for his appointment, as we have seen, was to assist the education authority with the examination of pupils in elementary schools nominated for admission to schools for the mentally deficient, and he immediately got down to assessing the size and nature of the whole problem of educational backwardness. The Mental Deficiency Act, passed in the year of Burt's appointment, had distinguished what were then termed idiots, imbeciles, feeble-minded, and moral defectives. Burt was concerned with all these groups, and also with the much larger group, with I.Q.s of between approximately 70 and 85, who were educationally backward without being classifiable as mentally defective.

The defective group, with I.Q.s below 70, constituted about 1·5 per cent of each age group in the school population. Roughly one-third of these were educationally rather than socially defective, and on leaving school many were decertified. Another third were borderline defectives, and capable of living in the community. The final third were institutional cases. By far the most important cause of mental deficiency, Burt believed, was an innate deficiency of intellectual ability. Looking at the family history of defectives, some form of subnormality was traceable in nearly 80 per cent of their ancestry. Environmental factors, such as malnutrition and

poverty, were of less importance than commonly supposed, and
mental deficiency resulting from factors operating after, during, or
just before conception he held to be comparatively rare. In diagnosing mental deficiency, data from various sources had to be evalu-
ated—environmental, genealogical, developmental, physical,
psychological and social—and the main point to be established was
whether the patient displayed such inefficiency in his daily adjustments as to render him a case for administrative action. Special
treatment was essential for defectives. First they should be ascertained as early as possible. Then the need was for adequate
accommodation and adequate training at schools or institutions
specially equipped for the task. Though no amount of training
could cure deficiency, such schools and institutions could train habits
and instil certain basic information. Severe cases had to be institu-
tionalised, but the less severe could be cared for in the community.
In relation to the commonly held views of the day Burt's views on
mental deficiency were enlightened, and his approach was humane.
He rejected the more extreme medical views on stigmata of
degeneration and moral deficiency, and he believed that something
useful could be done for defectives through training and supervision.
But holding as he did that genetic factors were the prime factors
responsible, he held out no excessively rosy hopes.

The backward group, partly because it was more numerous, and
partly because it created more problems within the schools,
commanded more of Burt's time. In 1918 his *Report on Backward
Children* was published. In it he defined the problem of backwardness, and made recommendations on curricula and teaching
methods. It was followed by a survey in Birmingham,[4] by
numerous other papers, and finally, some twenty years later, by
one of his major books, *The Backward Child* (1937). Burt defined
the backward group as consisting of those children, who, without
being mentally defective, would, in the middle of their school
career, be unable to do the work even of the class below that which
is normal for their age. Burt's estimate of the number of backward
children rested on his two large-scale surveys, one in London,[5] and
one in Birmingham (carried out with the assistance of a medical
officer, Dr Lloyd), and a smaller investigation in Warwickshire. In
the cities he estimated that at least 10 per cent of the school
population were backward, and in rural areas about double that
number. Backwardness was the outcome of multiple determination.
There was no single explanation of it, either biological or social. In

4. *Report of an Investigation upon Backward Children in Birmingham*. Birmingham
Education Committee, 1921.
5. Burt, C. L. *The Distribution and Relations of Educational Abilities*, 1917.

the average backward child at least three adverse factors were present. Environmental handicaps were conspicuously linked with backwardness – there was a 0·73 correlation with poverty, 0·89 with overcrowding, and 0·93 with infantile mortality. Many backward children came from poor home backgrounds, suffered from inadequate sleep and poor diets; and above all backwardness was closely associated with maternal inefficiency. The backward child commonly suffered from bad health, and was physically underdeveloped. All types of physical defect tended to occur more frequently among the backward than among the normal population, including sensory defects both visual and auditory, motor defects, and special conditions such as left-handedness and speech disorders. Into both these latter topics Burt made intensive investigations, and his long chapters on them in *The Backward Child* were important contributions to their study. Nevertheless these environmental and physical handicaps, though clearly associated with backwardness, were contributory rather than fundamental causes. They could be remedied given time, money and effort. Sixty to seventy per cent of backward children, however, were 'irremediably backward' as a result of 'a general inferiority of intellectual capacity, presumably inborn, and frequently hereditary'.[6] This conclusion might appear pessimistic, but to Burt it was a realistic appraisal of the problem, and did not rule out treatment. Burt, always a firm believer in selective education, thought that it was particularly important that the backward child should be segregated in special schools and special classes, where he could be provided with 'a special curriculum, a special time-table, and special teaching methods adapted to his narrower mind'.[7] He considered that far more could be done by way of remedial education and by means of special care and attention than was being done. So Burt's attitude can indeed more justly be termed realistic and practical than pessimistic. After all he devoted a considerable part of his life to assisting the backward, and he retained this interest long after his retirement. In 1962 he addressed the London Conference on the Scientific Study of Mental Deficiency, and in the last years of his life he contributed to *Forward Trends*, the journal of the Guild of Teachers of Backward Children, an organisation of which he became Patron. In 1963 the L.C.C.'s senior educational psychologist, Miss Margaret Proctor, paid eloquent tribute to the importance of Burt's work in the education of backward children.[8] It had indeed provided a large part of the background for the Board of Education's pamphlet on *The Education*

6. Burt, C. L. *The Backward Child*, 1937. p. 572.
7. *Ibid.*, p. 575.
8. Proctor, Margaret. *Forward Trends, VII*, 1963, 2.

of Backward Children (1937), and for the section on educationally subnormal children in the Ministry's pamphlet on *Special Education Treatment* (1946).

III

The concern of the L.C.C., as the education authority for London, with juvenile delinquency had been inherited from its predecessor, the London School Board. These responsibilities were extended and redefined in the Children Act of 1908, which, among many other provisions, required that Juvenile Courts should be constituted to examine children before committal to industrial and reformatory schools. The first decade of the century was a time of many new initiatives in the treatment of delinquents— probation, for example, and Borstals. Burt became caught up from the beginning of his appointment in this concern with delinquency. He was required to examine individual delinquents as part of his clinical duties, he made surveys of the distribution of delinquency in the London area as a whole, and in his spare time he carried out research. The outcome of all this work was the publication in 1925 of Burt's most widely read, and perhaps his best book, *The Young Delinquent*. Delinquency seemed to evoke all Burt's gifts, his clinical insight and sympathy, his sensitive awareness of the many-sided nature of the problem, and at the same time his scientific acumen and statistical expertise. Perhaps too he had a sneaking liking for the delinquent. Expounded with verve and literary skill, *The Young Delinquent* is certainly a masterpiece.

When Burt commenced his work on delinquency, continental ideas of a 'criminal type', derived from Lombroso, were still very prevalent. Havelock Ellis in his work *The Criminal* (1890) had popularised the view that criminals were regressions to 'a lower and older social state', and that children's crimes were often the result of 'moral insanity'. The Mental Deficiency Act of 1913 had endorsed the concept of 'moral imbecility'. Into this atmosphere Burt introduced a refreshing breath of common sense. 'Delinquency', he wrote, 'I regard as nothing but an outstanding example of common childish naughtiness.'[9] He rejected medical determinism and the concept of 'moral imbecility'. He regarded heredity as having a minor role to play in the causation of delinquency. In four-fifths of his delinquent cases he found no criminal history among the relatives, and he firmly asserted that 'hereditary and congenital traits are not to be deduced solely from the nature of the

9. Burt, C. L. *The Young Delinquent*, 1925, p. viii.

criminal actions themselves'.[10] The delinquent might display numerous underlying weaknesses, have more physical defects than normal controls, suffer from intellectual dullness and emotional instability, but he was, as a rule, not basically different from the normal child. Delinquency, like subnormality, was multiply caused. 'Crime', wrote Burt, 'is assignable to no single, universal source, nor yet to two or three; it springs from a wide variety, and usually from a multiplicity of alternative and converging influences.'[11] Among these influences those of environmental origin were of preponderant importance. Burt's studies of the ecology of delinquency covering the whole London County area convinced him that it was associated with certain types of environment, and he vividly portrayed the poor living conditions to which it was linked—overcrowding, broken homes, and the lack of recreational facilities. Poverty itself, his data suggested, could be overemphasised. Much more significant were defective family relations and defective discipline. The character of the street and neighbourhood was among the most prominent of the causal factors. Nevertheless Burt was not an environmental determinist, as so many of the sociologists appeared to be. In his view, 'It is the personal reaction to a given situation that makes a man a criminal, not the situation itself.'[12] Crime in the last resort was a conscious act, and psychologically motivated.

Burt's recommendations on treatment were enlightened. He was never sentimental. He recognised the need for punishment, and in extreme cases approved of birching, though he regarded it in 99 per cent of cases as a 'negative and desperate' remedy. Treatment should be based on a full investigation of each case and be tailored to the needs of the individual. 'In most cases what is clearly needed is not some single summary measure, but a sustained, bracing, educative training. . . . Its object is to train the child, little by little, and step by step, through tasks of increasing responsibility.'[13] It is a technique which clearly foreshadows the methods of behaviour therapy.

Burt's conclusions on delinquency were based principally on a detailed statistical and clinical study of 197 selected cases, twenty-eight of which were described fully in *The Young Delinquent*. His experience of delinquency, however, was much wider. His clinical work with delinquents extended over many years, and he had much case material at his disposal. His article on 'The Causes of Sex

10. Burt, C. L. *The Young Delinquent*, 1925, p. 25.
11. *Ibid.*, p. 599.
12. *Ibid.*, p. 188.
13. *Ibid.*, p. 535.

Delinquency in Girls',[14] for example, was based on a population of
113 prostitutes and incipient prostitutes. His interest in delinquency
continued after he had given up clinical work. He became a Vice-
President of the Institute for the Scientific Treatment of Delinquency, and continued to write on the problem. His work from the
beginning had helped to shape public opinion. It had had some
influence on the Departmental Committee on the Treatment of
Young Offenders, which reported in 1927, and as late as 1963 it was
regarded by J. B. Mays, a sociologist who went much further than
Burt in stressing the sociological aspects of crime, as 'outstandingly
important'.[15]

IV

As a clinical child psychologist Burt was concerned not only with
backward and delinquent children, but with maladjustment in
general. Though he never wrote an extended treatise on maladjustment, as he did on delinquency and on backwardness, he was called
on to deal with numerous cases of child neuroses. His projected
plan of describing 'group by group' the main forms of child
behaviour problems was never completed. He presented his views,
however, in outline in his lectures on *The Subnormal Mind* (1935),
and wrote with Margaret Howard an article on the nature and
causes of maladjustment among children,[16] as well as several earlier
articles.[17]

Burt's views on maladjustment were eclectic, and derived partly
from Freud and McDougall, and partly from his own statistical
analysis of personality assessments, an area in which he was among
the pioneers, being preceded in Britain only by Webb, a pupil of
Spearman's, who presented his doctoral thesis on character traits a
year before Burt's paper to the British Association.[18] Neuroses and
other forms of maladjustment were, according to Burt, essentially
psychogenic in origin. They were not 'nervous' in the proper sense
of that term, nor were they really 'diseases', but rather disorders of
a functional kind. Between neuroses and psychoses Burt believed

14. Burt, C. L. *Brit. J. Soc. Hygiene*, I, 1926, 251–71.
15. Mays, J. B. *Crime and the Social Structure*, 1963.
16. Burt, C. L. and Howard, Margaret. The nature and causes of maladjustment
among children of school age. *Brit. J. Statist. Psychol.*, V, 1952, 39–58.
17. Burt, C. L. The unstable child. *Child Study*, X, 1917, 61–79; The neurotic
school child. *Stud. in Mental Inefficiency*, IV, 1, 1923, 7–12.
18. Webb, E. Character and intelligence. *Brit. J. Psychol. Mon. Supp. III*, 1915.
Burt, C. L. The general and specific factors underlying the primary emotions. *Brit.
Ass. Ann. Rep.*, LXXXIV, 1915, 694–6.

that there was a difference in degree rather than in kind, the
psychotic being so severely disturbed that society was forced to
segregate him. These disorders were acquired rather than innate.
From Freud, Burt derived the view that maladjustments were often
the result of emotional conflicts of an unconscious kind, springing
from infantile experiences; from McDougall, his explanation of
many symptoms in terms of instincts, and a general dynamic
approach:

> To borrow the language of dynamic psychology, which
> McDougall made popular, the mental forces in the field must be
> taken into consideration quite as much as the mental forces in the
> individual. It follows that in any statistical investigation on the
> problem of the so-called maladjusted child, it will be essential to
> secure data, not only in regard to the child's personal character-
> istics— his general and special abilities, his health and physique,
> and his temperamental, emotional and moral characteristics, but
> also in regard to his past and present environment, at home, at
> school, and at work (if he is already employed) and during hours
> of play and recreation.[19]

Burt's own factor analysis of personality traits led him to favour a
general factor of emotionality, and a bipolar factor which he termed
'sthenic— asthenic'. In assessing personality the first and most
important point was to consider whether the man's general emotionality is normal, deficient, or excessive. Both deficient and
excessive emotionality tend to produce maladjustment, but the kind
of maladjustment will depend on whether sthenic (extraverted,
uninhibited) or asthenic (introverted, inhibited) tendencies pre-
dominate. Burt's classification of neurotic syndromes followed this
dichotomy— violence, temper, compulsions and obsessions being
sthenic, while neurasthenia, anxiety, phobias and so on were
asthenic. This terminology of Burt has not been generally adopted,
though the underlying distinction is not far removed from the more
widely accepted extravert-introvert typology, and, moreover, his
work in the field of personality has been somewhat overshadowed
by the more extensive work of his former pupils, R. B. Cattell and
H. J. Eysenck. However, Burt continued to show an interest in the
problems of maladjustment up to the 1950s. He was chairman of
the strong working party, comprising both medical and non-
medical members, which was set up by the British Psychological
Society, and which provided evidence for the Underwood Committee, appointed by the Minister of Education and reporting in

19. Burt, C. L. and Howard, M. *Loc. cit.*, 1952.

1955.[20] The historical information which Burt provided on the background of child guidance in Great Britain formed the principal basis of the second chapter in the Underwood report.

V

There are many scattered references in Burt's writings to the methods of treatment that he favoured. His approach was once again an eclectic one, and the overriding consideration was the need for adapting the treatment to the individual circumstances and problems presented by each case. In most straightforward cases Burt relied predominantly on what would now be called behaviour therapy, that is on processes of learning and relearning, on educational measures, habit-breaking and de-conditioning. This he applied both to delinquent cases, where he stresses the value of 'graded moral exercises', and to neurotic disorders. With the delinquent 'each succeeding day the task should be made a little stiffer than the last—the tempting opportunity still greater, and detection, in appearance at any rate, still less inevitable—until honesty has grown into a habit'.[21] With the neurotic 're-education is directed not so much towards the patient's thoughts as towards his habits . . . by dint of regular training it is sought to associate ideas with pleasanter emotions or with more rational habits. The final aim is to substitute a wholesome habit for a morbid one. The method resembles the process of de-conditioning.'[22] However, this kind of treatment was not always enough. More radical methods were necessary when 'complexes' were involved, and something like psychoanalysis then needed to be undertaken. Psychoanalysis had the merit of probing into underlying causes, and was generally required in obsessional cases.

Frequently with children Burt found that it was parents rather than children that required treatment. With neurotic cases he was insistent that punishment should be avoided, and with naughty children he held that improvement was often more likely if disciplinary control was relaxed rather than tightened. But he was not against firmness, nor did he rule out corporal punishment in extreme cases. His views were enlightened, rational and in general line with the most progressive views of the time. Only towards the end of his life did he begin to have some doubts about the wisdom of 'permissiveness' and progressive methods, and begin to place

20. *Report of the Committee on Maladjusted Children*, H.M.S.O., 1955.
21. Burt, C. L. *The Subnormal Mind*, 1935, p. 192.
22. *Ibid.*, p. 311.

more emphasis on strictness and discipline. But he never wavered in his belief that the prime requirement was the fullest possible investigation of each case. He claims a reasonable degree of success for the eclectic approach to treatment which he advocated. 'In London, of the cases referred to the psychologist's department and followed up for three years or more, 67 per cent showed marked improvement; of those referred to a psychiatrist only 53 per cent; of those left untreated, 47 per cent showed some degree of improvement. There was little difference in the type of cases included in the three groups; if anything, the first comprised the severest cases.'[23]

VI

The other group of children in which Burt was particularly interested was at the top end of the scale, the group of highly gifted children. It was part of his job at the L.C.C. to assist the education authority in the selection of scholarship candidates, and, as a Galtonian, he was quite naturally absorbed by the problem of what his master had termed 'genius'. True, scholarship winners did not quite coincide with geniuses in Galton's sense, but the problems were similar. 'For my studies of gifted children,' writes Burt, 'I have taken a borderline of 130 I.Q. . . . This is equivalent to defining them as the brightest 2½ per cent of the elementary school population of the same age. I adopted this figure because in general it appeared to discriminate those children who, when I first began my survey in London schools, were obtaining junior county scholarships for entry to secondary grammar schools.'[24] Within this group Burt distinguished a sub-group of 'exceptionally gifted' with I.Q.s of 150 and over. He believed that the number of gifted children was being underestimated, and certainly, because educational attainments did not always match innate intelligence, some of the gifted were being passed over for scholarship purposes. Giftedness, for one thing, did not necessarily show itself in the verbal ways required by the education system. So careful ascertainment was necessary. Environmental explanations of giftedness Burt believed were wholly inadequate, and in particular failed altogether to account for the fact that highly gifted individuals could spring from, and grow up in, a most unpromising milieu. To illustrate this he quotes the case of the son of an illiterate dockworker and his alcoholic wife, a young man whose I.Q. was 142 and who

23. Burt, C. L. *The Subnormal Mind*, 1935, pp. 351–2.
24. Burt, C. L. *The Gifted Child*, 1975, p. 50. (His article in *The Year Book of Education*, 1962, gives 3 per cent, and I.Q. of 128.)

eventually became a university professor.[25] Child prodigies of humble origin were of special interest to the hereditarian, and lent great weight to the hereditarian case. Equally weighty was the fact that children brought up in institutions in similar material and social conditions showed a wide range of ability, and occasionally were very bright. Burt records the cases of eight institutional children with I.Q.s of over 130, five of them known to be the illegitimate offspring of intelligent fathers. Although gifted children could occur in any social class, there was a tendency for the relative, though not the absolute, number to be greater in the higher occupational groups. 'A child from class I has a 1 in 5 chance of being gifted (I.Q. 130+), whereas a child in class II has only 1 in 14, and a child from class IV barely 1 in 200. But it is equally true to say that only about ¼ of the gifted children come from class I.'[26] Burt was much concerned with the wastage of talent. His follow-up studies suggested that 'at least one-third of the pupils in the higher educational categories have failed to obtain the type of education which their ability seemed to deserve'.[27] Not only was there frequently failure to ascertain the gifted, there was also failure to provide the special facilities and opportunities they needed. Equal opportunity did not, in Burt's view, require a deadening uniformity of treatment, it meant 'equal opportunity to make the most of differences that are innate'.[28] The gifted could benefit not only from special teaching and special classes, but there was a need for a new type of 'public school'— a 'super-selective' school for really talented pupils. This was in the national interest, as well as in the interest of the development of gifted children themselves. Burt strongly disapproved of the bias against the gifted manifested in the Plowden report—'the egalitarian scepticism of the whole concept of gifted-ness'.[29]

It would be quite wrong, however, to label Burt, just because he advocated the cause of the gifted, as an élitist and hostile to the working class. He was certainly not biased against the less advantaged members of society. The effect of his work at the L.C.C. was in fact to reduce the proportion of scholarships going to members of the privileged classes, and to double those going to working-class children.[30] The first duty of the psychologist, as he conceived it, was not to the gifted minority, but 'to do the best for the vast

25. Burt, C. L. Child prodigies. *New Scientist*, 14 October 1965; Burt, C. L. The gifted child. *Brit. J. Statist. Psychol., XIV*, 1961, 123–39.
26. Burt, C. L. The gifted child. *Loc. cit.*
27. *Ibid.*
28. Burt, C. L. *The Gifted Child*, 1975, p. 190.
29. *Children and their Primary Schools* (The Plowden Report), H.M.S.O., 1967.
30. Burt, C. L. The gifted child. *Brit. J. Statist. Psychol., XIV*, 1961, 123–4.

mass of the population, who, after all, consist of just ordinary mortals of average ability'. His second concern was towards the subnormal and handicapped, and then finally to the gifted.[31] The charge of élitism is a biased charge which fails to take account of Burt's work as a whole, singling out his help to the gifted, and neglecting his much greater help to the less fortunate.

Towards the end of his life Burt began to collect together some of the results of his earlier work on the gifted. In 1961 he wrote an article on gifted children,[32] and in 1962 he contributed a long introductory chapter to the *Year Book of Education* that was devoted to giftedness. The space race had by then brought the topic into favour. In the very last years of his life Burt wrote his final book, *The Gifted Child*, which was eventually published four years after his death. Besides this writing he lent his support to The Foundation for Gifted Children set up in 1968, and played a considerable part in the affairs of Mensa, the society for the intellectually able.

VII

The society known as Mensa was brought into being about the middle of the year 1946 in Oxford on the initiative of two barristers, Mr Roland Berrill and Dr L. L. Ware. Whether the idea was Ware's own, as he claims, or whether it was derived from a broadcast given by Burt in 1945,[33] in which the idea of 'a high I.Q. club' was adumbrated, cannot be established with complete assurance. The germ of the idea may possibly have been Burt's, but Burt was certainly somewhat disingenuous in his claims actually to have run groups prior to and similar to Mensa. The groups he refers to[34] bore no real resemblance to Mensa, nor was the University Club in Liverpool, which he mentions in the same context, remotely comparable, being nothing more than an ordinary dining and social club. There is, however, no doubt that Burt was interested in Mensa from its inception. He was in touch with Berrill from 1946; later he became President of the society and was much involved in its affairs.

The moving spirit in the early years of Mensa was undoubtedly Roland Berrill. He coined the very effective name of the society, and as its secretary guided its development. His eccentricities,

31. Burt, C. L. *The Gifted Child*, 1975, p. 190.

32. Burt, C. L. The gifted child. *Loc. cit.*, 1961.

33. There is no record of any such broadcast in the B.B.C. Archives or B.B.C. script department, however.

34. *Mensa Journal (International)*, No. 125, July 1969.

however, soon provoked a dispute among the membership, then quite small, and, disliking political intrigues, Berrill resigned in 1952. The society looked as though it might fade out, but two years later, in 1954, the present chairman, Mr Victor Serebriakoff, became secretary, and Mensa began to expand, at first slowly, and then more rapidly, becoming an international association with some 30,000 members in over sixty countries. Troubles, indeed, were by no means over. The history of Mensa has been a stormy one. It has attracted a small but noisy minority of frustrated geniuses, whose prickly antics have from time to time delighted the press. Nor have its aims and objects been easy to define. Burt's own primary object in his broadcast-proposal was 'a society which would bring together intelligent persons from every walk of life, scientific and technical, literary and artistic, commercial and industrial, manual workers and artisans as well as managers and members of the professional classes, and so provide some means for the interchange of first-hand experience and a mutual correction of impressions and views'.[35] The aims were more fully formulated in a Mensa brochure as (i) to seek members' opinions on current questions by postal question-naires; (ii) concern with the position of the intelligent in society; (iii) to provide volunteers for research workers who need a high I.Q. group for their work; to which was added later (iv) the fostering of intelligence, particularly through provision for gifted children. The only qualification for membership of the society was a score in a standard intelligence test higher than 98 per cent of people in general. When Serebriakoff analysed the membership in the 1960s academic, professional and managerial groups constituted the vast majority, seasoned with a handful of skilled artisans.

Burt's acceptance of the Presidency of Mensa in 1959 proved no sinecure. It involved him in a good deal of work almost to the end of his life, and, as some of the major rows developed during his period of office, the affairs of the society caused him a good deal of concern. His support for Mensa, however, never wavered, and his backing and advice were of great value to Serebriakoff in his efforts to cope with cranks and dissidents. There was a comic side to some of the controversies, from which Burt himself culled some wry amusement. Burt, as usual in a cause in which he believed, was lavish of his time. He read the proofs and commented in detail on Serebriakoff's history of the society.[36] He personally signed the Mensa appeal for funds in 1963. He wrote to the press, answered numerous requests for information, and was constantly being contacted on the telephone by enquirers who linked his name with

35. Burt, C. L. *The Listener*, March 1966.
36. Serebriakoff, V. *I.Q.: A Mensa Analysis and History*, 1965.

the society. He was, too, involved on occasion in personal problems, such as what to do about the suicidal tendencies of a boy with an I.Q. of 168. Throughout the last decade of his life Mensa was for Burt a continuing preoccupation, which contributed its share to the mounting prejudice against him which marked these final years. For Mensa was much disliked by egalitarian critics. As Liam Hudson noted, 'Many intelligent, honourable people feel that Mensa is a social evil, an institution which makes them feel inferior.'[37] It was regarded as an exclusive social club of cranky highbrows, based on élitist ideas, and hostile to the brotherhood of man. To these criticisms Burt became inured. 'We believe in a democratic society', he replied. 'This commits us to a belief in egalitarianism as regards political rights and educational and vocational opportunities, but it does not commit us to a belief that all men are born equal in natural ability.'[38] He saw advantages in having a society like Mensa to provide opportunities for research and support for the gifted in the community, and Burt stuck by his convictions in the face of mounting, and often unfair, criticism. The survival of Mensa owes most, no doubt, to the energy and ability of Serebriakoff, who rescued it when on the brink of collapse, but something, too, to the steady support of its President, Burt.

37. Hudson, Liam. Letter to Burt, 8 February 1966.
38. Burt, C. L. Letter, 7 December 1962.

CHAPTER SIX

Applied Psychology

I

In his work for the subnormal and the gifted Burt had become Britain's first professional applied psychologist. Earlier attempts to assess human beings, such as those for example made by the phrenologists at the beginning of the nineteenth century, had foundered as a result of their unsound theoretical basis. But Galton's psychometric work seemed to have changed the picture. As Sully put it in 1886, 'A sound scientific method of testing the strength of children's intellectual faculties has now become possible.'[1] Galton had experimented with the first crude psychological tests, and had developed statistical techniques for handling the resulting data. As early as 1881 adventurous schoolteachers had begun to try out the new methods on their pupils, and before long education authorities on the Continent were approaching psychologists for assistance in assessing school children. In 1897 the Breslau authorities enlisted the help of the German psychologist, Ebbinghaus, and in 1904 the French Minister of Public Instruction was instrumental in getting Binet to devise his first famous scale of intelligence. Even earlier, in 1890, Cattell in America had administered tests to American college students, and coined the term 'mental test'. Though mental tests were not the only tool in the armoury of the psychologists, they were, at the beginning of the century, the most important, and it was testing above all that enabled the psychologist to leave the laboratory and apply his newly acquired skills to practical problems. Burt's appointment to the L.C.C. in 1913 was the first official recognition in Great Britain of this new development in psychology.

Seven years earlier in 1906 Burt had commenced his work on testing for the British Association Anthropometrical survey initiated by Galton. The time was a momentous one in the history of psychometrics. Binet's original scale had just appeared in Paris; Spearman's factor theory, published in America in 1904, seemed to provide a justification for the concept of intelligence. There was a new note of optimism among psychologists, a belief that they had

1. Sully, J. *The Teacher's Handbook of Psychology*, 1886, p. 496.

something important to offer, and that a great many practical problems in education, child upbringing, mental disorder, and vocational life were on the way to solution. Burt shared in this optimism. By 1923, when he delivered the presidential address to the psychology section of the British Association, he believed that the whole field of individual psychology had been completely covered in the large, and that it was 'the duty of the state, through its school service, first to find out to what order of intelligence each child belongs, then to give him the education most appropriate to his powers, and finally, before it leaves him, to place him in the particular type of occupation for which nature has marked him out'.[2] From the time when his first article on intelligence appeared in 1909 until his death over sixty years later Burt was, in the words of *The Times* obituary notice, 'the leading figure in Britain in the applications of psychology to education, and the development of children, and to the assessment of mental qualities'.[3] The basis of Burt's work was mental testing and the statistical techniques for handling test results. Almost everything else he did in psychology derived from these foundations.

Burt's contribution to the field of mental testing was fivefold. Firstly, he was a pioneer in the construction of verbal group tests of intelligence; secondly, he was responsible for some of the more important revisions and standardisations of the Binet test for British use; thirdly, he devised a widely used battery of scholastic achievement tests; fourthly, he made a number of contributions to test technology; and, finally, he was among the leaders in the application of factor analysis to test results.

In his first investigations the tests Burt used followed the contemporary trend of employing simple measures of sensory discrimination, motor function, memory and association.[4] His results, however, showed that the simpler tests correlated poorly with 'general intelligence', and he came to the conclusion that 'the more complex the mental processes involved and the higher the mental level tested, the more completely did the experimental results correspond with the empirical estimates of intelligence'.[5] In Liverpool he turned, therefore, to the task of elaborating tests of a higher and more complex order than those previously employed. 'The highest mental processes of all are those classed together under

2. Burt, C. L. Psychological tests for scholarship and promotion. *The School*, XIII, 1925, 734–42.

3. *The Times*, 12 October 1971.

4. Burt, C. L. Experimental tests of general intelligence. *Brit. J. Psychol.*, III, 1909, 94–177.

5. Burt, C. L. Experimental tests of higher mental processes and their relation to general intelligence. *J. Exp. Pedagog.*, I, 1911, 93–112.

the term "reasoning". Tests involving reasoning had not before been applied.'[6] A secondary aim was to ascertain 'with what success they could be carried out upon a number of children at once . . . and by teachers untrained in psychological experiments'. Hence the verbal group test of intelligence, which was to play a major role in the testing movement of the twentieth century, was born, to be taken up later by the American Army in the First World War, and, after the war, by educational and guidance organisations of all the advanced countries of the world. Not all the tests Burt used in his Liverpool investigation were original. He adopted Ebbinghaus's completion test, the cancellation test first devised by Bourdon, and a modification of Galton's association test. The new tests he created included an analogies test, which has proved one of the most successful of verbal intelligence tests, and a test of syllogistic reasoning. A battery of fourteen tests in all was applied to groups of Liverpool secondary school pupils, both boys and girls, and Burt confirmed the conclusion that tests of logical inference and complex synthetic activity constituted the best tests of intelligence.

These Liverpool tests were followed later by a more comprehensive reasoning test, intended to be given to each child individually and orally.[7] The test consisted of fifty reasoning problems graded in years from seven to fourteen. It has not been widely adopted, partly because of its complexity, and partly because of the limited range of thinking processes it tapped. In constructing it Burt had recourse to his Oxford training in logic, but, as Vernon has pointed out, there is a certain arbitrariness in the choice of items. It was of some importance, however, as the starting point for Piaget's lifelong investigations into children's thinking, and as the basis for Burt's own view that all the elementary mechanisms essential to formal reasoning were present before the child leaves the infant school, that is, by the time the child reaches the mental age of seven.

Among the other verbal tests devised by Burt were a composite test for the Bradford Education Authority in 1920 consisting of opposites, analogies, completion and graded reasoning; the National Institute of Industrial Psychology Group Test 33, devised in 1923 and extensively used up to the 1960s; and the Northumberland Test devised for that county in 1925 following the earlier tests of Godfrey Thomson. Tests were becoming increasingly popular, and Burt could claim in 1924 that 'the successful widespread use of intelli-

6. Burt, C. L. *J. Exp. Pedagog.*, *I*, 1911, p. 95.

7. Burt, C. L. The development of reasoning in school children. *J. Exp. Pedagog.*, *V*, 1919, 68–77, 121–7. A short version of the test was included in *Mental and Scholastic Tests*, 1921.

gence tests remains among the most remarkable achievements of modern experimental psychology'.[8]

It was never Burt's intention that group tests should supersede individual tests such as those devised by Binet. He recognised that in many circumstances individual testing was necessary, and he devoted much effort to revising and standardising Binet's tests for British use. His work on the Binet scales was most thorough. His London revision included all the items from Binet's 1908 and 1911 scales, together with a number of memory tests added by American workers. The tests were reassorted in order of difficulty and age-assignments, and provided with British norms after having been tried out on over 3,500 London children. The tests were subjected to a detailed item analysis, correlated with educational attainments, and submitted to factor analysis. Burt regarded the Binet test as one of the psychologist's most useful tools in spite of the fact that it was by no means an entirely satisfactory test of innate intelligence. 'A child's proficiency in the Binet-Simon tests,' he states, 'is the complex resultant of a thousand intermingling factors. Besides the two essential items, the intelligence he has inherited and the age he has reached, a host of subsidiary conditions inevitably affects his score. Zeal, industry, good will, emotional stability, scholastic information, the accident of social class, the circumstance of sex—each and all of these irrelevant influences, in the one case propitious, in another prejudicial, improve or impair the final result.'[9] Hence the mental age score obtained was by no means infallible, and could not always be taken at its face value. As a practical psychologist Burt felt justified in making commonsense allowances and 'adjustments'. 'I did not take my test results just as they stood,' he writes. 'They were carefully discussed with teachers, and freely corrected whenever it seemed likely that the teacher's view of the relative merits of his own pupils gave a better estimate than the crude test marks.'[10] For the practical psychologist who had to work with teachers this was a sensible procedure; for the future researcher it could only be regarded as scientifically dubious. Nevertheless Burt believed in the value of the Binet scale and continued to work on it. He adapted the Terman revision, and when Terman and Merrill produced a new revised version in 1937 Burt and his colleagues at University College once again modified it for British use.[11] Still

8. Board of Education. *Psychological Tests of Educable Capacity*, H.M.S.O., 1924, p. 61.

9. Burt, C. L. *Mental and Scholastic Tests*, 1921, p. 187.

10. *Ibid.*, p. 280.

11. Burt, C. L. The Terman-Merrill Revision of the Binet Scale. *Mind, XLVII*, 1938, 101–3; The latest revision of the Binet tests. *Eugen. Rev., XXX*, 1939, 255–60; The revision of the Stanford-Binet Scale. *Occup. Psychol., XVII*, 1943, 204–6.

later, in the 1960s, he was consulted by the psychologists working on the new British Intelligence Scale (later published as the British Abilities Scales).

Scholastic or, as they are now usually termed, achievement tests were the other area of test construction to which Burt contributed. His series of tests for reading, spelling, arithmetic, writing, drawing, handwork and composition was widely used from the date of its publication in 1921 almost until his death. It was described in the *Mental Measurements Yearbook* in the 1950s as 'a standard work, indeed one of the classics of the field'.[12] As Burt pointed out,[13] achievement tests were rather similar to the group tests of attainment employed from 1862 onwards for checking standards in schools for purposes of grant payments. When payment by results began to fall into disuse towards the turn of the century there was still a need for measures of achievement, and both on the Continent and in Britain tests were devised for the purpose. In England P. B. Ballard and W. A. Winch (both psychologically trained and both inspectors of schools) and Professor J. A. Green of Sheffield were the principal pioneers. Burt followed in their footsteps, and the set of scholastic tests he devised for use in London in the first instance soon superseded all others. Ballard generously praised it as 'characterised by the scholarly care and thoroughness which we have learned to look for in everything that Mr Burt produces'.[14]

Towards the end of his life Burt was asked by a South African research student how in particular he compiled his reading tests, and he replied as follows:

1. The words, sentences and prose passages used in my tests were selected from a much larger preliminary collection. These in turn were taken (i) from various reading books currently used in the schools, (ii) from children's own talk and compositions, and (iii) from books or magazines which the children read out of school.
2. Teachers, several of them my own research students,[15] helped in the preliminary application of the tests, and in discussing

12. Buros, O. *IVth Mental Measurements Yearbook*, 1953. A fourth edition of *Mental and Scholastic Tests* appeared in 1962.

13. Board of Education. *Psychological Tests of Educable Capacity*, 1924, ch. I.

14. Ballard, P. B. Review of *Mental and Scholastic Tests*. *Brit. J. Psychol.*, XIII, 1922, 92–5.

15. The reference to postgraduate research students in this reply is probably an example of Burt's memory lapses. There is no mention of postgraduate students in the introductory note to the first edition of *Mental and Scholastic Tests*, and as Burt had no university position at the time he could have had no postgraduate students of his own.

the suitability of the shorter lists provisionally selected. This was necessary because a variety of methods of teaching reading was in vogue, resulting in slightly different vocabularies in each. So far as possible words common to all and representative of each were included.

3. The final selection was based on an item analysis. A random and representative sample of each age group was collected from a variety of schools, and each child was tested individually either by myself or one of my postgraduate research students who had worked with me. The teachers graded each child independently for reading ability, and a correlation coefficient was calculated for each item. Those items were finally selected which had the highest correlation.[16]

The systematic and thorough way in which Burt compiled his tests, which this passage reveals, helps to explain their long popularity. Much more questionable was the use that Burt himself later made of the scores obtained with his scholastic tests over a period of fifty years as evidence for a deterioration of educational standards.[17]

Of his ability in the field of test technology, however, there is no doubt. His claim in the preface to the second edition of *Mental and Scholastic Tests* may perhaps have been exaggerated, but there was an element of truth in it. 'A number of technical procedures that have since become commonplace in psychological investigations were then used almost for the first time,' he wrote, 'item analysis, tetrachoric correlations, the correlation of persons, the assessment of factor measurements by simple averaging, the method of scaling tests from percentage scores, the use of representative sampling, the application of partial regression equations— these were essentially new; indeed corrections for selection and partial regressions were sufficiently novel in psychological work to provoke considerable controversy at the time.'[18] As Burt was the first psychologist in Great Britain to engage in large-scale testing it is not surprising that he should be also among the first to apply novel statistical techniques. In doing so, however, he was borrowing rather than innovating. In his item analysis he employed Yule's 'coefficient of colligation'; in his partial regression equations for estimating the influence of schooling on Binet scores he also had recourse to Yule;[19] and he did not actually use, though he did mention,

16. Burt, C. L. Letter, 16 May 1967.

17. Burt, C. L. Intelligence and heredity. *Irish J. Psychol., III*, 1969, 75–94; The Mental Differences between Children, in *Black Paper II*, eds Cox, C. B. and Dyson, A. E., 1969.

18. Burt, C. L. *Mental and Scholastic Tests*, Preface to 2nd edn, 1947.

19. Yule, G. Udny. *Introduction to the Theory of Statistics*, 1910.

tetrachoric correlations, a technique which Pearson had devised in 1913. Nor is the correlation between persons that he refers to identical with the procedure later termed 'P' technique, since he was using it to compare the orders of difficulty found for items of the Binet scale by different investigators. The 'persons', in other words, are the testers, not the testees. None the less his techniques were a considerable advance over those being employed by most psychologists at the time, and he did introduce to psychologists several of the methods devised by statisticians in the first decade of the century.

Test technology was an area in which Burt retained his interest and his expertise. As a psychological adviser to the armed services in the Second World War, and to the Civil Service in the post-war period, he monitored the testing work of the army and civil service psychologists, and advised on methodology. Though he rarely attended meetings, Burt's personal advice and numerous memoranda made him a major force in the application of psychological techniques in the services, military and civil (see section IV below).

His contributions to test theory also continued. In his memorandum to the Hartog committee on examinations in the 1930s he extended the lessons learnt in the field of test technology to ordinary school and university examinations, and attempted to elucidate 'the marks of examiners' by means of factorial techniques.[20] After the war he turned to the problem of test construction in an article which it has been said 'sparkles with suggestive ideas'.[21] In it he criticised the haphazard construction of many tests, linked test construction to logic and information theory (then in its infancy), defined 'difficulty' as an attribute of test items, and discussed scaling in the light of general psychophysics.[22] This article, together with a later article on 'Test Reliability Estimated by Analysis of Variance',[23] was based on the roneoed laboratory notes which Burt prepared for his students, and which included memoranda on reliability, analysis of variance, and the construction and standardisation of tests; also, of course, in great detail on factor analysis, which is important enough to require a chapter of its own (see Chapter Nine).

There is no question that test technology in Great Britain owes a lot to Burt—a fact that was recognised when, in 1966, one of his

20. Burt, C. L. The Analysis of Examination Marks. In Hartog, P. and Rhodes, E. C. (eds) *The Marks of Examiners*, 1936.

21. Symposium of Service Psychologists, Advisory Committee on Defence Science. Memorandum by U.K. delegation, 1961.

22. Burt, C. L. Test construction and the scaling of items. *Brit. J. Statist. Psychol.*, IV, 1951, 95–129.

23. Burt, C. L. *Brit. J. Statist. Psychol.*, VIII, 1955, 103–18.

94 CYRIL BURT: PSYCHOLOGIST

former pupils, Dr Edgar Anstey, got him to write a Foreword to his own book on *Psychological Tests*.

By 1920 psychological testing had become of sufficient public importance for the Board of Education to refer the question of the use of tests in the education system to its consultative committee under the chairmanship of Sir Henry Hadow. A special sub-committee was set up to consider the matter, and three psychologists, P. B. Ballard, C. S. Myers and C. E. Spearman, were coopted. Burt himself was not a member, but he provided evidence, and was commissioned to write the historical chapter on the development of psychological tests for the report, which appeared under the title *Psychological Tests of Educable Capacity* in 1924. He also provided several technical appendices and a bibliography. It is obvious that the committee was to a very large extent swayed by his views. The words of the report often echo Burt's own statements almost verbatim. 'Intelligence tests claim to measure inborn intellectual ability, or "intelligence", which is envisaged as a purely abstract potentiality— an hypothetical quantity, postulated and defined, like most other scientific concepts, for the convenience of separate measurement.'[24] Within reasonable limits the I.Q. measured by intelligence tests is constant, except in a very small percentage of cases (such as canal boat children) where the necessary minimum of common environment was lacking. But, in general, 'the differences disclosed among individuals by means of intelligence tests are due to differences in native ability'.[25] The committee, therefore, recommended the use of tests to supplement examinations in English and Arithmetic for selection for 'free places' in secondary schools, and within the schools for classification, transference and individual diagnosis. It was noted, however, that 'any system of selection whatever, whether by means of psychological tests or by means of examinations, which determines at the age of eleven the educational future of children is and must be gravely unreliable'.[26] The report, which was reprinted in 1932, certainly encouraged local education authorities to adopt psychological tests, and paved the way for the later Hadow report on *The Primary School*, the Norwood report on *Curriculum and Examinations in Secondary Schools*, and the mass application of psychological testing, with not altogether happy results, to almost the entire child population of the country. For this, however, Burt was only partly and indirectly responsible. The report's warnings about selection at eleven, which

24. Board of Education. *Psychological Tests of Educable Capacity*, H.M.S.O., 1924, p. 65.
25. *Ibid.*, p. 75.
26. *Ibid.*, p. 108.

if not contributed by Burt certainly accorded with his views, were ignored when the final decisions were taken.

II

The first field in which tests were applied was that of education and child guidance. Here Burt was in almost at the beginning, and was certainly the first specialist in Britain. Several nineteenth-century British psychologists had grasped the potential value of psychology for education, and had written psychological textbooks for teachers. These books, however, tended to be of a philosophical nature, and were, for the most part, as the educator Sir John Adams observed, 'dull and unreadable'. The British Child Study Association, founded in 1894 with Sully's support, introduced a more empirical note, and its journal *Child Study* (at first named *The Paidologist*) contained a good many psychological articles, some by Burt, before ceasing publication in 1921. Another movement, known from its German origins as experimental pedagogy, also sprang up early in the twentieth century and relied extensively on the findings of psychology. Its organ, *The Journal of Experimental Pedagogy*, was eventually transformed into *The British Journal of Educational Psychology*. What Burt brought to these movements were a new professionalism, more clearly defined goals and more rigorous methods. With him educational psychology as a profession was born. From 1920 for half a century Burt's voice was influential not only in the development of educational psychology and child guidance, but in the shaping of educational policy. He promoted the use of tests for secondary school selection; he supported research into teaching standards and teaching methods; he assisted in the launching of child guidance clinics; he established training courses for educational psychology; and he gave evidence to various ministerial and other enquiries.

The first use of tests for secondary school selection would seem to be their use by the Bradford Education Authority in 1919. The tests used were those devised by Burt in Liverpool in 1911. Blackpool followed in 1922, Burt providing the standardised arithmetic tests, and working out correlations. Other authorities joined in, and also some public schools, for example Rugby. Meanwhile Godfrey Thomson had inaugurated the Northumberland scheme in 1921, to which Burt contributed a set of tests in 1925. By the time the Hadow committee had produced its report on *The Primary School* in 1931 its members had been persuaded that before the age of twelve 'children need to be grouped according to their capacity, not merely in separate classes or standards, but in separate types of schools'.[27] The process which culminated in the Education Act of 1944 had its beginnings in the early experiments of Burt a quarter of a century previously.

It was always Burt's belief that applications of this kind must be based on, and must be accompanied by, research. The need for research was a constant theme. As early as 1915 he was appealing for cooperation in research on behalf of the newly formed Research Committee of the Child Study Association.[28] He was a member of the British Association Committee enquiring into Mental and Physical Factors involved in Education, set up in 1916, and later in 1923 a member of the British Psychological Society's Committee for Research on Education, of which Susan Isaacs was the secretary. When the National Foundation for Educational Research was established after the Second World War Burt was made a Vice-President, and retained this position until his death. He was involved in nearly all the areas of educational research discussed in Schonell's articles on 'The Development of Educational Research in Great Britain'[29] and many of the theses in Blackwell's list were by Burt's pupils.[30] On the psychological side he was for long the king-pin of English educational research.

In child guidance Burt's influence was even more decisive. As Professor Seth remarked, 'Burt's massive scholarship and authority impended over the entire child-study scene.'[31] When child guidance in a technical sense actually began is largely a matter of definition. It is probably going too far to claim, as Burt did, that Galton's laboratory was 'virtually the first child guidance centre'.[32] Galton was far more interested in collecting statistics than in guiding individuals. Nor is it really justifiable to say that Burt and Keatinge in Oxford started the first child guidance clinic in England.[33] In 1905 Burt was still an undergraduate, and, although an enterprising one, undergraduates are not in a position to run child guidance clinics in any organised way. It was not until Burt got to London in 1913 that child guidance really started, and by then of course the Americans, Witmer and Healey, had already blazed the way. There is no doubt, however, that Burt, as L.C.C. psychologist, followed

27. Board of Education. *The Primary School*, H.M.S.O., 1931, App. III.

28. Burt, C. L. An appeal for cooperation in research. *Child Study, VIII*, 1915, 92.

29. Schonell, F. J. *Brit. J. Educ. Psychol., XVII–XIX*, 1947–1949.

30. Blackwell, A. M. List of researches in educational psychology and teaching method, 1918–1943. *Brit. J. Educ. Psychol., XIII–XV*, 1943–1945.

31. Seth, G. J. & Newsletter Ass. Educ. Psychol., 1972.

32. Board of Education. *The Primary School*, H.M.S.O., 1931, App. III.

33. *The Times*. Obituary Notice of Sir Cyril Burt, 12 October 1971.

closely in their tracks, and was operating a child guidance clinic from his Victoria Embankment office. Samples of his case reports are filed in the London Education Authority Archives from the year of his appointment onwards. Burt's psychological examinations were often supplemented by medical reports and by home visits either by himself or by care committee workers. All the ingredients of a child guidance service were present, and Burt continued to carry on this clinical work when he moved to the London Day Training College, and later to University College, as one among numerous other activities. In *The Young Delinquent* (1925) he outlined a plan for the establishment of more ambitious psychological clinics, staffed full-time by a minimum of two psychologists, one or more social workers, and a shorthand-typist. This plan caught the attention of a London magistrate, Mrs St Loe Strachey, who suggested that the Commonwealth Fund of America might be prepared to finance a demonstration clinic. A small meeting was called at the London Day Training College, where Burt was then quartered, and a letter, signed by several psychologists, the L.C.C. and other interested bodies, was sent outlining the proposal. The suggestion was favourably received. A Child Guidance Council was set up with Burt as chairman of the executive committee, and eventually in 1928 the London Child Guidance Training Centre was opened as a clinic in Islington with Dr William Moodie as Director. By that time a clinic in East London, financed by the Jewish Health Organisation and directed by Dr Emanuel Miller, had already been running for over a year. So the Islington clinic was not the first fully staffed clinic, though it was the first to provide comprehensive training for psychiatrists, psychologists and psychiatric social workers. In this development Burt had been the essential catalyst.

Nevertheless things did not turn out entirely as he would have wished. Although invited to serve as first Director of the clinic, Burt, whose ambitions had become increasingly academic, declined the offer, and the post went to the psychiatrist, Dr Moodie. It was not long before Moodie made it clear that in his view psychologists were to play a subordinate role in the clinics, and to be confined to the cognitive aspects of the mind and the measurement of intelligence.[34] This attitude was totally at variance with Burt's own conception of the part to be played by the psychologist. He held that 'psychologists are best suited to deal with the vast majority of cases referred to child guidance centres'.[35] He completely rejected

34. Moodie, W. *Child Guidance by Teamwork*, 1931.
35. Burt, C. L. Symposium on psychologists and psychiatrists in the Child Guidance Service: conclusion. *Brit. J. Educ. Psychol.*, XXIII, 1953, 8–28.

the view that psychology was concerned solely with the cognitive aspects of the mind: it was concerned, he insisted, with the whole mind. The proportion of cases in which pathological features were present was quite small, while social and environmental factors, with which psychiatrists were not specially trained to deal, were of preponderant importance. The lack of training of psychiatrists in normal psychology and statistical methodology ill-equipped them to direct child guidance establishments. Psychiatric diagnosis tended to be unreliable and the results of their treatment less successful than that of psychologists. Moreover he had a low opinion of the majority of psychiatrists, whom he regarded as 'the least intelligent medicals'.[36]

Burt's conflict with the medical profession was of long standing and persisted throughout his life. Coming from a medical family himself, he was well aware of the limitations of the average doctor's training. When he was appointed to the L.C.C. the medical officers resented his intrusion. They regarded the assessment of subnormality as their province, and were suspicious of the novel tests of the psychologist. Though some of the medicals, such as Dr Shrubsall, the mental subnormality expert, were mollified in the course of time, others remained hostile, and Burt's relations with his medical colleagues were far from cordial. Later he often crossed swords with psychiatrists, with Dr Moodie of the London clinic, and Dr Maberley of the Tavistock, with Dr Burns of the Birmingham Child Guidance Clinic, with Army psychiatrists, and above all with Dr Aubrey Lewis, the Director of the Maudsley Hospital and the leading British psychiatrist, whom he describes in a letter as 'my adversary'.[37] His views were forcibly expressed in the British Psychological Society's discussion on child guidance in 1942, in the British Educational Psychology Symposium in 1953[38] and finally in his comments on the Summerfield Report on *Psychologists in Education Services* towards the end of his life.[39] These final comments demonstrate how closely he kept in touch with events after his retirement, his clear grasp of the problems under discussion (remarkable at the age of eighty-six) and his practical common sense.

In spite of these disagreements the child guidance movement expanded greatly. When the Underwood Committee on Maladjusted Children reported in 1955, 'there were about 300 child

36. Burt, C. L. Letter, 22 October 1949.
37. Burt, C. L. Letter to Dr Marion Burt, 22 October 1949.
38. *Brit. J. Educ. Psychol.*, XXIII, 1953.
39. Burt, C. L. Psychologists in the education services. *Bull. B.P.S.*, XXII, 1968, 1–11.

guidance clinics, most of which were part-time: 204 of these were provided by local education authorities, a very few by voluntary bodies, and the remainder by regional hospital boards and teaching hospitals, which also provided the services of the psychiatrist for 143 of the clinics provided by the local education authorities'.[40] When the Summerfield Committee reported some years later, confining itself to the provision made by the local education authorities only, it noted '141 services covering 150 l.e.a.'s (93 per cent of all authorities) had establishments for 414 educational psychologists'.[41] Both reports recommended an expansion of the work, and an increase in the facilities for training educational psychologists and other child guidance workers.

In the training of educational psychologists Burt also played an important part. When he took up his position as Professor of Educational Psychology at the London Day Training College he did in effect provide training in educational psychology at the postgraduate level, and several child guidance workers, for example R. B. Cattell, were trained in this way. Soon after moving to University College an academic postgraduate diploma in educational psychology was established. This was a one-year course involving practical experience in schools and clinics, as well as formal instruction in child development, psychological assessment and remedial methods. The Summerfield Committee which considered the whole question of the training of educational psychologists in 1968 failed to give credit to Burt for these early initiatives. In educational psychology in England Burt was the leading pioneer.

III

Burt's applications of psychology extended, however, beyond the educational sphere. He made important contributions to vocational psychology, to military psychology, and to the use of psychological techniques in the civil service.

The birth of vocational psychology as a recognisable branch of applied psychology dates from just before the First World War when Hugo Münsterberg, then at Harvard, published his book on *Psychology and Industrial Efficiency* (1913). In it he mapped out the ground, and described experiments in the use of psychological methods in vocational selection. The war stimulated further developments in this area both in America and Europe, and in 1920 an

40. *Report of the Committee on Maladjusted Children*, H.M.S.O., 1955.
41. Dept. of Education and Science. *Psychologists in Education Services*, H.M.S.O., 1968.

International Association of Psychotechnics was founded. The Association devoted its first conference in Geneva entirely to the problems of vocational guidance. In England the main initiative came from the Cambridge psychologist, C. S. Myers, in whose laboratory Burt had worked as a part-time assistant in the early days of his L.C.C. appointment. In 1921 Myers succeeded in establishing the National Institute of Industrial Psychology. The Institute continued functioning for just over half a century, and one of its main areas of operation was vocational guidance. Quite naturally as a result of his earlier contact with Burt and Burt's growing reputation Myers enlisted Burt's aid. He was a member of the preliminary organising committee which led to the establishment of the Institute, and after its incorporation he was appointed a member of the Council and of the Scientific Committee. In the first year of the Institute's life Burt was asked to draw up a report on vocational research. This report was considered by the Executive Committee of the Institute towards the end of 1921 and, as a result, in the following year Burt was offered a half-time post with the Institute in order to organise its vocational department. Burt remained with the Institute for just over two years, during which he laid the foundations of the vocational guidance service which proved one of the N.I.I.P.'s main lines of activity throughout its existence.

Burt had already become concerned with the problems of vocational choice when working for the L.C.C., and early in 1915 had carried out a brief informal investigation with J. G. Cox. Owing to the war the experiment was discontinued, but Burt had obtained enough information to become convinced that vocational guidance using psychological techniques was a practical proposition. The N.I.I.P. appointment offered him the opportunity he needed to work out his ideas.

The main immediate requirement, he believed, was to review the field of vocational guidance in broad outline. Nothing systematic, apart from his own truncated preliminary study, had been done in Britain. The task, as he conceived it, involved a comprehensive study of the abilities and character of individuals, the devising of the necessary measuring instruments, a study of jobs and their requirements, and giving answers to certain practical administrative questions. It was also, of course, necessary to carry out a trial run of the proposed procedures in pilot form.

Burt began by drawing up a 'psychographic scheme' to serve as a basis for the collection of data on each individual to be assessed. The main headings were: (i) home conditions; (ii) physique; (iii) intellectual capacity, subdivided into (a) general intelligence, (b) specific capacities, (c) educational attainments; (iv) interests; (v) temperament and character. His scheme, with only minor modifications, provided the framework for vocational guidance at the N.I.I.P. throughout.

The measuring instruments were primarily tests. As vocational guidance was carried out principally on school leavers, many of them secondary school pupils over the age of sixteen, an intelligence test with a ceiling higher than that of the Binet scale was a main need. So Burt constructed a verbal intelligence test, N.I.I.P. Group Test 33, suitable for administration to older pupils and adults. With the less gifted testees there was a need for non-verbal tests, and one of Burt's assistants, Miss Frances Gaw, carried out an investigation with fourteen performance tests of intelligence, and constructed a battery suitable for less academic pupils.[42] The provision of tests for specific capacities and skills was a much more formidable task, but Burt and his assistants made a beginning. Even before his official appointment to the Institute's staff Burt had commenced working on tests for typists and shorthand writers. These were later developed into a set of clerical tests, which long remained in use.[43] Tests were also devised for dressmakers, milliners and engineering apprentices, and long before creativity became a fashionable topic, a series of tests for creative imagination was compiled. A beginning was also made with a study of the reliability of interview assessments of character qualities.

The first task in the correlative problem of job analysis was the determination of the intelligence requirement of occupations. The range of occuptions is enormous; so for practical purposes occupations had to be grouped. For a start a statistical analysis of the occupations actually entered by a large group of school leavers in a selected area of London was carried out by one of Burt's assistants, and occupations graded into eight main grades, from higher professional to casual and institutional. The intelligence level of each grade was estimated ranging from I.Q. 150+ for higher professionals to I.Q. 50— for institutional cases. Burt's table of occupational I.Q.s has been subjected to much recent criticism. He stated at the time that 'the figures finally arrived at are to be taken as nothing more than the roughest approximations',[44] but, he added, 'a rough numerical guide is better than no guide at all, or the

42. Industrial Fatigue Research Board. *Performance Tests of Intelligence*, Report No. 31, H.M.S.O., 1927.

43. Burt, C. L. Tests for clerical occupations. *J. Nat. Inst. Indust. Psychol., I*, 1922, 23–7, 79–81.

44. Industrial Fatigue Research Board. *A Study in Vocational Guidance*, Report No. 33, H.M.S.O., 1926, p. 15.

use of mere unformulated impression'. In a letter to one of his assistants, Miss Winifred Spielman (now Mrs Raphael), who was herself somewhat uneasy, Burt defended his position as follows:

> I must certainly make clear that the table is by no means based on guess work or *a priori* opinion as to the intelligence possessed by different strata of the community. So far as I remember the original start of the classification was some data obtained mainly in Liverpool when I was correlating the intelligence of children with their parents for semi-eugenic research on heredity and the difference of intelligence in different social strata. The next main source was the classification of ex-service examinees by the Civil Service Intelligence Tests. And all along, when I have tested children, even if I have not actually tested their parents (which, of course, I have only very occasionally done of recent years) I have usually kept a record of the apparent intelligence of their parents according to a standardised scale. This last is perhaps *a priori* guess work and might be omitted.[45]

The very shaky nature of these assessments is apparent from Burt's remarks in this letter, and unfortunately he was to make use of this data in later articles, subjecting it to some rather questionable statistical manipulations, and giving his readers little idea of its extreme unreliability.[46] Burt's own analysis of the requirements of occupations did not go much beyond this very rough estimate of intelligence levels, but rather fuller and more thorough analyses of specific occupations (dressmaking and engineering apprentice-ships) were carried out by his assistants.

While Burt was working at the National Institute of Industrial Psychology the Seventh International Congress of Psychology, the first such congress to be held after the Great War, took place at Oxford. Burt addressed the Congress on 'The Principles of Voca-tional Guidance',[47] and discussed, as well as the problems of assessment and job analysis, certain practical administrative ques-tions. At what age should vocational guidance be applied? As early as possible, he replied: which meant for elementary school children, by the age of fourteen. It was, he said, 'eminently desirable that every child before he leaves the elementary school should be made the subject of special study'. By that age the I.Q. was reasonably constant, and broad decisions could be made. What body should

45. Burt, C. L. Letter to Miss Spielman, 2 August 1925.
46. Burt, C. L. Ability and income. *Brit. J. Educ. Psychol., XIII*, 1943, 83–98; Intelligence and social mobility. *Brit. J. Statist. Psychol., XIV*, 1961, 3–24.
47. Burt, C. L. *Brit. J. Psychol., XIV*, 1924, 336–52.

undertake vocational guidance? The best agent in his view was the local education authority. It was an idealistic scheme, still imperfectly realised.

The small-scale experiment he carried out while at the N.I.I.P. in conjunction with the Industrial Fatigue Research Board provided encouraging results. One hundred school leavers, 52 boys and 48 girls, from three selected schools in a given area of London, were intensively examined and tested; then given vocational advice. After an interval of two years all the homes were revisited to discover how many of the children had obtained employment of the type recommended, and to compare their progress with that of the children who had not followed the vocational recommendations given to them. Burt's general summary of the results is worth quoting:

> The general outcome of the inquiry speaks strongly in favour of the methods used. The scheme has proved workable; the results unexpectedly successful. Judged by the after-histories of the several children, those who entered occupations of the kind recommended have proved both efficient and contented in their work. As compared with their fellows they are, on average, in receipt of higher pay; they have generally obtained promotion earlier; they have experienced fewer changes of situation; and they have incurred hardly a single dismissal between them. Over eighty per cent declare themselves satisfied with the work they have taken, and with their prospects and pay. On the other hand, of those who obtained employment different from the kind advised, less than forty per cent are satisfied. Among the latter group nearly half dislike their work, and among the former only one dislikes it, and that simply because it is not quite identical with what was originally advised . . . no great weight can be attached to these figures— yet, so far as they go, they are certainly encouraging.[48]

Later researches by other investigators, and follow-up studies of vocationally guided cases, were to add further confirmation of the value of the methods along which vocational guidance was established by Burt.

IV

Burt's involvement in military psychology was more marginal and advisory. In the First World War he played a part in the Psycho-

48. Industrial Fatigue Research Board. Report 33, H.M.S.O., 1926.

logical War Research Committee set up by the Psychology Sub-section of the British Association for the Advancement of Science, and which held its first meeting in January 1916 in the laboratory at University College with Spearman in the chair. The committee mapped out a number of problems for investigation, and appointed a number of sub-committees. The enquiries were on a small scale and supported by a meagre grant of £10. Burt himself was secretary to two of the sub-committees, and made responsible for the enquiries into social problems, for example the increase of juvenile crime during the war, and the psychological aspects of post-war educational reconstruction. He also made studies of the effects of air raids on London children. Subsequently, when war broke out again, he prepared a memorandum on the work of the committee as a whole, covering topics such as the selection of personnel, sensory and perceptual problems, fatigue, rumour and 'shell shock'.[49] He also appended a summary of work that had been carried out by both German and American psychologists between the wars.[50]

Burt's contribution to the application of psychology to the Second World War was limited by two factors, the evacuation of University College to Aberystwyth soon after war had broken out, and Burt's medical disabilities, which commenced almost immediately afterwards. Aberystwyth was an isolated spot, and Burt's disabilities prevented him from journeying far from his base. He rarely, therefore, attended meetings himself, but 'top brass' would from time to time turn up in Aberystwyth for discussions, and Burt was an inveterate writer of memoranda. Particularly in the area of statistics, his advice was extensively called upon.

The applications of psychology in the Second World War have been fully described elsewhere[51] and need not be detailed here. After sporadic preliminary trials a committee of psychologists was set up early in 1941 to advise on methods of selection in the Army. The committee comprised C. S. Myers of the National Institute of Industrial Psychology, James Drever, senior, of Edinburgh, and Cyril Burt. S. F. Philpott, his senior lecturer, deputised for Burt at meetings he could not personally attend. The committee recommended a new Directorate for the Selection of Personnel, and procedures for the testing and examination of recruits. The proposals were implemented in July 1941. About the same time the Admiralty

49. Unpublished Memorandum. *Psychology in War*, April 1942.

50. Burt, C. L. The military work of American and German psychologists. *Occup. Psychol., XVII*, 1942, 25–43.

51. Privy Council Office. *The Work of Psychologists and Psychiatrists in the Services*, H.M.S.O., 1947; Vernon, P. E. and Parry, J. B. *Personnel Selection in the British Army*, 1949; Ahrenfeldt, R. H. *Psychiatry in the British Army in the Second World War*, 1958.

had set up its Senior Psychologist's Department. The Air Force had already made arrangements with psychologists at the Universities of Cambridge and Oxford for the selection of aircrew and ground staff. From this time onward both psychologists and psychiatrists became heavily involved in war work, and all available personnel were mustered. In 1942 an expert committee was appointed to monitor and report on this work. The committee itself held thirty-two meetings, and sub-committees met even more frequently. Burt was asked to join this committee, but declined. 'I do not feel I can possibly travel up and down once a month and preserve my health for other jobs as well. My time can be better spent doing the actual work of standardising tests, instead of trying to justify them.'[52] The committee reported on its work in 1947.[53]

Even before getting roped into the official work of committees, Burt had taken advantage of the evacuation of school children to Aberystwyth to study the effects of evacuation and to write some sensible and helpful reports.[54] As usual he was quick off the mark and down to earth. When psychology had been put on an official basis Burt's own contribution was primarily statistical, and he was called on by all three services. Writing of the Army he says: 'Psychology has caught on amazingly. I expect it will mean quite a lot of busy work checking up on the results of the new proposed tests.'[55] Occasionally things happened on his doorstep. 'Work on War Office problems seems to be going quite well', he writes in 1942. 'They are now bringing a training regiment of new recruits for the Royal Artillery to Aberystwyth, and a lot of psychological testing is going on in the pier here. I have been down there once or twice to watch it.'[56] Together with his friend Professor Valentine he got involved in training problems, and each produced a memorandum on the application of psychology to Army training. Later in the war he joined an Admiralty committee concerned with selection problems. 'We are tremendously grateful for all your help', wrote the Chief Psychologist to the Admiralty.[57] From the Air Force he received the data of a big research on physical types and their relation to fitness for flying, as well as figures on the incidence of neurosis among aircrew. Then the Ministry of Infor-

52. Burt, C. L. Letter, 1 December 1942.
53. Privy Council Office. *Op. cit.*
54. Burt, C. L. *The evacuation of children under five.* Brit. Psychol. Soc., 1941; Incidence of neurotic symptoms among evacuated children. *Brit. J. Educ. Psychol.,* X, 1940, 9–15; The billeting of evacuated children. *Brit. J. Educ. Psychol., XI,* 1941, 85–98.
55. Burt, C. L. Letter, 16 June 1943.
56. Burt, C. L. Letter, 1 December 1942.
57. Letter from Chief Psychologist, 25 February 1945.

mation moved in, enquiring on methods of assessing the value of
publicity, and asking for his advice on sampling and the tabulation
of social survey questionnaire data. Visitors, too, came from abroad.
The head of psychological testing in the Australian Air Force spent
a few days in Aberystwyth, and his counterpart from Canada spent
a week. When Burt returned to London towards the end of 1944
war work got even heavier, and Burt sighed for the relative peace
of Aberystwyth. 'The difficulty is', he wrote, 'that so long as I am
in London it is very hard for me to refuse to attend the innumerable
committee meetings for the War Office, Air Ministry, Admiralty,
Ministry of Information, and Civil Service Commission. These
committees not only waste a horrible lot of time, but are not very
good for one's health. If I could only arrange to get away from
London for a few weeks, I should do far more work from outside
and probably improve my health.'[58] He complains that 'with all
this I am doing practically no work of my own. There is a great
demand for psychologists and psychiatrists not only for the fighting
services but also for post-war reconstruction. The psychological
work for the Air Ministry is still expanding, and here we seem to
be definitely useful if one can judge from the flattering reports we
get. The problem of selecting pilots who do not suffer from flying
stress is still engaging much attention. Proper selection, when it can
be carried out, seems to reduce the casualties enormously.'[59]

The bulk of Burt's statistical work for the services took the form
of unpublished memoranda, but two published articles, 'Validating
Tests for Personnel Selection'[60] and 'Statistical Problems in the
Validation of Army Tests',[61] give some idea of the kind of statistical
problems with which he was concerned—dealing with criteria
which yielded a threefold classification, the selectivity of samples,
demarcation lines in selection, and so on. His statistical expertise
made his advice enormously valued, particularly as he had a gift for
explaining things in lucid and non-technical language, and possessed
a sound sense of practical requirements. Lord Balerno, who became
Director of Army Personnel Selection in 1942, writes: 'I saw Cyril
Burt several times at meetings in his hotel and in Aberystwyth. I
was very much struck by him and his commonsense, which made
me consider him a very sane psychologist. There were other
psychologists whom I viewed with caution, but that was never so
with Burt. . . . Burt had a great deal to do with the establishment
of the other-rank selection system, and his advice was incorporated

58. Burt, C. L. Letter, 14 January 1945.
59. Burt, C. L. Letter, 11 December 1944.
60. Burt, C. L. *Brit. J. Psychol.*, XXXIV, 1943, 1–19.
61. Burt, C. L. *Psychometrika, IX*, 1944, 219–35.

into the system that was set up. . . . He was a very kind man, and out to help, and very courteous about it.'[62]

The success of service psychology during the Second World War, and particularly the publicity surrounding the War Office Officer Selection Boards, prompted the Civil Service Commission to consider using similar methods for the reconstruction competitions which it was proposed to hold following the end of the war in 1945. After the interruption of wartime the usual academic examinations were inappropriate, and selection boards on the Army model seemed to offer a solution to the difficulty. A Civil Service Selection Board was, therefore, set up, and selection on War Office lines introduced. When entry by academic examination was resumed in 1948 the Board (CISSB) was continued as an optional method of entry for a proportion of the candidates.[63] The decision to retain CISSB provoked a heated debate in the House of Lords in May 1948, Lord Moran and Lord Cherwell, Churchill's associates, in particular attacking psychological and psychiatric techniques. But CISSB survived, and in a modified and reduced form psychological methods are still employed in Civil Service selection.

In this development Burt's services were once again enlisted. He had as far back as 1920 constructed test papers for the Civil Service Commission.[64] In 1944 when post-war selection was under consideration Burt was again approached. At the end of 1944 he mentions 'very heavy work for the Civil Service', and the need to counter objections to the proposal to use psychological tests from Ernest Bevin, the Minister of Labour, who maintained that intelligence tests were unfair to the working class. To this Burt countered that it 'ignores the fact that intelligence tests, unlike the old type of examination, are supposed to pick out ability independent of educational opportunity'.[65] The following year he was involved in interviewing psychologists for the Boards. 'I was very annoyed at the time', he writes, 'with the Civil Service people for ringing up and insisting on my return [from Oxford] to interview the psychologists; but now the interviews are practically over I am very glad I did so. The posts are likely to be extremely important. If it succeeds psychology will be permanently established in the Civil Service.'[66] Burt continued for some time to assist the Civil Service Commission with advice, and in the selection of psycho-

62. Letter from Lord Balerno, 24 November 1975.
63. Civil Service Commissioners. *Memorandum on the Use of the Civil Service Selection Board in the Reconstruction Competitions*, H.M.S.O., 1951.
64. Burt, C. L. *Mental and Scholastic Tests*, 2nd edn 1947, p. 247.
65. Burt, C. L. Letter, 20 December 1944.
66. Burt, C. L. Letter, 16 April 1945.

logical staff, and he remained in touch with his former pupil, Dr E. Anstey, who became head of the research unit responsible for job analysis and test construction, and later Chief Psychologist to the Commission.

In both war and peace, therefore, Burt played an important part in the development of applied psychology in the public services of Great Britain. The first applied psychologist of 1913 had become the father figure of a considerable army of successors.

V

In 1950, indeed, it looked as though the cause to which Burt had dedicated himself even before he had graduated at Oxford had finally triumphed. Psychologists had been vindicated by their large-scale successes during the 1939–45 war. When peace returned psychology continued to be applied in the armed services, and the Civil Service had recently followed suit. The new Education Act of 1944 had resulted in a rapid growth of psychological testing for secondary school selection, and a little later the National Health Act of 1948 was to lead to the flowering of yet another branch of psychology, clinical psychology, in the National Health Service. It was probably the high water mark of the kind of applied psychology for which Burt stood.

It had certainly achieved successes, but an applied psychology based essentially on psychological testing possessed three weaknesses which led not indeed to a total collapse, but to a marked decline in its standing. It always lacked really secure theoretical foundations; it was largely divorced from developments in experimental psychology; it had little regard to sociological considerations.

Because of its lack of adequate theoretical foundations test construction, in spite of its statistical buttressing, was for the most part an *ad hoc* affair. Spearman, it is true, had at least seen the need to analyse 'The Nature of Intelligence and the Principles of Cognition', but the basis of his proposals was philosophical rather than experimental. The necessary empirical work had simply not been done, and it is only in recent years that developmental, comparative and clinical psychologists have begun to assemble the data. Burt himself made no serious attempt to work out a theoretical foundation for his tests. He had recourse to a miscellany of borrowed ideas from logic, neurophysiology and philosophical psychology. As the Canadian psychologist, G. A Ferguson, observed in 1954, 'at present no systematic theory, capable of generating fruitful hypotheses about behaviour, lies behind the study of human ability'.[67] This absence of theoretical foundations did not mean that psychological tests never produced results. Because of their empiricism, however, the results were uncertain, uneven, and difficult to interpret.

Even more worrying to many psychologists was the divorce of testing from the main streams of experimental psychology. Stimulated by the war, and by the problems generated by the adjustment of human beings to the products of high technology and to the stresses of combat, experimental psychology made considerable strides in the 1940s. This wartime work on man–machine interactions led to the establishment by the Medical Research Council of the Applied Psychology Unit in Cambridge in 1944, which unit has since its foundation been one of the most productive in applied experimental psychology, carrying out investigations, often as important theoretically as practically, into problems such as signal detection, skills, the effects of stress, short-term memory and perception. This kind of applied psychology was far removed from the applied psychology fathered by Burt, and far more in harmony with scientific developments in psychology.

The sociological weakness of the testing movement is a complex story, which will be considered more fully in Chapter Fourteen. Suffice it here to say that the testers paid inadequate regard both to the social components of human nature, and to the social consequences of their procedures.

The movement against testing grew among psychologists themselves even before the end of the Second World War. The Cambridge psychologist, E. G. Chambers, complained in 1943 that 'mathematical psychologists build elegant and dizzy numerical edifices, forgetting in their architectural zeal the flimsy foundations upon which their fabrics stand'.[68] After the war the critics grew more numerous. Sir Frederic Bartlett lent his considerable weight to the attacks on testing in his address to the XIIth International Congress of Psychology held in Edinburgh in 1948. Zangwill's widely-read *Introduction to Modern Psychology* (1950) pointed out in some detail 'the limitations of intelligence tests'. A few years later the use of tests for secondary selection, and indeed the whole concept of selection, came under heavy attack from Brian Simon;[69] and before long the campaign against selection was in full spate.

As the huge edifice of testing, for which Burt was to a considerable

67. Ferguson, G. A. On learning and human ability. *Canadian J. Psychol., VIII*, 1954, 95–112.

68. Chambers, E. G. Statistical psychology and the limitations of the test method. *Brit. J. Psychol., XXXIII*, 1943, 189.

69. Simon, B. *Intelligence Testing and the Comprehensive School*, 1953.

extent responsible, began to crumble, Burt felt more and more on the defensive, and more and more under personal attack as his charisma began to diminish. It even became hard for the younger generation of psychologists to realise how substantial his contributions had been in the fields of educational psychology, child guidance, vocational guidance and psychological testing. Indeed some of these contributions will surely endure, though the high confidence which led him to regard the whole field of individual psychology as established already on sound and scientific foundations, we can see now, was misplaced.

CHAPTER SEVEN

Developments in English Education

I

Outside psychology it was, of course, above all in the field of education that Burt was influential. Between the wars his views and his findings impressed themselves on the policy makers, particularly on the members of the Board of Education Consultative Committee, under the chairmanship first of Sir Henry Hadow, and then of Mr (later Sir) Will Spens, whose reports largely shaped the post-war reconstruction of the education system of England. 'Both the Hadow and Spens committees,' writes Van der Eyken, 'depended much on the evidence of the psychologists, and in particular on that of Professor Cyril Burt.'[1] Of this influence there can be no doubt. Though Burt was not himself a member of the Consultative Committee, he was frequently called upon to assist their deliberations. He provided the material for the historical chapter in one of their first reports, on *Psychological Tests of Educable Capacity* (1924), and, because of his extensive experience in the use of tests, greatly influenced the committee in coming to its conclusions. In the 1931 report on *The Primary School* Burt was responsible for the Appendix on the mental development of children between the ages of 7 and 11, which constituted the basis of the committee's own observations. Together with Sir Percy Nunn, Burt was co-opted to the drafting sub-committee and 'rendered invaluable help in the preparation of the report'. Similarly in the 1933 report on *Infant and Nursery Schools* Burt, assisted this time by Susan Isaacs, contributed the material on mental development in infancy. 'We attach particular importance to the evidence we have received from Professor Cyril Burt and Dr Susan Isaacs', stated the committee. In the Spens report on *Secondary Education*, published in 1938, Burt's influence was equally obvious. He not only provided a memorandum on the mental development of children from the ages of 11 to 16, but also a learned Appendix on Faculty Psychology and its bearing on the curriculum. The series of reports of the Consultative Committee

1. Van der Eyken, W. (ed.) *Education, the Child and Society*, 1973, p. 16.

has been described as 'hymns of praise to the "*g*" factor',[2] and Burt was one of the main protagonists of '*g*', or general intelligence.

Reports of consultative bodies have, over the last century, preluded major changes in English education. The report of the Bryce Commission on *Secondary Education* in 1895 paved the way for the Education Act of 1902 and the establishment of secondary schools run by local education authorities. The Hadow, Spens and Norwood reports prepared the ground for the tripartite scheme of grammar, technical and modern schools resulting from the 1944 Act, and the selection procedure at eleven-plus. The Plowden report of 1967 reinforced the moves towards comprehensive education which had been under way for over a decade. Well written and packed with information, these and other reports on almost every aspect of the educational system constitute landmarks in the history of English education. Nevertheless their originative role must not be exaggerated. As Kogan and Packwood observe, 'Many, probably most, committee recommendations are already being evolved within the education service. Many, perhaps too many, are the stock in trade of the education service for years before they are endorsed. But the committees can and do pick them up, study them, add the weight of evidence from the education service, and increasingly from outside research, codify and promulgate them. . . . They reflect the changes in the dominant social norms.'[3] If this is true, it would be unfair to hold the committees wholly responsible for developments derived from their recommendations, even when these were accepted without modification. It would be still more unfair to regard someone like Burt, who was not even a member of, but only a witness and adviser to, the Consultative Committee, as the architect of the selective system of schooling which emerged. Yet towards the end of his life he was cast in this role by many of his left-wing critics.

Educational committees have usually been progressive and enlightened in their views, and Burt was influential between the wars precisely because he represented the progressive thinking of his time. Before 1870, many lower-class children received no education at all. The Board Schools which the 1870 Act set up were explicitly concerned with the education of the working class. There was no question of progression to secondary schooling, and it was some years before large Boards, like the London School Board, established higher-grade elementary schools to make any provision at all for brighter pupils at the top of the age scale. The secondary

2. Kogan, M. and Packwood, T. *Advisory Councils and Committees in Education*, 1974, p. 6.
3. *Ibid.*, p. 5.

schools set up following the 1902 Education Act were a public supplementation of the older middle-class grammar schools, and until the 'free place' system was introduced in 1907 received very few working-class children. The 'free place', or scholarship, system required local education authorities to provide 25 per cent of places for pupils from elementary schools without fees in return for grant aid, and was the system in operation (though with a means test after 1933) until the 1944 Education Act was implemented. The 'free place' scheme was the first move in an egalitarian direction: it recognised that secondary schooling should be available even to working-class children, if they had the ability to profit from it. Only a year earlier in 1906 a report issued by the Board of Education Consultative Committee had declared that elementary schools and secondary schools prepared for different walks of life, 'the one for the lower ranks of industry, the other for the higher ranks and for the liberal professions'.[4] So the introduction of 'free places' was an important step towards social justice and mobility, even though it restricted secondary education in the case of working-class children to those of well above average academic ability.

The first noteworthy attack on this restriction came from the powerful pen of R. H. Tawney, who in his tract on *Secondary Education for All* (1922) argued that primary and secondary education should be conceived as 'stages in a single process through which all normal children ought to pass', and advocated full-time secondary schooling for all up to the age of 16. He declaimed against 'the intrusion into educational organisation of the vulgarities of the class system'. Influenced at least in part by Burt's work on the distribution of educational ability he still believed in diversity of educational provision. Equality did not mean identity; but no scheme of classification should be more than tentative, and 'all children should pass as a matter of course at the appropriate age to the secondary school'.[5] As a full member of the Hadow committee, and involved in the preparation of its reports on primary and secondary education, Tawney was almost certainly a more important influence than Burt in shaping the pattern of schooling to come.

The first Hadow report, on *The Education of the Adolescent* (1926), recommended that 'all children should be transferred at the age of 11 or 12 from the junior or primary school either to schools of the type now called secondary, or to schools of the type which

4. Board of Education. *Report of the Consultative Committee upon Questions affecting Higher Elementary Schooling*, 1906 (included in Van der Eyken (ed.) *op. cit.*, pp. 126–38).

5. Tawney, R. H. *Secondary Education for All: A Policy for Labour*, 1922, pp. 62–7.

is called central, or to a senior and separate department of existing elementary schools'. The age of compulsory school attendance should be increased to 15, and there should be 'a clean break' at the age of 11+. The reasons given for the choice of this age for the termination of primary schooling were firstly the arguments of the psychologists (including, of course, Burt), and secondly administrative considerations. However, Lord Eustace Percy, who was President of the Board of Education at the time, assures us that the break at about the age of 11 'did not originate with the Hadow report of 1926', and that by that date it 'had become commonplace among educational administrators in England'.[6] So this would seem to have been one of the matters in which the committee confirmed rather than originated the policy incorporated in its recommendations.

The 'clean break' at 11+ clearly involved in the committee's view a sorting process in which children were allocated to different types of school. Secondary schools for the less able children should have a mainly practical bias, and it was suggested that they should be termed 'modern' schools. It was piously hoped that 'the new modern schools should not become inferior secondary schools'. Children should be allocated to the appropriate type of school on the basis of a written examination, but 'a written psychological test might also be employed in dealing with border-line cases, or where examinations and teachers' estimates differ'. 'So long as the demand for higher education exceeds the supply,' noted the committee's report, 'some method of selection is inevitable.' But this was hopefully to be 'selection by differentiation' rather than 'selection by elimination', and there should be no finality in the allocation made at 11+.

The second and third Hadow reports buttressed these conclusions with data on the physical and mental development of children up to the age of 11, largely provided on the mental side by Burt. There was an added emphasis on intelligence, 'the mental capacity which is of most importance for intellectual progress', whereas 'special abilities rarely reveal themselves in any notable degree before the age of 11'. There is an interesting recognition that not all these abilities were due to heredity. 'There is now an increasing tendency', states the second report,[7] 'to believe that [earlier investigators] have underestimated the effects of the environment', and in the introduction it was stated that 'Professor Burt drew in his evidence a moving picture of the effects of a squalid environment, not only on

6. Percy, Lord Eustace. *Some Memories*, 1958, p. 99.
7. Board of Education Consultative Committee. *The Primary School*, 1931, ch. iii. (This chapter was mainly due to Burt.)

physical, but also, if the two can be distinguished, on mental energy.'[8]
Indeed 'the moral tone and the emotional atmosphere of the family
life may react profoundly upon the child's work in the school'.[9]

The economic depression of the 1930s retarded the implementation of the Hadow proposals. In 1933 Sir Henry Hadow retired
from the chairmanship of the Consultative Committee, and the
committee now under the leadership of Sir Will Spens turned its
attention in more detail to the reorganisation of secondary education
that the Hadow reports had proposed. The Spens report published
in 1938[10] was a crucial document in laying the foundations of the
new scheme of education, and of all the reports of the Consultative
Committee was perhaps the one most influenced by Burt, whose
authority, now that he had been translated to the Chair of
Psychology at University College, London, was at its height. The
Spens Committee accepted the break at 11+, and sketched in more
detail the pattern of secondary education to follow. In addition to
grammar and modern schools, it proposed an expansion of Junior
Technical Schools, and a reduction in the age of admission to these
schools from 13 to 11. Thus the tripartite plan, the roots of which
go back a good deal further, emerged as the pattern of the future.
The committee also explicitly considered, and rejected, the idea of
multilateral or comprehensive schools, though it rather inconsistently believed that 'the multilateral idea must be inherent in any
truly national system of education'. In sorting the children at 11+
into the three types of school the committee, advised by Burt, stated
that 'general intelligence is the most important factor determining
work in the classroom', and believed that 'with few exceptions it is
possible at a very early age to predict with some accuracy the
ultimate level of a child's intellectual power, [though] . . . this is
true only of general intelligence and does not hold good in respect
of specific aptitudes and interests'. Selection at 11+ was not to
depend wholly on intelligence tests, however. The wishes of
parents and the assessments of teachers were to play a part, and
there should be a possibility of reallocation at the age of 13. The
committee laid great stress on parity of status between schools, and
suggested means of attaining it.

The Spens Committee was further required to look in detail at
the content of education, and devoted much of its report to the
question of the curriculum of secondary schools. Here again Burt's

8. Board of Education Consultative Committee. *The Primary School*, 1931, ch.
iii, p. xix.

9. *Ibid.*, ch. iii.

10. Board of Education Consultative Committee. *Secondary Education with
Special Reference to Grammar Schools and Technical High Schools* (Spens Report),
1938.

evidence carried considerable weight. The committee was impressed by 'the great advance in the science of psychology' in the past forty years. In spite of this the curriculum of the grammar schools in particular was still based on the outmoded faculty psychology of the nineteenth century. 'The traditional psychology of the earlier nineteenth century, with its emphasis on faculties and its belief in the doctrine of formal discipline or mental transfer, played an important part in perpetuating a curriculum common to all pupils. It was tacitly assumed that most boys and girls were equipped with the same mental endowments, that most of them developed in much the same way and at almost the same rate of progress, and that all learned by the same methods. Little attention was paid to individual differences in interests or abilities. If it was objected that the content of the curriculum was uninteresting or difficult, it was agreed that at any rate it was good for mental training. Too frequently, however, little effort was devoted to the selection of content appropriate to the needs, interests and ability of the pupils, and time and attention were concentrated on drill and exercises.' All this was pure Burt, and Burt provided an Historical Note on Faculty Psychology[11] in support of these observations. Thus the committee noted with approval that 'the emphasis in educational theory has shifted from the subject to the child'.

Shortly after the Spens report was published in 1938 war broke out, and no immediate steps were taken to implement its recommendations. However, surprisingly early in the war, and well before victory was in sight, attention turned to problems of post-war reconstruction. The Beveridge report on Social Insurance appeared in 1942, and a year before this, in 1941, the President of the Board of Education, Mr R. A. Butler, appointed a further committee under the chairmanship of Dr Cyril Norwood, to consider the curriculum and examinations in secondary schools. The Norwood committee reported in 1943,[12] almost simultaneously with the Board of Education's own White Paper on *Educational Reconstruction*, which formed the basis of the Butler Education Act of 1944. The Norwood committee covered much the same ground as Spens, and came broadly to identical conclusions. But its report was much less scholarly, and much more dogmatic. No evidence was taken from Burt or any other psychologist, and the findings of psychologists were subtly distorted. The committee was dominated by traditionalists who had 'no sympathy with a theory of education

11. Board of Education Consultative Committee. *Secondary Education with Special Reference to Grammar Schools and Technical High Schools* (Spens Report), 1938, Appendix IV, pp. 429–38.

12. Committee of the Secondary School Examination Council. *Curriculum and Examinations in Secondary Schools* (Norwood Report), 1943.

which proposes that its aim can be dictated by the provisional findings of special sciences'. 'Education must be ultimately concerned with values which are independent of time or particular environment.' Experience, not psychology, was enough to show that children fall into three broad groups, the academic type, the technical type, and the practical type, and there must, therefore, be three types of curriculum, and three types of school to cater for them. Parity of esteem was certainly desirable, but it 'cannot be conferred by administrative decree nor by equality of cost per pupil. It can only be won by the school itself'. Allocation to different types of school must be made primarily on the basis of teachers' judgments, though intelligence tests, which the committee regarded as still of an experimental nature, might be used supplementarily.

When the Norwood committee was sitting Burt was not in London. He had moved with a great part of University College to Aberystwyth. But it is doubtful if, even had he been readily available, he would have been consulted. The committee, consisting wholly of educationists and educational administrators, called on evidence from teachers, commercial organisations and professional bodies, but clearly did not think it worth consulting psychologists or social scientists. Not surprisingly Burt was critical of the report, and voiced his objections immediately in the *British Journal of Educational Psychology*.[13] He even seemed to go back on some matters with which previously he had been agreeable. Thus he expressed doubts on the desirability of 11+ as the age of transition. 'The grounds for allocating children to schools of different types at the early age of 11 are administrative rather than psychological', he now maintained. He objected also to the delineation of three types of child based on their possession of qualitatively different specific aptitudes, verbal, mechanical and practical, rather than on 'all-round innate capacity'. 'It would', he stated, 'only be in very exceptional cases that such types as are envisaged by the Norwood report display themselves so early as 11 or 12.' He protested also at the 'precarious plan of relying solely on subjective impressions of teachers'. 'The Norwood committee', he added, 'seems scarcely to have realised the large and growing part played by tests of intelligence.' And he perspicaciously asked whether 'once the children have been sent to some special types of school at the age of 11 there is really much likelihood of any large re-sorting at a later age'.

It is hard not to feel that some of these criticisms by Burt were actuated by pique against the neglect of psychological evidence,

13. Burt, C. L. The psychological implications of the Norwood Report. *Brit. J. Educ. Psychol.*, XIII, 1943, 126-40.

including his own, and that they masked a basic agreement with the recommendations, which in principle did not differ so much from those of the Spens committee, which he had earlier approved.

The Spens-Norwood plan of tripartite selective secondary education became incorporated into the education system following the Education Act of 1944 and the school-leaving age was raised to 15 to provide for a minimum of four years' secondary schooling following the sorting process at 11+. In the words of the Board of Education White Paper,[14] the aim was to provide all children with 'efficient full-time education suitable to the child's age and aptitudes'. The system was official policy for nearly twenty years until in 1965 a Labour government declared its intention to end selection at 11+. It was to linger on in certain areas much longer. The selective system was opposed from the start by many left-wing thinkers, and before long its rigidity had revealed defects and it had incurred widespread unpopularity. Its whole basis came increasingly under attack during the 1950s and 1960s. As early as 1948 the National Association of Labour Teachers came down in favour of comprehensive schools. Selective schooling, they declared, was bound to perpetuate class divisions. 'So long as this stratification of children at the age of eleven remains it is in practice useless to talk of parity in education or of equal opportunity in later life.' Even streaming was undesirable, and as for intelligence tests they were 'pseudo-scientific' devices 'the purpose of which is to create an intellectual aristocracy, an élite, by excluding from opportunity as many as possible'. 'It is high time', stated their report,[15] 'that we forgot the unverified assumption that only a small percentage of our children have sufficient native ability to move on to advanced work of a high standard.'

All these criticisms were taken up in more detail by Brian Simon in his *Intelligence Testing and the Comprehensive School* (1953). Fundamentally, argued Simon, 'the present selective and graded system of schools serves the needs of a class-divided society'. He even went so far as to assert that 'the theory that children can be divided into different groups, that they have fundamentally differing mental capacities which determine their whole future development, is derived from the theory and practice of intelligence testing'. Indeed, this entire theory and practice, according to Simon, was fallacious, and led to profoundly harmful results. The way forward was through comprehensive secondary schooling.

Simon's arguments were ideologically rather than scientifically

14. Board of Education. *White Paper on Educational Reconstruction*, 1943, p. 7.
15. National Association of Labour Teachers. *The Comprehensive School: its History and Character*, 1948.

based, and were backed by little hard evidence. But, before long, experience of selective education began to reveal certain weaknesses. The report on *Early Leaving* (1954) issued by the Central Advisory Council for Education provided statistics which demonstrated the high rate of wastage among working-class children who had secured grammar school places, and the relatively poor examination marks of those who stayed the course. There was certainly no equality of outcome, even if there was equality of opportunity. Two years later Floud, Halsey and Martin's study, *Social Class and Educational Opportunity* (1956), showed that the sons of non-manual workers not only had a better chance of obtaining entry to a grammar school, and improved their chances with each fresh increase in the number of available places, but made better use of their opportunities in the schools. Size of family and parental attitudes were influential factors in determining both success in the selection examination and achievement in the grammar school. In a later study of ability and attainment in the primary school Douglas (1964) compared middle-class and working-class children of equivalent I.Q.s between ages 8 and 11 and showed that the middle-class children were three times as successful as working-class children in obtaining grammar school places.[16] He attributed the results to differences not merely in parental attitudes, but to the effect of the neighbourhood and social background. It looked as though too much weight was being put on the I.Q. and other variables were being ignored. To these doubts as to the fairness of the selection procedure were added criticisms of its damaging effects in the schools. Coaching for intelligence tests became rife, and was proving quite effective in raising I.Q.s. Vernon's studies suggested that a single practice test could raise the I.Q. by 5 points and intensive coaching by as much as 15 points.[17] Besides introducing an arbitrary factor into selection, the need to coach produced undesirable distortions in the curricula of many schools. After it had been in operation for ten years, as Anthony Crosland pointed out in his book *The Future of Socialism* (1956), the 11+ examination had come to be bitterly disliked and resented. Though some of the objections, in Crosland's view, were exaggerated, nevertheless 'the school system in Britain remains the most divisive, unjust and wasteful of all aspects of social inequality'.[18] By the middle 1960s, as a result partly of this unpopularity, and partly an increasing volume of sociological evidence, these views were more and more widely accepted, and the move towards comprehensive education gathered momentum. Not only were the

16. Douglas, J. W. B. *The Home and the School*, 1964.
17. Vernon, P. E. *Intelligence Testing*, 1952.
18. Crosland, C. A. R. *The Future of Socialism*, 1956, p. 188.

administrative paraphernalia and the undesirable outcomes of selection attacked, but the basic psychological theories on which the whole system was founded came under fire. The Robbins report on *Higher Education* (1963) was the first official report to give voice to these objections. According to Robbins it was 'highly misleading to suppose that one can determine an upper limit to the number of people who can benefit from higher education'. There was no such thing as a fixed 'pool of ability', and 'the belief that there exists some easy method of ascertaining an intelligence factor unaffected by education or background is outmoded'. The committee's researches had indicated that 'the differences between children of the same potential but different backgrounds widens progressively'.[19] The whole basis of the edifice erected on the basis of the Spens and Norwood reports was being undermined by statements and findings such as these, and Burt's reputation was inevitably implicated in the collapse.

The Plowden report on Primary Schools[20] went further, and in place of the doctrine of equal opportunity, which had inspired most of the reforms in English education since the beginning of the century, substituted the doctrine of 'positive discrimination', which implied the special favouring of those handicapped by disadvantageous environmental backgrounds. The Plowden committee, influenced by sociologists rather than by psychologists, stressed the environmental factors underlying scholastic achievement, and although not denying that genetic factors played a part in intelligence, defined intelligence as 'generalised thinking powers which have developed from experience in and out of school'.

The rapid growth of comprehensive education and the setting up of educational priority areas marked a new phase in English education, and the beginning of a strenuous endeavour to achieve not simply equality of opportunity, but, as Halsey termed it,[21] 'equality of outcomes'. This, perhaps not unexpectedly, soon produced a reaction from those who considered that educational standards were being jeopardised, that bright children were being penalised, and that biological facts were being ignored. The *Black Papers* edited by Cox and Dyson[22] gave expression to these fears, and the disappointing results of the new experiments in Britain, and equally from similar experiments overseas, forced even Halsey

19. Committee on Higher Education. *Higher Education*, H.M.S.O., 1963, ch. vi.
20. Central Advisory Council for Education. *Children and Their Primary Schools* (Plowden Report), 1967.
21. Halsey, A. H. (ed.) *Educational Priority*, H.M.S.O., 1972.
22. Cox, C. B. and Dyson, A. E. (eds) *Black Paper I*, 1969; *Black Paper II*, 1969; *Black Paper III*, 1970.

to admit that 'the essential fact of twentieth century educational history is that egalitarian policies have failed'.[23] Particularly weighty was the American study by Jencks,[24] which provided a mass of data to prove that educational reform cannot bring about educational or social equality. Jencks's striking conclusion was that 'the character of a school's output depends largely on a single input, namely the characteristics of the entering child. Everything else—the school budget, its policies, the characteristics of the teachers—is either secondary or completely irrelevant.'[25] According to Jensen[26] this was basically because educability depended primarily on intelligence, and intelligence was primarily a matter of inheritance.

All this led to heated controversies in which scientific evidence was soon swamped by ideological bias. Into these controversies Burt was increasingly dragged in the last few years of his life. Because of his belief in the selective system, his stubborn adherence to the doctrine that intelligence was mainly inherited, his continued faith in the value and justification of intelligence tests, and his caustic attacks on his sociological and educational opponents, he became indeed a central figure in the controversies, and an arch-exponent of all that 'progressive' thinkers had come to hate. There is no doubt that he resented the onslaughts on what one correspondent termed 'the arrogant educational psychologists led by Sir Cyril Burt'.[27] He complained to his sister that 'the labour educationists, who are out to build what they call a classless society, have launched ludicrous attacks on my views.'[28] His views, perhaps, were never quite so reactionary as they came to be regarded, though there was one feature of them which raised quite natural revulsion and scepticism—his total denial that the limits set by natural endowment could ever be outgrown. As he put it in his article in the *Irish Journal of Education*,[29] 'A definite limit to what children can achieve is inexorably set by the limitations of their innate capacity', and thus no improvements in the quality of their education can ever make any difference. This extreme statement, however, did not wholly do justice to his views, which we must examine in somewhat more detail.

23. Halsey, A. H. (ed.) *op. cit.*
24. Jencks, C. *Inequality*, 1972.
25. *Ibid.*, p. 256.
26. Jensen, A. R. *Educability and Group Differences*, 1973.
27. Price, G. Letter to *New Statesman*, 29 November 1968.
28. Burt, C. L. Letter to Dr Marion Burt, 3 March 1970.
29. Burt, C. L. Intelligence and heredity: some common misconceptions. *Irish J. Educ.*, III, 1969, 75–94.

II

Burt's views on education, like most of his views, remained remarkably consistent throughout his life. Well in advance of their time when he entered the educational world before the First World War, his views did not alter with developments in educational theory and practice, and by the end of his life they were out of tune with many so-called 'progressive' trends of the time.

No doubt one important factor shaping Burt's outlook was his own personal educational history. He himself started his schooling at a London Elementary Board School among working-class children. Apart from a cultivated home background he had few advantages, and it was by ability and hard work that he won scholarships first to Christ's Hospital, and then to Oxford and Würzburg. What he himself had done, other able children could also do. The doors were not firmly closed to talent, and it was his aim to see that they were opened still wider. Burt never identified ability with class, though there were, he believed, as a matter of demonstrable fact, differences in class averages. But because of the numerical preponderance of the working class, there were large numbers of bright working-class children, and equality of opportunity regardless of social origin was a basic tenet of Burt's educational philosophy. Selection was grounded in biological, not primarily in social, considerations. As he put it, 'in education equal opportunity means opportunity to make the most of differences that are innate'.[30]

This Galtonian philosophy, which Burt had early come to accept almost as a matter of faith, confirmed him in the views derived from his own personal experiences. Individual differences in talent and character were a fundamental fact of human nature; these differences were partly a matter of nature and partly a matter of nurture; but nature was of preponderant weight, and must be taken into account in the educational process. Galton was also, he held, right in thinking that it was only through the application of measurement and quantitative techniques that proper account could be taken of individual differences, and education be turned at least in part into a scientific discipline. Hence Burt's emphasis from the beginning of, and throughout, his career was on psychometric methods. Much of his educational work was based on the collection of statistical data, on measures and norms of performance, and, derived from these, on an analysis of the underlying patterns of abilities and character traits. These analyses showed, Burt maintained, the dominant role of universal general factors, such as

30. Burt, C. L. General ability and special aptitudes. *Educ. Res., I*, 1959, 3–16.

'innate general intelligence' and 'general emotionality'. If these general factors could be accurately estimated, then children could be guided into educational channels which accorded with their innate make-up, and much maladjustment and frustration avoided. At least in the field of ability Burt believed that intelligence testing had made sufficient progress to enable this to be done with a fair degree of precision.

These fundamental beliefs naturally led Burt to support a selective system of education. Children differed so widely that they could not effectively be educated together at the secondary stage. He approved, therefore, of the principle of selection, though critical of some of the detailed arrangements proposed by the Norwood committee. In 1957 he commended the judicious report of the British Psychological Society on Secondary School Selection.[31] And in 1959 he himself set out his own views on 'The Examination at 11+'.[32] He criticised the rigidity of the provisions for transfer, and the neglect of the warning given by the Hadow committee. Dividing lines had been made too sharp, and readjustments too difficult. By the age of 11 special aptitudes were only just beginning to reveal themselves, and mistakes in placement could easily arise. Nevertheless the 11+ examination making use of intelligence tests, standardised papers in English and Arithmetic, and teachers' reports enabled predictions to be made that correlated 0·80 with educational outcomes. Selection of some sort was essential, and 'the 11+ examination was by far the most trustworthy way of identifying those who possess the highest ability'. Burt dismissed as of little importance some of the criticisms commonly made of the 11+ examination, namely that the results could be substantially influenced by coaching, and that it imposed too great a nervous strain on many children. 'It should,' Burt declared, 'be an essential part of the child's education to teach him how to face a possible beating on the 11+ (or any other examination), just as he should learn to take a beating in a half-mile race, or in a bout with boxing gloves, or a football match with a rival school'—a comment which possibly overlooked the long-term and often irreversible effects of the 11+ decision!

In the last years of his life Burt restated his views on 'The Organisation of Schools' in *Black Paper III*.[33] He again criticised the 1944 Act in details, but affirmed his unchanging belief in

31. Vernon, P. E. (ed.) *Secondary School Selection*, 1957.
32. Burt, C. L. The examination at 11+. *Brit. J. Educ. Studies*, VII, 1959, 99–117.
33. Cox, C. B. and Dyson, A. E. (eds) *Black Paper III*, 1970, pp. 14–25. See also Burt, C. L. General ability and special aptitudes. *Educ. Res.*, I, 1959, 3–16.

selective schooling. He denied that there was any evidence to suggest that the attainments of the great mass of average pupils was any better in comprehensive schools, and maintained that the abolition of selection particularly hit brighter children from working-class backgrounds. It was only sensible to concentrate really good teachers, of whom there was a shortage, where the brightest pupils were congregated. So far from agreeing with the Plowden doctrine of 'positive discrimination' Burt insisted that it made economic sense to focus resources on the gifted rather than on the innately dull. In fact the system he would have preferred was the system he had himself grown up in, where bright pupils of exceptional ability, the top 2 or 3 per cent, were picked out by scholarship examinations and accorded privileged treatment. This seemed to him better than the 20:80 cut which the 11+ examination brought about. Special treatment for the very gifted, and, at the other end, special treatment for the subnormal, with the large majority of children in between, streamed in a diversity of schools and classes, more or less sums up his views on the ideal organisation of schools.

It was not only his advocacy of selection that brought Burt into conflict with a growing body of educational opinion, but also his increasing doubts as to the value of 'progressive' methods in education, and his conviction that these had led to a decline in standards in the basic subjects, which showed itself not only in deteriorating performance in the schools, but to weaknesses at still higher levels. His long experience as an examiner in Colleges of Education convinced him that standards of English composition had deteriorated, and that fewer teacher-trainees could express themselves in clear and logical prose—a gift which Burt himself certainly had to an unusually high degree. He was not wholly opposed to 'progressive' methods; they had a place, he held, in the education of the duller children. But they were no substitute for the disciplined effort that should be demanded from average and bright pupils. He blamed Piaget, towards whose work he was always ambivalent, for the more undesirable consequences of the 'playway', and when creativity became a vogue in the 1960s he was scathing in his attacks. 'With children, I find, most of the ideas that can be pinned down as resulting from their own original invention are painfully naive and misleading.'[34] He, therefore, deprecated the popular notion of encouraging originality in those of average or less than average intelligence. 'Today what is needed most of all is an ability to appreciate and aim at sound, valid and relevant thinking, rather than inventive or creative thinking. . . . Self-

34. Burt, C. L. Letter to Dr P. Wason, 26 November 1969.

control is a far higher virtue than self-expression.'[35] All of which sounded very reactionary, and provoked a good deal of unpopularity.

In support of his views Burt asserted that educational standards had appreciably declined in the half-century since he commenced work as an educational psychologist, and he attributed this to progressive education. In his contribution to *Black Paper II* he wrote:

> If we go back to the period just before the war, or again just before the First World War, the overall trend has shown, not an improvement, but, if anything, a decline. Judged by tests applied and standardised in 1913–14, the average attainments in reading, spelling, mechanical and problem arithmetic are now appreciably lower than they were 55 years ago. The deterioration is most marked in English composition. Here the vogue is for 'creativity'. Bad spelling, bad grammar and the crudest vulgarisms are no longer frowned upon, but freely tolerated. Instead of accuracy the teacher aims at self-expression; instead of clear and logical thought or precise description of facts, he—and still more often, she—seeks to foster what is called 'imagination'. At the same time parents and members of the public at large are beginning to wonder whether the free discipline, or lack of discipline, in the new permissive school may not largely be responsible for much of the subsequent delinquency, violence, and general unrest that characterize our permissive society.[36]

Not surprisingly, these observations provoked a storm of protest from teachers and teachers' organisations, and a demand for the evidence upon which they were based. The *Sunday Times*, often critical of Burt, took the matter up, and called him an 'extremist'.[37] In an article published shortly afterwards in *The Irish Journal of Education*[38] Burt supplied data collected, he said, from various surveys and reports from 1914 onwards by an assistant, Miss M. G. O'Connor, purporting to demonstrate this decline. Amplifying his published statements in a letter to the Secretary of the National Union of Teachers Burt said:

35. Burt, C. L. Creativity in the classroom. *J. & Newsletter Assoc. Educ. Psychol.*, II, 2, 1968, 3–8.

36. Burt, C. L. The mental differences between children. In Cox, C. B. and Dyson, A. E. (eds), *Black Paper II*, 1969.

37. *Sunday Times*, 12 October 1969.

38. Burt, C. L. Intelligence and heredity. *Irish J. Educ.*, III, 1969, 75–94.

In the early 1960s I was asked to revise [*Mental and Scholastic Tests*] for a fourth edition, and with the aid of my former research students (many of them teachers) I endeavoured to collect fresh data, to see how far it was necessary to revise the standardisation. To my surprise very little revision was necessary compared with the 1920 standardisation. Owing to the First World War the level in 1920 was a little below that of 1913–14. Recent changes, expressed in terms of the 1914 standardisation, are given as percentages in the article you quote. If you would look again at the figures, you will see that they are by no means large— 4·6% down in accuracy of reading, 7·5% in mechanical arithmetic, and 8·9% in spelling. . . . To describe the very small changes in the figures reported as 'a very serious accusation' is surely a rhetorical exaggeration.[39]

These statements of Burt did not satisfy the critics. As was pointed out by G. F. Peaker, an able school inspector who was also a competent statistician, norms of performance can only be compared if the samples are comparable, and as there had been a decline in the socio-economic standing of Inner London during the half-century in question the samples were not comparable, and it was necessary to supply a correction factor to the figures obtained. When this was done a small improvement rather than a decline in standards was the result.[40] There is, of course, other evidence which supports Burt's position, but what is certain is that Burt's own data were not convincing. After his death more serious accusations were made— but these we shall examine in Chapter Twelve.

All this brought Burt into much ill-odour. 'Cyril Burt has done education a disservice by allowing his name to be associated with a piece of party electioneering propaganda', wrote one teacher.[41] He became regarded as a reactionary, and a defender of class distinction in society. At the same time there was a considerable body of opinion, reflected in the contributors to the *Black Papers*, who looked up to him as a protagonist of educational sanity and the maintenance of standards. The attacks upon him certainly went too far, were often unfair, and occasionally vicious— which is not saying that his views were not open to criticism. It is, however, quite untrue that Burt was an upholder of established class distinctions. His political views were on the liberal side; he adhered to no political party, and certainly was by no means conservative in his sympathies. 'I am not a patriotic person', he wrote to one lady

39. Burt, C. L. Letter, 28 October 1969.
40. Peaker, G. F. Memorandum, November 1969.
41. Letter, October 1969.

friend,[42] and he was never particularly friendly to the 'establishment'. His knighthood was bestowed by a Labour government; he addressed, and was sympathetic to The Progressive League, to which Crosland, Healey, the Huxleys, Bertrand Russell, and other forward-looking persons belonged; and Eysenck has correctly observed that he was, if anything, left of centre politically. His views on education were not motivated by political considerations or class bias; they were derived from his fundamental belief in innate individual differences in capacity on the one hand, and on standards of value on the other. His conclusions were the logical outcome of his premises. They were biologically, not politically, inspired. Given his views on the nature of intelligence he could hardly have concluded otherwise. Whether his views on the nature of intelligence were sound, and whether his data were scientifically reliable, are different questions.

The controversies surrounding Burt's last years tended to eclipse his earlier contributions to the advancement of education. The arrangements that followed the Education Act of 1944 may not have been perfect: but they represented a considerable advance on what had obtained before. Burt in his advice to the Hadow and Spens committees helped to promote this advance. In London he assisted many working-class children to obtain secondary education, and had greatly improved the methods for educating the subnormal and the backward. He was among the pioneers in the 'child-centred' approach, and in child guidance. And his work in psychometrics was, at the time, in Sir Robert Blair's words 'a unique contribution to the scientific study of educational problems'.[43] Had Burt ceased writing on education after the Second World War his reputation as a progressive educator would have been generally acclaimed.

42. Burt, C. L. Letter to Mrs Beatrice Warde, 28 June 1956.
43. Blair, Sir Robert. Prefatory Memorandum. *The Distribution and Relations of Educational Abilities*, 1917.

CHAPTER EIGHT

University College, London

I

Burt's appointment in 1932 to the Chair of Psychology at University College, London, marked the climax of, and at the same time a turning point in, his career. He had succeeded to what was, at the time, unquestionably the senior chair of psychology in the country. There were then, indeed, only five such chairs in the whole of Great Britain, two in London, and one each in Cambridge, Edinburgh and Manchester, and the Cambridge and Edinburgh chairs dated only from 1931. So Burt had reached the top of the tree at the age of 49. At the same time it was for him a watershed. Up till 1932 his energies had been directed primarily towards applied problems; after 1932 he turned mainly to theoretical and methodological questions.

When the University College Chair of Psychology fell vacant in 1931 on Spearman's retirement, Burt was an obvious successor. Sully, the pioneer of child study, had turned a philosophically orientated department towards psychology of a scientific kind, and opened a small laboratory in 1897. Burt's own teacher, McDougall, had been in charge of this laboratory from 1900 to 1907, combining it for part of the time with his Oxford duties. In 1907 Spearman had been appointed Reader, and he succeeded to the Grote Chair of Mind and Logic in 1911. The title of the chair was changed to Psychology in 1928. In addition to this psychological ancestry Galton himself had had close links with the College, and had endowed a Chair of Eugenics, to which Karl Pearson, who had been Professor of Applied Mathematics since 1884, transferred in 1912, and held until his retirement in 1933. Burt's outlook, background and training were perfectly attuned both to the department and to the College, and the main lines of work established under Spearman's direction were precisely those which Burt himself wished to pursue. As Burt himself pointed out, 'From the days of Sully and McDougall the Department has stood for something unique in the history of British Psychology— the study of the individual.'[1]

Burt's main aim in taking up the chair was to continue the tradition which had been established by his predecessors. Spearman had built up a small, but powerful, research school centring on the investigation of human abilities and personality traits employing psychometric and factor-analytic methods. It was the first really live and important school of psychological research in Great Britain. To quote an earlier account: 'Research students eventually came to him from many parts of the world, and Spearman steered them into a coordinated scheme of research, thus ensuring that his students added something to a planned edifice instead of dissipating their energies on diverse trivialities. The result was in many ways impressive. Seven out of the first ten, twelve out of the first twenty of the *Monograph Supplements* of the *British Journal of Psychology* were written by those who had worked with Spearman, and Spearman's own book, *The Abilities of Man* (1927), is largely documented by the research of his pupils.'[2]

Burt's own contact with Spearman went back to his Oxford student days, when both were associated with the British Association psychometrical project. Spearman had already published his famous 1904 paper, which is generally regarded as the origin of factor analysis. Burt's own first investigation into intelligence was explicitly undertaken 'with a view to testing in practice the mathematical methods of Dr Spearman'.[3] The text of this paper was submitted to Spearman before publication. Burt asked Spearman for his criticisms and suggestions, and Spearman sent back four foolscap pages of detailed comments, most of which were accepted by Burt and incorporated with acknowledgements in the published version of his paper. Burt was very deferential to Spearman, who was twenty years senior to himself, and wrote, 'I cannot say how much I owe to your papers, as well as to your personal encouragement and suggestions'.[4] Between 1909 and 1931 Spearman and Burt, though their views on certain matters diverged, were frequently in touch and remained on good terms. 'I called on

1. Burt, C. L. Farewell Address to the University College Psychological Society, June 1950. For the history of the department, see Flugel, J. C. A Hundred Years or so of Psychology at University College, London. *Bull. Brit. Psychol. Soc.*, No. 23 (May 1954), pp. 21–31.

2. Hearnshaw, L. S. *A Short History of British Psychology, 1840–1940*, 1964, p. 201.

3. Burt, C. L. Experimental tests of general intelligence. *Brit. J. Psychol.*, III, 1909, 95.

4. Burt, C. L. Letter to Spearman, 19 May 1909. Burt Archives, Liverpool University.

Professor Spearman and Flugel this afternoon', Burt wrote, 'at University College. . . . Spearman was very nice. He made me an honorary member of the laboratory, and pressed me to come and have tea, and work there, whenever I liked.'[5] He became intimate with Spearman's family, and one of Spearman's daughters writes, 'Cyril was a delightful "uncle" to me when I was a child, taking me to the zoo, pantomimes, and even sliding down our stairs with me on a tin tray.'[6] This long-standing personal link between the two men rendered the transition from Spearman to Burt propitious and smooth. The way in which Burt later on turned against Spearman, and attempted to belittle his achievements, was among the more discreditable episodes in Burt's career, and will be examined later. But even in the 1930s Burt was already beginning to question Spearman's position as the originator of factor analysis. Stephenson states that Burt several times let hints drop in lectures that 'he, Burt, was the initiator of factor methods',[7] and in an exchange of letters between Burt and Spearman in 1937–39 questions of priority were beginning to rankle. The correspondence in which Spearman's blunt brevity was confronted by Burt's evasive prolixity is revealing of both men.[8] While Spearman was alive Burt did not dare to do more than 'drop hints'. After Spearman's death the campaign of belittlement became increasingly unrestrained, obsessive and extravagant. In 1932, however, this was still far in the future, and Burt took over under favourable auspices. His old friend, Jack Flugel, who had worked in the department since 1909, and had risen from being a Demonstrator to Associate Professor, was no doubt disappointed in not getting the chair, but he was much too balanced and good humoured an individual to bear a grudge, and his friendship and loyalty to Burt remained undiminished. As Flugel himself put it, 'There can be no doubt that in Burt the College found a successor worthy of the great tradition which Spearman had established, and that in particular Burt developed and carried further the lines of research which Spearman had so well begun.'[9]

II

The change in Burt's personal circumstances were, indeed, far

5. Burt, C. L. Letter to his mother, undated.
6. Letter from Mrs Forman, 6 November 1976.
7. Letter from W. Stephenson, 1 December 1976.
8. Spearman–Burt correspondence, Burt Archives.
9. Flugel, J. C. *Loc. cit.*, p. 30.

greater than the change in the department. As he himself put it ten years after his retirement, 'After I was transferred from a Chair of Educational Psychology to one of General Psychology, I am afraid I became increasingly out of touch with children, parents, teachers and educational administrators.'[10] Contacts were not broken off completely: problem children from London schools were still referred to the department; research students were given facilities in schools and clinics; and Burt retained certain links with the National Institute of Industrial Psychology and other bodies. But the focus of Burt's concentration changed decisively, and the massive supply of data and case material available to him when he was on the staff of the L.C.C., as he was up to 1932, largely dried up, except indirectly through the projects of postgraduate students.

Another important change in Burt's circumstances about the time of his transfer to University College was his marriage in April 1932 to Joyce Woods, one of his former students at the London Day Training College. Burt was then 49 years of age, and, although he was notoriously attracted to women, his devotion to work was even greater, and he was generally regarded as a confirmed bachelor. His wife was twenty-six years younger than himself. She had taken an honours degree in English and History at King's College, London, and then did her year's teacher training at the L.D.T.C. After qualifying she took a temporary post as teacher of English at the Guernsey Ladies College for two terms, but she disliked teaching and failed to get another post for which she applied. Instead she married Cyril Burt. Burt himself, it is said, was strangely unenthusiastic about the whole affair and, because of morbid doubts about his own constitution, determined never to have children. The enterprise seemed fantastic to most of their friends, particularly as temperamentally they were very different. Joyce was lively, sociable and sporting. She enjoyed tennis, badminton, and other active sports. Cyril loathed sports of all sorts, and disliked casual social intercourse. The marriage held until the war. Joyce, with the financial help of her husband, took a medical course, which she had always wanted to do, and, after qualifying, specialised in gynaecology, taking the F.R.C.O.G. examination, and eventually becoming distinguished in her profession. Both preferred their own work to each other's company, and at first boredom, and then antipathy developed. Cyril's own medical knowledge was considerable. He had grown up in a medical home, worked in the Physiological Laboratory at Oxford with McDougall, and for five years was with Sherrington in the Liverpool Medical

10. Burt, C. L. Letter to the Secretary of the Secondary School Examination Council, 8 August 1960.

School. He had absorbed an enormous amount of medical information, and his omniscience made his wife feel perpetually inferior. In
the specialism of gynaecology she was at least her own mistress! When
the war broke out and Cyril was evacuated to Aberystwyth she did
not follow her husband, but obtained hospital posts in Surrey, Oxford
and London, visiting Aberystwyth for occasional holidays and week-
ends. The final break came in 1952, when she left their London flat
never to return. There is no doubt that Burt felt bitter and resentful at
his wife's desertion. He refused to initiate divorce proceedings, and
his wife, who set up an establishment with another man, to the end of
her life called herself Lady Burt. No direct communication took place
between them, and Burt deleted his wife altogether from his will. She
survived him by only three years.

At first these changed circumstances did not greatly affect Burt's
work. The Burts moved to a flat in Eton Road, Hampstead, and Burt
developed a new routine. The mornings, which he nearly always
spent at home, were devoted to his own work. A former member of
staff, who knew him well, stated that he always regarded his own
work as of greater importance than the running of the department,
and that he delegated a lot of departmental business to members of his
staff, and particularly to Dr Philpott. He disliked committees and
administration, and rarely attended Professorial Board meetings
unless his department was directly involved. Inevitably, however, he
had to take his turn as Chairman of the Board of Studies, Chairman of
the Board of Examiners, and convenor of the Higher Degrees Sub-
committee for Psychology. His own department he ran on a light
rein, and with a minimum of red tape. When he had to make decisions
he made them expeditiously.

During the first ten years of Burt's occupancy of the chair things
went well. The department was of manageable size, and Burt was still
reasonably fit. Not only did he have time to produce three major
books— *The Subnormal Mind* (1935), *The Backward Child* (1937) and
Factors of the Mind (1940)— he wrote numerous articles, broadcasted
frequently, gave several series of extension lectures, and contributed
weightily to various public enquiries, including the Spens Committee on secondary education, and the International Examinations
Enquiry. He was certainly greatly assisted in getting through this
huge volume of work by employing, and personally paying for, his
own secretarial assistance. Professorial salaries in the 1930s were not
very magnificent (Burt was appointed at a salary of £1,000 per
annum); but Burt was abstemious, and the wages he paid were modest. He had already commenced the practice of employing his own
assistants while at the London Day Training College, when Miss
V. G. Pelling, who had worked with him at the National Institute of

Industrial Psychology, helped him with testing and secretarial work. Shortly before he moved to University College he engaged Miss Gladys Bruce, who remained with him until her death in 1958. A neurotic and withdrawn woman she took to Burt, who seemed to understand her. She was an efficient stenographer and typist, and helped Burt enormously in the preparation of his books, in his extensive correspondence, and in the typing of the numerous memoranda and sets of notes for students that he was constantly producing. She was prepared to work late hours, and would often stay until nine or ten at night typing correspondence or reports. Unfortunately she was not very systematic in her filing, so there are comparatively few records remaining from the time of her secretaryship. But there is no doubt that it was her help that enabled Burt to get through the quantity of work that he did.

In the department Burt had a small but efficient team of assistants. Flugel, who had been a member of the staff for over twenty years, took the abnormal and social psychology, and added the psychoanalytic spice. Between 1926 and 1940 he was aided by Pryns Hopkins from Yale, who was established in the department in an honorary capacity. S. J. F. Philpott, the other longstanding member of the staff, was responsible for experimental psychology and the running of the laboratory. Appointed by Spearman in 1920 after taking a degree in the natural sciences, he was one of the mainstays of the department. 'Perhaps the most characteristic thing that I can say about Philpott', writes Flugel, 'is that . . . I cannot recollect a single occasion on which he refused to give help or advice to me or anyone if it were in his power to do so, at whatever inconvenience to himself. . . . Philpott was a man whom to know was to respect and love.'[11] Dogged rather than brilliant in his research on work curves, he eventually became antagonised by Burt's unappreciative, almost contemptuous, attitude towards him, and relations between the two became exceedingly strained. He was highly regarded, however, by most of his fellow psychologists, and in 1948 was elected President of the British Psychological Society, having served as Treasurer and Deputy-President for nearly twenty years. The more junior members of the staff, William Stephenson, Constance Simmins and Grace Studman, were appointed as research assistants only shortly before Burt's accession to the chair. Stephenson, whose own views on factor problems came to diverge from those of Burt, writes, 'During the years 1931–1937 at University College I had no reason ever to doubt Burt's helpfulness; he was benign and compassionate. But I was never invited by either Burt or Flugel to enter into any close personal relationship such as I had with

11. Flugel, J. C. *Loc. cit.*, p. 29.

Spearman.'[12] The social cement of the department was provided, as is quite often the case, by the technician, J. T. Raper, and his wife, who worked as a secretarial assistant, rather than by any member of the academic staff. 'Raper', writes Flugel, '*was* the department—inasmuch as, somehow or other, he had to be consulted about everything, by staff, students and visitors alike. . . . His personality was such that it is quite likely that many students will remember him more vividly than any of their official teachers.'[13]

A university department, in spite of being part of a larger community, is often very much a world of its own, and relations with allied disciplines are far from close. The University College professoriate in Burt's day included some eminent men whose interests overlapped with Burt's, but no very fruitful relations appear to have developed. Karl Pearson was still there until 1933, but there had been bitter antagonism between him and Spearman, and it was only when his son, Egon Pearson, succeeded him that relations between psychology and biometrics improved, without, however, leading to much active collaboration. In the Galton laboratory R. A. Fisher was occasionally consulted by Burt, but Burt did not till later get interested in quantitative genetics. The philosophers John MacMurray and A. J. Ayer were critical of psychology, and Ayer, writes Burt, 'was fond of pulling our psychological legs'. Report has it that Burt was not particularly popular with his colleagues (who included, among others, J. B. S. Haldane, Herbert Dingle, L. S. Penrose and J. Z. Young), nor very closely involved with them. J. Z. Young in the Anatomy department says that he never had any contact with Burt. In fact Burt had no great regard for most of his contemporaries, particularly his younger contemporaries, and he made disparaging comments on J. Z. Young's Reith Lectures. After the intimate and close-knit community of the London Day Training College the atmosphere surrounding Burt was distinctly less warm and congenial. However, he was a remarkably self-sufficient person, and simply got on with his work, and especially with his own writing and varied outside commitments.

III

To his students, of course, Burt was an enormously impressive person. He had a dazzlingly brilliant and well-stocked mind,

12. Letter from W. Stephenson, 1 December 1976.
13. Flugel, J. C. *Loc. cit.*, p. 29.

immense expertise in areas, such as statistics, where they were mere beginners, a fund of practical experience, and great powers of lucid exposition. He was an acknowledged master at whose feet they were proud to sit. The number of students at the time of his appointment was small, comprising some twenty undergraduate honours students spread over three years, and a dozen postgraduates. In the pre-war period there was no great expansion. The balance of the department was towards research rather than undergraduate teaching, and Burt himself took a primary responsibility for postgraduates, though Flugel and Philpott assisted in their own areas of interest. Burt's undergraduate teaching consisted mainly in the first-year introductory course, which he believed should be undertaken by the head of the department. This was a comprehensive course covering the whole area of psychology, with a good deal of emphasis on sensation, perception and cognitive processes, intelligence, attention, personality, physiological and biological psychology (with some reference to the mind–body problem) together with some lectures on applications and methodology.

The impressions of a student in the late 1930s are worth quoting:

Burt was the best of the 40 or 50 lecturers I heard at various times during my five years at London University. His voice was pleasant and cultured, but in no sense affected. He spoke with great fluency, never hesitating for words and never using unusual or technical language unless it was impossible to convey the meaning accurately. His lectures appeared to be spontaneous . . . he referred to notes only to produce reference or cite data. His talks were extraordinarily well-balanced, informative and lively. He drew upon an immensely wide background of knowledge, but he carried his learning lightly. He was punctilious in points of detail, but never pedantic. Burt had the gift of tuning to the intellectual level and state of knowledge of his audience. Thus he never talked over the heads of his listeners nor did he ever insult them by labouring explanation unduly. And he achieved this without cheapening or falsifying his subject matter. He never projected his personality for effect. He commanded attention by his obvious interest in what he was presenting, and by his mastery of the material. . . . In presenting the work of any psychologist he was scrupulously fair in setting out what the man was trying to do and the difficulties he had to overcome. He always stressed the positive achievements before indicating weaknesses. It was impossible listening to him to be sure whether he inclined to one school or another. . . . He spiced his lectures with occasional epigrams and shafts of wit, but he always introduced them to bring a point home, never as ends in themselves. . . . After hearing Burt once I never missed one of his lectures avoidably.[14]

The abler students in particular appreciated Burt's teaching; but there were complaints from the rank and file of inadequate tutorial instruction and an insufficiency of written work; in fact this sparked off a signed protest in the late 1930s which caused Burt some distress. Flugel agreed that the students had a case and that undergraduates were being sacrificed to research; essays and tutorials were too few; and he suggested ways of improving assistance to the junior members of the department. This seems to have been a passing cloud, and relations with students in the pre-war days at least were generally good.

With postgraduates, of course, Burt's contact was closer. The department attracted students from many parts of the world, and among the many able researchers who worked under Burt were E. Anstey, J. Cohen, Agnes Crawford, Ruth Griffiths, M. Hamilton, A. R. Jonckheere, M. M. Lewis, J. B. Parry, and F. W. Warburton from Great Britain; Cicely de Monchaux, A. J. Marshall, and Florence Schonell from Australia; D. W. McElwain, T. P. H. McKellar, and C. F. Wrigley from New Zealand; A. Lubin from the U.S.A.; H. J. Eysenck from Germany; El Koussy from Egypt; and M. Desai from India. Many of these were to hold influential positions in Britain and abroad, and were to express their warm appreciation for the help and encouragement they received from Burt. Even Eysenck, not lavish in his praise, expressed consistent appreciation of Burt's teaching. Few among them were prepared to give credence to the attacks made on Burt's integrity after his death.

Nevertheless the postgraduate school was not without its weaknesses. There was an enormous wastage among the postgraduates. Barely four out of every ten students who registered, successfully completed their courses. There was little of the concerted planning that had been evident under Spearman. The topics researched into covered an enormous range of subjects: child psychology, social psychology, personality, testing, factor analysis, aesthetics, humour, imagery, visual perception, work curves, etc. Each thesis was a unit in itself rather than a brick in an edifice. Many of the theses supervised by Burt himself were highly competent pieces of work, but with a few exceptions they did not contribute directly to any body of data that he was master-minding. Some cohesion, however,

14. Communication from Dr J. B. Parry, 1977.

was provided by means of special seminars for postgraduates, held twice a week and instituted to prevent undue concentration on narrow fields of enquiry. These seminars were well attended, and lively and stimulating discussions took place. But one postgraduate student noted a characteristic of Burt which provides an important clue to his character—in all the discussions that took place Burt 'had to win'. His superior range of knowledge and technical expertise usually made this easy; but when opposition appeared he showed that he had to win the argument at all costs, a characteristic that appeared very frequently in later controversies. Nevertheless the help and encouragement that he gave to his postgraduates was deeply appreciated. 'I can express nothing but gratitude for the help and encouragement he gave me', wrote one of his former students, 'and I have spoken to others who feel the same way. I found him easier to communicate with on paper than by discussion, but this may be a comment on me rather than on him.'[15] Burt himself, it would seem, preferred to make his comments on students' work in writing rather than orally, and his detailed criticisms were often of a voluminous nature. This again points to another of his characteristics. He was cognitively rather than emotionally involved in his relations with people, and rarely established close and intimate friendships. There were a few exceptions, mainly women, but throughout his life he was essentially a 'loner'.

Not all the postgraduates were engaged in research. A few were recruited for the Academic Diploma in Psychology, the regulations for which were revised soon after Burt's appointment, and provided for training in industrial, educational and social psychology. Training for the educational section was located at University College, and was under Burt's charge, assisted by Miss Simmins, and, after her resignation, by Miss Keir. According to Miss Grace Rawlings, who briefed the Summerfield Committee in the 1960s, the diploma course prior to 1946 was not regarded as a recognised qualification for educational psychologists. 'We have always been most emphatic that candidates for the Diploma prior to 1946 were not trained as educational psychologists, and therefore not considered eligible for such posts in local authority services.'[16] The grounds for this non-recognition were firstly that non-graduates were sometimes admitted to the diploma, and secondly that practical training was inadequate. Burt replied that 'the pre-war regulations expressly state "the object of the diploma course is to afford facilities for instruction in certain branches of applied psychology to students intending to take up practical work in various fields", and section

15. Communication from Dr J. B. Parry, 1977.
16. Letter from Miss Grace Rawlings to C. L. Burt, 25 November 1968.

B is explicitly concerned with educational psychology. Does not this imply that students successfully pursuing this course *were* in fact "trained educational psychologists"? . . . The lectures and demonstrations I myself gave were based on my experience as educational psychologist for the L.C.C. . . . The Tavistock Clinic assisted with the clinical training required by the regulations.'[17] In his review of the Summerfield Committee Report on Educational Psychologists Burt seemed anxious to claim priority in their training, maintaining indeed that it went back to London Day Training College times in 1923.[18] It is difficult to understand why Burt should have been so concerned about so trivial a matter, which turned on the precise definition of 'adequacy of practical training' and 'recognition'. Some training was certainly given in the 1930s, and this became fully regularised and recognised when the regulations for the diploma were amended in 1946.

IV

In September 1939, just before the University was due to commence the session, war broke out, and the department of Psychology, together with various departments of University College, was speedily evacuated to the University College of Aberystwyth in Wales. There it remained until the autumn of 1944.

These years in Aberystwyth were to have a marked effect on Burt's personality. Although, as we have seen, he was called in to assist in the application of psychology in the armed services, for five years he was removed from the centre of the stage, and isolated from a great deal that was taking place in psychology. With many of the new developments he was out of sympathy, and when he returned to London there were many new faces and new trends. At the same time his self-confidence was shaken by the deterioration of his health, and by the virtual breakdown of his marriage. Though masking his troubles beneath an unruffled exterior, he became increasingly hypochondriac and cautious, and, when challenged or crossed, increasingly edgy and difficult. His relations with colleagues and some of his abler students became strained; his behaviour to them began at times to generate distrust, and even dislike. Honours and triumphs still lay before him, but the supremely confident days ended in 1940 with the publication of his last major work, *The Factors of the Mind.*

17. Burt, C. L. Letter to Miss Rawlings, 28 November 1968.
18. Burt, C. L. Psychologists in the Education Service. *Bull. Brit. Psychol. Soc.,* *XXII*, 1969, 1–11.

Aberystwyth, of course, had its compensations. It was, wrote Burt, 'a delightful and beautiful spot, and the natives are astonishingly kind'. Burt enjoyed the sea air and the walks in the vicinity. But more than that he revelled in the freedom from committee work, and in the more intimate atmosphere of the place. Aberystwyth, he stated in his autobiographical sketch, 'brought back the conditions I have always preferred—the chance to live intimately with a tiny group of colleagues and students, as members of a harmonious family'.[19] Student numbers were reduced to a handful, and most of the postgraduates took up other activities, or remained in London. The college ruling was that no research students should be located in Aberystwyth unless their research was directly contributing to the war effort. This ruling was relaxed to some extent from 1941 onwards, but postgraduate numbers did not pick up again till 1944, and did not reach their pre-war volume until 1945. So Burt, for the first time in years, had some freedom from the pressure of business. His staff, of course, was also reduced. Philpott accompanied him to Aberystwyth for the duration; Flugel joined them after a year, and in deference to the susceptibilities of a Welsh community was asked to play down psychoanalysis! J. S. Wilkie visited periodically to give physiology lectures.

The students who remember the Aberystwyth days all speak in almost rapturous terms of their experiences. 'Burt's handling of his group of students, most of whom had come to psychology after taking up some other career previously, and who were nearer 30 than 20 years of age, was most stimulating, and produced an atmosphere which must have been unique for any department', wrote one former student. 'The relationship was often one of mutual stimulation rather than that of teacher and student. This was very different from the one prevailing at the time among University College of Wales departments with which we came into contact.'[20] Another student described her relations with Burt as follows:

Those who were students of Professor Burt at Aberystwyth during the war remember a close personal contact with him— informal and brilliant lectures sitting round his dining room table; chance meetings with him as he walked along the promenade. With luck and perhaps some skill, one could meet him occasionally at the end of his Sunday afternoon walks, and be invited back to afternoon tea, for which his housekeeper always seemed able to provide cottage cheese sandwiches and fresh cakes, and at which Professor Burt entertained his guests with lively

19. Burt, C. L. An autobiographical sketch. *Occup. Psychol., XXIII*, 1949, 20.
20. Letter from Dr W. H. Hammond, 30 November 1976.

and unrepeatable stories about high officers in the War Office and Civil Service. I recall too the small kindnesses, such as allowing me to store a large trunk in the basement of his house, and allowing others to have a weekly hot bath— hot water seemed to be in remarkably short supply in Aberystwyth lodgings. Essays were returned with detailed typed comments, sometimes as long as the essay itself, always helpful and constructive comments. . . . He produced and distributed sheafs of notes on statistics and factor analysis, and on many other topics, which were models of clarity and of simple expositions of complex material— a starting point for further reading on that topic.[21]

No doubt in this small, close-knit, exiled community the students saw much more of Burt than had been possible in the London days.

His own ménage was a peculiar one. His wife came rarely to Aberystwyth— so rarely, that one student who saw a lot of Burt was unaware even that he was married. The German housekeeper engaged by Mrs Burt just before the war was interned soon after reaching Aberystwyth, and another housekeeper, Miss Elizabeth Dean, was engaged. Described as 'a skinny 57 year old, slightly microcephalic, with wispy hair, looking much older in her tremulous condition', she took to Burt with devotion and remained as housekeeper as long as he was in Aberystwyth, and in touch with him until his death. The other member of the ménage was, of course, the indispensable secretary, Miss Gladys Bruce.

So Burt was well served and looked after while in exile. The problem which soon arose was his health. This is such an important matter that it will be discussed more fully in Chapter Thirteen. For the present we may note that his medical troubles began very soon after he arrived in Aberystwyth. In February 1940 he was complaining of nausea, and started dieting. A week later he comments, 'The incidental benefit is that I can manage to do a good deal more mental work. Previously I used to get very lazy after lunch, but with the lighter diet I am more alert.'[22] Dieting, however, did not cure the problem, and in December 1941, after further attacks of nausea and giddiness, Ménière's disease was diagnosed (see p. 278). At this period only his left ear was involved; twenty years later his right ear was similarly affected. The disease was to incapacitate him, and restrict his movements for the rest of his life, though the acute phases were transitory. Not only did it make him reluctant to travel, but it partly deprived him of hearing, at first not too seriously, but later, after involvement of the right ear, increasingly severely. Burt

21. Communication from Dr Agnes Crawford, 1971.
22. Burt, C. L. Letter to his sister, 14 February 1940.

was stoical in the face of these disabilities. He never whined in public, and he never stopped working, though he increasingly excused himself from invitations that he did not particularly relish.

In the early days of the war, however, he was straining to do more. In May 1940, when the war situation was at its most critical, he wrote to the superintendent of a mental hospital near Pershore in Worcestershire 'suggesting that I might perhaps be useful in a mental deficiency institution and so release a doctor'.[23] It was not until somewhat later that military psychology got launched and Burt's advisory work commenced. This at least made him feel useful; but it by no means satisfied his urge to be doing something. So he took advantage of local opportunities and, assisted by a research student, Miss Enid John, made a study of children evacuated from the cities, publishing several papers in 1940–41.[24] And he got interested in the question of bilingualism, two of his research students, Miss M. A. Davidson and Miss I. M. Slade, carrying out an investigation of 'The Effects of Bilingualism on the Intelligence Test performances of a group of Welsh University Students'.[25] The sojourn in Aberystwyth was never just a seaside rest cure!

Burt himself, too, with more time on his hands began to look again at some of the masses of data that had been collected while he was at the L.C.C. This led to the publication in June 1943 of his article 'Ability and Income'.[26] This was a highly important article, marking, perhaps, a watershed in Burt's career. First of all, two of his 'practical conclusions' for the first time evoked a good deal of unpopularity—the conclusions namely that (i) 'The foregoing results suggest the view that the wide inequality in personal income is largely, though not entirely, an indirect effect of the wide inequality in innate intelligence', and (ii) 'they do not support the view (still held by many educational and social reformers) that the apparent inequality in intelligence of children and adults is in the main an indirect consequence of inequality in economic conditions'. Burt had not stated matters in quite so provocative a way before. But secondly, and more seriously, this was chrono-logically the first of Burt's articles the integrity of which was later challenged. It was the first paper in which he referred to the results of his twin studies, and in coming to some of his conclusions about social class Burt indulged in some extremely questionable statistical

23. Burt, C. L. Letter, 23 May 1940.

24. Burt, C. L. The incidence of neurotic symptoms in evacuated children. *Brit. J. Educ. Psychol.*, X, 1940, 9–15; The billeting of evacuated children. *Brit. J. Educ. Psychol.*, XI, 1941, 85–98; The Evacuation of Children under Five. In *Under-fives in Total War*, Brit. Psychol. Soc., 1942.

25. Davidson, M. A. and Slade, I. M. Unpublished report.

26. Burt, C. L. Ability and income. *Brit. J. Educ. Psychol.*, XIII, 1943, 83–98.

manipulations, as indeed he himself to some extent admits in the paper. These charges will be examined more fully later. Here it may be noted that the writing of this paper (if we allow the usual period of a year between writing and publication) coincided with the height of his Ménière attacks.

We shall see later that Ménière's disease is often accompanied by various psychological symptoms. This may well account not only for certain lapses of judgement in 'Ability and income', but also for the sharp deterioration in his relations with Dr Philpott which occurred while they were in Aberystwyth. Academic bickering is not an uncommon phenomenon, and no great notice might be taken of it, did it not throw a good deal of light on Burt's character.

Philpott, we have already noted, was appointed to a lectureship by Spearman in 1920. After carrying out research on the use of the cinema in education, he became interested in Spearman's ideas on the fundamental importance of oscillations of cognitive efficiency, and he devoted the rest of his life to the study of work curves and their fluctuations. His major publication was a monograph on 'Fluctuations in Human Output'.[27] He later summarised his findings in his presidential address to the British Psychological Society as follows:

> In brief the essential facts are that (i) single curves vary widely in outline, although (ii) grand total curves, based on many experimental records, tend to resemble one another, i.e. they approach a standard system in their ups and downs, a system such that at the moment one grand total curve is at a trough others tend to be at troughs and vice versa. . . . In 1932 I suggested a theory [of these fluctuations] in terms of natural rhythms. Let there be a pool of possible waves each of characteristic period and trough sequence, from which on any given occasion the subject takes a random sample with which to constitute his curve for the given experiment. If the samples are relatively small with reference to the size of the pool as a whole, then findings (i) and (ii) above would follow. The wave system set up by single random samples would give a standard end result, that given if all the waves of the pool were simultaneously excited. Adding to this general statement I have, of course, suggested that the waves of the pool are periodic in log time with periods that are whole number multiples of the unit $p = \cdot 0016$ on the scale of log time, all trough sequences being such that they meet in a universal common trough at time $T_0 = 4 \cdot 076 \times 10^{-23}$ seconds from the moment of starting work. These are the first two constants ever

27. Philpott, S. J. F. *Brit. J. Psychol. Monogr. Supp. XVII*, 1932.

suggested in psychology. They represent a revolutionary change in our notions of mental work.[28]

It must be admitted that Philpott's work was both abstruse and difficult to understand, and that it was not proved either as revolutionary or as fruitful as he himself supposed. But it was honest work, patient work, and perfectly harmless. It hardly deserved the pulverising disdain with which Burt treated it, or the barrage of memoranda and letters which poured scorn on it. The memoranda and letters that landed on Philpott's doorstep early in 1944 amounted to well over 30,000 words! The letters alone during the three weeks between January 7th and 27th added up to some 16,000 words! On the peak day, January 10th, no less than 8,000 words were typed. The last and longest letter was commenced just before midnight. What demonic force drove Burt to such extravagant and absurd lengths? Why did he think it necessary to spend hour upon hour of his time, and to sit up half the night, to make this devastating attack on a colleague upon whose devoted labours the functioning of the department largely depended, and to whom staff and students alike were deeply attached? Why these lengthy screeds addressed to someone with whom a chat would have been easy and far more appropriate? And it was not merely the volume of material that was infuriating, but its tone. Burt himself was somewhat apologetic about this:

Let me apologise for handing over those documents to you yesterday on the spur of the moment without explanatory note. I quite appreciate the fact that the way I word my memoranda must be rather alarming. Gladstone addressed Queen Victoria as though she were a public meeting. I write memoranda to myself as though I were the editor publishing controversial articles. I find it easier to write about people in the third person. It must sound very stilted and pugnacious when the third person finds it handed to himself over the doorstep. I hasten to explain, therefore, that this sort of stuff is merely meant in the first instance to clear my own mind.[29]

Equally riling was the snide humility that kept on creeping in.

I really do not think, as you so repeatedly say, that your very original work has been neglected because of any purblind prejudice. I think the trouble is that the reader has to spend so

28. Philpott, S. J. F. *Quart. Bull. Brit. Psychol. Soc.*, *I*, 4, April 1949, 133.
29. Burt, C. L. Letter to Dr Philpott, 10 January 1944.

much time on trying to grasp the lines of proof. This is no doubt due, not to any shortcomings on your part, but first of all on the complexity of the subject, secondly to the fact that after all most psychologists are frightfully busy with their day-to-day routine work, and thirdly perhaps to the fact that where mathematical arguments are concerned we are nearly all Goddam idiots. I suppose after all that the majority of psychologists in this country, like Flugel and myself, are really Arts people, and are mere amateurs in dealing with what you term 'elementary algebra'.[30]

And then just to be nasty he wrote in another letter, after a visit to the department by the Provost, 'The Provost noted that there was a good deal of work going on in connection with work curves, and I think he rather wondered how that helped the war effort. This is only gossip arising out of conversation at the luncheon to which he went after his discussion with you in the laboratory.'[31] And so it went on and on. After all this the two men were not on speaking terms; in fact one Aberystwyth student said she never saw them speak to one another during their last two years there. For Burt to write as he did in his autobiographical sketch about 'the chance to live intimately with a tiny group of colleagues and students as members of a harmonious family' seemed to those who knew the facts to be not merely disingenuous but insolent. Philpott, it seemed, could be wholly ignored. It was this kind of conduct, even more than his opinions, that brought upon Burt in his later years so much distrust and hostility. The relations between Burt and Philpott never mended. Burt consistently blocked any promotion for Philpott, and, beneath his bland exterior, never relented. Philpott in weary resignation came eventually to the conclusion that Burt was mentally unbalanced— which possibly had an element of truth in it. It is difficult to believe that this kind of friction would have occurred before Burt's health problems became exacerbated by the development of Ménière symptoms. The Aberystwyth period was in more ways than one a climacteric in his career.

V

In 1944 it was decided that University College should reassemble in Gower Street for the session commencing in October. The war was still on, and flying bombs were still falling. But the end was in

30. Burt, C. L. Letter to Dr Philpott, 12 January 1944.
31. Burt, C. L. Letter to Dr Philpott, 27 January 1944.

sight, and the prospects of floods of new students released from the forces made it desirable to get back to normal working. So Burt and his department left Aberystwyth as the October term commenced, and established themselves in their old quarters in London. Conditions were far from easy. The college had been hit by bombs, and some of Burt's own papers had been lost. Housing, too, was a problem, as much property had been damaged or destroyed.

For Burt it meant a considerable upheaval. He had to find somewhere to live, and he had to replan his domestic arrangements. There was uncertainty as to his wife, who now had a job at the Radcliffe Infirmary in Oxford, and a small house there which she shared with medical colleagues. Would she return to London and live with him again? Eventually in 1947 she did, obtaining a post at King's College Hospital, and for a time the marriage was revived. Meanwhile the housekeeping problem was solved by the release of his former German housekeeper, Miss Erna Neuburger, from internment on the Isle of Man, and in November 1944 he found somewhere to live, the spacious and attractive flat at 9 Elsworthy Road, overlooking Primrose Hill, where he was to remain until his death. It had a large living room with views over the hill, and plenty of space for storing his bulky library and his masses of papers, as well as accommodation for his complex domestic arrangements. It had two main disadvantages—it was cold, and inadequately heated; and it was expensive. After his wife left him it proved a severe drain on his resources. But it certainly gave him an agreeable environment for the evening of his life. He believed there could not be a nicer flat in London, and it enabled him to indulge his liking for walking. He could stroll on Primrose Hill, and even walk over the hill and through Regents Park almost all the way to College.

After his return to London there were still officially four more years before Burt was due to retire. In actual fact, owing to the difficulty the college had in finding a successor, he stayed for six years. This was, perhaps, the busiest time of his life. With the cessation of the war student numbers increased rapidly, and before long the pre-war enrolment in psychology was vastly exceeded. In his report on the department in 1947, the year before he was due to retire, Burt notes that undergraduates taking psychology had increased from 5 in 1931 to 103 in 1947, and postgraduate research students from 12 in 1931 to 71 in 1947, of whom 37 were registered for Ph.D.s. The department, still in its old cramped quarters, and with inadequate staff and equipment, was under heavy pressure. In 1944 his oldest friend and colleague, Jack Flugel, had retired; but new lecturers were, of course, appointed to cope with the load, and

A. Summerfield, M. Hamilton, J. Whitfield, Cecily de Monchaux, Gertrude Keir, Grace Rawlings, and Charlotte Banks joined the staff. But the infra-structure of the department remained much as it was, and Burt reverted to his pre-war routines. The pressures on him were immense, and his health was far less sound than it had been before the war, though the severe Ménière attacks of Aberystwyth days had abated. The surprising thing was how much he managed to cope with: the departmental load; college and university committee work, which he could no longer avoid; calls on his time from government departments and other public bodies; the editing of, and writing for, a new statistical journal; and finally the production of a larger number of articles for publication than at any other period of his career. The bibliography of his writings in *Stephanos*[32] lists no fewer than seventy-three items for the six years 1945–50. It was certainly an astonishing achievement.

And it coincided with the showering on Burt of public recognition in a variety of forms. First, and, of course, foremost, was his knighthood in 1946, when he was the first psychologist to be so honoured. In 1948 an honorary D.Litt., to add to his pre-war LL.D. from Aberdeen, was bestowed on him by the University of Reading, at a congregation where the Prime Minister, Mr C. R. Attlee, was another recipient. In 1950 he was elected a Fellow of the British Academy, and in the same year an honorary Fellow of his old Oxford college, Jesus College. Together with these honours went many eulogies. On his knighthood he received a huge fan mail from old colleagues and former students, from fellow psychologists, from distinguished figures like Sir Charles Sherrington (then approaching 90 and in a nursing home), Lord Woolton and Sir Julian Huxley, and from Miss Ellen Wilkinson, M.P., the Minister of Education in the Labour Government, who wrote, 'So much of the work in which you have been a pioneer is now playing an increasingly important part in education.'[33] It was, of course, because of his work for education and for the armed services during the war that the honour of knighthood was primarily conferred. But there was a genuine warmth in many of the tributes, which went far beyond giving recognition for useful work performed. In his address to the congregation on the occasion of the Reading D.Litt., Professor A. W. Wolters, Professor of Psychology and a long-standing admirer, spoke of his constant kindness and friendship to all, and told Burt that he was responsible for 'the best that British Psychology has so far produced, even though you try to

32. Banks, Charlotte, and Broadhurst, P. L. (eds) *Stephanos: Studies in Psychology presented to Cyril Burt*, 1965.
33. Letter from Miss Ellen Wilkinson M.P., 17 June 1946.

hide your light under a bushel of factors'. 'He has enriched scientific literature with a series of classics, one of which, *The Young Delinquent*, is famous beyond the world of psychology.'[34]

Beneath the glittering surface, however, not all was well. Burt's health was far from restored; he and his wife were never properly reconciled; and his conduct was beginning to antagonise a growing number of both colleagues and students. Amid the many new faces and new ideas in psychology his predominance no longer went unchallenged, and he was not always too scrupulous in attempting to get his way. In fact Burt began to acquire the reputation of a thoroughly devious character, for whom the sobriquet 'The Old Delinquent' seemed quite apt.

This is what a former colleague from another college has to say on the matter:

When I went to Bedford College in 1945 I had nothing but respect and liking for what I knew of him. We hadn't been in close contact, but he had always been amiable and helpful to me. It was only very gradually as I saw him in action on Boards of Studies and Examiners, and had occasional informal contacts with him that I began to disapprove of what he did, and in the end came to the conclusion that in some respects, he just had a bad character. It seems an old-fashioned thing to say. I was unfortunately chairman of one or two meetings in which we had to prevent him, by an actual vote, from getting his own way in some unreasonable demand, and he never forgave me for allowing this to happen. We remained on very polite terms, never had a cross word, but we had no use for each other. . . . [However,] although I thought him unscrupulous in ordinary university matters I had naively never even imagined that the lack of scruple could extend to scientific work.[35]

An example of this deviousness, and also of the way in which he browbeat Philpott, occurred in connection with the establishment of Eysenck's clinical diploma at the Maudsley Hospital.

Burt was the most determined opponent of the Diploma, and Aubrey Lewis the main supporter. Finally there came a meeting at which it was definitely agreed that the diploma should be established with Eysenck's proposals accepted in outline. Philpott was secretary to the Board, and when his minutes came round

34. Wolters, A. W. Address to Reading University Degree Congregation, June 1948.
35. Harding, D. W. Letter, 29 October 1976.

before the next meeting this very definite decision had been changed into an agreement that the discussion should be continued. Aubrey Lewis arrived at the meeting in a state of controlled seething, and of course objected to the minutes of the previous meeting. Burt blandly expressed his impression that we had not actually made a decision, but everyone else had to say that the minutes were wrong, and the item was altered as Lewis wanted. When I spoke to Philpott afterwards he said rather sheepishly that, of course, he knew it was wrong, but Burt had absolutely insisted on his phrasing it as he did.[36]

Students, too, began to experience his devious ways. The incident that took place with Professor A. D. B. Clarke and his wife in their student days is of particular importance, as it sowed the seeds for their later role as instigators of doubts as to Burt's integrity. The Clarkes after graduating at Reading enrolled as Ph.D. students with Eysenck at the Maudsley Hospital. Since Eysenck was not then a recognised teacher of the University they had formally to register with Burt, who was one of the examiners for their theses.

After the Ph.D. vivas [writes Clarke] Burt said that we were both to glance at some brief summaries he had made of our theses and approve them, because 'I like to publish some of the more promising results'. These summaries proved to be a little inaccurate. We corrected them, and almost forgot about the incident. In the autumn, to our astonishment, we found two articles under our authorship in the *British Journal of Educational Psychology* implicitly attacking Eysenck. We did not recognise them as the same summaries (of which of course we had no copies) we had corrected at University College. Our theses had indeed been critical of the 'dimensions of personality' approach, but the whole emphasis of 'our' articles was slanted. We went personally to apologise to Eysenck, who, hearing our disclaimer, was exceedingly generous, saying that this sort of ploy was typical of the old man. When I asked him for advice he suggested that I should let the matter drop. Nevertheless I wrote an angry letter to Burt, and was told that he thought we were out of the country and hadn't therefore sent galley proofs. By this stage we had become quite clear that Burt was dishonest, and predictably he later quoted 'our' two articles as independent support for his attack upon Eysenck.[37]

36. Harding, D. W. Letter, 29 October 1976.
37. Clarke, A. D. B. Letter, 23 September 1976.

Of course, not all students had experiences of this kind. In a large department not all students, even postgraduates, came closely into contact with the Professor. Burt's charisma was still potent, and his intellectual powers dazzling and undimmed. He was still to most students a figure to be revered. In the year of his retirement they decorated his room with flowers on his birthday, and the farewell party in June 1950, when he eventually retired, was the biggest party for which the college had ever catered.

> We began with sherry on the lawn [Burt wrote to his sister] and we then lined up to be photographed. The dinner itself was marvellously arranged. There must have been 150 people present. . . . Joyce was presented with a magnificent bouquet of roses, and the table was all decorated with flowers. . . . After we had eaten as much as we could Jack [Flugel] proposed a toast. He made a most amusing speech, which consisted in a semi-humourous biography interspersed with incidents that I had almost forgotten. Then the President of the Student Psychological Society seconded the toast and made the presentation. They seem to have collected nearly £130 to purchase a calculating machine, and as they also had a lot over they also got a typewriter. After that I had to reply, and there was the usual singing and cheering. . . . The whole thing was full of bright ideas and must have involved an enormous amount of thought and energy. Joyce's bouquet had been bought that morning at Covent Garden by a couple of students who got up at half-past four. The menu card was an enormous affair with a hand-painted design of young delinquents on the front, and a space inside for the signatures of all present.[38]

So eighteen years after he had succeeded Spearman Burt's tenure of the Chair of Psychology at University College came to an end. The problem that had exercised the college and university authorities for some three years was 'who was to follow him?'

VI

The question of a successor was far from easily answered. Burt was extremely eminent; the department of psychology had established a tradition of a special sort, unlike that of most other departments in the country. Before the war the number of universities with departments of psychology was small, and hence there were few

38. Burt, C. L. Letter to his sister, 25 June 1950.

psychologists around with both the necessary academic standing, and the kind of interests the department required. The younger psychologists had nearly all been engaged in war work, had had little time to publish, and were light on teaching experience. The task of the selection committee was made more difficult by marked disagreement among its members, and particularly a long-drawn-out tussle between some of the medical members of the committee and Burt who was pulling wires and doing all he could to get the man he wanted appointed. In a letter to his sister he admitted, 'The retiring professor is not supposed to exert his views on the subject, but things do not work out that way. I was really responsible for stopping them appointing that rather ineffectual gentleman from Canada, and putting in the American professor, who with all his faults is not quite so bad as L—— would have been.'[39] Burt was desperately concerned that the tradition of individual psychology should be preserved, and did all he could to influence the committee in this direction. In a memorandum he wrote on the department he maintained that it would be a mistake to appoint either a psychologist specialising in pure or general psychology or an eminent experimentalist. Other departments in the country catered adequately for this sort of psychology. The man he thought who would continue the tradition of the department was Alec Rodger, who had been head of the vocational guidance department of the National Institute of Industrial Psychology, and during the war senior psychologist at the Admiralty. The medical members of the committee backed William Line, a British-born psychologist who had been educated in Canada and then taken a Ph.D. under Spearman. He held a chair in Toronto, and had been Director of Personnel Selection in the Canadian Army during the war. After months of debate the committee failed to agree, and the two external advisers, Professor Bartlett of Cambridge and Professor Pear of Manchester, were unable to resolve matters. Burt's appointment was renewed for the 1948–49 session while the debate continued.

In June 1949 matters were still unsettled, and Burt wrote to his sister as follows:

The discussion about my successor has been going on throughout the whole of the term. The Provost has continually asked me to see him about the matter and has taken a very sensible line in the discussion with me. Unfortunately, however, the medical members of the committee have proved very skilful in their various devices for attempting to get their own way. At the last committee

39. Burt, C. L. Letter to his sister, 14 December 1951.

meeting they asked the Provost if I could be persuaded to absent myself in case there were criticisms of my department which could be ventilated more freely if I was not actually there. I agreed, on the understanding that I should return to answer any important criticisms and to discuss the actual proposals. But by raising irrelevant issues throughout the morning (so I am told) until lunch-time they managed to get the actual decisions rushed through at the very last moment before I was sent for. I think the Provost must have been taken by surprise, because he sent for me to say that he himself did not agree with their decision. The man we were hoping would be chosen as my successor received a majority of the votes, but it was then agreed that the majority was not large enough to enable any action to be taken. Very ingeniously they suggested that the candidate himself would not like to come to a college where there was a strong opposition to his appointment. Accordingly they suggested that a commission should be formed to run the department for next session. They seem, however, to have rather over-played their hand, and other professors have got very restive. They are inclined to think that the three medical people concerned are trying to get too much power in the college. As a result there has been a strong reaction against them among the other heads of departments who have come forward very nobly in defence of psychology. I think the final outcome will probably be the complete reversal of the original decision.[40]

In the event Burt was asked to carry on for yet another session, and the search went on. Burt himself approached various persons, asking them if he could put forward their names. Dr Thouless of Cambridge was canvassed, and replied 'It was very kind of you to suggest putting my name forward for the U.C. chair. My answer is regretfully and emphatically "No".'[41] R. B. Cattell doubted whether the college could provide the kind of facilities to which he had become accustomed in America. Even Eysenck, whose relations with Burt were then rather cool, and who was only in his early thirties, was approached, but declined, as he did not know precisely what the duties of a professor were, and feared that clerical and administrative tasks might interfere with his research. Other refusals came from Rex Knight of Aberdeen, and from Zangwill, then at Oxford. Almost every available psychologist in the country was considered. Some were rejected by the committee; others declined the invitation. The deadlock was eventually broken by the emerg-

40. Burt, C. L. Letter to his sister, 14 June 1949.
41. Thouless, R. H. Letter to Burt, 6 April 1949.

ence of the American psychologist, Roger Russell. In 1949 Professor Russell of the University of Pittsburgh had accepted an invitation from the Institute of Psychiatry (Maudsley Hospital) to come to its psychological department to set up an animal psychology laboratory. The proposed research lay mainly in the field of genetic studies into the inheritance of temperamental qualities, and was closely integrated with the research work on dimensions of personality carried out by Eysenck and his collaborators. Russell was invited to apply for the chair, and agreed to do so. At last a candidate had appeared who satisfied both parties on the committee. So Roger Russell was appointed to succeed Burt, and Burt finally retired at the end of the summer term, 1950.

Burt's retirement, however, was at first not complete. For one thing there was a large number of research students working in areas of Burt's speciality, and it was agreed that he should continue to supervise twenty-three of these students with an appointment as 'Special Lecturer'. Professor Russell also asked him to continue with a certain amount of lecturing. The outcome was an unhappy one. Professor Russell writes about the matter as follows:

> Listening to and talking with Burt convinced me that he was a 'great man' among his contemporaries internationally. After my appointment to the chair I urged the UCL Professorial Board to agree to Burt continuing to lecture after his retirement, as well as having the perks of an Emeritus Professor. They—and the Provost—conceded reluctantly, for my request broke a long-standing custom of the college. One reason for the concession, as I recall, was that Burt had some astronomical number of postgraduate students still registered under his supervision. I soon realised why there had been reluctance in acquiescing to my proposal. Very soon after my tenure began Burt started a series of complaints about changes I, after full discussion with the staff, had begun to introduce. His discussion with me grew increasingly disharmonious, a fact which distressed me very much. I recall some telephone conversations in which I did relatively little of the talking. Finally I sought advice from members of the appointments committee which had selected me. Upon their advice I discussed the situation with the newly arrived Provost, Sir Ifor Evans, and Burt was informed that the college's custom of not continuing the services of retired professors would become effective. . . . I think it is a pity that Burt could not have retired as gracefully as Flugel did. In my experience he was intolerant of those who held different views than his own and of those he thought might be challenging his pre-eminence. I believe that

your search will uncover instances which suggest that he was egocentric to a degree which led him to protect his position at almost any cost.[42]

So Burt had to be informed by the Provost that his links with the department were to be severed. Actually, two years later, he was permitted to give two introductory lectures to the child psychology students, and he gave an occasional lecture on statistics in Professor Egon Pearson's department. But his special brand of psychology rather rapidly faded out. He commented some years later in a letter, 'The American professor who followed me at University College was one of those who hold that the proper study of man is rats, and most of the work in the field of individual human psychology passed to the Institute of Education.'[43] He felt that the department had lost prestige, and when Russell resigned to return to America in 1957, he hoped once again to influence the selection committee to appoint a candidate favourable to his type of psychology, but again without success.

Thus his connection with the college ended in the bitterness of defeat. His efforts to preserve the Galtonian tradition had failed.

42. Letter from Professor R. W. Russell, Vice-Chancellor, Flinders University, South Australia, 15 November 1976.
43. Burt, C. L. Letter to Mrs Warde, 10 July 1959.

CHAPTER NINE

Factors of the Mind

I

From the time of his appointment to the University College chair in 1932, till 1963 when he finally handed over control of the *British Journal of Statistical Psychology*, factor analysis was one of Burt's principal fields of interest. The main aim of factor analysis is to reduce a complex matrix of observed measures to a more meaningful set of basic underlying factors, in the same way, for example, as the whole range of visible colours can be described in terms of the three dimensions of hue, brightness and saturation. Factor analysis is a mathematical technique which demands considerable algebraic and geometric expertise. Burt, though not by training a mathematician, had a natural talent for, and acquired by assiduous study a high competence in, the necessary branches of mathematics. His work was well regarded not only by psychologists working in this area, but by those mathematicians who eventually became interested in factorial methods. Burt himself regarded his factor-analytic work as perhaps his most important achievement. When *Factors of the Mind* was completed in 1940 he wrote to his sister, 'I have just finished a rather large book embodying many years of work and which I think may prove to be a more lasting contribution to psychology than anything else I have yet written.'[1] This may have been an overestimation on Burt's part. The book was certainly unfortunate in appearing just after the outbreak of war. But this alone does not account for its relative neglect. It was too wordy and philosophical to appeal to mathematical psychologists, and after the war was overshadowed by more down-to-earth American writers.

Burt's first acquaintance with factorial techniques arose through his contacts with Spearman while still an Oxford student. He employed factor analysis on a small scale in his early investigation into intelligence, and a few years later undertook a factorial analysis of emotional traits, one of the first excursions into the statistical analysis of personality. In London he applied factorial techniques to the analysis of educational abilities, and to some of the psychological

1. Burt, C. L. Letter to his sister, 27 May 1940.

tests he was employing. These early ventures were not worked up in any detail. Factor analysis remained secondary to Burt's essentially practical interests, and Burt's recognition of Spearman's leadership was virtually complete.

In the second phase of Burt's factorial work, from his appointment at University College to Spearman's death in 1945, factor analysis moved increasingly to the centre of the stage. Burt elaborated his views much more fully, and his grasp of the mathematics and methodology of factor analysis became much firmer and deeper. His views in several respects diverged from those of Spearman, though he still publicly acknowledged Spearman's priority and pre-eminence in the field. This period culminated with the publication of *Factors of the Mind* in 1940.

In the final phase, which lasted from 1947, when he launched the statistical journal with Godfrey Thomson, until the early 1960s, Burt produced a stream of articles on the mathematics and conclusions of factor analysis, and also largely rewrote the early history of the subject. In this phase he was mainly concerned in de-throning Spearman as the founder of factor analysis, and asserting his own claims to priority as the first user of factorial method in psychology.

II

It is universally agreed by every leading factorist, except Burt in the final phase of his factorial work, that factor analysis had its origins in Spearman's 1904 article in the *American Journal of Psychology*.[2] 'No single event in the history of mental testing', wrote Guilford,[3] 'has proved to be of such momentous importance as Spearman's proposal of his famous two-factor theory in 1904.' Spearman had noted a hierarchical arrangement in the table of correlation coefficients between diverse mental tests and marks, and proved that this could be explained mathematically if each test or mark was measuring two factors—a central, or general, factor present throughout, and specific factors confined to each separate measure. Spearman proposed a somewhat laborious but simple formula (his famous tetrad difference equation) for diagnosing hierarchical arrangement, and he identified his general factor with the central function of 'intelligence', though he preferred simply to use the symbol 'G'. He later equated it with 'mental energy', and the

2. Spearman, C. E. General intelligence objectively determined and measured. *Amer. J. Psychol.*, *XV*, 1904, 201–93.

3. Guilford, J. P. *Psychometric Methods*, 1936, p. 459.

specific factors with the various 'engines' by which this energy was employed.

Spearman's work came under almost immediate attack. Karl Pearson objected to the correction formulae used by Spearman to adjust correlations for sampling errors. At the British Association meeting in 1910 he scathingly attacked the idea that 'somehow good correlations can be extracted from bad experimental data by sheer mathematical manipulation'. A few years later Godfrey Thomson questioned Spearman's main conclusion, demonstrating experimentally that the hierarchical arrangement of correlation coefficients did not necessarily depend on a general factor, but could be explained by the laws of chance.[4] The mind, he held, was a comparatively undifferentiated complex of innumerable bonds and influences, which mental tests 'sampled'. The factors which emerged as a result of statistical analysis had no real existence but were merely coefficients, changing both with the tests and with the population tested. Nevertheless in the course of time Thomson came to accept the practical value of postulating a general factor.[5]

In the long term more important were the further developments which Spearman's work stimulated. These included modifications of the two-factor theory itself, and the elaboration of the mathematical basis of factor analysis. According to Spearman's original formulation the general factor and the specifics could account for the whole of the observed correlations, and no other factors need be postulated provided the battery did not contain tests that were obviously akin. Burt, as we shall see, was one of the first to question this parsimonious viewpoint, and in the 1920s and 1930s it became increasingly clear that certain broad group factors were required over and above 'g'. The American statistician and psychologist, T. L. Kelley, in 1928, while still accepting the general factor, postulated a number of group factors—verbal, numerical, spatial, etc.[6] In England in 1931 William Stephenson, a member of Spearman's own department, demonstrated the existence of the verbal group factor,[7] and shortly afterwards W. P. Alexander and El Koussy produced evidence in favour of a practical or spatial factor.[8] The number of factors continued to grow. Thurstone in 1938 dispensed

4. Thomson, G. H. A hierarchy without a general factor. *Brit. J. Psychol., VIII*, 1916, 271–81.

5. Thomson, G. H. *The Factorial Analysis of Human Ability*, 1939.

6. Kelley, T. L. *Crossroads in the Mind of Man*, 1928.

7. Stephenson, Wm. Tetrad differences for verbal sub-tests. *J. Educ. Psychol., XXII*, 1931, 255–67.

8. Alexander, W. P. Intelligence concrete and abstract. *Brit. J. Psychol. Monogr. Supp. 19*, 1935. Koussy, El. The visual perception of space. *Brit. J. Psychol. Monogr. Supp. 20*, 1935.

with 'g' altogether and replaced it by eight primary mental abilities.[9] By 1959 Thurstone's eight factors had expanded into Guilford's one hundred and twenty,[10] and the simplicity of Spearman's early model, which was one of its attractions, seemed totally to have vanished. Nevertheless there would be universal agreement now that some group factors at least are necessary, and that Spearman's two-factor theory was too parsimonious to account for the facts. Indeed Spearman himself in his later formulations accepted restricted group factors.[11]

The strengthening of the mathematical basis of factor analysis began with the work of Maxwell Garnett, a lecturer in Karl Pearson's department of statistics, who later became secretary of the League of Nations Union. Garnett was really the originator of multiple factor analysis. As soon as the possibility of several factors, rather than just two, had been envisaged, a method to enable a matrix of test correlations to be analysed directly into its components, rather than through the laborious calculation of tetrads, was desirable. Garnett[12] proposed the essential formulae of multiple factor analysis, which were later taken up by American workers, Kelley, Hotelling and Thurstone. Thurstone's method of multiple factor analysis, which was particularly influential, was first published in 1931, and first employed by Alexander in Britain in 1935.[13] In certain respects, however, it had been anticipated by Burt in his work on educational abilities in 1917, though at that time Burt had not worked out the method in any detail. Hotelling's method of 'principal components' was less widely used, but is interesting in its resemblance to Pearson's 'lines of closest fit' proposed in 1901. There is nothing to indicate, however, that Hotelling was directly influenced by Pearson's work.[14] As a result of these developments factor analysis, by the late 1930s, had become of much more interest to mathematicians themselves, and A. C. Aitkin, M. S. Bartlett, and D. N. Lawley in particular had turned their attention to the mathematical foundations of the subject, leading to a much clearer formulation of its possibilities and limitations. The introduction of computers in the 1950s made more elaborate mathematical procedures technically possible. As a result factor analysis became a respectable and not unimportant branch of multivariate analysis. With all

9. Thurstone, L. L. *Primary Mental Abilities*, 1938.

10. Guilford, J. P. Three faces of intellect. *Amer. Psychol., XIV*, 1959, 469–79.

11. Spearman, C. E. and Wynn Jones, Ll. *Human Ability*, 1950.

12. Garnett, J. C. M. On certain independent factors in mental measurement. *Proc. Roy. Soc. (A), XCVI*, 1919, 102–5.

13. Thurstone, L. L. Multiple factor analysis. *Psychol. Rev., XXXVIII*, 1931.

14. Hotelling, H. Analysis of a complex of statistical variables into principal components. *J. Educ. Psychol., XXIV*, 1933, 417–41, 498–520. Pearson, K. The lines of closest fit to a system of points. *Phil. Mag., II*, 1901, 559–72.

these developments Burt kept closely in touch, and was broadly in sympathy, though he continued to prefer his own hierarchical factorial structure to the more elaborate proposals of workers like Guilford and Cattell.

Concurrently factor analysis had been expanding the scope of its applications. Originally it had been concerned with the analysis of human abilities. It soon began to be applied to assessments of personality. Spearman's pupil, E. Webb, and Burt himself were the pioneers in this venture.[15] In 1915 Webb's monograph on character was published, and at the British Association meeting of the same year Burt reported on 'The General and Specific Factors underlying the Primary Emotions'.[16] Burt was later to extend this enquiry and apply factor analytic methods to temperament, aesthetic judgments, and physical measurements. He was also among the first, if not the first, to correlate persons as opposed to tests, factorising the results; to analyse the marks of examiners factorially; and to see the relevance of factorial methods to problems entirely outside the field of psychology; in other words to generalise factor analysis as a technique applicable to all multivariate problems, and to almost any form of measurement.[17] It has indeed in recent years been applied to economics, agriculture, botany, and the social sciences, as Lawley and Maxwell have noted.[18]

III

The first clear evidence of Burt's interest in factor analysis is his inaugural article on 'General Intelligence', published in 1909, only five years after Spearman's seminal paper.[19] The investigation he then reported, it will be remembered, 'commenced with a view to testing in practice the mathematical methods of Dr Spearman' (p. 95), and answering the question whether anything that might be named 'general intelligence' could be detected. Thirteen tests were intercorrelated, and the results analysed using the tetrad equation, which was derived from Spearman's work. The theoretical values calculated from the tetrads were compared with the observed coefficients, and the agreement between theoretical and observed

15. Webb, E. Character and intelligence. *Brit. J. Psychol. Monogr. Supp. III*, 1915.

16. *Annual Report of the British Association*, 1915, pp. 694–6.

17. Burt, C. L. *Marks of Examiners*, 1936, p. 260; *Factors of the Mind*, 1940, p. xii.

18. Lawley, D. N. and Maxwell, A. E. *Factor Analysis as a Statistical Method*, 1963.

19. Burt, C. L. Experimental tests of general intelligence. *Brit. J. Psychol., III*, 1909, 94–177.

values was found to be so close that it was roughly equal to the probable error. 'A neater agreement between observation and theory could scarcely be desired' (p. 163). Nevertheless Burt did note that 'the tendency for subordinate groups of allied tests to correlate together is discernible, but small' (p. 164). There is no evidence in Burt's 1909 article, as he subsequently claimed,[20] that he proceeded to subtract the theoretical figures from the observed correlations and to factor analyse the residuals, thus inaugurating multiple factor analysis, nor is there any reference at all to Pearson's method of principal components which Burt professed to be using from 1907 onwards.[21] Indeed he states in his 'Autobiographical Sketch'[22] that he addressed an informal undergraduate society known as the Delian Society, which met in his rooms, on Pearson's lines of closest fit as early as 1904. There is, however, nothing but Burt's statement to support this claim, and there are several grounds for doubting it. In particular there is conclusive evidence that Burt lacked the mathematical competence at this stage of his career to understand Pearson's article. In a letter to Spearman, Burt commented on his mathematical immaturity in 1909 (five years after the Delian meeting) as follows: 'My own immature ideas of what a hierarchy might be were coloured by my own equally immature ideas about correlation, if I can call them my own, for what little I knew about correlation was in those days derived directly or indirectly from your work: Pearson and Brown got added later in footnotes.'[23] All the evidence suggests, therefore, that Burt's first venture into factor analysis was wholly derivative from Spearman's work and his conclusions not appreciably different from Spearman's. Burt's claim to have enlarged Spearman's two-factor theory into a three-factor theory as early as 1909 is not supported by the published reports of his work.[24]

Burt's second factor-analytic investigation was the research he carried out in Liverpool with R. C. Moore into 'The General and Specific Factors underlying the Primary Emotions'. The investigation was very briefly reported in the Annual Report of the British

20. e.g. Burt, C. L. *Brit. J. Psychol. (Stats), I,* ii, 1948, 95–106; and *II,* ii, 1949, 98–121.

21. Burt, C. L. In Appendix to Chapter II, Butcher, H. J. *Human Intelligence,* 1968, p. 68.

22. Burt, C. L. In Boring, E. G. *et al, History of Psychology in Autobiography, IV,* 1952, p. 61.

23. Burt, C. L. Letter to Spearman, 6 November 1937. (Spearman-Burt correspondence, B.P.S. Archives.)

24. See Burt, C. L. *Factors of the Mind* (1940), ftnt. p. 140, and compare Burt, C. L. The experimental study of general intelligence. *Child Study, IV,* 1911, 92–100.

Association,[25] no details being given of the methodology employed or of the mathematical working. The basic data were estimates of emotional tendencies linked to McDougall's instincts using two samples, one of children and one of adults. Burt derived from the correlations a general factor of emotionality, and showed that the residual partial correlations could be arranged cyclically. His later account of the investigation ran as follows: 'In a research carried out with R. C. Moore in which both impressionistic assessments and objective tests were used we applied the modified Pearsonian procedure ("simple summation") to determine the general and specific factors underlying the primary emotions. We found a large general factor of emotionality, and two significant bipolar factors distinguishing first what we called "sthenic" from "asthenic" emotions . . . and secondly "euphoric" from "dysphoric" emotions.' (Burt, 1915, 1950.)[26]

This investigation was certainly important as one of the first attempts to apply factor analysis to the field of personality, and the concept of 'general emotionality' played a central role in Burt's psychology from 1915 onwards. His later account, however, is both inaccurate and misleading. Burt did not use objective tests, only estimates of emotional tendencies; he did not employ modified Pearsonian procedure (simple summation) until the data were reworked many years later; and he did not at the time derive two significant bipolar factors. Burt read back into this investigation far more than it originally contained, and since the pronoun 'we' clearly implies that these procedures and findings related to the period when he and Moore were working together in Liverpool his later account must be regarded as a fabrication.

Burt's third use of factorial techniques was the most elaborate and significant of his early ventures. It was carried out while he was L.C.C. psychologist and involved an analysis of school marks by a sample of 120 school children, aged from 10 to 12, on thirteen different measures (composition, arithmetic, reading, handwork, etc.).[27] Of the 78 resulting correlations all were positive and all but four significant. Each measure was repeated, and the calculated reliabilities inserted in the diagonals of the correlation table.[28] Clearly a considerable degree of hierarchical arrangement obtained.

25. *Annual Report of the British Association*, 1915, pp. 694–6.

26. Burt, C. L. The early history of multivariate techniques in psychological research. *Multivariate Behavioral Research, I*, 1966, 37–8. The reference, Burt 1950, is to The Factorial Study of the Emotions. In Reymert, M. L. (ed.) *Feelings and Emotions*, 1950.

27. Burt, C. L. *The Distribution and Relations of Educational Abilities*, 1917.

28. Burt, however, omitted the reliabilities when he went on to analyse specific correlations, and extract group factors.

Burt went on to calculate the theoretical values of the correlations on the assumption that a single common factor was solely responsible. There proved to be several striking discrepancies between the observed and the theoretical values, indicating the presence of group factors. Burt identified the general factor with what he termed 'general educational ability'. This had been assessed by the children's teachers, and though largely overlapping with general intelligence, which had been independently assessed, was not identical with it. Burt next removed the influence of 'general educational ability', employing a multiple correlation technique, and drew up a table of residual correlations. He then tested for significance, only 25 of the 78 residual correlations attaining an acceptable level. Burt concluded that these residuals could be explained by postulating four group factors: arithmetic, language, memory and composition. But there was not a sharp demarcation between them, and he suggested not a hierarchical arrangement, but a circular chain of overlapping factors.

This investigation was in several respects a landmark. It more clearly demonstrated the presence of group factors than any previous analysis had done, and it introduced a number of procedural innovations which anticipated the 'centroid' method developed by Thurstone in the 1930s. Burt later summarised his essential contributions as:[29] (i) substituting reduced self-correlations for correlations of unity in the diagonal (a procedure that he preferred to Thurstone's 'communalities'); (ii) substituting 'simple summation' for 'weighted summation' as a practicable method of approximation; (iii) testing residuals for significance before extracting supplementary factors to reduce the number of factors to the *minimum* number of significant factors. His claim, however, that these procedures were derived from Pearson's 1901 paper seems unfounded, since there is no reference at all to Pearson's paper in the 1917 report, and nothing to suggest that Pearson's formulae were being employed.[30]

No significant further developments in Burt's factorial work took place while he was with the L.C.C. In a report to the Education Officer in 1922 he discussed the bearing of the factor theory on the organisation of schools and classes. This was reprinted in an abridged form in the second edition of *Mental and Scholastic Tests*.[31] He considered that pupil allocation should be based not only on general intelligence, but on group factors, verbal, mathematical and

29. Burt, C. L. L'Analyse Factorielle: Méthodes et Résultats. *Collôques Internationaux du Centre National de la Recherche Scientific*, Paris, 1955.

30. The formulae of which he made use were in fact Udny Yule's. See Burt, C. L. *Mental and Scholastic Tests* , 2nd edn, 1947, p. 270.

31. Burt, C. L. *Op. cit.* Memorandum III, Appendix V.

manual. But types were only tendencies, and in any case were not prominent before the age of 11 or 12. He later carried out factor analyses of various group and individual tests, and of selected items from the Binet scale, using the same methods he had employed in his 1917 report. In his memoranda, again included in the second edition of *Mental and Scholastic Tests*,[32] he now emphasised more strongly his divergencies from Spearman both in his conclusions and his methods.

Factor analysis during this phase of Burt's career had been an adjunct to his main practical tasks, and neither psychologically nor mathematically had his conclusions and his methods been worked out in any detail.

IV

The key advances occurred when Burt moved to University College and largely gave up his applied work. He now had time to devote himself to methodological and theoretical questions, and factor analysis before long had moved to the centre of the stage. For a period of twenty years from 1935 to 1955 it was indeed his principal, though never an exclusive, focus of interest.

His first full-scale consideration of the subject was in the Memorandum on 'The Analysis of Examination Marks', which he prepared in 1935 for the International Institute Examinations Enquiry, directed by Sir Philip Hartog.[33] Burt saw that the marks of examiners could be analysed in terms of the factorial models originally devised by psychologists for analysing test scores. As a result of the work of Garnett, Thomson and Burt himself in Britain, and Kelley, Hotelling and Thurstone in America, Spearman's simple theory of two factors had become greatly elaborated, both psychologically and mathematically. Empirical evidence for various group factors had accumulated, and Burt, falling back on his Oxford logic, suggested that a four-fold scheme could be employed to embrace all possible components. He termed the four main types of factor, universal, particular (or group), singular and chance.[34] Applying this to examination marks it was possible to analyse marks as comprising four components: (i) those which *every* examiner treats as relevant; (ii) those which *some* of the examiners

32. Burt, C. L. *Op. cit.* Memorandum I, Appendix IV; and Memorandum II, Appendix V.

33. Hartog, P., Rhodes, E. C. and Burt, C. L. *The Marks of Examiners*, 1936. Memorandum by Burt, pp. 245 314.

34. *Op. cit.*, p. 259.

treat as relevant; (iii) those which only *one* examiner treats as relevant; and (iv) any elements which may arise from many minor accidental influences, that is, from the effects of chance. The aim of the exercise was to estimate the hypothetical true marks of candidates from the weighted average of the marks given by several different examiners, adjusting the marks of individual examiners for differences of scale, estimating the accuracy of individual examiners' marking, and the correlation between the marks of each examiner and the hypothetical true marks. Burt provided a full mathematical exposition of the steps involved, deriving his equations by means of determinants and matrices. For his introduction to matrix algebra he was indebted to a mathematically-minded inspector of schools, Dr W. F. Sheppard, whose book *From Determinant to Tensor* was published in 1923. Burt also endeavoured to show that 'by adopting a broader mathematical basis . . . the seemingly divergent formulae put forward [by various factorists] are in their essential nature merely variants or alternative simplifications of one general conception'.[35] For practical purposes the 'simple summation' method he himself had proposed in his earlier investigations gave 'reasonable approximations'.

There is no doubt that Burt's memorandum on factorial methods applied to examination marks represented a considerable advance on Spearman's mathematical appendix to *Abilities of Man* (1927), just as Burt's 'four-factor' theory was an advance on Spearman's original 'two-factor' theory. Nevertheless Burt still gave Spearman full credit for being the father of factor analysis: 'it should be observed', he wrote in a footnote, 'that Spearman's highly original work has formed the starting point of almost all the mathematical investigations upon this and kindred problems.'[36] No mention has been made at this stage of Pearson's 1901 paper, even when referring to Hotelling's 'principal components'. So either Burt was unfamiliar with Pearson's paper, or he did not consider it to have any relevance to factor analysis. The other significant feature of the *Marks of Examiners* Memorandum was the fact that Burt was applying factor analysis not to the examinees but to the examiners. Psychologists had for the most part hitherto been interested in the subjects, usually children, whom they had been testing. In this enquiry Burt was concerned with the testers, in this case the examiners, themselves.

35. *Op. cit.*, p. 309. In an article on 'Methods of factor analysis with and without successive approximation' (*Brit. J. Educ. Psychol., VII*, 1937, 172–95) Burt made a fuller comparison of various methods of analysis, including that proposed by Kelley in *Essential Traits of Mental Life*, 1935.

36. *Op. cit.*, p. 257.

The suggestion that persons might be correlated as well as tests originally goes back to Stern.[37] Burt, however, seems to have been the first to employ the technique in experiments at the Institute of Education and during his early days at University College. He applied it to children's preferences for different school subjects, and to aesthetic preferences.[38] Its underlying rationale and its implications were more fully treated in an important paper, 'Correlations between Persons', in 1937.[39] In this paper Burt formulated 'the reciprocity principle', that 'the factors obtained by correlating persons are identical with those obtained by correlating tests'. The validity of this principle, and indeed the legitimacy of correlating persons at all, has been widely questioned. Arguments with Stephenson, who attacked the reciprocity principle, continued to the end of Burt's life, his final paper on the subject being published posthumously.[40] The differences between Burt's standpoint and that of Stephenson, who had stolen a march on Burt in his 1936 paper,[41] were fully set out in their joint contribution to *Psychometrika* in 1939. In Godfrey Thomson's view reciprocity can only be found in a very special sample of people, who are all of average ability, and in a very special sample of tests which are all of average difficulty.[42] His standpoint also forced Burt to defend negative factor loadings and bipolar factors. Burt disagreed with Thomson's comments, and went on to elaborate his views in several papers published in American journals[43] and in his article on 'Methods of Factor Analysis with and without Successive Approximation'.[44]

Meanwhile he was engaged on his major work, *The Factors of the Mind*, which appeared the year after war had broken out. This was intended to be, and indeed was, a definitive statement of Burt's standpoint. It consisted of three parts: Part I in which he expounded his views on the logical and metaphysical status of factors in psychology; Part II in which he discussed the relation between different methods of factor analysis, including correlation between

37. Stern, W. *Differentielle Psychologie*, 1911.
38. See Burt, C. L. Appendix III to the Hadow Report on *The Primary School*, 1931; and Burt, C. L. *How the Mind Works*, 1933. Thomson, however, doubts whether Burt really appreciated at the time the implications of what he was doing (*Factorial Analysis of Human Ability*, 1939, p. 199).
39. Burt, C. L. *Brit. J. Psychol.*, XXVIII, 1937, 59–96.
40. Burt, C. L. The reciprocity principle. In *Science, Psychology and Communication: Essays honoring Wm. Stephenson*, eds Brown, S. R. and Brenner, D. J., 1972.
41. Stephenson, Wm. The inverted factor technique. *Brit. J. Psychol.*, XXVI, 1936, 344–61.
42. Thomson, G. H. *The Factorial Analysis of Human Ability*, 1939, ch. xiv.
43. Burt, C. L. Factor analysis by submatrices. *J. Psychol.*, VI, 1938, 339–75; The unit hierarchy and its properties. *Psychometrika*, III, 1938, 151–68.
44. Burt, C. L. *Brit. J. Educ. Psychol.*, VII, 1937, 172–95.

tests and between persons, general factor methods and group factor methods, and simple summation and weighted summation methods; and Part III in which he applied factor analysis to the problem of temperamental types, and a demonstration of the reciprocity principle. An Appendix contained working methods for computers, but because of the recent appearance of Thomson's and Thurstone's books rigorous algebraic proofs of the essential formulae were omitted. In the Preface to the book Burt refers to 'the remarkable lead of Professor Spearman', and states that 'Spearman's pre-eminence is acknowledged by every factorist'.[45] Spearman's work, he notes later in the book, 'after all inspired, directly or indirectly, the numerous alternative methods put forward to supplement or supersede it'.[46]

Yet he is at pains to emphasise his differences from Spearman in two essential respects: firstly in his formulation of the four-factor theorem; and secondly in his account of the metaphysical status of factors. The four-factor theorem, which Burt had first propounded in the *Marks of Examiners*, was now set out more fully, and derived from logical principles, in fact from the logic of the schoolmen. 'The measurement of any individual for any one of a given set of traits may be regarded as a function of four kinds of components: namely, those characteristic of (i) all the traits, (ii) some of the traits, (iii) the particular trait in question wherever it is measured, and (iv) the particular trait in question as measured on this particular occasion. This I regard as the fundamental logical postulate from which all factor theories must necessarily start.'[47] And Burt went on to show that the various theories were just special cases of the more fundamental four-factor theory. His aim here, as it was when he was considering the methods of factor analysis, was to provide a solution sufficiently general to embrace all rival formulations. Obviously the validity of Burt's solution depended on the generality of the scholastic-type logic upon which it was based; if this were questioned his formula lost much of its power.

On the metaphysical status of factors his objections to Spearman were more apparent than the consistency of his own views. Spearman had proposed that the general factor of ability could be identified with mental energy, and the specific factors with the 'engines' through which it operated. Burt objected to this realistic interpretation. 'Our factors', he wrote, 'are to be thought of in the first instance as lines or terms of reference only, not as concrete

45. Burt, C. L. *Factors of the Mind*, 1940, pp. v, x.
46. *Op. cit.*, p. 269.
47. *Op. cit.*, p. 103.

psychological entities.'[48] In the first place factors are descriptive only, they are principles of classification, and they are to be regarded 'nominalistically', not 'realistically'. They are like lines of latitude and longitude, simply 'an abstract frame of reference', not actual entities. Causal explanations, of the sort Spearman employed, were anyhow old-fashioned from a scientific point of view, and now superseded by statistical and quantum mechanical accounts. In a fluid and uncertain world the stability of factors was only relative. Their value was in the improved, but still tentative, predictions which they enabled the psychologist to make. It all sounded very modern, and in tune with the latest theories of physics.

Burt, however, did not hold consistently to this viewpoint. He went on to claim that factors did reveal 'the structure of the mind'. 'The philosophical theory that I should offer . . . might be described as a modernisation of the old Platonic doctrine of ideas. Its main principle would be that reality is best described in terms of "forms", "structures", or "gestalten",'[49] which he went on to say possessed a certain causal efficacy. Here he comes down in favour of a Platonic, 'realistic' view of factors, which is strictly incompatible with the 'nominalistic' account of factors as merely descriptive. And in later articles Burt expounded at some length his conclusions on the 'structure of the mind' disclosed by factor analytic work.[50] A difficulty, of course, was that many alternative factorial solutions were mathematically possible, and that a choice between them had to be made on non-mathematical grounds. So the conclusions were really preconceptions, tidied up perhaps, but not essentially discoveries. Hence, perhaps, we can detect a certain disillusionment with factor analysis when Burt concedes that 'factorial psychology will have to be very largely superseded by the functional and genetic study of the mind'.[51] Several years later he wrote to his sister, 'I wish I had time to take up individual peculiarities in physiology. It is so much more satisfactory to be able to get at something concrete, instead of the highly abstract things one deals with in statistical psychology.'[52]

The Factors of the Mind, nevertheless, was unquestionably a landmark both in Burt's career, and in the history of factor analysis. It was the culmination of many years' work, and the most theoretically important of all Burt's books. It considered the status

48. *Op. cit.*, p. 18.
49. *Op. cit.*, p. 232.
50. Burt, C. L. The structure of the mind. *Brit. J. Educ. Psychol., XIX*, 1949, 100–11, 176–99; The Factorial Study of the Mind. In *Essays in Honour of David Katz*, 1951, pp. 18–47.
51. Burt, C. L. *Factors of the Mind*, 1940, p. 245.
52. Burt, C. L. Letter to his sister, 20 February 1952.

and methodology of factor analysis more thoroughly and more philosophically than anyone else had done, and it contained a great deal of material amplifying Burt's earlier publications on correlations between persons and the factorial analysis of temperament. With its publication in 1940 and the onset of the war Burt's factorial work fell into abeyance for a number of years, apart from a few minor exercises such as his 'A Factor Analysis of the Terman-Binet Tests', and his work on 'A Factor Analysis of Body Measurements for British Adult Males'.[53]

The death of Spearman in 1945 left Cyril Burt and Godfrey Thomson as the standard-bearers of factor analysis in Great Britain, and in 1947 they came together to edit jointly the new statistical journal launched by the British Psychological Society. The final phases of Burt's factorial work are contained mainly in the pages of this journal.

V

Between 1947 and the middle 1960s Burt wrote nearly thirty articles on factor analysis, many of them substantial, and he commenced the preparation of a second edition of *The Factors of the Mind*. This was first proposed as early as 1947. A Preface was drafted in 1954, and revised in 1957. Work on the revision proceeded fitfully until about 1965, after which it appears to have been abandoned in a half-finished and inchoate condition. The aims of this phase of Burt's factorial work were broadly threefold: to amplify and refine his mathematical treatment of factors; to collate the results of factor analysis; and to rewrite the early history of factorial work.

Mathematically Burt set out to show that factor analysis was one of a family of multivariate techniques. As such it had a close affinity with the analysis of variance devised by R. A. Fisher. Burt's very first contribution to the new statistical journal was 'A Comparison of Factor Analysis and Analysis of Variance'.[54] He noted in a subsequent article that 'Fisher[55] in discussing analysis of variance describes his purpose as an endeavour by a process of abstraction to isolate causes into a number of elementary ingredients or factors', and that his use of the term 'factors' suggests 'something more than

53. Burt, C. L. and John, Enid. A factor analysis of the Terman-Binet tests. *Brit. J. Educ. Psychol.*, XII, 1942, 117–21, 156–61; Burt, C. L. and Banks, Charlotte. A factor analysis of body measurements for British adult males. *Ann. Eugen.*, XIII, 1947, 238–56; Burt, C. L. Factor analysis and physical types. *Psychometrika*, XII, 1947, 171–88.
54. Burt, C. L. *Brit. J. Psychol. (Stats)*, I, 1947, 3–26.
55. Fisher, R. A. *Design of Experiments*, p. 100.

a merely nominal similarity between factor analysis and analysis of variance'.[56] Nevertheless there were differences in starting point and in emphasis, as Burt notes in his article. Again factor analysis, though related to, must be distinguished from, canonical analysis. 'In canonical analysis the criterion is external (as in Spearman's earlier papers on intelligence) while in factor analysis the criterion is derived from the internal evidence of the tests or trait measurements.'[57] At this point Burt began to question Spearman's right to be regarded as the founder of factor analysis, and began to claim priority for Pearson and himself. We shall return to these claims shortly. Meanwhile his mathematical contributions continued. He developed his group factor method, and the idea of subdivided factors arranged hierarchically; he discussed tests of significance in factor work, tests which had too often been ignored; he considered the problem of the identification of factors in different populations, and the problem of negative factors and sign reversals; and he produced articles on special problems such as the factor analysis of qualitative data, and factorising measures made upon a single individual. These were useful contributions, to which a brief non-mathematical account cannot do full justice.

The number of new factor analyses carried out by Burt in this period were few—after all he no longer had data coming in on a sufficient scale to make this possible, and so he was dependent on re-analysing old data or material collected by others. He was more concerned in collating the results of past analyses, and assessing what they added up to. Burt believed that factor analysis had made a great deal of progress in elucidating what he called 'the structure of the mind', and indeed he went so far as to claim that 'probably all the more important group factors have now been approximately identified'.[58] He admitted that the choice of factors depended on prior, non-quantitative hypotheses, and as his own preference was for the scheme of hierarchical levels which he derived from Spencer, Sherrington and McDougall, it is not surprising that his conclusions fitted this pattern. They were set out in a number of papers, and perhaps most clearly in his contribution on 'The Factorial Study of the Mind' to the David Katz Festschrift.[59] Here Burt adopts the broad division between the cognitive and the orectic aspects of mind, distinguishing in each area a general factor—general intelli-

56. Burt, C. L. Tests of significance in factor analysis. *Brit. J. Statist. Psychol.*, V, 1952, 109–33.

57. Burt, C. L. Factor analysis and canonical correlations. *Brit. J. Psychol. (Stats)*, I, 1948, 95–106.

58. Burt, C. L. The structure of the mind. *Brit. J. Educ. Psychol., XIX*, 1949, 199.

59. *Essays in Honour of David Katz*, 1951, pp. 18–47.

gence and general emotionality respectively. The cognitive aspect was then divided into a hierarchical arrangement of group factors at various levels, the sensori-motor, the perceptual, the associative and the relational, with elaborate sub-divisions within each level. On the orectic side, after the general factor has been eliminated, two bipolar factors (sthenic and asthenic, euphoric and dysphoric) remain. Burt went on to consider acquired emotional traits, such as interests and ideals, artistic appreciation, social attitudes, neurotic traits and moral qualities. Apart from the recognition accorded to general intelligence and to a lesser extent general emotionality, and to certain major group factors, the scheme has carried little conviction among psychologists. It was too much shaped by preconceptions, based on too limited and unreliable experimental data, and was altogether too formal and jejune to recruit many adherents. It would seem that factor analysis, though developing considerable mathematical sophistication, and proving of value in specific applied problems, has yielded remarkably little in the way of hard conclusions to the science of psychology.

VI

The rewriting of the early history of factor analysis was Burt's other concern, perhaps his dominant concern, during the final period of his work. This is a strange story. Burt's account has convinced few; it is totally at variance with the evidence and replete with misrepresentations; it might be dismissed as an unimportant aberration of Burt's declining years were it not for the fact that it provides documentary evidence for the peculiarities of his personality, and, probably, for a pathological streak in his make-up.

When he wrote *The Factors of the Mind* Burt was not greatly concerned with historical background. He accepted the orthodox view, that factor analysis originated with Spearman's 1904 article. 'My indebtedness to earlier writers, particularly to Spearman (whose brilliant work has after all inspired, directly or indirectly, the numerous alternative methods put forward to supplement or supersede it) will be obvious.'[60] 'Spearman's pre-eminence is acknowledged by every factorist . . . my own obligation is a personal one as well: the generosity that he showed in encouraging and criticising my early work has continued to the present day.'[61] In *The Marks of Examiners* he had earlier observed that 'Spearman's highly original work has formed the starting point of almost all the

60. Burt, C. L. *Factors of the Mind*, 1940, p. 269.
61. *Ibid.*, p. x.

mathematical investigations upon this and kindred problems'.[62] Spearman was certainly the starting point of Burt's own work on intelligence. Burt wrote in his first published paper, 'The investigation reported in the following pages was commenced with a view to testing in practice the mathematical methods of Dr Spearman . . . the mathematical part of the work is especially indebted to the generous advice and assistance of Dr Spearman. . . . Dr Spearman and Mr McDougall have been kind enough to read through my manuscript and to allow me to make use of their criticisms and to embody their suggestions.'[63] The correspondence between Spearman and Burt relating to this 1909 article on intelligence is extant, and confirms the help given by Spearman. This correspondence completely invalidates the account given by Burt from 1947 onwards concerning the models he used in this early work. The correspondence which took place in 1937 resulted from a claim made by Burt in an article in the *British Journal of Educational Psychology* of that year[64] that the 'proportionality criterion' which he had used in 1909, though derived from an article of Spearman and Krüger, was in fact first employed by Burt himself. The equation (later known as the tetrad equation) was in fact supplied by Spearman in a letter to Burt dated 23 June 1909.[65] After the claim in Burt's 1937 article Spearman wrote, 'I am a little concerned with the *priority* of this enunciation of the "proportionality criterion". I am afraid throughout all these years I have been rather claiming this priority for myself, on the strength of my letter to you being dated 23rd June, 1909, whereas your article in the *British Journal of Psychology* was only published in December 1909.'[66] In answer to this letter of Spearman Burt completely withdrew his claim. 'There can be hardly any real doubt', he wrote. 'The whole idea of a hierarchy is your own; and since the essence of a hierarchy is its proportionality, surely you have a prior claim here.' Burt went on in a very deferential way suggesting that if there were any divergencies between Spearman and himself he (Burt) was probably wrong. I have 'been wondering where precisely I have gone astray. Would it be simplest for me to number my statements, then like my schoolmaster of old you can put a cross against the point where your pupil has blundered, and a tick where your view is correctly interpreted.'[67] Up to 1940, therefore, we have a clear

62. Burt, C. L. *Marks of Examiners*, 1936, ftnt p. 257.
63. Burt, C. L. *Brit. J. Psychol.*, III, 1909, 95–6.
64. Burt, C. L. *Brit. J. Educ. Psychol.*, VII, 1937, 185 (ftnt).
65. Spearman–Burt correspondence. Burt Archives, University of Liverpool.
66. *Ibid*. Letter from Spearman to Burt, 10 November 1937.
67. *Ibid*. Letter from Burt to Spearman, 12 November 1937.

admission as to Spearman's priority and Spearman's responsibility for the methods adopted by Burt in his 1909 article.

It was not until 1947 that Burt began to put forward a different story. In fact we can be fairly certain that the revised version took root in that, or the previous, year. In the full annotated bibliography on the history of factor analysis which he circulated to students in the mid-1940s there is no mention of Pearson's 1901 papers. Every important reference is listed, commencing with the paper by Bravais on errors (1846) and going up to Thomson's *Factorial Analysis of Human Ability* (1939). In a lecutre on 15 February 1944, according to the notes taken by a student, Dr Agnes Crawford, he stated that factor analysis proper commenced with the work of Oehrn in 1889; Krüger and Spearman read his dissertation and applied and developed his method. Pearson, once again, simply does not come into the picture. Two years later in a lecture on 14 May 1946, according to notes taken by the same student, the calculation of communalities for filling in the diagonals of the correlation table was carried out according to a formula of Spearman's in his (Burt's) early work on intelligence. So by the middle of 1946 the new story has not been born. We can detect its very tentative beginnings in his contribution to the Michotte Festschrift published in 1947. Here Burt wrote, 'The idea that a positive correlation between two variables may be explained by a common "factor" or by common "elements" (to use the term that appears most frequently in early writers) is found in Galton, Pearson, Edgeworth and other statisticians.'[68] Burt goes on to express his indebtedness to Karl Pearson, but does not at this early stage refer to Pearson's 1901 articles upon which later he lays so much stress. Spearman's role was played down, and his conclusions misrepresented. Spearman did not, as Burt stated, propose 'the identification [of general intelligence] with general sensory discrimination';[69] he held merely that 'discrimination has unrivalled advantages for investigating and diagnosing the central function', and added that 'Discussion as to the psychical nature of this fundamental function has been reserved until a more complete acquaintance has been gained concerning its objective relations.'[70] Burt was perfectly well aware of Spearman's position on this matter as he had added a footnote to page 165 of his 1909 article to clarify it.[71] So he was unquestionably misrepresenting it in his Michotte paper.

68. Burt, C. L. In *Miscellanea Psychologica*, ed. A. Michotte, Louvain, 1947, pp. 49–75.
69. *Ibid.*, p. 53.
70. Spearman, C. E. *Amer. J. Psychol.*, XV, 1904.
71. Burt, C. L. *Brit. J. Psychol.*, III, 1909.

The new story was developed in rather more detail in the revised notes on factor analysis Burt handed out to students in the 1947–48 session and in Burt's inaugural article in the new statistical journal which he jointly edited with Godfrey Thomson, the first number of which appeared in October 1947.[72] Here he noted that 'the idea of reducing a number of correlated variables to an equal number of uncorrelated variables by choosing the "principal axes of the correlation ellipsoid" to represent the new dimensions appears to have been first put forward by Karl Pearson',[73] though he refers to Pearson's article in *Biometrika*, not to that in the *Philosophical Magazine*[74] which he later designated as the *fons et origo* of factor analysis. In the same article he went on once again to misrepresent Spearman's position when he wrote, 'The arguments which Spearman proposed . . . were proofs, not of the presence of "general intelligence", but of its identity with "general sensory discrimination" and of the absence of any other factor.'[75]

A month later Burt reviewed Thurstone's *Multiple Factor Analysis* (1947).[76] He objected to Thurstone's identification of 'the type of factor analysis current among British psychologists' with Spearman's views, and with the commonly held belief that multiple factor theories followed the general factor theory after an interval of some years. On the contrary, wrote Burt, 'the very first suggestion ever put forward for factorising a correlation table was based on a multiple factor principle, and consisted precisely in the "principal axes solution" [of Pearson]. . . . This procedure, put forward more than 45 years ago, is absolutely identical with that so warmly praised by Thurstone towards the close of his book. . . . Spearman's first paper, to which Thurstone so often refers, followed Pearson's suggestion by about three years . . . in point of time, therefore, the "theory of a single general factor" appeared as a simplified substitute for a multiple factor theory.'[77] Burt then went on to claim that what was called a 'three-factor hypothesis' was put forward in his 1911 paper in *Child Study*,[78] though in actual fact there is no reference in the article to any factor other than the general

72. Burt, C. L. A comparison of factor analysis and analysis of variance. *Brit. J. Psychol. (Stats)*, I, 1947, 3–26.

73. *Ibid.*, p. 21.

74. Pearson, Karl. On the systematic fitting of curves to observations and measurements. *Biomet.*, I, 1901, 265–303; The lines of closest fit to a system of points. *Phil. Mag.*, II, 1901, 559–72.

75. Burt, C. L. *Loc. cit.* p. 14.

76. Burt, C. L. *Brit. J. Educ. Psychol.*, XVII, 1947, 163–9.

77. *Ibid.*, pp. 164–6.

78. Burt, C. L. Experimental study of general intelligence. *Child Study*, IV, 1911, 77–100.

factor, and nothing at all to suggest the presence of any group factor.

The story has now clearly developed considerably. Spearman has been dethroned as the father of factor analysis. Pearson, Burt alleged, had anticipated him by three years, and multiple factor theories, far from being a development from Spearman's work, were the source of it. Moreover, Burt has begun to make claims about his own early work, which are demonstrably contrary to the truth. The new story is strikingly different from that accepted by Burt himself seven years previously in *Factors of the Mind* and still handed out to students only a year before. What is the explanation for the change? We cannot be completely certain, but there were probably two decisive influences: firstly, Spearman's death in 1945, and secondly, the publication of Thurstone's book on *Multiple Factor Analysis* in 1947. Had Spearman been still alive it would hardly have been possible for Burt to write as he did in the statistical journal without evoking a devastating rejoinder from Spearman. The Spearman–Burt correspondence that took place between the years 1936 and 1939 shows that Spearman was not disposed to tolerate any specious claims on Burt's part. Spearman's death, therefore, removed an inhibition. Thurstone's book, on the other hand, provided a provocation. Burt, who was distinctly anti-American in his attitudes, was provoked, as his review of the book makes clear, by Thurstone's disregard of British work other than that of Spearman. Burt felt that the methods being advocated by Thurstone had in fact been anticipated by British workers, and that Thurstone was not giving them credit for this. He himself had anticipated Thurstone's 'centroid' method, and the 'principal axes' method praised by Thurstone was identical with the procedure described by Pearson in *Biometrika* in 1901. In spite of the fact that Thurstone makes no mention of Pearson in his account, it is highly probable that it was Thurstone's chapter on the 'principal axes' method that alerted Burt to the significance of Pearson's paper, since there is no earlier reference to it in Burt's writings. So the ground had been prepared for the new story and the seeds sown. It is doubtful, however, whether the seeds would have germinated but for pathological changes in Burt's personality, which will be examined later.

From this point on the new story grew rampantly. In the second issue of the statistical journal Burt returned to it in his article on 'Factor Analysis and Canonical Correlation'.[79] Here he made a distinction between canonical analysis in which the criterion is external, as in Spearman's early paper (in this case teachers' estimates of intelligence), and factor analysis in which the criterion

79. Burt, C. L. *Brit. J. Psychol. (Stats)*, I, ii, 1948, 95–106.

is derived from the internal evidence of the tests (as in his own 1909 paper). So he concluded, 'Spearman did not attempt to "factorise" his tables as we now understand "factorisation". . . . Nowadays . . . the methods in common use follow the principle first adopted in my paper of 1909. This consisted in taking the observed correlation table as a whole, and finding what I call the "highest common factor", i.e. the factor which gave the closest fit to all the observed coefficients. To obtain such a factor as this we have to adopt the principles previously adopted by Pearson for calculating what he termed the "lines of closest fit".'[80] This claim wholly ignores the fact that Burt's 1909 work was entirely derived from Spearman, and it was Spearman who had suggested the method of calculating the theoretical values of the hierarchy. Pearson was not mentioned in the 1909 paper except as a critic of Spearman, and according to Burt at the time Pearson's arguments could be dismissed. A perusal of Burt's article makes it perfectly clear that Pearson had no influence on it whatever, and the matter is clinched by the correspondence that took place between Spearman and Burt in 1937.

Later in the same year in a discussion on 'The Factorial Study of Temperamental Traits' Burt claimed that the factor analysis of emotional traits that was presented to the British Association in 1915 was 'based essentially on the method suggested by Karl Pearson in 1901 for the analysis of physical characteristics (*Phil. Mag., II*, 559–72). It differed from Pearson's in two main respects, namely (to use terminology that has since become current), (i) in seeking to determine the *minimum* number of orthogonal factors needed, rather than the *maximum* number, and (ii) in substituting *simple* sums for the *weighted* sums that Pearson's formula strictly required.' This account of the 1915 investigation is completely fictitious.[81]

In 1949 Burt began his article on 'Alternative Methods of Factor Analysis' with the statement that 'there can be little question that the problem and fundamental principles of what psychologists call "factor analysis" are due essentially to the pregnant suggestions of Galton and Karl Pearson', adding that 'in early discussions of factorial procedures in psychology during the years 1905 to 1915 the statistical proposals of Galton and Pearson were constantly cited', and complaining that writers who entered the field at a later date, like Thomson in Britain and Thurstone in America, seemed

80. Burt, C. L. *Brit. J. Psychol. (Stats), I*, ii, 1948, p. 101.
81. Burt, C. L. The factorial study of temperamental traits. *Brit. J. Psychol. (Stats), I*, iii, 1948, 178–203. See pages 159–60 above.

to be unaware of Pearson's article on 'lines of closest fit'.[82] In fact
no writer on factor analysis before 1940, either in Britain or
America, referred to Pearson's 1901 articles, apart from a brief
reference in Brown's *Essentials of Mental Measurement* (1st edn,
1911) in a passage that was deleted from the second edition. Nor is
there any indication that Burt himself was aware of them, since
there is no significant reference in any of his writings prior to
1947.[83] In the same article Burt makes exaggerated claims relating
to his own early work, maintaining that his 1909 investigation was
the first attempt to calculate factors from complete correlation
tables. In fact all he did was to compare the obtained correlations
with the theoretical correlations derived from Spearman's formula,
sum the deviations, and compare them with the average probable
errors. He never, as he put it, contended 'that instead of aiming at
a *maximum* number of common factors a safer policy was to aim at
a *minimum*'.

Burt intensified his attack on Spearman later in 1949 in an article
on 'The Two-Factor Theory'.[84] In it he set out to demonstrate that
'the Galton-Pearson school has after all provided the model, or at
least the main line of development for factorial work in psychology.
From a mathematical standpoint the methods of factor analysis in
vogue at the present time resemble in their general approach, not so
much the somewhat specialised technique which Spearman proposed on the basis of his own somewhat specialised hypotheses, but
rather the older procedures first outlined by Edgeworth and Karl
Pearson for reducing correlated variables to uncorrelated components.' He then amplified his contention that Spearman had not
really employed factor analysis at all, and he contrasted his own
work which he claimed was from the start based on Pearson. 'The
principle eventually adopted (in my 1909 investigation) was
suggested by Pearson's procedure for fitting theoretical values to
contingency tables in cases of manifold association.' Far from Burt
having followed Spearman and relied on his advice, Burt now
claimed that he took a different route and that he was in disagreement
with Spearman from the start. He also maintained that in his own
earlier researches 'the results strongly suggested a small but discernible tendency for groups of allied tests to correlate together'.[85] In
the original article he was at pains to point out that the residual

82. Burt, C. L. Alternative methods of factor analysis. *Brit. J. Psychol. (Stats)*,
II, ii, 1949, 98–121.

83. There is an incidental reference to the *Phil. Mag.* article in *Factors of the Mind*,
p. 340, ftnt. in connection with probable errors.

84. Burt, C. L. *Brit. J. Psychol. (Stats)*, II, iii, 1949, 151–78.

85. *Ibid.*, p. 174.

correlations were less than three times the probable error and could be ignored. There was no question at this stage of any 'three-factor' theory. The emphasis was entirely on the confirmation of Spearman's hypothesis of a general factor.

It would be tedious to analyse in detail the numerous articles between 1950 and 1968 in which the same story was repeated and elaborated. The claims got more and more extravagant. 'In the early days of factorial work—say from 1909 to 1924—all those who attempted to factorise complete correlation tables would, I think, have given Pearson's method, if not pride of place, at least priority of place.'[86] This is totally absurd in view of the fact that Burt himself never mentioned Pearson's articles before 1947, and Thomson, the other leading British factorist, stated that he did not regard Pearson's 'lines of closest fit' as having anything to do with factor analysis.[87] Burt even went so far as to maintain, in his contribution to the Katz Festschrift in 1951, that in Spearman's early work the term 'factor' was not employed, except incidentally in reference to such non-mental influences as age and sex.[88] This statement, which was repeated in 1966,[89] is again quite untrue. Spearman stated in reviewing his data that 'the central factor varies from less than one fifth to over fifteen times the size of the accompanying specific ones', and he provided a table showing 'the ratio of the common factor to the specific factor'.[90] Though the terms 'factor' and 'function' were interchangeably used, Spearman was already employing the term 'factor' in the connotation given it in factor theory. The culmination was reached in the Appendix on factor analysis attached to chapter II of Butcher's *Human Intelligence*.[91] Here Burt, who wrote the Appendix, stated that 'in psychology [factor analysis] was in fact first used by Burt to decide between three alternative hypotheses', and he added, 'this method was first used by Burt and his research students in early studies from 1907 onwards. It is essentially a simplification of the method proposed by Karl Pearson (1901) commonly known as "principal components".' Thus Spearman was dethroned, and Burt himself elevated in his place! No deferential withdrawal now on the question of priority! Burt was the first! It seems almost a classic example of the

86. Burt, C. L. The influence of differential weighting. *Brit. J. Psychol. (Stats)*, *III*, 1950, 113.

87. Thomson, G. H. Letter to Mr D. F. Vincent, 7 August 1952.

88. Burt, C. L. In *Essays in Honour of David Katz*, 1951, p. 33.

89. Burt, C. L. The early history of multivariate techniques in psychological research. *Multivar. Behav. Res.*, *I*, 1966, 24–42.

90. Spearman, C. E. Intelligence objectively determined and measured. *Amer. J. Psychol.*, *XV*, 1904, 273, 276.

91. Butcher, H. J. *Human Intelligence*, 1968, appendix to ch. ii by Burt, p. 66.

killing of the father king. And indeed it is more than probable that there were pathological features in this bizarre saga.

A discussion of the pathology must be left to a later chapter. Suffice it to say that it shows many of the marks of a delusional system, growing from small beginnings into a blind and warping compulsion. The seeds were probably present in the 1930s, as Stephenson has noted and the Spearman–Burt correspondence confirms, but their development was inhibited by Spearman's authority. From 1947 onwards their growth was rapid, and the new story was repeated with obsessive frequency in article after article and with growing elaboration. Not content with this, Burt picked on younger psychologists who had innocently adhered to the orthodox account, wrote to them and castigated them for crediting Spearman with factor analysis. Some, like the statistician, Patrick Slater, caved in: 'Thank you very much for your extremely interesting letter,' he replied to Burt, 'about the early development of factor analysis. My statement that it originated with Spearman was taken straight from Vernon's book. . . . I am quite prepared to believe that the tradition that factor analysis originated with Spearman is a myth, like the traditional association of the steam engine with Watt.'[92] Others like D. F. Vincent of the National Institute of Industrial Psychology were not so easily browbeaten. On 3 October 1951 Burt wrote to Vincent as follows: 'A correspondent has drawn my attention to your interesting discussion about Spearman's work on factor analysis in last month's number of *Psychology at Work* , and points out that your account of Spearman's contributions differs a little from that given in the statistical section of the *British Journal of Psychology* . . . . Factor analysis certainly began in 1901, but it began with two important contributions published by Karl Pearson describing the method of principal axes. In that year and a year or two later Pearson came to Oxford and described his methods: and it was then that McDougall and I got interested in these techniques.'[93] This led to a protracted correspondence between Burt and Vincent. Vincent made a critical study of Burt's published articles and analysed their misrepresentations, contradictions and evasions. This analysis was never published because Vincent believed that no publisher or journal would agree to accept it, such was Burt's reputation at the time.[94] It was Vincent who in the end broke off the interchange, because, as he said some years later to another correspondent, 'I should not get a simple answer to a simple question. I should get half a dozen

92. Slater, P. Letter to Burt, 25 June 1951.
93. Burt, C. L. Letter to D. F. Vincent, 3 October 1951.
94. I am indebted to Mr D. F. Vincent for providing me with copies of his correspondence with Burt, and for his detailed comments on the exchanges. These are now available in the Burt Archives at the University of Liverpool.

foolscap sheets of typescript, all very polite and very cordial, raising
half a dozen subsidiary issues in which I was not particularly interested, and to which out of politeness I should have to reply, and that
would entail a considerable expenditure of time looking up references. I should then get more foolscap pages of typescript raising
more extraneous issues. That has been my previous experience, and
after the first letter my problem has been how to terminate the correspondence without being discourteous.'[95]

To these compulsive letters to younger psychologists were added
almost certainly 'fake' letters to his statistical journal. The most
notorious of these was the letter purporting to have come from
'Jaques Lafitte' in 1954. This was supposed to have been a rejoinder
to a review by 'F. N. Harper' of a book by R. B. Cattell. The letter
began, 'In commenting on the origins of factor anaylsis the reviewer
of Dr Raymond Cattell's book overlooks one very misleading
statement. Dr Cattell declares that "Spearman's demonstration in
1904 that a single factor runs through most mental tests . . .
presented the first formal and adequate statement of factor analysis."
Surely the first formal and adequate statement was Karl Pearson's
demonstration of the method of principal axes in 1901.'[96] The letter
ran to nearly four closely printed pages, some 3,500 words! In sty[l]
and in content it was indistinguishable from the writings of Burt.
The unknown French psychologist 'Jaques Lafitte', apart from
references to Binet and Voltaire, seemed wholly dependent on
Anglo-Saxon sources, and wholly a disciple of the post-1947 Burt.
The reviewer who was criticised, 'F. N. Harper', was also most
probably Burt himself!

Did Burt know what he was doing in concocting the story he so
obsessively attempted to put over? It is difficult to say with
certainty, but perhaps in the end he became a victim of his own
delusions. He never seemed to have appreciated the complete
contradiction between his new story and the evidence, and to his
own considered statements before 1947. He never made any attempt
to justify his change of viewpoint; the earlier evidence he misquoted
and falsified. Yet he had no compunction in repeating his story to
a top level gathering of factorists meeting in Paris in 1955, when he
might have known that it would be regarded with incredulity. As
one discussant remarked, 'les exposés historiques de Sir C. Burt et
Mlle Banks m'ont beaucoup surpris, par la façon dont ils parlent
des travaux de Spearman. Cela renverse tout ce que j'ai appris et

95. Vincent, D. F. Letter to C. F. Wrigley, 23 October 1958.
96. 'Lafitte, Jaques'. *Brit. J. Statist. Psychol.*, *VII*, 1954, p. 61.

tout ce que je savais dans ce domaine.'[97] This apparently total blindness to the implausibility of his story suggests that a delusional system had taken over; that he had come to believe in what he was saying, and that he twisted the evidence accordingly. If not deluded how, when he was preparing the second edition of *Factors of the Mind*, could he go solemnly and systematically through his earlier text and delete every favourable reference to Spearman, while incorporating a new historical section which was entirely at variance with his previous account—and do all this without any attempt at explanation or justification? Could any well-balanced individual have supposed he could get away with this?

Two further questions remain. Is there any element of truth in the new story? Why were Burt's inconsistencies and misrepresentations not exposed by his colleagues? As we have seen, Burt's contention from 1947 onwards was that Pearson founded factor analysis in his 1901 articles, that his (Burt's) work was derived from this source and not from Spearman at all, and hence that he (Burt) was the first factorist in psychology. We can say at once that these claims by Burt about his own early work were completely false. But what about Pearson's role? In their standard work on *Factor Analysis as a Statistical Method* Lawley and Maxwell have this to say on the relation of Pearson's method of principal axes to factor analysis: 'When analysing the structure of covariance (or correlation) matrices two approaches, which formally resemble each other to some extent but have slightly different aims, are currently employed. One is principal components analysis following Pearson (1901) and Hotelling (1933), while the other is factor analysis and stems from the work of Spearman (1904, 1926). In the interest of clarity, it is advisable to distinguish between these two approaches. . . . The principal components method . . . is a relatively straightforward method of "breaking down" a covariance or correlation matrix into a set of orthogonal components or axes equal in number to the number of variates concerned. . . . In contrast . . . the aim of factor analysis is to account for, or explain, the matrix of covariances by a minimum, or at least a small number, of hypothetical variates or "factors".'[98] According to Lawley and Maxwell, therefore, the techniques though different are related. It would, of course, have been perfectly legitimate for Burt to have pointed out this relationship, and the relevance of Pearson's 1901

97. Collôques Internationaux du Centre National de la Recherche Scientific, Paris, 1955. Burt did not attend in person. His paper was read by Dr Charlotte Banks.

98. Lawley, D. N. and Maxwell, A. E. *Factor Analysis as a Statistical Method*, 1963.

articles to the problems that factorists had been concerned with. He could have commented on their neglect by all earlier factorists, including himself and Hotelling, whose method was closely allied to that of Pearson. What Burt was not entitled to do was to claim that as a matter of historical fact Pearson's articles were the decisive influence in the early days of factor work, and the main inspiration of his own first endeavours. This claim is entirely contrary to the evidence and involved a falsification of history.

Why were these falsifications and misrepresentations not exposed by his colleagues at the time of their perpetration? The reasons are complex. Probably very few psychologists were aware of the full extent of Burt's fabrications. The readership of the statistical journal was a small one. In the early 1950s fewer than 100 members of the British Psychological Society subscribed to it. Burt's articles were long and wordy. Mathematicians were interested in the mathematics, not in the historical padding; and non-mathematicians avoided the articles altogether. So they were probably little read. Those who spotted the oddity of Burt's views either dismissed it as an unimportant quirk, or, in deference to Burt's eminence and reputation, either said nothing, or merely expressed surprise. Godfrey Thomson, Burt's joint editor, should perhaps have spoken up before his death in 1954. It appeared that he was uneasy, but deferred to Burt's superior historical knowledge, and, as joint editor, he probably hesitated to rock a boat that was in some danger of foundering altogether. His friendship with Burt moreover had been of long standing. So Thomson did not openly protest. Critics like D. F. Vincent and C. B. Frisby of the National Institute of Industrial Psychology also thought it prudent to remain silent. Burt was, after all, an eminent member of the N.I.I.P. Council and a former member of their staff. In my own *Short History of British Psychology* I noted the discrepancy between Burt's early and late views on Spearman's work, but did not pursue the matter in detail, and I must admit that at that time I had not read through all Burt's articles on factor analysis and collated them with his early writings.[99] So Burt's historical fiction was not exposed; rather it tended to be simply ignored. It has had little effect on the history of factor analysis; but it provides convincing documentary evidence for Burt's culpability. He falsified history in the interest of self-aggrandisement. That he was guilty of malfeasance there can be no reasonable doubt. The only question at issue can be, was he guilty *simpliciter* or guilty with diminished responsibility as a result of pathological influences? This is a question to which we shall return.

99. Hearnshaw, L. S. *A Short History of British Psychology*, 1964, p. 198.

VII

In spite of the aberrations of his later years, Burt's contribution to the development of factor analysis must not be underestimated. His early work was a most important exemplification and extension of Spearman's original theory. He was one of the pioneers, and, as his algebraic sophistication increased, he became a master of the mathematical procedures involved and a leading factor theorist, retaining his technical grasp and facility into late old age. At the same time the techniques he advocated were practical and realistic, and before the days of computers were extensively used in Britain. He was certainly one of the first to apply factorial techniques in the field of personality, and his pupils, Eysenck in England, and Cattell and Wrigley in America, have built on the foundations he laid. He was the first, or among the first, to develop inverted factor techniques, and to correlate persons instead of tests. Though his elaborate scheme for 'the structure of the mind' has not found acceptance in detail, the hierarchical idea as such has much to commend it, and his insistence on general factors can be defended on theoretical grounds. Though the yield of factor analysis for the science of psychology has been disappointingly meagre, there is no reason to doubt that in principle it is a perfectly legitimate technique. After all Mendel, from a statistical analysis of his crossing experiments, arrived at the conception of underlying 'characters', which later work was to identify with genes and DNA molecules. There is no reason why statistical analysis should not enable tentative conclusions to be reached with regard to human abilities and traits of personality. Burt himself regarded such conclusions as provisional and in need of confirmation by experimental and perhaps neurological research. In one area, the difference between verbal and spatial ability, split-brain experiments already seem to have provided confirmation of the factorists' findings. Factor techniques may at present have lost the popularity they enjoyed in the 1930s; they may have been overambitious in their aims, and exaggerated in their claims: they are nevertheless more than an historical curiosity, and Burt's contribution to their development was in several respects a significant one, even if we cannot accord him Spearman's crown. It is lamentable that he should have blotted his record by the delinquencies of his later years.

CHAPTER TEN

Years of Retirement

I

Burt gave up his chair at University College, London, in September 1950. He died on 10 October 1971. He enjoyed, therefore, just twenty-one years of retirement. Throughout this period he kept up a ceaseless stream of activity, writing innumerable articles, reviewing books and manuscripts, editing the statistical journal of the British Psychological Society, examining, broadcasting and lecturing, dealing with a huge correspondence, and keeping abreast of what was going on in the psychological, educational and scientific worlds. Though dogged by uncertain health he was constantly on the go, and he maintained a high level of intellectual activity and drive right up to the last few weeks of his life.

Burt had never been a sociable or clubbable man, and the routine into which he settled on retirement suited him well. His domestic affairs had been arranged by Lady Burt before she finally separated from him, and these arrangements worked smoothly until the end of his life. He was indeed extremely fortunate in retaining the services of a devoted companion and housekeeper, Miss Gretl Archer, a cultivated woman of Austrian birth, who looked after his daily needs. Miss Archer came to Elsworthy Road in 1950. Up till 1958 she was engaged mainly on domestic duties; after the death of Miss Bruce, Burt's secretary, however, she undertook in addition a good many secretarial tasks. She could not take shorthand, but she could type, and she was systematic in her filing of correspondence; so for the last fourteen years of Burt's life most of his correspondence is extant. Most important, however, was the fact that she was a sympathetic listener, and shared many of Burt's interests in the arts, religion and scientific discovery. She had an immense admiration for Burt, and was captivated by his erudition. Without her devoted help Burt could not possibly have achieved the huge output of his twenty-one years of retirement.

His day began early with a simple breakfast in bed, when he would read *The Times*, any manuscripts that had been sent to him, and his morning mail, answering letters by hand, or scribbling out answers for typing. He would usually be in his study by ten o'clock, and with a short break for coffee, work on till lunch at one. Whenever possible—that is, when his health and the weather permitted—he would stroll on Primrose Hill or in Regents Park in the afternoon, then indulge in light reading around tea time, and perhaps, before his hearing deteriorated, playing the piano, or amusing his Siamese cat, Simmie, of which he was extremely fond. Then came more work before dinner at 7.30 p.m.; and work again until 11.30 p.m. or midnight. It was a strenuous day, involving seven to eight hours work as a rule, and even when relaxing on his bed, he would frequently be fiddling with his calculating machine or jotting down notes. Of course, there were sometimes interruptions when visitors came to tea, or somebody wanted an interview, or when there was some particularly interesting programme on a scientific subject on radio or television. In the 1950s he would still go out to meetings and deliver lectures in person; in the 1960s, owing to an increasing loss of hearing as well as Ménière and other troubles, he rarely left the flat except for his strolls and rather infrequent outings.

It may perhaps seem surprising that under these comparatively favourable conditions, and with this diligent routine, Burt did not produce any major work during his years of retirement, and that, in spite of the erudition displayed in many of his publications, there were in some of the most important of them serious inadequacies. It is necessary, in passing judgment on this period of Burt's work, to view it in its total context, both personal and situational. His unremitting toil was less productive, and less free from blemishes, than it might have been, as a result of psychological and economic forces which led him to divert a good deal of his energies into relatively unfruitful channels.

His economic situation during these years of retirement was by no means satisfactory. The truth is that Burt was compelled to work right up to the end of his life just to make ends meet. The pension he received was far from adequate for his needs. He retired on a pension of £767. 12s. od. from the L.C.C., supplemented by £50 from University College. The college pension was increased by stages from 1956 onwards, reaching £657 by 1969. In the last full year before his death Burt received by way of pension the total sum of £1574. 15s. od. He did not qualify for any state pension until he had reached the age of eighty; this then brought him in a meagre £3 per week. In 1970 the salary of a senior professor was approximately £5000; so Burt was receiving by way of pension less than one third of the salary he would have been entitled to. He had an expensive establishment to keep up. His flat was a roomy one, and excellently situated; but it was a heavy drain on his resources. The landlord was Eton College, and after back-door pressure from an influential friend of Burt (unbeknown to Burt himself) was persuaded to reduce the annual rent from £550 to £450. This figure did not include rates. Rent and rates together amounted to £642 in 1970, that is over 40 per cent of his official pension. The place was a large one to heat and to keep clean. His heating and lighting bill in 1970 amounted to £210, and cleaning to £312. So the total outgoing on his flat in that year came to £1164. In addition he paid his housekeeper wages of £4 per week, and was also, of course, responsible for her maintenance. His bills for extra typing, postage, telephone and so on amounted to nearly £100. Though he lived simply there were, from time to time, the inevitable extras, such as a bill for £354 for decorations in 1968. (In 1967 his prostatectomy cost him £150.) How then did he manage to square his budget? He had a small additional income of about £500 from building societies, bank deposits and other investments, which came to him partly through the generosity of his sister, as his own savings had been depleted through paying for his wife's medical education. He had, too, a steady income of several hundred pounds a year from royalties, as his books continued to sell well. But these additional sources were hardly adequate to meet his regular expenses, much less pay for extras or occasional luxuries. When in 1965 his housekeeper wanted to recarpet his large sitting-room he wrote to his sister, 'I am afraid I rather demurred. This year my expenses will vastly exceed my income, and I should like to know how much the annual deficit is likely to be before spending money on the "House Beautiful".'[1] This may have been a more difficult year than most, but he always had to be careful, and he always had to earn to bring in the extra needed to balance his accounts. So a good deal of his time during retirement was spent on 'pot-boiling' jobs, in particular, examining and reading manuscripts for publishers.

The average professor is glad to be released from the burden of examining on his retirement. In Burt's case he continued to take on a huge load of examining up to the last year of his life. In 1970 he comments on 'the usual collection of Ph.D. theses'. But he did far more than this. He regularly examined theses for The College of Preceptors, marked papers in the psychology of advertising (400–500 scripts), together with hundreds of scripts for colleges of education and the University of London Institute of Education. Not unnaturally, he would complain of exhaustion after the examination season was over. For a man in his eighties it was an incredible load to go on carrying.

1. Burt, C. L. Letter to Dr Marion Burt, 21 June 1965.

Even more remarkable was the constant stream of manuscripts sent to him by publishers for critical assessment. Allen and Unwin, the University of London Press, and Penguin Books all made use of his services and greatly valued his reports. In this job there is no doubt that Burt excelled. He was prompt and businesslike; his reports were lucidly written, were penetrating, but at the same time fair, in their criticisms, and were often extremely helpful in their constructive suggestions. Between 1959 and 1971 he reviewed no fewer than 246 manuscripts (including a number of foreign books for possible translation into English) from Allen and Unwin alone. The last report was despatched a fortnight before his death. His reports were often packed with erudition: to take just one example, in commenting on a book on 'Psychosocial Dynamics' he wrote:

The following statements seem to be open to criticism or correction and deserve the author's reconsideration:

1. On p. 114 it is alleged that in 1792 Joanna Southgate at the age of 52 proclaimed that she was about to give birth to the Messiah and died 12 years later. This is probably a slip of the memory for Joanna Southcott (born 1750 not 1740) who announced that in October 1814 she would give birth to 'Shiloh', and who died in October 1814 (not 1804).

2. We are told that the 'absolutism of the Pharaohs' left 'no room for individual variation and impeded social advance'. In point of fact during the first XIX dynasties Egyptian civilisation made astonishing advances, and the literature and art under the XVIII dynasty indicate a wide scope for individual variation.

3. The reference to 'the invention of the steam engine in ancient Alexandria', which remained 'unused because it did not fit into the framework of the existing order', seems misleading as it stands: the machine presumably referred to was simply a laboratory model constructed by Hero (c. 160 A.D.) to demonstrate some of the principles expounded in his *Pneumatika*. It consisted essentially of a horizontal tube, pivoted at the centre on a vertical tube, and ending with two nozzles bent at right angles: when steam was passed from below into the tubes, the horizontal arms rotated like a lawn sprinkler. (The principle embodied is that of the steam turbine rather than the 'steam engine', viz reaction).

4. The choice of 'two frogs of the same genus' to illustrate the relative lack of differentiation among lowlier animals is rather unfortunate. The genus *Rana* contains over 200 species. The bull frog, the flying frog, the leopard frog, and the edible frog display

striking differences; and 'the experimental biologist testing the reactions' (of frogs) *does* find marked individual differences.[2]

It was this spontaneous outflow of varied, massive, often recondite and detailed, learning on a whole variety of subjects, scientific, artistic, historical, philosophical, religious and literary that so impressed those who came into contact with Burt. It is not surprising that the publishers, and often the authors themselves, were highly grateful for his comments and advice. In 1968 Burt received a letter from Mr Foster of the University of London Press which ran, 'I have been conscious in recent months of the exceptional help you have been giving us in connection with some forthcoming publications . . . and am concerned lest we should have overburdened you. . . . Apart from thanking you most sincerely for all that you have done to solve some of our problems, I should like to make some recompense to you for all the trouble you have taken on our behalf. The modest reading fees that we have sent you from time to time are quite inadequate, and I should like to send you a cheque for £100 as a rather more tangible expression of our gratitude.'[3]

In May 1971, less than five months before his death, Burt read the manuscript of a philosophico-psychological book for Penguin. In addition to a 3,000-word report Burt provided a 33-page appendix of 'Supplementary Comments' (15,000 words) with acute, but at the same time constructive, notes, on the manuscript, and again an astonishing outflow of erudition. For instance, the author's

account of how the Devil came to be called Lucifer is misleading (he is probably confusing it with the story of Ormuzd and Ahriman). . . . The introduction of the word into English (Isaiah XIV. 12) is due to a misunderstanding; the author should look at the Hebrew 'Hellel ben Sachar (lit. 'shining one', 'son of the dawn god'). These are two of the honorific titles given to the Babylonian monarch. The chapter is a 'taunt-song (see v. 3 R.V.) triumphing over the defeat of Nabonidus by Cyrus (539 B.C.). The word 'hell' is a misleading translation for 'Sheol' ('underworld'). 'Hellel' also means 'praiseworthy one': (from the same verb as 'Hallelu-jah'). . . . The Latin translation 'Lucifer' is not a noun, but (as in the Hebrew) an adjective; in Latin its metaphorical meaning is 'bringer of safety', and was occasionally

2. Burt, C. L. Report to Allen and Unwin Ltd, 12 March 1963.
3. Letter from Mr H. S. Foster, 16 January 1968.

used (like 'Augustus') as an honorific title of potentates by late Latin writers.[4]

All this, and much more, was vintage Burt. The Penguin director who received the report wrote 'I am overwhelmed by the detailed and thorough way in which you have approached this manuscript, and I am enormously grateful. I feel it would be derisory to pay you 30 gns, and I propose to pay you 75 gns.'[5]

So the reviewing of manuscripts did bring in much-needed cash. Yet Burt's motives in undertaking this work were not merely mercenary. 'It is a job which I enjoy and often profit by', he wrote to Allen and Unwin, and obviously he put into it far more than mere duty required. Burt was not a mercenary man; he thought little about money, except through necessity, and he was often generous within the limits of his means. His one extravagance was the flat in which he lived, and even this was not really an extravagance, but a necessary basis for the kind of life he partly chose, and partly was obliged to lead. If he was to stay on there, and remain professionally active, he had to keep up a certain amount of 'donkey work'. He did this manfully, and rarely, if ever, complained. There was something admirable in the way he coped, and kept going almost up to his death. Only two months before the end Burt, in giving an account of his activities to his sister, wrote, 'in the main I have been engaged on making money'.[6] If in these twenty-one years of retirement no major work came from his pen, if there are shortcomings in some of his important papers, perhaps the explanation partly lies in the pressure of routine work he was compelled to keep up.

II

Not all his retirement activities were as professionally unproductive as examining and assessing manuscripts. Some of his major lectures were important statements of his position, and while in the 1950s he was still delivering them in person, they attracted large audiences, and sometimes substantial fees. The attendances at several of his public lectures exceeded the thousand mark; at the University of London Institute of Education, for example, in 1953, and at New Cross in 1955. On the occasion of his Hobhouse lecture on 'The Contribution of Psychology to Social Problems', delivered in 1952,

4. Burt, C. L. Report to Penguin Books Ltd, 19 May 1971.
5. Letter from Penguin Books Ltd, 24 June 1971.
6. Burt, C. L. Letter to Dr Marion Burt, 5 August 1971.

the large hall was packed, and more than 200 persons were turned away. His Bingham lecture on 'The Inheritance of Mental Ability', delivered in 1957, attracted a distinguished audience, and brought him a substantial fee of $500 (nearly £200 at the then rate of exchange). 'I attempted', he wrote to his sister, 'a rather popular style of lecturing, but to my horror I found confronting me a large number of professors, etc. The college has given me a list of people who applied for reserved seats, and it includes eleven professors (of different subjects), nearly all the psychologists, Fraser Roberts, representatives from the American Embassy, the U.S. Educational Commission, and one Dutchman who had flown over specially for the lecture. Mrs Bingham had also flown over from America to present an illuminated scroll to mark the occasion.'[7] His friend, Mrs Beatrice Warde, commented enthusiastically; 'to epitomise such a tremendous study and drive home its salient points in fifty minutes, *and* make the whole thing crackle with wit—oh, it was superb! . . . And what an audience you drew! It was packed to standing-room. The fire regulations were flouted, and every stair-case occupied, the corridor leading to the main hall jammed fifteen deep.'[8] Other important lectures included the Convocation Lecture of the National Children's Home on 'The Causes and Treatment of Backwardness', given in Birmingham (1952), for which he received a fee of £105; the Maudsley Lecture on 'The Assessment of Personality' (1954); the Galton Lecture on 'The Meaning and Assessment of Intelligence' (1955); and the Godfrey Thomson Lecture on 'The Applications of Mathematics to Psychology' (1957). Throughout the 1950s he was able to attract large and enthusiastic audiences. In 1960 Burt took the chair at Aubrey Lewis's Hobhouse Lecture, but after that he rarely again appeared on public platforms. Invitations to lecture continued to come in, but he declined them, or very occasionally agreed to prepare a script to be read on his behalf. In 1960 he was invited to deliver the 25th Anniversary Address to the Psychometric Society in Chicago 'as the most eminent person in the area'. But by this time a transatlantic trip was beyond him. His last major addresses (neither of them delivered in person) were the F. W. H. Myers Lecture on 'Psychology and Psychic Research' (1968), which was published in an amplified form by the Society for Psychic Research; and the important Lee Thorndike Award Lecture on 'The Inheritance of General Intelligence', which he revised in the last few weeks of

7. Burt, C. L. Letter to Dr Marion Burt, 22 May 1957.
8. Letter from Mrs B. Warde, 23 May 1957.

his life, and which was posthumously published in the *American Psychologist*.[9]

In addition to these public events Burt still kept up in the 1950s occasional university lecturing. He lectured annually to Dr Oakeshott's students at the London School of Economics, and in the department of child development in the University of London Institute of Education. In 1950 he broadcast a series of eight talks on 'The Study of the Mind'. Burt had broadcast fairly regularly in the 1930s and 1940s, and was regarded as a good broadcaster by the B.B.C., with a natural and easy manner at the microphone. The 1950 series was markedly less successful than the earlier broadcasts. Burt himself seemed to realise this and attributed it to the deterioration in his hearing, 'which prevents me from knowing quite what my voice is doing, and so is rather apt to lead to a little mental confusion'.[10] The B.B.C., in spite of a good rating for the first talk, regarded the series as 'disappointing'; adding that 'the approach lacked flexibility and was basically academic . . . the talks did not have the excitement and sense of contemporaneity . . . too many issues seemed dated.'[11] After that Burt only gave the occasional talk on radio, which included a couple of broadcasts on Radio Free Europe in 1962–63, and in 1969 he made a successful television appearance for the B.B.C., the cameras coming round to his flat.

If the 1960s brought a decrease in the amount of lecturing and broadcasting, they also brought an increase in journalistic demands, as Burt got more and more embroiled in controversies of interest to the public— controversies about intelligence, selective education and educational standards. The peak was reached in 1969, following the article in the *Irish Journal of Education*, in which he spoke on the decline of educational standards, and his *Black Paper II* contribution on 'The Mental Differences between Children'.[12] During that year he wrote fourteen articles in response to requests; as he said in a letter to his sister, 'I am kept very busy writing for newspapers, weeklies and technical journals, replying to criticisms from labour egalitarians, who don't like what I said in *Black Paper II*.'[13]

All this was time-consuming, though perhaps not quite as time-consuming as the committee work in which Burt was still involved in the 1950s. He was chairman of the British Psychological Society's working party on maladjusted children, which produced in 1951 a long report for the Underwood committee. This assignment

9. Burt, C. L. *Loc. cit.*, *XXVII*, 1972, 175–90.
10. Burt, C. L. Letter to the B.B.C., 28 September 1950.
11. Report, B.B.C. Archives.
12. Cox, C. B. and Dyson, A. E. (eds) *Black Paper II*, 1969, pp. 16–25.
13. Burt, C. L. Letter to Dr Marion Burt, 15 December 1969.

prompted Burt to look at his own material on maladjustment, collected while he was at the L.C.C., and to analyse it factorially. It led to the publication in the statistical journal of an article by Cyril Burt and Margaret Howard on 'The Nature and Causes of Maladjustment among Children of School Age'.[14] 'The analysis of case histories, and the greater part of the calculations, have been carried out by Miss Howard.' This was the first appearance of Miss Howard on the scene.

Burt participated in several other working parties and committees. He produced a memorandum for the British Psychological Society's working party on mental deficiency (1954), sat on the organising committee for the International Congress of Criminology (1954), was consulted by the Home Office Advisory Committee on Young Offenders (1960), and was much involved in the experiments initiated by Sir James Pitman, and conducted by John Downing, on the Initial Teaching Alphabet. He kept closely in touch with this project from its first proposal in 1953–54 until the appearance of the research report in 1966, producing several critical memoranda. He also contributed an 'evaluation' to the *I.T.A. Symposium* published by the National Foundation for Educational Research in 1967. Although critical of some of Dr Downing's statistical work, Burt considered that 'the elaborate investigations . . . have been entirely worthwhile . . . we now know far more about the process of reading and of learning to read than we did before the experiments were undertaken, and valuable experience has been gained in regard to practicable methods of research in this bewildering field of education'.[15] In a recorded statement he contributed to a discussion meeting held at the British Psychological Society conference at Edinburgh in 1969 Burt linked the I.T.A. experiments with his own early work as L.C.C. psychologist, and raised a number of problems for further research.

Burt's interest in educational psychology remained lively until the end of his life, and when the Association of Educational Psychologists was formed in 1964, Burt became its Patron. This was far from a sinecure: the chairman of the Association, R. S. Reid, was frequently in touch with him, and Burt contributed regularly to the Association's *Journal and Newsletter*, some twenty articles in all. He was nearly as generous in his contributions to *Forward Trends*, the official journal of the Guild of Teachers of Backward Children, of which he was also Patron. And then there was Mensa, and its high-flyers, whose problems, as we have seen, were no less demanding; and up to 1963 the British Psychological

14. Burt, C. L. and Howard, Margaret. *Brit. J. Psychol. (Stats)*, V, 1952, 39–59.
15. Burt, C. L. Unpublished report.

Society committees in which Burt was involved, its Council, and its 'wretched' (to use his adjective) publications committee. In this he was involved as editor of the statistical journal, the tangled story of which must be reserved for a separate section.

All in all, these activities consumed much time. He was in fact often over-committed, as he complained to his friend, Valentine, in 1955: 'By the way', he wrote, 'you must not picture me as always sitting over books and figures. During the last week or two I have hardly been able to sit down over my work for more than half an hour or so together. I seem always to be running off to lectures, examinations, committee meetings, social gatherings and the like. In fact ever since I have been back from Malvern I have said with a sigh, "Now at last I can get down to *The Factors of the Mind*"; but that dull and happy day still seems to move on and on like the rainbow.'[16]

III

For the first thirteen years after his retirement perhaps Burt's most onerous task was the continued editing of the British Psychological Society's statistical journal. This journal had been founded with the title *British Journal of Psychology (Statistical Section)* in 1947 under the joint editorship of Cyril Burt and Godfrey Thomson. The aims of the journal were stated as 'the publication of original or expository articles dealing with the following subjects: (*a*) quantitative methods in all branches of psychological research; (*b*) mathematical and statistical techniques for the evaluation of psychological data; (*c*) researches and results of researches of which a main feature is the application of such methods.'[17] In a letter to Godfrey Thomson, Burt stressed the need to avoid excessive technicality. 'I gather that everybody is rather anxious that the journal should not be too unintelligible or too dull for the general psychologists. I would suggest that a prudent policy would be to start with issues which, if possible, would have a fairly wide appeal, and so build up and eventually educate a reading public in this country. That means that at the outset we should aim at a technical level a little lower than that of *Psychometrika*.'[18] Burt later interpreted this as meaning the publication of 'not so much short researches, as fairly lengthy expository reviews of the latest developments'.[19] This attempt to

16. Burt, C. L. Letter to C. W. Valentine, 10 November 1955.
17. Prospectus issued by the British Psychological Society.
18. Burt, C. L. Letter to Godfrey Thomson, 19 February 1947.
19. Burt, C. L. Letter to Mrs B. Warde, 6 October 1956.

secure a broad readership was not very successful. At the end of the tenth year the circulation among the society's members had only just reached one hundred, and the total circulation was only 249. The journal was not paying for itself, and was proving a financial burden to the society. In fact, during the first five years the losses had amounted to £3350, and there seemed little sign that the journal would pay its way. Its appeal was obviously minimal.

The trouble lay partly with the high cost of printing statistical material, and partly with the contents of the journal itself. The journal was originally published by the University of London Press, whose estimate was chosen from three submitted. As the U.L.P. were Burt's own publishers he was naturally strongly in favour of this choice, and their estimate was competitive. The estimates did, however, assume a circulation before long of 500 copies, and this figure was never reached during the period of Burt's editorship. For this the contents of the journal were probably to a large extent to blame. There was an over-loading of articles on factor analysis, and an excessive number of articles by Burt himself. Nearly one-third of the material in the first two volumes was contributed by Burt personally, and over the seventeen years when he was joint or sole editor, he supplied no fewer than 63 articles or long critical reviews under his own name, and almost certainly others under pseudonyms. Before his association with the journal ended, some of his articles, which were extremely lengthy, had not the remotest connection with statistical, or any other branch of mathematical, psychology— for example, articles on 'Hebrew Psychology', 'The Sense-Datum Theory' (20,000 words) and 'The Psychology of Value' (40,000 words). The journal became, and indeed had been in effect from the start, a vehicle for Burt, and he even referred to it as 'my journal'.[20]

In the early 1950s this brought Burt, who on Thomson's death in 1954 became sole editor,[21] into increasing conflict with the officers and council of the British Psychological Society. The members of the society had expressed at Annual General Meetings a good deal of dissatisfaction with the society's publications. The complaints were directed not solely at the statistical journal; in fact, it was the *British Journal of Medical Psychology* that in particular came under fire by reason of its heavily psychoanalytic bias. As a result of this discontent the B.P.S. Council set up an *ad hoc* publications

20. Burt, C. L. Letter to Dr Marion Burt, 8 November 1955.
21. Godfrey Thomson asked the B.P.S. Council if he might resign from his Joint Editorship in October 1949. He was persuaded to continue on the understanding that Burt did most of the work. Burt in effect was sole editor from 1950 onwards (B.P.S. Council Minutes 1222 and 1248, October and November 1949).

committee in 1953 which recommended various changes in the editorial control and business management of the society's journals. A standing committee on publications was established to deal with all matters relating to journals, and the editorship of journals was to be restricted to a normal period of five years, and a maximum of six. It was clear to the committee that unless the losses on the statistical journal could be reduced it might have to cease publication altogether. So immediate steps were taken in an endeavour to make it pay. These involved proposals for an increase in the price of the journal, which Burt was very reluctant to accept, and a change in the publishing arrangements, which he was even more unwilling to accept. The society, however, under a strong President, Professor Rex Knight of Aberdeen, got its way, and it was decided that the University of Aberdeen Press should print the journal, and that the society's officers (Secretary and Treasurer) should constitute themselves publishers. Burt was bitterly opposed to this arrangement. As an expert in typography he did not like the Aberdeen University Press, and complained that they had insufficient experience of setting mathematical material; and he accused the officers of the society, not entirely without justification, of knowing nothing about publishing. The arrangement certainly did not work well. Aberdeen was a long way off; there were delays in the production of the journal; and it continued to make losses. The discussions in the publications committee became increasingly acrimonious. Burt began to accuse the officers of wanting to wind up the statistical journal altogether and to replace it with an experimental journal. 'At the moment', he wrote, 'except for the President [Dr Strauss] who is now in hospital, all the officers are hostile to the statistical journal, partly because it has proved so expensive, and partly because they want to launch an experimental journal and a journal on clinical and social psychology to rival the existing journals of experimental and medical psychology, which refuse to kow-tow to the society.'[22] Burt's suspicions were largely unfounded. The society was quite prepared to run a statistical journal provided it could be made to pay, but it saw little prospect of it paying while Burt remained editor. Moreover Burt had been editor for ten years, either jointly or solely, and according to the recent ruling of the publications committee editors of the society's journals were to hold office for a maximum term of six years. Hence, to put the matter in Burt's words, 'on the only occasion I was absent from a Council meeting the opponents of the journal took the opportunity to move a vague resolution, the effect of which was that the President suggested that, as in the view of the publications committee no

22. Burt, C. L. Letter to Mrs B. Warde, 11 November 1956.

editor should serve for more than five years, I would perhaps be willing to resign. I think the hope was to put in an editor who would gradually turn the journal into an experimental and perhaps a clinical journal. But in the end Dr Whitfield was actually nominated.'[23]

The appointment of J. W. Whitfield as joint editor with Burt in 1957, and the decision to transfer the publication and printing of the journal to the London firm of Taylor and Francis, persuaded the Council to grant it a new lease of life. Moreover some financial assistance had been provided by Mrs Beatrice Warde, a close friend of Burt. The full story of this friendship must be reserved to a later section. A woman of immense drive and ability, Mrs Warde was a devoted admirer of Burt. Not only could Burt do nothing wrong, he was, for her, the torchbearer of the new age, in which science, religion and humanity would all be reconciled in a splendid synthesis. For her the statistical journal was the gospel of the new age, and to keep it going, and Burt in charge, appeared in her eyes virtually a religious duty. So she devised a plan for subsidising the journal, but doing so in such a way that the money was to go, not to the society, but to Burt personally. Not unnaturally the society hesitated to accept an arrangement, the implications of which directly conflicted with the decisions of its publications committee. To Mrs Warde, whose account of the negotiations came mainly from Burt, the society and its officers appeared monsters of ingratitude. 'I don't think I've ever heard of a case in which a warm-hearted donor was met with more frigid unforthcomingness', she complained, and as for the Council's treatment of Burt she regarded it as 'intolerable'. After tortuous and protracted negotiations a compromise was reached. Burt was to remain editor jointly with Whitfield for a time, and Mrs Warde did assist the journal financially. In 1960 Burt nominally handed over the editorship to Whitfield, but remained as 'assistant to the editor'. Whitfield, an able Cambridge Psychologist who had been appointed to the University College staff by Burt's successor, was far from well, however, and far from businesslike, and the journal was once again verging on shipwreck. Burt was more or less forced to take over control again, and *de facto* continued to run the journal until 1963. Burt's behaviour, however, again brought him into conflict with the society, and evoked some extremely sharp comments from the President of the society (Professor James Drever, Jnr). He accused Burt of 'regarding the *British Journal of Statistical Psychology* [as it was now known] as to some extent a private journal of your own', and went on, 'The statistical journal suffers from a mixture of

23. Burt, C. L. Letter to Mrs B. Warde, 16 December 1957.

editorial highhandedness and inefficiency that is unique in my experience. I can only suppose from your letter that the Council of the B.P.S., despite changes in membership, has been consistently prejudiced over the last ten years.'[24]

In 1963 the Whitfield–Burt regime came to an end. In that year Dr R. J. Audley, another member of the University College staff, was appointed editor, again 'with the assistance of Cyril Burt'. Officially Burt remained assistant throughout Audley's period of editorship from 1963 to 1968. But matters between them soon came to a head. Burt still wanted to control the way the journal was run; difficulties and tension developed between him and Audley; and in the end Audley had to exert his authority and take full charge. There is no doubt that this was a severe blow to Burt. For seventeen years he had poured into the statistical journal a large investment of time and energy; it had become the main vehicle for his reports and the expression of his views; as editor he had not merely an autocratic control over the contents of the journal, but an established place in the psychological world. And now all this had been wrested from him. The tenacious way in which he held on to his editorial role over so many years and against so much opposition indicates how important it was for him. For the journal Burt's departure was the beginning of better times. Within three years of Audley becoming editor its subscribers just doubled, and by 1970 were approaching one thousand, nearly four times what they had been in 1956. The journal, which had changed its title to *The British Journal of Statistical Psychology* in 1953, became *The British Journal of Mathematical and Statistical Psychology* in 1966, widening its scope and attracting more subscribers. After 1964, apart from an occasional book review, Burt contributed only once more to the journal, and this was the important article on 'Quantitative Genetics in Psychology', which he wrote towards the end of his life.[25] The relinquishing of editorial control, hard as it was for him to take, at least relieved him from an enormous burden of writing, correspondence, attending meetings, and all the routines of editing. But he was by then eighty years of age, and the opportunity for a final *magnum opus* had effectively passed.

IV

Burt had many plans for the revision of books, for collections of papers, and for new books, but with two exceptions—the fourth

24. Drever, J. Letter to Burt, 31 May 1961.
25. Burt, C. L. *Brit. J. Math. Statist. Psychol.*, XXIV, 1971, 1–21.

edition of *Mental and Scholastic Tests* (1962), and his posthumously published *The Gifted Child* (1975)—none of these plans came to fruition. As was noted in the previous chapter, a revision of *The Factors of the Mind* was broached as early as 1947 and occupied Burt at intervals up to 1965, when it was abandoned. Another project, about which the publishers, Allen and Unwin, were very pressing, was for a third, revised, edition of *How the Mind Works*. This book, based on broadcast talks by Burt, Ernest Jones, Emanuel Miller, and William Moodie, was originally published in 1933, and a second, somewhat revised, edition appeared in 1945. Originally half the book was by Burt, and half by the three psychiatrists. In 1963 Allen and Unwin enquired of Burt, 'Have you been able to make any progress with the revised edition which was to consist only of your own material? It is still continually asked for.'[26] 'Can we make it worthwhile to give this book precedence over your many other jobs?' they asked a few weeks later.[27] The next year the publishers offered to provide an assistant to do some research. In 1967 Burt wrote saying that he had completed a first rough draft, but added that further drastic revisions were needed.[28] After that no more is heard of the venture.

Throughout the 1950s and 1960s Burt toyed with other projects which came to nothing. In 1956 the University of London Press wrote suggesting a book on 'The Meaning and Assessment of Intelligence'. The idea appealed to Burt, but appears never to have been taken up. Burt himself at one time hoped to write on the 'Psychology of Music', but he abandoned this project because of increasing deafness.[29] Four or five proposals for volumes of collected papers were discussed with publishers. In 1968 Burt sketched an outline plan for a collection of papers on individual differences, to be published by Penguin Books, including a new introductory chapter, the study of monozygotic twins (1966), social mobility (1961), class differences in intelligence (1959), the gifted child (1962), the factorial study of the emotions (1950), and formal training (1939). In 1969 Methuens approached Burt suggesting a collection of papers on intelligence and heredity, and finally in 1971 he wrote, 'I am supposed to be making two books suggested by the University Press out of collections of my papers. The papers overlap so much, and are so often out of date, that this

26. Letter from Allen and Unwin Ltd, 27 August 1963.
27. Letter from Allen and Unwin Ltd, 11 September 1963.
28. Burt, C. L. Letter to Allen and Unwin Ltd, 15 May 1967.
29. Burt, C. L. Letter to Mrs B. Warde, 13 January 1957.

VII *Cyril Burt and J. C. Flugel (left): on the way to Canada for the meeting of the British Association, July 1924*

VIII *The Burt family: on the occasion of Dr and Mrs Burt's Golden Wedding, July 1930*

XI *Cyril and Marion Burt: 1952. Taken on Primrose Hill by Cyril Burt's secretary, Miss Bruce*

XII *Cyril Burt: about 1960. In the London Zoo*

IX Cyril Burt:
aged 49

X Cyril Burt:
aged 64

XIII Cyril Burt: replying to the Stephanos *presentation, 19 October 1965*

*XIV Cyril Burt: aged 88. Taken by Professor A. R. Jensen in August 1971,
two months before Burt's death*

means re-writing them all. . . . The publishers seem most interested in "Mind and Consciousness".'[30]

The one project which was completed at the time of Burt's death
was *The Gifted Child*. An agreement for a book of approximately
300 pages was signed with the University of London Press on 11
August 1964. Burt originally envisaged a book 'similar to *The
Backward Child* in size and treatment'.[31] A book rather less than a
third the size of *The Backward Child* was eventually completed just
before Burt's death. It was published on 11 August 1975, exactly
eleven years after the original agreement had been signed.

Burt had always tended to be overambitious in the projects he let
himself in for, and there is a record of abandoned schemes from
quite early days. He contracted to write a 70,000–80,000 word book
on experimental psychology for Methuens in 1911; a 350-page book
on 'The Psychology of Individual Differences' for the Cambridge
University Press in 1912, and a book on 'The Mental and Physical
Welfare of the Child' for Staples in 1947. None of these saw the
light of day. Clearly there was always a tendency for Burt to take
on too much. In his retirement this tendency was accentuated,
partly because of 'bread and butter' commitments which he had to
undertake, partly because of the routines in which he got enmeshed,
and partly because he overtaxed his declining powers. This decline
he commented on as early as 1957 when working on the revision of
The Factors of the Mind: 'I find it increasingly difficult to sustain
attention to an abstract string of argumentation, and what used to
take me a couple of days now usually takes a week, and has to be
carefully revised because of the stupid little slips that creep in.'[32]
Five years later he again noted, 'My attention and reasoning powers
are deteriorating very markedly, so while I can write statistical
arguments without too many stupid slips I want to make the most
of my time, chiefly revising *Factors of the Mind* when I can get down
to it.'[33] A few months later he again commented on declining
powers: 'My mind certainly seems to be ageing. Three quarters of
an hour logical thinking is as much as I can do at one spell; and
especially if I am tired with walking. I can do very little in the
evening. What I write has to be checked and re-written many times
before it is fit for the printer. Most of the mistakes are quite
childish.'[34]

In assessing the achievements of Burt's final years allowances

30. Burt, C. L. Letter to Dr Marion Burt, 5 August 1971.
31. Burt, C. L. Letter to R. S. Reid, 3 December 1970.
32. Burt, C. L. Letter to Mrs B. Warde, 16 December 1957.
33. Burt, C. L. Letter to Dr Marion Burt, 2 July 1962.
34. Burt, C. L. Letter to Dr Marion Burt, 13 March 1963.

must be made not only for his declining powers, but for the conditions under which he was working, and for the loads, extraordinary for a man of his age, which he was attempting to carry. It is perhaps not surprising that many overambitious projects were not completed, and that some of his work was flawed. We must return to these matters later, but it is also important to give credit for what Burt did achieve in positive terms during these years of retirement. His bibliography, omitting popular articles and ephemera, but including a number of posthumous publications, lists some 200 titles in the twenty-one years of his retirement. This is an average of nearly ten articles, published lectures, or critical notices a year, or one about every five weeks. Roughly one-third of these were published in the statistical journal, the remaining two-thirds in a large variety of journals, compendia or pamphlets.

Apart from his articles on factor analysis and other statistical topics that were dealt with in the last chapter, his publications during this period can be classified under six main headings:

1. *General psychology and the history of psychology:* including articles on general psychology in symposia on scientific developments; contributions to the *Encyclopaedia Britannica*; a survey of British psychology during the first half of the twentieth century; an account of Hebrew psychology; and studies of particular psychologists, such as Galton, Binet, McDougall, together with a good many obituary notices of his contemporaries.

2. *Philosophical psychology and methodology:* including articles on mind and consciousness; the psychology of value; the sense-datum theory; aesthetics; scientific method; the principle of indeterminacy; the field concept, etc.

3. *Intelligence, giftedness, and the inheritance of ability:* including his important articles on quantitative genetics; monozygotic twins; social mobility; the distribution of intelligence, as well as several items on gifted children.

4. *Educational problems and educational psychology:* including educational guidance, selection and streaming; educational standards; problems of reading and backwardness.

5. *Parapsychology:* a topic in which Burt became increasingly interested in his later years: apart from his Myers lecture, noted above, his principal papers have been collected together by Anita Gregory in a volume entitled *E.S.P. and Psychology* (1975).

6. *Typography:* including a monograph, *A Psychological Study of*

Typography (1959), and several articles on typography generally, and on the typography of children's books in particular.

The contents of these various groups of articles have been, or will be, more fully examined elsewhere in this book. For a man between the ages of 68 and 88 it is an impressive, and indeed astonishing, volume of work, even more so when other pressures and various medical disabilities, which will also be discussed later, are taken into account. But we have not yet considered all that was involved in Burt's daily routine during these years. In addition to lectures, articles, editing, the assessment of manuscripts, examinations and committees, there was also his huge correspondence—letters from his family, friends, admirers, fellow psychologists, critics, opponents, people asking for help and advice, cranks and criminals—to most of whom he answered promptly, and often at considerable length. Burt must have been one of the most assiduous and remarkable letter-writers of his time!

V

For Burt, particularly during his years of retirement, letter writing was an extremely important channel of communication. He was not a social man, and shunned most of the social contacts and relaxations that the average individual enjoys. He had a few regular, and a sprinkling of occasional, visitors to his flat. But he had very few close friends, and, apart from his sister in Malvern, no immediate family. What he did have was an enormous circle of professional contacts, and a large body of admirers, and with these he kept in touch mainly through correspondence. At a rough estimate he would write something approaching 1500 letters a year. A great many of these would be in his own beautifully legible handwriting, and no copies would be kept. Important letters were typed, and copies filed. From 1958 onwards the files are systematic and full. Burt was a fluent letter writer, and many of his letters were of extraordinary length, at times amounting to a dozen, or even twenty, pages. The time he devoted to correspondence must have been prodigious.

Two sets of letters stand apart because of their regularity and volume—his letters to his sister, Dr Marion Burt, and his letters to his friend, Mrs Beatrice Warde. It is unusual for a brother and sister to correspond as fully and frequently as Burt and his sister, and even more unusual for the correspondence to cover so wide a range of topics.[35] Not only did Burt provide a running commentary on his activities and his state of health, but there were besides many discussions on matters theological, cultural, and scientific. It was almost as though Burt was engaging in a process of continuing education in all those areas in which his knowledge was so extraordinary. Thus in answer to a query about Hipparchus and Ptolemy he would think nothing of sending back four pages of detailed information about these ancient astronomers; or on another occasion, he would discuss the decline of theological scholarship among the Anglicans (there was no one to approach Lightfoot, Westcott, Sanday or Streeter, and the best seemed to be among the Wesleyans and Presbyterians); or, when replying to comments on a portrait of Nefertiti, he would discuss how Egyptian hieroglyphics were translated: or again explain the difference between the chemical structure of Penicillin and Cephalosporinin (the side chains were similar, but one had a hexagonal and the other a pentagonal nucleus). The correspondence is of particular value for the information it provides on Burt's psychosomatic condition. He was intensely interested in matters of health, and his sister, being a medical practitioner, was someone with whom he could discuss his and her symptoms. It also provides a good deal of detailed information about his attitudes and interests.

The correspondence with Mrs Beatrice Warde, during the years in which it continued, almost reached the region of the fantastic. It began in October 1954, and ended with Mrs Warde's death in September 1969. Unfortunately, comparatively few of Burt's letters to Mrs Warde have been preserved—only the copies of typed letters, mainly concerned with the statistical journal. On the other hand, all, or nearly all, of Mrs Warde's letters to Burt, running into thousands, are extant, and give some idea of their relationship. How many letters Burt wrote in reply it is impossible to say precisely; but, as he was conscientious in answering mail, they also, though not so numerous, must have reached the thousand mark.

Beatrice Warde was born in New York, the daughter of the American writer, May Lamberton Becker, and Gustav Becker, composer and music teacher. After graduating at Barnard College she obtained a post in the typographic library of The American Type Founders Company. In 1925 she came to Europe with her husband, Frederic Warde, a typographical designer, from whom she separated more than ten years before his death in 1939. Settling in England Mrs Warde joined the Monotype Corporation as editor

35. Though a good many of Burt's letters to his sister have been preserved from 1940 onwards, and some from earlier years, Dr Marion Burt destroyed all her own letters to her brother soon after his death.

of *The Monotype Recorder*. There, together with Stanley Morison, she did much to establish the reputation of the Corporation as a leader in the field of typography. She travelled extensively in its interests, not only throughout Great Britain, but throughout the English-speaking world. *The Times* obituary described her as having 'a personality that combined intelligence, energy and generosity in rare degree'. Her famous 'Credo', which begins 'This is a printing office, crossroads of civilization . . .', still hangs in many printing offices all over the world.

The correspondence began when Burt wrote to Mrs Warde, then unknown to him personally, on 16 October 1954 as follows:

Dear Mrs Warde,

I wonder whether I might ask your advice regarding suitable monotype faces for a journal which I edit for the British Psychological Society (specimen enclosed)? I was encouraged to do so by the Librarian at the St Bride's Institute, who, I fancy, approached you with one or two questions on my behalf two or three weeks ago.

When the journal was first started in 1947 we selected Times Roman, and, to save paper and fit the requirements of offprints, were advised that the type should be set solid, and that free use of 8-point type should be made in the text. Now that we are getting away from wartime conditions, I think that we might aim at a more attractive page, with type more freely leaded, and the smallest type-face reserved solely for footnotes.

For financial reasons we are forced to change our printer, and we thought we might take the opportunity of reconsidering the general style of printing.

Of the three type-faces recommended by the Royal Society for mathematical work, I myself prefer Imprint. But perhaps that is merely because the Oxford University Press was able to produce an attractive looking volume for me in this type (it did not contain any mathematical formulae). I believe, however, that, owing to recent developments, the cheapest method of printing higher mathematical works is in Modern Series 7. This appears to have been increasingly used for mathematical work; and the recent book on *The Printing of Mathematics* is set in this type.

Although I think most of us who belong to an older generation have what we consider to be mild aesthetic prejudices against the so-called Modern faces, possibly we should be well advised to change to this type-face.

If it is not trespassing too much on your time and kindness, my colleagues and I would be very grateful to have your advice.

Yours sincerely,

Cyril Burt

So it began. Burt had been, of course, for a long time interested in typography, and in 1954 returned once again to an intensive study of the matter from a psychological standpoint, the first-fruits of which were his article, 'A Psychological Study of Typography', in the statistical journal.[36] So there was common ground from the start between him and Mrs Warde. But they soon found that they had much more in common than typography. Mrs Warde was deeply interested in history, culture and language. She described herself as 'a sophisticated, Europeanised, papistical worldling'. She had indeed a remarkably lively mind, and a warm, extroverted temperament. An enthusiastic convert to Catholicism, she at the same time displayed a keen, though perhaps somewhat prejudiced, interest in scientific developments, subscribing regularly to *The Scientific American*, and passing on her copies to Burt. So the correspondence soon began to range very widely; Mrs Warde effervescent and full of enthusiasms; Burt stimulated to pour out in his more matter of fact way his immense fund of knowledge, writing for example about the history of Gregorian chants, explaining what 'bits' meant in information theory, discussing the translations of the Bible, and including passing comments on himself, his work and other psychologists. The correspondence remained in some ways strangely formal. They never got on to first name terms. Burt always began his letter 'Dear Mrs Warde . . .' and ended 'Yours very sincerely . . .': while to Mrs Warde he was 'Dear Professor . . .' or 'Dear Sir Cyril. . . .' Nevertheless it became an important ingredient in both their lives. 'I look with greater favour on this humming, practical life of mine, because you find it amusing', she wrote to Burt.[37] Before she retired from The Monotype Corporation in 1960 Mrs Warde was continually on the move. Wherever she went she wrote to Burt—from hotels, planes, ships, trains— often daily, sometimes even twice a day. 'I have never once in the past five years, never once, come back to my hotel after an out-of-town lecture or speech without starting a letter to you before I put the light out.' So letters poured in to 9 Elsworthy Road, from all over the country and the world. Whenever there was a fixed address to write to, Burt replied, and Mrs Warde thanked him for his 'wonderful letters'. 'My gratitude for what you do and *are* wells up

36. Burt, C. L. *Brit. J. Statist. Psychol.*, *VIII*, 1955, 29–57.
37. A great many of Mrs Warde's letters are not fully and properly dated.

in such measure as to go straight to God in thanksgiving.' Her letters were replete with flattery, no doubt entirely sincere. 'How different you are from the typical academical: how much richer in mind, broader in background, more generous in spirit.' 'The thought of your wisdom and kindness kept me from just throwing the whole human race overboard—you are the daimon in that midden.' Though Burt seems to have preserved an amused detachment in the face of this barrage, there are reasons to think that it meant a great deal to him. It gave him a window on the world; it saved him from emotional loneliness; and it no doubt fortified his ego, often beleaguered by critics and suspicious colleagues. In addition there were more tangible spin-offs; substantial financial subventions to help the statistical journal (some paid to the society, some to Burt personally to cover offprints, promotional literature, etc.); the loan of a Grundig tape-recorder; and introductions to some of her friends such as Mrs Rosalind Heywood, the psychic researcher, and Dr Buros of the *Mental Measurements Yearbook*. Mrs Warde became a not-infrequent visitor to Elsworthy Road, sometimes just for tea ('It was strange and wonderful', she wrote, 'to have had that enjoyable hour of tea, and wondering about religion at Elsworthy Road in company with one of my principal Idols in this world'), sometimes for an evening ('It was very nice', wrote Burt, 'to spend the evening in pleasant conversation instead of grinding away at my desk over these tedious papers for journals, books and other authorities who demand long written reports.'). It was a sad loss to Burt when Mrs Warde collapsed and died suddenly at her home in Epsom on the night of 14 September 1969. On her writing table was found a half-finished letter to her 'Dear Professor'.

To no other correspondents was there the same ceaseless stream of communications as to his sister and to Mrs Warde. The rest of the world, however, was by no means neglected! And the sample of those who received his letters was a wide one, ranging from the eminent to the distressed and rejected. Julian Huxley discussed with him the number of gifted persons in the population, and Marghanita Laski the heredity of men of genius; Sir Peter Medawar wrote thanking Burt for his comments on his Reith lectures, and stating, 'I do hope that the case for a substantial inborn element in intellectual ability is now won and over'[38] (a statement which contrasts rather conspicuously with his letter to *The Times* in 1976, 'The expression innate intelligence should henceforth be dropped from the language'[39]). An interesting set of letters were the letters Burt exchanged with Arthur Koestler from 1963 onwards. Burt, having

38. Letter from Sir Peter Medawar, 3 November 1960.
39. *The Times*, 3 November 1976.

critically read and commented on the manuscript, wrote a Preface
to Koestler's *Act of Creation* (1964), and then Koestler contributed
a chapter to *Stephanos* (1965). This led to a correspondence on creativity, laughter, behaviourism and related topics. Koestler visited
Elsworthy Road and talked to Burt. There was an obvious sympathy
between them in their mutual rejection of 'reductionism'. Many
people wrote to ask for comments and advice, and were grateful for
the help they received. Thus Michael Young of the Institute of Community Studies asked for comments on his paper on social mobility,
and replied 'Thank you very much again for your helpful comments.
You really are amazingly helpful to beginners.'[40] He was constantly
advising psychologists, psychiatrists and others on statistical problems, methodology or the presentation of material. Professor Warburton of Manchester sent him some queries on partial correlation:
Burt responded with a highly technical and penetrating reply extending over seven pages.[41] Later Warburton passed on to Burt his draft
report on the Initial Teaching Alphabet, and when he received Burt's
comments wrote 'I find it difficult to express my gratitude for the
tremendous amount of trouble you have taken in correcting this bulky
report.'[42] In 1969 Dr Guntrip of Leeds sent Burt the draft of his book
on 'The Self', and received back an eighteen-page letter of comments.
Also in 1969 Burt and Dr Wason of University College exchanged a
highly interesting set of letters on reasoning. It would take pages to
list all those with whom Burt corresponded, and all the topics he
discussed in his letters.

He was lavish in his help and advice, and many, besides the
eminent, benefited. Some of those who wrote to him were total
strangers; some were people in trouble. With one prison inmate he
corresponded for many years. 'You were the guide-post to my new
life', he told Burt, 'for your letters and friendship killed the
bitterness I had towards society and mankind.' Parents with problem
children; lonely spinsters frustrated through having to care for
senile and difficult parents; bright Mensa members who felt they
were not realising their potential; psychiatric patients doubtful
about the treatment they were receiving; students in difficulties
with their researches; school children with projects—all these, and
more, would write to him, and to all he would generously respond.

The generosity and kindness expressed in these letters reflected one
side of Burt's character, perhaps the dominant side; other letters
reflected his less admirable qualities, his cantankerousness and a certain deviousness. He was extremely sensitive to those who in any way

40. Letter from Michael Young, July 1961.
41. Letter from C. L. Burt, July 1969.
42. Letter from F. W. Warburton, 5 May 1968.

seemed to challenge his authority in his own areas of competence, and promptly jumped in to the attack. To take an example: In March 1963 Burt read Dr. J. McLeish's *The Science of Behaviour*. McLeish's remarks on intelligence and intelligence testing, written from a left-wing standpoint, provoked Burt, and he immediately counter-attacked. The letter of six closely typed foolscap pages (roughly 4,000 words) setting out his objections began as follows: 'Dear Dr McLeish, I obtained your book, *The Science of Behaviour*, as soon as it appeared, and found it most interesting. I shall no doubt be asked to write a review or critical notice of it for one of the society's journals in the near future, but before I discuss it in public, I should, merely as a matter of courtesy, like to make sure that I do not misinterpret your meaning.' Then followed six pages of detailed criticism, which, as Burt had not in fact been asked to review the book, really constituted a gratuitous attack. The letter ends, rather characteristically, with apologies for the 'excessive bluntness as well as the excessive length' with which Burt has made his points. This led to an exchange of letters, in which as was usually the case in the controversies in which Burt took part, no one seemed satisfied, because of 'misunderstandings' and 'communication gaps'.[43]

Liam Hudson found exactly the same thing when Burt upbraided him for his review in *New Society* of Serebriakoff's Mensa history. Burt and Hudson had from time to time corresponded before on other matters, and following Burt's letter on the Mensa review Hudson wrote in some exasperation:

What strikes me so forcibly about our correspondence, and what has worried me increasingly over the last four or five years, is the difficulty we psychologists experience in communicating our ideas to each other. I find myself in the odd and distressing position of being at sixes and sevens with yourself— a man whose work I greatly admire, and with whom I believe I agree not only on all matters of psychological principle, but in nearly all technical details as well. All that I can detect between our respective positions are a few niceties of technique and a few nuances of sympathy. And yet the misapprehensions obvious in our correspondence would give the impression that we occupy positions of polar opposition. . . . In conclusion might I chide you for your latest letter to *New Society*. . . . The first sentence of your second paragraph is a frightful misrepresentation of my view. . . . You do me the honour of quoting my article directly in five places, and on every occasion you get me wrong! This strengthens my feeling that you have tended to view my work as

43. Correspondence between C. L. Burt and J. McLeish, March–April 1963.

unworthy of your detailed attention. One mistake in a direct quote is of course a scholar's licence—but five out of five does suggest a certain disregard.[44]

In controversies of this kind Burt could be both slippery and unscrupulous. He would misrepresent his opponents and blur the issues. Beneath a polite exterior and apparent reasonableness was a steely determination to get the better of the argument, and to humiliate his opponents. Into these controversies he was prepared to throw much effort, and, in the last decade of his life, as his views became increasingly unpopular, more and more of his time was absorbed by them.

In the huge flow of his correspondence, which continued unabated until a couple of weeks before his death, the different facets of Burt's complex personality are well reflected.

VI

There were few breaks in the busy routine of Burt's life from the time of his retirement in 1950 to the day of his death in October 1971. Before his final hospitalisation he had two earlier spells in hospital, for a broken ankle in 1960, and a prostatectomy in 1967. These were his only real cessations from activity. His annual holidays in July or August were never complete breaks; he had reading to do, and sometimes writing as well. His recreations tended to be intellectual ones, and to be seriously pursued.

He read very widely throughout his life, and it was his practice to make full and careful summaries of any book that really interested him. The range of his reading was astonishing, embracing philosophy, theology, science, history, biography, literature, musicology, and, of course, psychology and the biological sciences closely related to it. With all his other commitments it is incredible that he managed to get through so much as well as keep his eye on the periodical literature. He was a regular reader of *The Times, The Times Literary* and *Educational Supplements, Nature, The Scientific American, The New Scientist,* and other periodicals. He was discriminating in what he read, preferring the experts to the popularisers. Among the philosophers he read Ayer, Braithwaite, Polanyi, Popper, Russell, Ryle and Wittgenstein—a remarkable list for one educated at Oxford in the hey-day of Oxford idealism. He was enormously interested in the progress of both the physical and the biological sciences—in cosmology, quantum theory, molecular

44. Letter from Liam Hudson, 24 February 1966.

biology and neurophysiology. He kept abreast, too, of the technological background of science. He not only read about computers,
but in 1955 went to see the computer at J. Lyons and Co. when
computers were still a novelty. He studied Scott on transistors,
Hallows on television, and Sutton on rocketry. In a different sphere
he kept abreast of the discoveries of the archaeologists. He read
Woolley on Abraham, Glanville on life in Ancient Egypt, and
Child on the Aryans. Equally he maintained a lively interest in
events of the recent past. He read Churchill, the Jenkins biography
of Asquith, and Bullock's Hitler. He was constantly looking back
at the classics of the past. In 1963 he made a detailed summary of
Newton's *Principia*; he studied Galileo's works in the original Latin
or Italian. When relaxing he would browse in a Shakespeare play or
a detective novel.

There were three areas in which Burt retained a very special
interest—astronomy, theology and music. He was a keen amateur
astronomer, not only keeping abreast of the technical literature, but
observing the heavens himself. He read Hoyle, Spencer Jones,
Lovell and Gamov, and also more specialised books like Stetson's
Sunspots and their Effects. He had his own little telescope (a 2½-
inch instrument) with which he would star-gaze. In 1957 he
compiled a star map of his own; in 1959 he made a special effort to
see the occultation of Regulus by Venus; and in 1961 he made
observations on Mercury. In 1965 (at the age of 82) he got up at
4.30 a.m. to observe a comet. He studied the Nautical Almanac,
and noted the movements of Jupiter's major satellites. In January
1971, just before his 88th birthday, he rose before breakfast to see
Venus, Jupiter and Mars together in the dawn sky. He was
fascinated by space exploration, and the latest advances of cosmo-
logical theory.

In theology Burt had been interested from his early days. In 1963
in answer to a questionnaire on religious belief and mystical
experience he summarised his religious position as follows:

I should prefer to say 'Metaphysical Monotheist'. But if this fits
in with none of your categories, the best labels would be
'Christian' (where 'Christ' = 'Messiah' = Isaiah's 'suffering servant' = Jesus, NOT the pre-existent Christ of Paul and the Fourth
Gospel, much less the second 'person' of the 4th century creeds);
and as regards denomination 'Liberal Anglican'. So far as theology
is concerned I ought to be called a Unitarian (though I have
little sympathy for their writings, and have never attended their
places of worship). As regards the critical problems (historical
accuracy, message of Jesus, *Formgeschichte*, eschatology, etc. I

have been most influenced by continental writers (Strauss, Harnack, Bultmann) though I believe they carry scepticism too far. The views of Manson, Vincent Taylor and Canon Lightfoot seem a better compromise. Many very advanced Anglicans, who have been influenced by higher criticism and their knowledge of Church history seem to me to be in effect Unitarians (Dean Inge, Bishop Barnes, etc), and I certainly think the Anglican Book of Common Prayer the best existing form of communal worship (provided one treats the creeds as thoroughly dated).[45]

Burt, though not a frequent churchgoer, showed a profound intellectual interest in religious history and theology. He became quite proficient at Hebrew, and his theological reading was extensive and serious. He made ten pages of detailed notes on Wand's *The Four Great Heresies*. He studied Narborough's *Epistle to the Hebrews* and Moule's *Epistle to the Colossians*. He read Ryle on *Genesis*, Burrows on *Gnosticism*, and Otto on *The Idea of the Holy*, to name but a few. Among his papers are notes on eastern and other religions, and the draft of a book to be called 'The Pros and Cons of a Religious Metaphysic'. Theologising was in fact one of his recreations. 'By way of giving myself a real holiday last Easter I spent a lot of time getting down on to paper all the ancient, modern, and hitherto uninvented arguments for the existence of the Deity that I could think of, and then tried to work them out as though they were problems in the calculus of probability. I found that all the arguments taken by themselves were rather weak—usually a little over 50 pro as compared with rather less than 50 contra; but the cumulative result of the whole collection became quite impressive.'[46]

The third area in which Burt showed a special interest was music. This again was a long-standing love going back to his schooldays. He was a competent pianist and organist, dabbled in musical composition, and, as was usual with Burt, engaged in serious musicological studies. He had a detailed knowledge of Wagner's operas; made a minute analysis of some of Beethoven's symphonies; and was planning a book on the psychology of music when deafness intervened. His deafness, indeed, was a heavy tribulation, as it debarred him eventually from one of his few real recreations, playing the piano. He continued to listen to broadcast concerts as long as possible, but in the end he had to fall back on reading scores, which he could do with some facility. 'When I read the score of Bruch's G Minor Concerto and hear in my mind's ear the solo melody of

45. Burt, C. L. Letter to Basil Smith, 9 September 1963.
46. Burt, C. L. Letter to Mrs Warde, 11 October 1956.

the Adagio, I doubt if any hedonic tone attaches to the *sound* of my mental violin, and yet I enjoy the music almost as much as if I were listening to it at the Festival Hall.'[47]

It was fortunate for Burt that the companion of his retirement years, Miss Archer, shared his three main interests and saved him from loneliness; for visitors to Elsworthy Road were not numerous. About the only regular visitor was Dr Charlotte Banks, one of his former assistants at University College. She was faithful and constant in her attendance, usually coming in for tea on Saturday afternoons. Burt looked forward to these occasions, and when she did not turn up notes the fact in his diary. She would sometimes join in Christmas festivities at Elsworthy Road, too. Before his death in 1964, Professor C. W. Valentine, one of Burt's oldest friends from Würzburg days, would visit occasionally; but as both men aged, contacts became less frequent. Other psychologists would turn up at times to discuss special problems, including a number of visitors from abroad—Hotelling, the factorist, for example, and Jensen. Jensen was among his last visitors. 'Next week', Burt wrote to his sister in the August before his death, 'the notorious Professor Jensen is again coming to tea. He's excellent!'[48] Jensen had visited him the year before, and Burt then wrote, 'Jensen keeps me pretty busy. He is coming again to-night with sheets of correlations and factor analysis.'[49] Visitors, however, were not so very frequent, and, judging from Burt's engagement diaries, weeks would sometimes go by with no callers other than Charlotte Banks.

Burt himself got out for short strolls whenever he could. His flat was favourably situated on the edge of Primrose Hill, a pleasant open space with trees and a low slope rising to 219 feet and giving views over London, as well as access on the far side to the more extensive area of Regents Park with its floral and zoological gardens. So when the weather was fine it was easy for Burt to stroll out, and, if he felt like it, walk for a couple of miles in attractive surroundings. He kept up this practice of exercise to the very last. His last recorded walk was on 16 September 1971, when he walked to the nearest seat, but noted in his diary 'could hardly walk last lap'. In earlier years he would also enjoy visiting museums and galleries. Sometimes he had a serious purpose, as, for example, when he visited the genetics exhibits at the Natural History Museum; at other times he went purely for enjoyment, to the Tate Gallery, Wallace Collection, or Victoria and Albert Museum.

47. Burt, C. L. The psychology of value. *Brit. J. Statist. Psychol., XVI*, 1963, 59–104.
48. Burt, C. L. Letter to Dr Marion Burt, 5 August 1971.
49. Burt, C. L. Letter to Dr Marion Burt, 11 August 1970.

In the summer Burt escapted from London, usually for three or four weeks, to enjoy a short holiday. Before the war he had been fond of continental travel, but he never went abroad after the 1930s mainly because his Ménière troubles made him nervous of going far afield. In the 1950s and in the 1960s, up to 1968, he spent his summer vacations in Malvern, where his parents had retired and where his sister continued to live. He enjoyed walking on the Malvern hills, and it was while doing this that he fell and broke his ankle in 1960. After a period in a nursing home he made a good recovery, and, though thereafter he had to be careful, he resumed his walking on subsequent visits. The last Malvern visit took place in 1968. For the three remaining years of his life his holidays were spent on the south coast at Bognor Regis. His last holiday was in June–July, 1971. On his return he wrote to his sister, 'Our three weeks at Bognor are over, and we returned yesterday afternoon . . . we had wonderful weather and could get out both morning and afternoon every day . . . most of the time it was too hot to think of sitting in motor cars. However, on Tuesday we drove to Chichester to see the Cathedral again, and then on to a little village called Bosham.'[50]

Shortly after he got home Burt was complaining of stomach pains. These came and went. By the end of August Miss Archer noticed signs of jaundice. His doctor visited him on August 30th, and again on August 31st when he took blood tests. On September 7th a consultant was called in, and it was suggested that the trouble might be gallstones. Burt kept on walking and taking gentle exercise, but he complained of fatigue and drowsiness. He managed to complete his Thorndike lecture on 'The Inheritance of General Intelligence' on August 21st, and then concentrated on completing the manuscript of *The Gifted Child*. On September 27th he was advised to go into hospital for further observation. There his condition deteriorated fairly rapidly, and he died on 10 October 1971 at the age of 88 years and 7 months. The cause of death was cancer of the liver.

50. Burt, C. L. Letter to Dr Marion Burt, 17 July 1971.

CHAPTER ELEVEN

Subsidiary Interests

Before we pass on to consider some of the controversies that arose after Burt's death, and to attempt an assessment of his life and work, we must pause briefly to deal with a number of subsidiary topics in which he displayed long-continuing interest, and to which he made significant contributions. Three areas in particular absorbed a considerable amount of his time and energy, namely, the psychological study of typography, and psychology of aesthetics, and parapsychology or psychical research.

I

Burt's interest in typography went back to pre-First World War days, and arose as a result of discussions then being held about the printing of school books. School medical officers, whose appointment had become a statutory requirement in 1907, soon began to suspect that the poor printing of many school texts severely handicapped children with poor eyesight, and aggravated their already defective vision. In 1912 the education section of the British Association set up a special committee to study the problem, and reports were included in the proceedings of the Association for the years 1913 to 1917. Burt was interested in these discussions from the beginning, and as soon as he got to London it was one of the matters he took up. In his first annual report he wrote, 'At the request of the Committee the influence of the spacing adopted in reading books upon the accuracy and fluency of reading was investigated by the medical research officer and the psychologist. 127 children, of varying ages and from various schools, were tested individually upon four different occasions with pages printed in four different fashions, differing either in type or in spacing. It was found that within certain definite limits, and for all but the youngest and poorest readers, differences in spacing had little or no influence compared with other factors.'[1] The medical research officer referred to was Dr James Kerr, an unconventional and dynamic character,

1. L.C.C. Report of the Council's Psychologist, February 1915, p. 4.

who in 1907 had been transferred from the post of school medical officer to that of 'consulting medical officer', and had become chiefly concerned with special inquiries and research. He was progressive in his views, a member of the Fabian Society, and, among other things, a competent statistician. He was one of the few medicals with whom Burt got on well. In the investigation of children's reading material Dr Kerr dealt with the clinical aspects, and Burt undertook a series of experiments in the classroom and the laboratory. The results of the inquiry were communicated to the British Association committee, and included a tabulated set of standards showing the size of type and the style of printing suited to pupils of different ages. Older type-faces, such as Caslon, were preferred to the more modern types, which children often found confusing. Sans-serif type, in particular, was shown to be less easy for them to read. The committee's recommendations carried considerable weight with the publishers of school books.

So Burt was early introduced to the arcana of typography. The whole topic was one that fascinated him. It seemed to provide a focus for his many-sided interests. He became absorbed in the history of printing and its aesthetics; in the subtle differences between type-faces and their effect on legibility; and in the applicability of experimental designs and psychophysical methods to the solution of some of the practical questions that arose. He became an expert in typography who could hold his own with the leaders in the field, and who was looked up to with respect by people such as Stanley Morison and Mrs Beatrice Warde of the Monotype Corporation. He was, however, too busy with other things to take the question up again until after the Second World War.

It was not until his final years at University College that Burt actively returned to the study of typography. The stimulus for his renewed interest was the proposal to launch the statistical journal. Soon after the plan had been put forward Burt, with the help of some of his students, began a series of preliminary investigations on legibility and on the typographical preferences of educated adults, and he took up again, with more sophisticated methodology, his earlier experiments on school children. He came to regard the problem as basically a problem of communication— in this case communication by means of visible symbols— and hence as falling under the general aegis of communication theory. 'Analogous to the audible "noise" which interferes with the accurate transmission of audible information, there is a visuo-mental interference or "blur" which impedes the accurate transmission of visible infor-

mation.'[2] He suggested that a symbol-to-blur ratio might correspond to the communication theorists' signal-to-noise ratio. His
own experiments, which he went on to describe, he regarded as
only a very tentative beginning in the experimental study of
typography. The comparative crudity of psychological measurement did not justify very refined analysis of the results. Two factors
were clearly involved in typographical preferences, the legibility
factor and the aesthetic factor. Legibility, according to Burt, was
itself 'the resultant of many different factors— the size, the form, the
thickness or boldness of the letters, the width of the line, the
distance between successive lines, the texture of the paper, and the
intrinsic interest of the subject matter itself.'[3] But that was not all,
and Burt added that 'printed material proves more legible, and
reading becomes quicker and more accessible, when the material is
set in a type which the reader finds, often without realising it,
aesthetically attractive'.[4] In his experiments Burt investigated all
the variables involved and their interactions, using Fisher's Latin
square design. The investigations, though only of a pilot nature, led
to a number of publications; his article in the statistical journal, his
Cambridge University Press monograph, and his contribution to
the 1960 Year Book of Education on 'The Typography of Children's
Books'.[5] The combination of erudition, methodological sophistication and practicality which Burt's work in this area displayed
brought it well-merited acclaim. It was among his best and least
controversial pieces of work, as well as being one of the few strictly
experimental investigations that he carried out.

II

If Burt's interest in typography went back to the time of the First
World War, his interest in aesthetics went back even further.
According to his autobiographical sketch[6] his first talk to the Delian
Society in Oxford was on the psychology of aesthetics. His interest
was enhanced during his stay in Würzburg in 1908 by his contacts

2. Burt, C. L. The psychological study of typography. *Brit. J. Statist. Psychol.*,
VIII, 1955, 29–57.

3. *Ibid.*, p. 32.

4. Burt, C. L. The Printing of Children's Books. *Year Book of Education*, 1960,
p. 255.

5. Burt, C. L. A psychological study of typography. *Brit. J. Statist. Psychol.*,
VIII, 1955, 29–57; *A Psychological Study of Typography*, 1959; *Year Book of
Education*, 1960, p. 225.

6. Burt, C. L. In Murchison, C. (ed.) *History of Psychology in Autobiography*,
IV, 1952, p. 60.

with Külpe, who, he had noted in one of his letters, was 'great on the psychology of aesthetics'.[7] It was kept alive by his friendship with Valentine, whose first book on *The Experimental Psychology of Beauty* appeared in 1913, and whom Burt assisted half a century later in the preparation of the enlarged book with the same title that was published in 1962. Burt himself had considerable artistic gifts; he could draw quite well, and he was, as we have seen, a very competent and erudite musician. His knowledge in all the arts went far beyond that of the usual amateur, and his powers of artistic appreciation were analytic and acute. This comes out particularly in some of his letters.

> Those who write books on 'How to look at Pictures' insist that you must spend time over pictures. They will usually tell you that the best painters do not intend their pictures to be hung in galleries where the spectator merely gives a single glance and passes on. There are plenty of painters who insisted on exhibiting only one picture at a time and expected you to remain in the gallery at least a quarter of an hour. If I go to the Orangery in Paris to enjoy Monet's 'Water Lilies' I spend far longer there than I should if I dropped in to listen to a symphony at the Queen's Hall.[8]

And again with regard to music, he wrote:

> I have noticed frequently when following orchestral music on scores that my attention is directed by the score to something that I had never noticed before; e.g. in the Overture to the Meistersingers the way in which three tunes are given simultaneously on the last three or four pages, or again how the apprentices' motive on the flutes is made to accompany the repeated tonic chords during the last few bars. I find it quite amusing to watch one instrument, e.g. the drum, solely through a particular movement that I have heard twenty times before. It seems clear that the composer could not possibly have expected anyone to appreciate all the points of the music at first hearing, but he exercised his ingenuity so that each time you come back to his music your attention would still find something new to feast on.[9]

Burt also, of course, had read widely in the literature of several

7. Burt, C. L. Letter to his sister, 27 July 1908.
8. Burt, C. L. Letter to J. B. Parry, 28 April 1939.
9. Burt, C. L. Letter to J. B. Parry, 28 April 1939.

languages (Greek, Latin, Hebrew, French, German and Italian, as well as English), and was familiar with writings on aesthetics and Western cultural history from the time of Plato and Aristotle onwards. He was indeed magnificently equipped to make an outstanding contribution to the psychology of aesthetics, and it is unfortunate that his work in this field hardly went beyond pilot investigations, encouragement to students, and a number of incomplete sketches. Burt was often annoyingly and inexplicably casual in publishing the results of his own researches, and details had to be extracted from him almost forcibly by enquirers. In the case of his aesthetic experiments the brief published accounts given by Burt himself have to be supplemented by reference in Cattell, Bulley and Valentine, by articles and theses by his students, and by comments in his unpublished correspondence.[10] Had he focused his energies in this area with greater concentration he could certainly have written a better book than his friend Valentine. As it was, his promise and potential were never realised.

His own experiments in aesthetics began in Liverpool, where he first met Margaret Bulley, with whom he later collaborated in London under the auspices of the B.B.C. No details of these early experiments were published. When he got to London Burt became interested in the drawing ability of school children, and in the testing of artistic ability for purposes of vocational guidance. His study of children's drawings resulted in his discussion of the development of artistic talent, and his scale of children's drawings, which were both included in *Mental and Scholastic Tests* (1921). His work on artistic ability in connection with vocational guidance was undertaken when he was working at the National Institute of Industrial Psychology, but was not included in the Industrial Fatigue Research Board report on vocational guidance.[11] It involved a factorial analysis of artistic ability, and is briefly referred to in Burt's 1949 article on 'The Structure of the Mind', where he wrote:

For purposes of both educational and vocational guidance it proved necessary to determine, so far as possible, what is the precise psychological nature of the abilities that are ordinarily called 'aesthetic' or 'artistic' and to measure such abilities if they exist. So far as I am aware, the earliest factorial studies were those undertaken in 1919 with the assistance of the staff and students at

10. Cattell, R. B. *A Guide to Mental Testing*, 1936, p. 52; Bulley, Margaret. *Have you Good Taste?*, 1933; Valentine, C. W. *Experimental Psychology of Beauty*, 1962.
11. Industrial Fatigue Research Board. Report No. 33. *A Study in Vocational Guidance*, H.M.S.O., 1926.

the St Martin's School of Art, and continued at other schools of art maintained by the L.C.C. The tests we employed were mainly pictorial (ranking picture postcard reproductions), but tests of poetical and musical appreciation, and of skill in imaginative sketching and painting were also included. The testing and the analyses were undertaken jointly with Miss V. G. Pelling, at that time my assistant in the vocational guidance department of the N.I.I.P.[12]

As a result of the enquiries Burt began to postulate a 'general factor for artistic ability' common to the three major arts, painting, music and poetry. As Valentine notes, 'the only evidence of a common factor in the appreciation of all the three arts . . . is that provided by the work of Burt and Pelling'. In response to Valentine's request Burt produced some further details as to the methodology and the results of these tests, and they are given in Valentine's book.[13] They were never written up by Burt himself.

At the London Day Training College several of Burt's students dabbled in aesthetics, but it was not until he had moved to University College that work of a more serious kind was undertaken. During the 1930s he collaborated with his former Liverpool acquaintance, Margaret Bulley, in experiments sponsored by the B.B.C.; he carried out the experiments with pictures briefly described in *How the Mind Works* (1933); and he encouraged a number of his ablest postgraduate students, including H. J. Eysenck and J. B. Parry, to work in the field of aesthetics, as well as introducing seminars on aesthetics into his teaching programme.

The B.B.C. enquiry involved only nine artistic judgments of paired objects, which were illustrated in *The Listener* (pairs of chairs, bookcases, wine glasses, jewellery, coffee pots, two-handled jars, teapots, voiles and embroidery). However, some 6,000 replies were received. The responses were compared with the judgments of six leading art experts, who were practically in entire agreement as to the better of each pair. There was a very high level of concordance between the judgments of these experts and those of the general public. Miss Bulley discussed the experiment in her book *Have you Good Taste?* (1933), to which Burt provided a statistical appendix. He was later to cite these results in support of his belief in the objectivity of values. 'In all our tests', he observed, 'the minor differences between individuals were entirely swamped

12. Burt, C. L. The structure of the mind. *Brit. J. Educ. Psychol., XIX*, 1949, 194.

13. Valentine, C. W. *The Experimental Psychology of Beauty*, 1962, p. 421.

by the general agreement',[14] which suggested to him that values were objectively real.

The experiments mentioned in *How the Mind Works*[15] involved a series of fifty picture postcards, some by classical masters, some by second-rate artists, and some at the level of 'the crudest and most flashy birthday card that I could find at a paper shop in the slums'. The test consisted in arranging the fifty cards in order of artistic merit. The test was given to eleven expert art critics and artists, whose rankings correlated at nearly the 0·9 level. It was then administered to various groups of adults, art students, grammar and elementary school children, and infants aged from 6 to 8. The total population tested numbered 657. Once again Burt never published the detailed results of his experiment and it was left to Valentine to extract the actual figures from him. 'The main point that Burt stressed', notes Valentine, 'is that there is a decided resemblance between the orders produced by different groups and also between their orders and those of the experts. Hence there must be some general principle or tendencies underlying the various attitudes.'[16] In his discussion of the nature of artistic appreciation which formed part of his broadcast talk Burt admitted that there were various types of aesthetic reaction and various subjective elements involved in artistic judgment; nevertheless he maintained that his results pointed to the existence of an underlying general and objective factor. 'We see beauty because it is there to be seen.'[17] So, he went on, 'I am tempted to contend that aesthetic relations, like logical relations, have an independent, objective existence: the Venus of Milo would remain more lovely than Queen Victoria's statue in the Mall, the Taj Mahal than the Albert Memorial, though every man and woman in the world were killed by a passing comet's gas.'[18] He proceeded in his broadcast to consider the nature of beauty, arguing that beauty was concerned with order and arrangement; that in this order there must be some sort of unity, but at the same time variety and diversity, if interest was to be retained. 'A sense of beauty arises only when we look at an object that is more or less complex.'[19]

Problems of aesthetics were adopted as thesis topics by a dozen or so research students during Burt's tenure of the University College chair. Several of these were concerned with factor-analytic

14. Burt, C. L. The psychology of value. *Brit. J. Statist. Psychol., XVI*, 1963, 93.
15. Burt, C. L. *et al. How the Mind Works*, 1932, ch. xv, The Psychology of Art, pp. 267–310.
16. Valentine, C. W. *The Experimental Psychology of Beauty*, 1962, pp. 146–8.
17. Burt, C. L. *How the Mind Works*, 1932, p. 294.
18. *Ibid.*, p. 307.
19. *Ibid.*, p. 297.

studies, and it emerged that in addition to the general aesthetic factor there were subordinate factors, some connected with subject matter (painting, music, literature, etc.), and others dependent on temperamental differences, in particular the two marked bipolar factors indicating a preference for classical *vs* romantic, and realistic *vs* impressionistic styles. Burt discussed some of these results in his articles on the factorial analysis of emotional traits,[20] and the matter was taken further by Eysenck, who carried out his work as a postgraduate student in Burt's department, in a number of articles and books.[21] Another main aspect of Burt's aesthetic theory, the doctrine of complexity, was examined fully by another postgraduate student, J. B. Parry, in a thesis entitled 'The Role of Attention in Aesthetic Experience', which brought out the part played by complexity and variety in the attentive or apperceptive process.[22] Both these researches were interesting not only in themselves, but also in bringing out Burt's superb qualities as a supervisor, at any rate with his abler students working on problems that really interested him. Perhaps because, during the latter stages of these investigations, the college had been evacuated to Aberystwyth, while the students themselves remained in London, an unusual amount of correspondence was generated. These letters from Burt bring out both his critical powers and also the richness of the knowledge he had at his disposal. Often his letters, which might easily run to 5,000 words or more, are masterpieces replete with information and ideas, and they were poured out in profusion.[23]

After his retirement Burt did not lose his interest in aesthetics and he continued to write on aesthetic questions up to the last few years of his life. He defended his concept of a general aesthetic factor against the attacks of critics; in a long article on the general theory of value he presented arguments in support of the objectivity of values, substantiating these arguments with the results of an empirical investigation; he enlisted information theory in support of some of his views; and he further concerned himself with the problem of aesthetic education. What he did not do was to synthesise

20. Burt, C. L. The factorial analysis of emotional traits. *Char. & Pers., VII*, 291–9.

21. Eysenck, H. J. An experimental and statistical investigation of some factors influencing aesthetic judgments. Ph.D. Thesis, University of London, 1940; The general factor in aesthetic judgments. *Brit. J. Psychol., XXX*, 1940, 94–102; Type-factors in aesthetic judgments. *Brit. J. Psychol., XXXI*, 1941, 262–70; *Dimensions of Personality*, 1947, ch. vi; *Sense and Nonsense in Psychology*, 1957, ch. viii.

22. Parry, J. B. Ph.D. Thesis, University of London, 1940.

23. Burt, C. L. Letters to Eysenck and Parry. Burt Archives, University of Liverpool.

his varied contributions to aesthetics into a comprehensive treatise on the subject.

Among the critics one of the most persistent and able was R.A.M. Gregson of Canterbury University, New Zealand. Gregson argued that while the presence of a general aesthetic factor might be interpreted as an indication of a common aesthetic perception of an objective reality, it might equally be regarded as 'the artifact of a common culture imposing a conformity of responses on a population of subjects who will, within physiological limits, value any properties . . . for reasons which are a mixture of the aesthetic and non-aesthetic. Burt had not indicated how his statistical demonstration could be part of an *experimentum crucis* between an absolutist and a subjectivist aesthetic theory.'[24] In refuting this objection Burt had recourse to the high agreement between works of art from many periods of human history, and to a cross-cultural study by one of his research students, Dr Aydin Cancardas, who secured rankings from persons of different nationality and different cultural backgrounds, and still found comparatively high correlations.[25] Gregson's intervention, however, was principally important in that it stimulated Burt to write his long article on 'The Psychology of Value', which though rather inappropriately taking up a large part of one issue of the *British Journal of Statistical Psychology*, was nevertheless an immensely erudite piece of work, setting out Burt's aesthetic standpoint more fully than anywhere else.[26]

His previously expressed viewpoint was categorically reaffirmed: 'Beauty is an irreducible characteristic which cannot formally be defined, but only intuitively apprehended, like the quality "yellow" or the relations "before" and "after".' In a world that was partly, but not perfectly ordered, aesthetic intuition grasped the element of order.[27] The various subjective theories, hedonic, expressive, emotive, which Burt went on to examine with a considerable parade of scholarship, failed to provide satisfying explanations; cognitive, rationalist and intuitive theories, on the other hand, came much nearer to doing so. Burt then went on to back up his arguments with the results of an empirical investigation carried out over a long period of years and with the help of several co-workers, and aimed at collecting introspective reports on judgments involving aesthetic and moral values. The population tested, Burt stated, amounted to

24. Gregson, R. A. M. *Brit. J. Statist. Psychol.*, *XIV*, 1961, 72–4.

25. Cancardas, A. A comparative study of tests of aesthetic appreciation. Ph.D. Thesis, University of London, 1954. (Miss Cancardas commenced her research under Burt's direction in 1943.)

26. Burt, C. L. The psychology of value. *Brit. J. Statist. Psychol.*, *XVI*, 1963, 59–104.

27. Burt, C. L. and Williams, E. D. *Brit. J. Statist. Psychol.*, *XV*, 1962, 77.

just over two hundred persons, about four per cent of whom were 'experts' (i.e. 'highly educated, and conceivably influenced by their specialised knowledge or theories'). The test situations, eight in number, were described, and a table presented the percentage replies under various categories given by the 'experts' and by the rest of the sample. The experiment was never completely written up, nor elsewhere described, by Burt. On the basis of the evidence provided by it Burt concluded, first that the vast majority of persons 'regard both aesthetic and ethical judgments as assertions of fact', and secondly 'most of them also maintain that their judgments are based on direct apprehension of these valuable qualities and of the different degrees in which they are manifested.'[28] Burt admitted that this evidence could not conclusively prove the point, but he maintained that 'nevertheless when the results of an experimental enquiry as well as the general voice of common sense in almost every age and community agree in supporting the objectivity of value we are clearly faced with strong presumption in favour of that conclusion'. As was so often the case with Burt, the historical, critical and theoretical discussion of the problem was impressive, but the empirical evidence much less convincing. His scholarship was dazzling; his science, weak.

Burt's scholarship was equally apparent in his long and interesting review of Moles's *Information Theory and Aesthetic Perception* which he contributed to the *Journal of Aesthetic Education*.[29] Burt was obviously up to a point sympathetic to Moles's distinction between 'semantic information' and 'aesthetic information'. Both were concerned with order and ordering, and information theory could certainly throw light on aesthetic problems. Nevertheless there were for Burt difficulties in wholly absorbing aesthetics into information theory:

With the doubtful exception of certain types of architecture, no mathematical formula can ever express the entire character of a work of art, much less provide plausible rules for aesthetic composition. Let me cite just one notable example. Many amateur typographers, from the days when the French *Academie des Sciences* appointed a commission on the subject, have attempted to design elegant type-faces in accordance with explicit geometrical principles. All such attempts have failed. The outcome is invariably a set of frigid, lifeless, ill-proportioned characters; and the same is true of all other would-be scientific compositions,

28. Burt, C. L. The psychology of value. *Loc. cit.*, p. 91.
29. Burt, C. L. Information Theory and Aesthetic Education (Review). *J. Aesth. Educ.*, I, 1966, 55–69.

including both mathematical architecture and the mechanical products of electronic music. As Ruskin, Roger Fry, Clive Bell and other literary and artistic critics have so constantly insisted, the aesthetic quality of any beautiful object, whether work of art, or work of nature, must always include that unpredictable ingredient which results from life and mind. Always there must be an element of indeterminacy.[30]

To say that art was unpredictable did not, however, mean that it was heaven-given and unteachable. Indeed, in his discussions of artistic education Burt insisted that in spite of the rarity of creative genius of the highest order, artistic gifts were widely distributed, and educable. '*Some* capacity for artistic production, and still more obviously *some* capacity for artistic appreciation is inherited by everyone, but left for the most part untrained and undeveloped.' Thus, 'almost every boy and girl is capable of some degree of artistic education in nearly every direction, and it is the duty of the teacher to study the interests and aptitudes of each individual child. . . . Art in the broadest sense is the most powerful factor for shaping the aspirations of the growing child, and the surest instrument for refining character and moulding ideals.'[31]

In an area where Burt was so talented and so knowledgeable it is a misfortune that he never managed either to prosecute his empirical studies more thoroughly, or to synthesise the historical, philosophical and psychological material, of which he had so extensive a command, more comprehensively. He has left us instead with an intriguing and stimulating collection of fragments.

III

The third field of special interest that we must consider is that of psychical research, or parapsychology as it is now more generally termed. There is no doubt that Burt's introduction to psychical research was due mainly to McDougall. McDougall, though not convinced of all the findings of the psychical researchers, was satisfied that telepathy, at least, had been proved, and that telepathic phenomena were incompatible with materialism.[32] He was indeed to become sufficiently sympathetic to the aims of the Society for Psychical Research to be chosen as its President in 1920, and when,

30. Burt, C. L. Information Theory and Aesthetic Education (Review). *J. Aesth. Educ., I,* 1966, p. 69.

31. Burt, C. L. Psychological aspects of aesthetic education. *J. Aesth. Educ., II,* 1967.

32. McDougall, W. *Body and Mind,* 1911, p. 349.

later on, he moved to Duke University, he helped to promote the famous experiments of Dr Rhine. Burt never hesitated to acknowledge his debt to McDougall in more ways than one, and, writing to Thouless in 1948 he stated, 'My interest in the subject [of psychical research] goes very far back. McDougall, as you know, was always very attracted to the subject . . . even as students he started us taking an interest in such problems; and I dabbled in the matter quite a lot when I was at Liverpool, owing to the tradition left there by Oliver Lodge.'[33] Burt's interest, however, was until quite late in his life fairly marginal, and his attitude somewhat sceptical. Significantly, he did not become a member of the Society for Psychical Research until 1959. When, in 1935, he lectured on psychical research at Gresham College he held that 'the results achieved by psychical research are for the most part slender and unconvincing. Nevertheless a few facts of supreme importance have been discovered and established.'[34] The established facts, however, related to matters such as hypnotism rather than psychical research proper, and Burt went on to say that though the recent experiments of Rhine and Coover were interesting, nevertheless he still remained 'somewhat of a sceptic' as far as telepathy was concerned.

Burt, however, was sufficiently interested to encourage and collaborate with Dr S. G. Soal, a lecturer in mathematics at Queen Mary College, London, in the 1930s. In 1929 Soal had carried out a large-scale investigation on the clairvoyant perception of objects at a distance, with negative results. When Rhine's results were published in 1934 Soal attempted to repeat his card-guessing experiments. Many of these experiments were carried out in Burt's laboratory between 1934 and 1939. The results of over 128,000 card-guessing trials carried out with 160 subjects were once again negative, but on re-analysing the data Soal found that two of the subjects were scoring significantly on cards one or two places ahead of, or behind, the card actually focused by the agent. Soal regarded this as strong evidence not only for telepathy, but for precognition. Burt's own part in these experiments was slight, but he was led on to a small-scale pilot investigation into the generality of paranormal activity, that is the possible existence of a general factor underlying all paranormal manifestations. He concluded that 'the scant evidence at present available would certainly seem to support the hypothesis of a general paranormal factor', though he went on to maintain that there was really nothing 'paranormal' about so-called psychical

33. Burt, C. L. Letter to Dr R. H. Thouless, 13 April 1948.
34. Burt, C. L. In Gregory, A. (ed.) E.S.P. and Psychology, 1975, ch. I.

gifts.[35] His attitude was by now clearly more sympathetic than it had been in 1935, and just before he was due to retire from University College he received an invitation from Thouless, a firm supporter of the Society for Psychical Research, to let his name go forward as Senior Research Consultant to the S.P.R.[36] Burt, however, had other irons in the fire, and declined the invitation. It was ten years before his attention turned again towards the paranormal, and it was once more Soal who provided the stimulus.

In 1959 Soal, and a collaborator, Bowden, wrote a book on a remarkable pair of young cousins living in a remote part of Wales who demonstrated extraordinary telepathic powers.[37] In a long series of card tests carried out between August 1955 and April 1957 scores far exceeding chance were frequently recorded. Occasionally runs with one hundred per cent successes were obtained. These impressive results, however, were dismissed by an anti-psychical critic, C. E. M. Hansel, as due to 'trickery',[38] and this provoked Burt to write a long (45-page) review of Soal's work in his statistical journal,[39] in which he examined the evidence, analysed the arguments of Hansel and the sceptics, and indulged in speculations of his own to account for the facts, which seemed to him to have been established beyond reasonable doubt. 'Alike for their success and for the care with which they have been concluded, the experiments here recorded', Burt maintained, 'are unrivalled in the whole corpus of psychical research.' This led him on to consider the problem of consciousness, which became for him a central concern during the last decade of his life. 'Whatever else they may be, paranormal manifestations are all modes of consciousness.' And, once the nature of consciousness was grasped, paranormal phenomena ceased to be so peculiar and special. 'Once we recognise that all cognition, whether normal or paranormal, implies a unique kind of relation, then the anomalies of which Rhine and others make so much begin to disappear.' Burt then went on to outline a 'field theory of consciousness' in which 'the consciousness of a given individual, so far as it has location, resides in the environment around him rather than inside his head'. Fields of this type could inter-penetrate and inter-act.[40] To think in terms of a three-

35. Burt, C. L. *Psychology and Psychical Research*, S.P.R., 1968, p. 6.

36. Thouless, R. H. Letters to C. L. Burt, 10 April 1948; 23 March 1949.

37. Soal, S. G. and Bowden, H. T. *The Mind Readers*, 1959.

38. Hansel, C. E. M. *New Scientist*, V, 1959, 457.

39. Burt, C. L. Experiments on telepathy in children. *Brit. J. Statist. Psychol.*, XII, 1959, 55–99.

40. Dr G. D. Wassermann of the University of Newcastle upon Tyne accused Burt of plagiarism in putting forward these ideas. Wassermann had propounded an almost identical theory in his paper in the *Ciba Foundation Symposium on*

dimensional universe made up solely of tangible objects was to beg the question. Burt's lengthy review ended with a statistical appendix. The arguments with Hansel, however, continued, and provoked Burt to a further long 'reply', in which he maintained that a 'psychic universe consisting of events and entities linked by "psychic" interactions, obeying laws of its own, and interpenetrating the physical universe and partly overlapping it' was quite conceivable.[41]

In the last ten years of his life Burt wrote a good deal on psychical research. Seven of his articles, including two not previously published, were collected by Anita Gregory in the book *E.S.P. and Psychology*, which appeared in 1975.[42] The collection, however, did not include the most important piece of work, his F. W. H. Myers Memorial Lecture published by the Society for Psychical Research in 1968.[43] This was a scholarly and impressive exposition of Burt's position, linking paranormal phenomena, so-called, to the general nature of consciousness. It was because these phenomena seemed to provide a decisive argument against behaviourism and physicalism that Burt became so interested in them. Psychical research became for Burt, during this final period an integral part of his metapsychological system, and in his Myers lecture and other articles he developed his theory of consciousness and of mind–brain relationships. Burt had always been a dualist. As he put it in a letter to Arthur Koestler in 1967, 'there must be a ghost in the machine'.[44] He went on in his Myers lecture and elsewhere to develop the idea of independent psychic fields, postulating two types of psychic field, 'related rather like electrical and magnetic fields in the theory of electro-magnetism'.[45] The field of passive consciousness is determined largely by the changing processes within the brain; the field of active consciousness, or 'psychon', on the other hand, is a kind of Leibnizian monod with a possibly infinite life-time. Not only might the psychic fields of different individuals overlap, thus

Extrasensory Perception, (1956), pp. 53–73. Though it is quite possible that Burt may have been influenced by this source, it is difficult to prove direct plagiarism decisively. Burt was obviously influenced by a considerable variety of sources. A lengthy, heated, and inconclusive correspondence between Burt and Wassermann took place in 1959 (Burt Archives, University of Liverpool).

41. Burt, C. L. *Brit. J. Statist. Psychol.*, XIII, 1960, 179–88.

42. Burt, C. L. *E.S.P. and Psychology, op. cit.*, 1975.

43. Burt, C. L. *Psychology and Psychical Research*, S.P.R., 1968. Burt's claim that he was 'one of the very few surviving members of the Society who have had the privilege of listening to Myers himself' must be regarded with some scepticism. Myers died on 17 January 1901, when Burt was still a schoolboy, and it seems highly improbable that he ever had an opportunity of hearing him. Burt's early 'memories' were often faulty.

44. Burt, C. L. Letter to A. Koestler, 2 May 1967.

45. Burt, C. L. Myers lecture, p. 49.

accounting for telepathic experiences, but there might well be a sort of 'oversoul'—'a kind of group mind formed by the subconscious telepathic interaction of the minds of certain persons now living together perhaps with the psychic reservoir out of which the minds of individuals, now deceased were formed, and into which they were re-absorbed on the death of their bodies'.[46] This active 'psychon' was something that acted according to its own laws. Psychology was, therefore, a science in its own right, and not dependent on material data. 'The psychic factor must be conceived as functioning as a universe which is governed, not by causal laws, but by the laws of probability'—a claim which Burt maintained was not contrary to, but in line with, modern physical theory.[47]

The role of the brain in the psychophysical organism was, according to Burt, to serve first as a detector (not a generator) of consciousness, and secondly as an inhibitor of, or guard against, the multitude of influences to which its clairvoyant powers laid it open. 'Our sense organs and our brain operate as an intricate kind of filter which limits and directs the mind's clairvoyant powers, so that under normal conditions attention is concentrated on just those objects or situations that are of biological importance for the survival of the organism and its species.'[48] Burt believed that these hypotheses were in line with the latest neurophysiological findings, particularly those of Eccles. The very ordinary chemical processes of brain cells could not actually generate consciousness, though there was no reason why they should not be constructed to detect, select and amplify psychical influences. The mode of action here, however, was not physical, but psychical. 'The effect of voluntary choice on the nerve impulses in the brain must itself be a form of psychokinesis.'[49] In this way the active 'psychon' could direct the body, and, indeed, Burt made clear in his review of Alister Hardy's Gifford lectures, he believed in 'the supreme importance of consciousness in deciding the direction and furthering the progress of animal evolution', rather than explaining evolution in terms of natural selection alone.[50]

This was all pretty heady stuff of a frankly speculative nature. Burt, however, was by now convinced of the genuineness of a sufficient corpus of paranormal phenomena to give it plausibility,

46. Burt, C. L. Myers lecture, p. 85.
47. Ibid., p. 41.
48. Ibid., p. 59. A theory of this kind had been put forward by M. M. Moncrieff in The Clairvoyant Theory of Perception, 1951. Burt refers to Moncrieff's book on p. 43 of his Myers lecture.
49. Burt, C. L. The evidence for paranormal phenomena. Int. J. Parapsych., III, 1961, 77–87.
50. Burt, C. L. Evolution and parapsychology. J.S.P.R., XLIII, 1966, 403.

though he admitted that faking and wish-fulfilment could not always be ruled out. There are, he noted, 'comparatively few who can resist the temptation to indulge in a little faking, fishing, and even bare-faced prevarication, when things go wrong'.[51] But he added, 'Are not all of us tempted at times in much the same way?'— possibly a revealing bit of introspection! Unconscious self-deception was also a factor to be reckoned with. Nevertheless he concluded that 'the probabilities in favour of telepathy are far stronger than against it'. The facts, once accepted, demanded a speculative interpretation. 'Since the physicist, whenever his observations and experiments seem to require it, does not scruple to postulate entirely novel entities and entirely novel modes of interaction, there can be no reason why the psychologist or parapsychologist should not postulate irreducible psychic entities and irreducible psychic modes of interaction, if these help him to interpret the anomalous data with which he is faced.'[52] Or, as he said in his Myers lecture, 'The psychologist should have the courage to forge his own concepts and postulates on the basis of what he, as a psychologist, observes.'[53] But Burt never committed himself wholly to the empyrean, and at the end of his Myers lecture he came back to earth: 'Such concepts must be invoked as a last resort, and then scrupulously defined and re-defined, so as to yield corollaries which can be empirically tested, and so either confirmed or else finally refuted.'[54] It was an area in which Burt himself did little empirical testing, and a great deal of speculation; but he brought to his speculations an unusually rich store of knowledge, so that they constitute a stimulating, if problematical, contribution to metapsychological theory.

51. Burt, C. L. Parapsychology and its implications. *Int. J. Neuropsychiat.*, II, 1966, 363–77.

52. Burt, C. L. Psychology and Parapsychology. In Smythies, J. R. (ed.) *Science and E.S.P.*, 1967, pp. 61–141.

53. Burt, C. L. Myers lecture, p. 49.

54. *Ibid.*, p. 103.

CHAPTER TWELVE

Posthumous Controversies

I

Burt's reputation survived his lifetime. Not long before his death the American Psychological Association bestowed on him its Edward Lee Thorndike Award, a high honour which had never previously been accorded to a foreigner. Burt worked on his Thorndike address in the last summer of his life and it was published posthumously in the *American Psychologist*.[1] The esteem in which he was held by educationists in Britain was indicated by the opening of the Sir Cyril Burt School for maladjusted children in the London Borough of Beckenham shortly after he died. In the obituary in *The Times Educational Supplement*[2] Burt had been described as 'Britain's most eminent educational psychologist', and in the Cattell *Festschrift* which came out a little later he was called 'dean of the world's psychologists'.[3] Nobody then anticipated the criticisms and onslaughts to which his work was shortly to be subjected.

Of course, while he was still alive, Burt's views and conclusions had often come under attack, and these attacks mounted in strength during the last decade of his life. Up to the end of the 1940s he had not been a controversial figure. It was the establishment of the tripartite, selective scheme of secondary education following the 1944 Education Act, and the widespread use of intelligence tests to decide the destiny of multitudes of children, that brought Burt's work into the focus of public attention and made it a special target for criticism. Burt, and a good deal of what he stood for, became anathema to left-wing, egalitarian critics, like Brian Simon.[4] The whole concept of intelligence came under fire. It was denied that it could be adequately measured by tests; that it was a constant quantity, largely innate in origin; and that it had any educational relevance. The rising school of educational sociologists, of whom

1. Burt, C. L. The inheritance of general intelligence. *Amer. Psychol., XXVII*, 1972, 178–90.
2. *The Times Educational Supplement*, 15 October 1971.
3. Dreger, R. M. (ed.) *Multivariate Personality Research*, 1972, ch. xi.
4. Simon, B. *Intelligence Testing and the Comprehensive School*, 1953.

A. H. Halsey was an increasingly prominent member, began to point out the class bias of intelligence testing.[5] Psychologists, like Alice Heim and D. H. Stott, before long joined in the growing band of critics. There seems little doubt that it was these criticisms that led Burt to take up the cudgels, and turn again to the exposition of his views and to a search for evidence to support them. He began his important article on 'The Evidence for the Concept of Intelligence'[6] with a paragraph on 'Current Criticisms', and noted that 'The concept of intelligence, and the attempt to measure intelligence by standardised tests, have of late furnished a target for vigorous attack.' None of these attacks, however, even when they were, like Simon's, clearly politically motivated, went beyond the bounds of the usual academic controversies; and nobody publicly questioned the competence and integrity of Burt's work, even when they disagreed with it.

In the 1960s the attacks became more venomous. Burt described McLeish's *The Science of Behaviour*,[7] in particular, as a 'libellous book', and went out of the way to answer the charges that had been levelled against his own work. One of the main purposes of his second main article on monozygotic twins[8] was to reply to the criticism of McLeish and other writers. Towards the end of the decade, after the publication of the *Black Paper* articles, and his contribution to the *Irish Journal of Education*, in which he produced evidence for a decline in academic standards in London schools and blamed 'progressive' education, the attacks spilled over into the public press. Highly critical articles appeared in the *Sunday Times*[9] and elsewhere. Burt was described as 'an extremist', and identified with right-wing, and, through his association with Jensen, 'racist' groups. In a letter to his sister, written early in 1970, Burt complained that 'the labour educationists who are all out to build what they call a classless society, keep launching ludicrous attacks on my views'.[10] Many of the criticisms were, indeed, clearly politically motivated and unfair.

All these attacks Burt survived. He was an expert controversialist, who relished argument, and usually gave far more than he got. His critics were, for the most part, far less erudite and agile than he was himself, and it is an indication of their incompetence that they were

5. Halsey, A. H. and Gardner, L. Selection for secondary education. *Brit. J. Sociol., IV*, 1953.

6. Burt, C. L. *Brit. J. Educ. Psychol., XXV*, 1955, 158–77.

7. McLeish, J. *The Science of Behaviour*, 1963.

8. Burt, C. L. The genetic determination of differences in intelligence. *Brit. J. Psychol., LVII*, 1966, 137–53.

9. *Sunday Times*, 12 October 1969.

10. Burt, C. L. Letter to his sister, 3 March 1970.

not able at the time to make out a much more damaging case against him. So Burt's professional reputation was not seriously impaired during his lifetime. Even those who distrusted Burt personally, and regarded him as a devious character, did not publicly express their views; and only a few of them (Dr Frisby of the National Institute of Industrial Psychology, Professor L. S. Penrose and possibly a few others) suspected that his scientific work was unsound. In the Memorial Address that I myself delivered at St Mary's Church, Primrose Hill, eleven days after Burt's death, I commented without compunction on his world-wide reputation and outstanding gifts.[11] There seemed no good reason to suspect that Burt would not soon be enshrined in the psychologists' pantheon among the founders of the subject.

II

Burt had not been in his grave a full year before criticism, far more penetrating than anything he had been subjected to while alive, was directed against his work on the inheritance of intelligence, and in particular his reported findings on twins.

Burt had commenced collecting material on twins soon after his appointment as L.C.C. psychologist. He had specially mentioned this to Dr Kimmins, the chief inspector to whom he was responsible, as one of the topics he was interested in. His contacts with schools and institutions in the London area enabled him to identify twins, and his access to the records enabled him to spot twins that had been separated early in life. There is no doubt that with the assistance of teachers, medical officers and social workers Burt was able to build up, during the time he was at the L.C.C., a body of material on twins, as well as collecting data on other family relationships. The eminent geneticist, Dr Fraser Roberts, has testified to having been through Burt's data with him[12] and both Professor L. Hogben and Professor R. B. Cattell in the 1930s were assisted by Burt in obtaining twin material.[13]

Burt's first published reference to his own twin data was in his

11. Hearnshaw, L. S. Obituary. *Bull. Brit. Psych. Soc., XXV*, 1972, 86.

12. Fraser Roberts, J. A. *The Times*, 19 November 1976. Dr Fraser Roberts informs me that he spent a whole day going through Burt's figures, probably about 1955.

13. See Herrman, L. and Hogben, L. The intellectual resemblance of twins. *Proc. Roy. Soc. Edin., LIII*, 1933, 105–29; Cattell, R. B. and Molteno, E. V. Contributions concerning mental inheritance. *J. Genet. Psychol., LVII*, 1940, 31–47.

1943 article on 'Ability and Income'.[14] He here reported 156 pairs of non-identical (dizygotic, DZ) twins and 62 pairs of identical (monozygotic, MZ) twins, of whom 15 pairs had been reared apart.[15] The correlation between the I.Q.s of the DZ twins was 0·54, between those of the MZ unseparated 0·86, and for the MZ separated 0·77. Burt did at times claim that his results for twins had been published previously in a succession of L.C.C. reports and in theses,[16] but no trace of such reports nor any reference to them remain in the authority's archives. Nor did any of his postgraduate students work on twin material.

Burt's next report was twelve years later in his article, 'The Evidence for the Concept of Intelligence'.[17] Thanks, he said, to his assistant, Miss Conway, the number of cases, particularly for the small but crucial groups of MZ twins reared together or apart, had been increased. The totals now reported were 83 MZ twin pairs reared together, and 21 pairs reared apart, as well as 172 DZ pairs all reared together and 984 siblings (of whom 131 were reared apart) and 287 foster children. The table of correlations included group and individual tests of intelligence, 'final assessments' for intelligence, scholastic attainments (general, reading and spelling, arithmetic) and various physical measures (height, weight, head length, head breadth, eye colour). Between 1943 and 1955 the twin population had increased by 16 DZ pairs and 42 MZ pairs, six of the additional MZ pairs being reared apart. Neither in this report, nor in the earlier one, were any but the most sketchy details provided about the investigation. The data were, indeed, never presented in a manner commensurate with their importance.

The 1955 article was followed a year later by a mainly theoretical article on 'The Multifactorial Theory of Inheritance and its Application to Intelligence'.[18] The correlations for MZ separated twins were repeated, this time to four places of decimals, and correlations for both 'adjusted assessments' and unadjusted group tests given for parents and children, siblings, and fathers and mothers. No further details were given apart from reliability indices. The correlations

14. Burt, C. L. *Brit. J. Educ. Psychol.*, *XIII*, 1943.

15. Burt's figures for the various groups do not tally with the total of 189 cases that he gives. Jensen (*Behav. Genet.*, *IV*, 1974, Table I, p. 9) also seems to be wrong in giving 62 as the number of MZ twins together. 62 was the total number of MZ twins, together and separated.

16. For example, Burt, C. L. *Brit. J. Educ. Psychol.*, *XIII*, 1943, ftnt. p. 89. Also letter to Dr Nichols, National Merit School Corporation, Evanston, Ill., 17 March 1964.

17. Burt, C. L. *Brit. J. Educ. Psychol.*, *XXV*, 1955, 158–77.

18. Burt, C. L. and Howard, Margaret. *Brit. J. Statist. Psychol.*, *IX*, 1956, 95–131.

were used to assess the percentages of variance attributable to genetic and environmental influences respectively, and these worked out, using 'adjusted assessments', to about 87 per cent to be ascribed to genetic constitution and 13 per cent to environmental factors.

In 1957 Burt delivered the Bingham Memorial Lecture, his subject being 'The Inheritance of Mental Abilities'.[19] Although he now professed to have collected 'over 30' cases of MZ twins reared apart, the correlations reported were those of his 1955 article. No precise figures for the number of subjects in each group (MZ, DZ, etc.) were given, so we know neither the exact number of his separated MZ group, nor whether there were changes in any of the other groups.

Burt himself did not report on twins under his own name again until 1966, when his article on 'The Genetic Determination of Intelligence: a Study of Monozygotic Twins reared together and apart' was published.[20] However, there were two articles under the name of J. Conway in which the number of separated MZ pairs was now stated to be 42—an incredible doubling of the number of this rather rare group in the space of three years![21] By 1966 the MZ separated group had grown to 53 pairs, and there were changes reported in the sizes of all the other groups, some by way of addition, and others, strangely, by way of subtraction. In spite of changes, sometimes large, in the sizes of the groups, the correlations in many cases remained identical to three places of decimals! But nobody at the time seemed to have noticed this. The figures for MZ separated twins given in this article were repeated in Burt's later publications, his Thorndike lecture, and his posthumously published *The Gifted Child*, though he informed Dr Sandra Scarr of Yale University in a letter[22] that three additional pairs of such twins had been discovered since his 1966 article had been written, and he sent her a revised table of I.Q. scores which included these three extra pairs. His published writings, however, make no mention of them.

For various reasons Burt's work on twins and other kinship relationships was highly influential. Firstly, Burt had shown an impressive mastery of quantitative genetics. He was, as Jensen observed, 'the first psychologist to understand thoroughly and to use the important contributions of Fisher, Haldane and Mather in

19. Burt, C. L. *Amer. Psychol.*, XIII, 1958, 1–15.
20. Burt, C. L. *Brit. J. Psychol.*, LVII, 1966, 137–53.
21. Conway, Jane. The inheritance of intelligence and its social implications. *Brit. J. Statist. Psychol.*, XI, 1958, 171–90; Class difference in general intelligence. *Loc. cit.*, XII 1959, 5–14.
22. Burt, C. L. Letter to Dr Sandra Scarr, 22 May 1971.

biometrical genetics', and 'in the theoretical aspects of application
of quantitative genetics to psychometric data, Burt was outstandingly ahead of all the others of his time'.[23] Secondly, Burt claimed
to have accumulated a larger population of separated MZ twins than
any other investigator. Newman, Freeman and Holzinger had
reported 19 pairs of separated MZs; Shields, 37 pairs; and Juel-
Nielsen, 12 pairs. So Burt's population fell not far short of that of
the other three studies put together. Moreover he had reported a
large number of other kinship correlations, some of which were
unique in the literature (e.g. uncle-nephew and second cousins).
And thirdly, as Kamin noted, 'the most important feature of the
Burt study is its purported demonstration that the environments in
which twins were reared were not at all correlated'.[24] So Burt's
work became perhaps the principal, though of course by no means
the only, buttress of the hereditarian case. The whole issue was
brought into the centre of public debate in 1969 as a result of
Jensen's notorious article in the *Harvard Educational Review*,[25] in
which he made considerable use of Burt's findings.

The unsoundness of the empirical foundations of the Burt edifice
was first exposed by Dr Leon Kamin of Princeton University in a
colloquium held in the Psychology Department in April 1972.[26]
The attack was repeated before a wider audience in the University
of Pennsylvania on 19 September 1972, and at a number of other
American universities over the next few months. Thousands of
mimeographed and xeroxed copies of these talks were circulated,
and in May 1973 Kamin addressed the Eastern Psychological
Association in Washington, D.C. So his views were already widely
disseminated prior to the publication of his book *The Science and
Politics of I.Q.* in October 1974.[27] In this book Kamin minutely
dissected the major studies purporting to demonstrate the heritability of the I.Q., and found inadequacies in all of them. He concluded
that 'the assumption of genetic determination of I.Q. variation in
any degree is unwarranted', and that there were no grounds for
rejecting the environmentalist hypothesis. It is hard for an unprejudiced reader not to feel that a great many of Kamin's criticisms
are distinctly captious, and unfortunately he did not subject the
studies supporting the environmentalist case to the same rigorous

23. Jensen, A. R. Kinship correlations reported by Sir Cyril Burt. *Behav. Genet.,*
IV, 1974, 25.
24. Kamin, L. *The Science and Politics of I.Q.*, 1974, p. 35.
25. Jensen, A. R. How much can we boost I.Q. and scholastic achievement?
Harvard Educational Review, XXXIX, 1969, 1–123.
26. On the question of priority see Kamin, L. *Bull, B.P.S., XXX*, July 1977, p.
259.
27. Kamin, L. *The Science and Politics of I.Q.*, 1974 (Penguin, 1977).

scrutiny. So his work must be regarded as biased. Nevertheless his criticisms of Burt's work were extremely damaging, and, for the most part, wholly justified.

Kamin's criticisms of Burt's twin studies can be subsumed under four main headings: firstly, there was a lack of precise details as to the methods used to collect the data, and as to the populations tested; secondly, there were conflicting and contradictory statements in the various reports; thirdly, there were careless errors; and finally, and most damaging of all, there were remarkable, and indeed wholly incredible, consistencies in correlation coefficients derived from changing sample sizes.[28]

Firstly, lack of precise details: there was, Kamin pointed out, 'no way of knowing what tests were administered at what times'; there was 'no precise information on how test scores were adjusted, on the basis of teachers' comments, to provide "final assessments" ', or as to how parental I.Q.s were obtained; nor was there any information given about the sex of the twin pairs, the extent and duration of their separation, nor their precise age at testing. It is only fair to say that this lack of detail had worried a number of enquirers before Kamin came on the scene.

Secondly, Kamin pointed to a number of conflicting and inconsistent statements with regard to the assessment of economic and cultural status and intelligence, and with regard to the number of children in institutions. Even some of the I.Q.s and social class ratings were discrepant. Thus, 'the two dullest twins were reported to have I.Q.s of 66 in 1966. The list later circulated by Burt gave them I.Q.s of 68 and 63.' Kamin might also have observed that at the other end of the scale the two brightest had I.Q.s of 136 and 137 in 1966, and these were given as 131 and 132 in the subsequently circulated list.

Thirdly, there were a number of careless errors in Burt's tables, some of which were pointed out to him and admitted before his death. These were a relatively trivial matter. The fourth criticism, relating to the invariance of many of the correlations, however, was decisive. Although the sizes of Burt's samples of MZ twins, DZ twins, and siblings all changed from one report to another, many of his correlations, some twenty in all, did not. They remained constant to three places of decimals. This was wholly incredible. For example, the correlation for the group tests of intelligence for MZ twins reared apart was 0·771 for 21 pairs in 1955, and for 53 pairs in 1966; and that for MZ twins reared together was 0·944 for 83 pairs in 1955, and for 95 pairs in 1966. An occasional coincidence might have been acceptable, but not twenty such coincidences in a

28. Kamin, L. *The Science and Politics of I.Q.*, 1974 (Penguin, 1977), ch. iii *passim*.

table of sixty correlations. There was obviously something wrong with Burt's work. Kamin made no further accusations. He simply concluded 'the numbers left behind by Professor Burt are simply not worthy of our current scientific attention'.[29]

The conclusions reached by Arthur Jensen, whose standpoint was totally opposite to that of Kamin, were almost identical. Jensen had for many years been an admirer of Burt. He heard, and was deeply impressed by, the Bingham lecture given by Burt in 1957, and Burt's work was a major influence in the development of his own viewpoint. Jensen visited Burt and had long discussions with him during the summers of 1970 and 1971. In his obituary notice in *Psychometrika* Jensen described Burt as 'one of the world's great psychologists', who left on him 'a total impression of immense quality, of a born nobleman'.[30] When it came to the detailed examination of Burt's kinship correlations Jensen, nevertheless, was forced to admit that they were full of inadequacies, inconsistencies, improbabilities and downright errors.[31] He noted not only 'the higher than ordinary rate of misprints in Burt's published tables', but also 'sheer inaccuracies in Burt's tabulation of the correlations from Newman *et al*.' He commented on the enigmatic shrinking of some of the samples between 1955 and 1966 with strangely inconsistent effects on the correlations. He also deplored the lack of precise detail. So though full of admiration for Burt's technical mastery of quantitative genetics, he had to conclude that 'the correlations are useless for hypothesis testing. Unless new evidence rectifying the inconsistencies in Burt's data is turned up . . . I see no justifiable alternative conclusion in regard to many of these correlations.' In a letter to *The Times*[32] Jensen argued that nothing more than carelessness was involved in Burt's discrepancies, and he repeated this contention in a later contribution to the *American Psychologist*.[33]

In the same year (1974) that Kamin's and Jensen's critiques of Burt's data appeared in America, Alan and Ann Clarke in England, in the third edition of their *Mental Deficiency*, commented not only on 'a number of puzzling features' in Burt's twin studies, but also on the suspiciously perfect regression to the mean in his parent-child I.Q.s— suspiciously perfect because it would only be predicted with random mating, whereas in human populations assortative

29. Kamin, L. *The Science and Politics of I.Q.*, 1974 (Penguin, 1977), p. 47.
30. Jensen, A. R. *Psychometrika, XXXVII*, 1972, 115–17.
31. Jensen, A. R. Kinship correlations reported by Sir Cyril Burt. *Behav. Genet., IV*, 1974, 1–28.
32. Jensen, A. R. Letter to *The Times*, 9 December 1976.
33. Jensen, A. R. Burt in perspective. *Amer. Psychol., XXXIII*, 1978, 499–503.

mating was the rule. They concluded that Burt's 'findings are by no means so firm as some subsequent authors have interpreted them'.[34]

Three years after Burt's death, therefore, there were growing doubts as to the validity of his twin studies and other reported data on kinship. At least some of his work in this area was, to say the least, so obviously careless and slipshod that it could no longer be taken seriously. Towards the end of 1976, however, much more grave charges were made, and to these we must now turn.

III

In *The Times* of 16 October 1976 a mysterious advertisement appeared in the Personal Columns: '*Sir Cyril Burt*. Could Margaret Howard or J. Conway who helped Sir Cyril in studies of the intelligence of twins or anyone else who knows them tel. (reverse charges) Oliver Gillie, 01-485 8953.' It turned out that Oliver Gillie was the medical correspondent of the *Sunday Times*, and in that paper eight days later (24 October 1976), prominently on the front page, appeared the sensational headline, 'Crucial data was faked by eminent psychologist', and alongside was a photograph of Burt. The article, signed by Oliver Gillie, commenced: 'The most sensational charge of scientific fraud this century is being levelled against the late Sir Cyril Burt, father of British educational psychology. Leading scientists are convinced that Burt published false data and invented crucial facts to support his controversial theory that intelligence is largely inherited.' Four main charges were levelled against Burt by Gillie: firstly, Burt often guessed parental I.Q.s and treated his guesses as hard scientific data; secondly, there was no evidence that the two women, Margaret Howard and J. Conway, who were supposed to have collaborated with him in his twin studies, ever existed; thirdly, that the concordant correlations noted by Kamin could only have been arrived at by working backwards to make the observations fit the answers; and fourthly, that Burt fabricated data to fit the predictions of his favoured genetic theories. The gravity of these charges was magnified, Gillie made clear, by reason of the influence which Burt's work had exercised on the establishment of selective education in Britain, and on pronouncements about racial differences in intelligence by Jensen and Eysenck. If Burt's figures were faked it was a matter not only of scientific but of political and public

34. Clarke, A. D. B. and Clarke, Ann M. *Mental Deficiency*, 3rd edn 1974, ch. vii.

concern. *The Times* took up the issue the following day,[35] with the headline 'Theories of I.Q. pioneer completely discredited', and went much further than Gillie in suggesting not only that the very idea that intelligence is largely determined by heredity had been undermined, but that most of Burt's earlier work was equally suspect.

The controversy that these articles aroused soon reverberated round the world. Over the next six weeks no fewer than fifty-two letters were published in the correspondence columns of *The Times*, together with a leading article on November 10th, and the scandal got a mention in many prominent daily, weekly and professional journals on both sides of the Atlantic. Actually there was nothing substantially new in the Gillie article except the charge of fraud itself. Most of the material had been collected from Kamin, Jensen, and the Clarkes. The mystery of the 'Burt ladies', Miss Howard and Miss Conway, had been spotted early in 1975 by Professor J. Tizard of the University of London Institute of Education, after he had attempted without success to contact them to resolve certain problems connected with Burt's work. Gillie's charge regarding the 'missing ladies' was directly derived from Tizard; his charge about parental I.Q.s from the Clarkes. All Gillie did was to expose and sensationalise the problems. In Tizard's words, 'Gillie's article made public, and added substance to, things that a number of psychologists had been saying for some years, though in more circumspect language.'[36]

There were two main reasons for the turmoil which followed the *Sunday Times* allegations. Firstly, the Burt case touched on the sensitive and politically emotive heredity *vs* environment controversy; and secondly, though there were perfectly legitimate grounds for suspicion, the charge of fraud, by any acceptable judicial standards, had not in fact been proved. So there was ample scope for controversy not only between hereditarians and environmentalists, but between pro- and anti-Burt factions. One of the principal Burt defenders was his old pupil, Professor John Cohen of Manchester University, who described Burt as 'a polymath of Renaissance dimensions', maintained that his work was 'meticulous, thorough and painstaking', and rejected the fraud charge 'lock, stock and barrel'.[37] And as for Miss Howard, Cohen recollected meeting her in the late 1930s. 'Her roundish face, her pleasing smile, her brown eyes and bobbed auburn hair, her slightly tinted spectacles, and her competence in mathematics' had made, appar-

35. *The Times*, 25 October 1976.
36. Tizard, J. The Burt affair. *Univ. of London Bull.*, No. 41, May 1977, p. 4.
37. Cohen J. The detractors. *Encounter*, March 1977, pp. 86–90.

ently, an impression on his memory which forty years had not dimmed. Eysenck equally insisted that there was no evidence which would support anything other than the charge that he (Burt) made errors of estimation and calculation, and rejected the Gillie accusation as a political smear campaign, an attempt at character assassination.[38] 'I think the whole affair', he wrote to Burt's sister, 'is just a determined effort on the part of some very left-wing environmentalists determined to play a political game with scientific facts. I am sure the future will uphold the honour and integrity of Sir Cyril without any question.'[39] Jensen, Cattell and others made the point that if Burt had set out to fake his results he would have made a much better job of it. To leave so many invariant correlations was 'a curious mistake for a cunning forger to make'.[40]

In response the anti-Burt party simply repeated and, indeed, stepped up their allegations. The Clarkes maintained that Burt's errors were always in a direction that lent support to his views, that he was guilty of irregularities which could not be dismissed as carelessness, and concluded that he was 'either a fraudulent scientist, or a fraud as a scientist'.[41] Kamin, who earlier had not suggested fakery as an explanation of Burt's curious results, now considered that 'the charges of scientific fraud clearly have some substantial basis',[42] and in a letter to Science[43] implied that Burt's early work, dating back to Liverpool days, was unsatisfactory and tainted.

In this tangle of charges and counter-charges the two most balanced assessments of 'the Burt case', as it had come to be known, were those of Nicholas Wade in Science and Professor J. Tizard in the Univeristy of London Bulletin.[44] Wade summed up his review by saying: 'it would be of some historical interest to know whether the flaws [in Burt's data] resulted from systematic fraud, mere carelessness, or something in between. The facts so far available do not allow any of these explanations to be ruled out.' Professor Tizard, whose suspicions lit the fuse which set off the whole explosion, in a judicial review of the resulting devastation, assessed the evidence fairly; and though he felt compelled to condemn Burt as a scientist,

38. Eysenck, H. J. The Times, 12 November 1976; The Burt case. Encounter, January 1977, p. 19.

39. Eysenck, H. J. Letter to Dr Marion Burt, 16 November 1976.

40. Wade, N. I.Q. and heredity. Science, CXCIV, No. 4268, 26 November 1976, p. 919.

41. Clarke, A. D. B., Clarke, Ann M. and McAskie, M. The Times, 13 November 1976.

42. Kamin, L. The hole in heredity. New Scientist, 2 December 1976.

43. Kamin, L. Science, CXCV, 21 January 1977.

44. Tizard, J. The Burt affair. Univ. of London Bull., No. 41, May 1977; Wade, N. I.Q. and heredity. Science, XCXIV, No. 4268, 26 November 1976.

paid tribute to many of Burt's personal qualities. He concluded by asking, 'Who can say what really motivated him as a person?' Tizard's impartial magnanimity contrasted strikingly both with the uncritical adulation of some of Burt's supporters, and with the rancorous denigration of his detractors.

IV

How can these conflicting and divergent viewpoints be resolved? There is clearly a need for further investigation, and for evidence to replace innuendo and suspicion. Unfortunately, not all Burt's papers were preserved following his death. His housekeeper, Miss Archer, had to vacate the rented flat as soon as she could, and move to smaller premises. Burt's books were disposed of to various universities, and nobody was available to spend weeks sorting through Burt's papers in detail. My instruction to Miss Archer was, 'Keep as much as possible. If in doubt the best policy is to keep and send to me.'[45] Finally Miss Archer was forced to rely mainly on her own judgment. 'In the end,' she wrote, 'I decided to burn all the papers which, as far as I knew, had been already published, but was not quite sure about the material in 2–3 large boxes in the attic. So one evening when Michael Young brought Liam Hudson along to see me, I took them upstairs, showed them the boxes and told them I don't know anything about statistics, but guess they contain the material he had accumulated for his articles on twins, which were published, but I was still in doubt whether I should destroy it or not. They both thought I could burn the whole material (consisting of bundles of test sheets with name and age of the children given at the top, long strips of figures and calculations, etc.) if it had already been used for publication.'[46] To this Professor Liam Hudson adds: 'There was really no point whatever in preserving them: only Professor Burt himself could have reassembled and reworked them, should there ever have been cause to do so. Whether they dealt specifically with his twin studies, or with some other project, I do not know.'[47] There is, in fact, no certainty that the material in the boxes did relate to twins, and some reason to think, as we shall see, that most of it at any rate did not. What is beyond doubt is that Burt himself left no instructions as to the disposal of his papers, and Miss Archer herself accepts full responsibility for what happened to them. It must also be emphasised that, although a considerable

45. Hearnshaw, L. S. Letter to Miss Archer, 14 February 1972.
46. Archer, G. Letter to Dr Urbach, 10 May 1975.
47. Hudson, L. Letter to Miss Archer, 24 May 1975.

amount was destroyed, a very great deal was preserved, including the bulk of Burt's correspondence from 1955 onwards, and his diaries from 1953 to the end of his life. Though the evidence provided by these does not answer every question, or resolve every problem, it does fill in some gaps, and does enable us to reconstruct in some detail Burt's life during the last critical years. Together with biographical material from earlier times, and information from his published writings themselves, this evidence enables us to narrow down the possibilities to a very few.

After examining it we can say with complete certainty that neither Burt nor any of his alleged assistants carried out any field work after 1955, and it is probable that all his data, such as it was, had been collected prior to his retirement in 1950, most of it, indeed, prior to the Second World War. Burt certainly added no data himself after leaving University College, and there is no evidence of any contact or communication with any assistants. Moreover Burt not only had no research funds at his disposal, but it appears that he never even applied for financial assistance. It would not have been difficult for him to have obtained funds from at least three sources: the Medical Research Council, the Leverhulme Trust, and the Nuffield Foundation. However, he received no grants from any of these bodies, and the M.R.C. and the Leverhulme Trust say that he never even applied for support. The Nuffield Foundation are unwilling to give information about rejected applications, but it is unlikely that, had Burt applied, his request would have been turned down. So it is clear that Burt not only did not collect data, but had no serious intention of collecting it following his retirement.

Burt's accounts of how and when the data on twins were obtained are conflicting, and cannot all be true. In a letter to Eysenck, written less than three months before his death, Burt said: 'Most of our own studies of separated twins were accumulated bit by bit between 1913 and 1939. We began with a very elaborate scheme including temperamental as well as intellectual assessments, and first-hand notes on home conditions. . . . As my work increased I had to give up the time-consuming visits to homes, and the job of estimating non-cognitive traits. Most of the later cases (including a few post-war) were simply tested at school; results checked by teachers; socio-economic status obtained from care-committee workers. We did not bother with addresses',[48] for which Eysenck had asked. This account rings true, and agrees broadly with the account supplied to Professor C. Jencks of Harvard early in 1969. 'All the assessments [of I.Q.]', he wrote to Jencks, 'were made in the course

48. Burt, C. L. Letter to Professor Eysenck, 27 July 1971.

of routine work—usually scholarship or 11+ examinations at 10–11½, occasionally in connection with the certification of children nominated for mentally defective schools. . . . If, as was often the case, a certain amount of travel was required to examine the separated twin, then the job was usually delegated to Miss Conway or Miss Howard.'[49] Burt was not involved in routine testing after his retirement, so this places the testing before 1950 at the latest. The accounts given in his published papers, however, were quite different. In 1955 he mentioned, besides surveys carried out in London schools, 'further data collected by Miss Conway' who, 'thanks to numerous correspondents', had been able to increase the number of cases, particularly for the small but crucial group of MZ twins reared together or apart.[50] In 1959 it was stated that many of the cases had been ascertained through personal contacts, which, on the face of it, implies precisely the opposite of 'routine work'.[51] In a letter to Professor Lloyd Humphries of the University of Illinois written in 1968 Burt stated that since his Bingham lecture, published ten years previously, 'we have added considerably to the number of our separated MZ twins'[52]— again a direct contradiction of what he later wrote to Eysenck. His published claims to have collected no fewer than thirty-two pairs of separated MZ twins between 1955 and 1964 (when his 1966 article was sent for publication) conflicts, therefore, with a good deal of other evidence, some of it supplied by himself.

What, then, are we to believe? On this issue the evidence from diaries is decisive. Though there are some gaps in the diary record, the diaries are so nearly complete, for fifteen of the last eighteen years of Burt's life, and record so many trivia (haircuts, tea in the garden, walks on the hill, the temporary disappearance of the cat, etc.) as well as listing engagements of his own and visitors to the flat (even the weekly Saturday visits of Charlotte Banks), that we can be reasonably confident that no important activity or contact has been omitted. On the basis of this evidence we can be sure that Burt himself did not collect any data on twins, or any other topic, during these years, and that he was never visited either by Miss Howard, or by Miss Conway, or by any other assistant actively working for him. Nor is there any trace among his carefully filed correspondence of any communication from any of these supposed assistants. It has been suggested that he might have received communications by telephone, but in view of his disabilities of

49. Burt, C. L. Letter to Professor Jencks.
50. Burt, C. L. *Brit. J. Educ. Psychol., XXV*, 1955, 167.
51. Conway, J. *Brit. J. Statist. Psychol., XII*, 1959.
52. Burt, C. L. Letter to Professor Lloyd Humphries, 11 November 1968.

hearing it is extremely unlikely that he would have relied solely on telephone messages for important research data.[53] We are forced, therefore, to the conclusion that the accounts given in Burt's published papers were false, and that a measure of deception was certainly involved.

But this does not solve all the problems by any means. In particular it does not explain why Burt, who was an extremely able person, did such a botched job of deception, and left so many loose ends and contradictions in his reports. Confining ourselves for the moment to the twin studies, it must be noted first that both Burt's major papers, the 1955 paper and the 1966 paper, were written in pique and in answer to his critics. Nearly all Burt's work during the period of his retirement was, in fact, mainly of a defensive kind, designed to uphold the Galtonian standpoint against environmentalist and other attacks. These attacks came in two main waves, in the years 1953–56 (Simon, Heim, Floud and Halsey),[54] and in the years 1963–64 (McLeish, Robbins, Douglas).[55] His two twin articles of 1955 and 1966 were his rejoinders, as he himself makes clear, and were motivated by a determination to get the better of his critics. They were not, in the proper sense, research reports, written calmly and painstakingly, following the patient collection and cool analysis of the data. They were written in haste and anger. We know from Burt's diary that the paper published in 1966 was commenced on Wednesday, 13 May 1964, and completed on Tuesday, 19 May 1964. It was revised on Friday, June 12th, before being sent off to the *British Journal of Psychology*, and further revisions took place during the following year prior to publication. But it took less than a week to write, and, as the first section of the article points out, it was essentially an attempt 'to answer the questions and criticisms raised by Dr Shields, Dr McLeish and other writers'. We must not forget, too, that Burt was all the time heavily involved in other activities— in 1964, for example, he read and reported on twenty-one manuscripts for Allen and Unwin, wrote other articles, acted as examiner, reviewed books, sometimes at length, and wrote hundreds of letters. In such circumstances careless mistakes are likely to occur, and some of Burt's errors were

53. When he took over the editorship of the *Brit. J. Statist. Psychol.* in 1963 Professor R. J. Audley discovered that 'C.B. found it difficult to understand anything said over the phone' (Letter, 29 November 1977). He had to communicate with him in writing or by visits.

54. Simon, B. *Intelligence Testing and the Comprehensive School*, 1953; Heim, Alice. *The Appraisal of Intelligence*, 1954; Floud, J. E., Halsey, A. H. and Martin, F. M. *Social Class and Educational Opportunity*, 1956.

55. McLeish, J. *The Science of Behaviour*, 1963; Committee on Higher Education (Robbins Report), 1963; Douglas, J. W. B. *The Home and the School*, 1964.

obviously just careless; for example, the inaccuracies in his tabulation of Newman's correlations, and the 33, instead of 3, investigations of siblings reared apart, both noted by Jensen.[56] Burt, strangely enough, though quick to spot errors in the work of others, was quite often slipshod in his own writing. There are a good many small inaccuracies in his autobiographical sketches (errors of dating and misreporting). McAskie checked the accuracy of a sample of bibliographical references from Burt's kinship papers and found that 20 per cent of the entries contained one or more numerical errors.[57] Burt himself was well aware of this tendency to inaccuracy in his later years. 'My attention and reasoning powers', he wrote in 1962, 'are deteriorating very markedly. So while I can write statistical arguments without too many stupid slips I want to make the most of my time.'[58] In the following year he said, 'My mind seems to be ageing. Three quarters of an hour's logical thinking is as much as I can do at one spell; and especially if I am tired with walking, I can do very little in the evening. What I write has to be checked and re-written many times before it is fit for the printer. Most of the mistakes are quite childish.'[59] In his letters, too, we find uncorrected instances of what he himself termed 'senile paragraphia'; for example, 'no other sometimes' for 'no other symptoms' in a letter to his sister.[60] He also complains of poor memory. It is important, too, to remember that Burt's articles were never submitted to friendly criticism. For many of them he was his own editor.[61] He had no close associates who matched him in ability and were capable of criticising him on equal terms. So he was deprived of a very necessary corrective. Carelessness, then, partly the result of haste and partly the result of emotional involvement and declining powers, was assuredly a contributory ingredient in the final product.

It was not, however, the only ingredient. There was also deception— deception about his assistants, and deception as to when the data were collected. Though there is some evidence that Miss Howard and Miss Conway, the two women who were supposed to have assisted him in his twin studies, were real people, yet, as we

56. Jensen, A. R. Kinship correlations reported by Sir Cyril Burt. *Behav. Genet.*, *IV*, 1974, pp. 10, 20.

57. McAskie, M. Carelessness or fraud in Burt's kinship data. *Amer. Psychol.*, *XXXIII*, 1978, 496–8.

58. Burt, C. L. Letter to his sister, 2 July 1962.

59. Burt, C. L. Letter to his sister, 13 March 1963.

60. Burt, C. L. Letter to his sister, 17 May 1965.

61. The 1966 article on monozygotic twins published in the *Brit. J. Psychol.* was read by two referees, one a very distinguished scientist, who recommended its publication. (Communication from Professor A. Summerfield, editor of the journal at the time.)

have pointed out, it is certain that they were not in contact with him in the late 1950s and 1960s. Confirmation for the existence of Margaret Howard comes not only from Professor John Cohen (see p. 236), but from a twin who was tested by her, and who writes:

> I had my intelligence assessed by Miss Howard, who I know was doing research in this field under Burt, together with another woman whose name I knew began with 'C', but my recollection of the full name escaped me until the present prompting of seeing it in print. These two were visiting Aberystwyth, but were not in fact registered there. I understood their research to be one involving individual intelligence testing, some of which was being carried out in Wales, but I cannot after this interval of time recall any more about the research.[62]

Miss Conway's existence is more shadowy. She may have been the woman whose name began with 'C', mentioned in the letter just quoted. Her earliest mention by Burt was in his 1943 article on 'Ability and Income',[63] and there seems no good reason why, at that time, Burt should merely have invented her. Neither Howard nor Conway were registered students of London University, though that, of course, would not have prevented them from coming by invitation to meetings in the department of psychology at University College in the 1930s. Burt's description of Miss Howard as a 'research student' in one of his 1955 articles[64] was, therefore, technically incorrect. It is much more probable that both Howard and Conway were L.C.C. social workers. This is how they were described by Burt in a letter to Dr Nichols of Evanston, Illinois, in 1964—'the council's social workers, Miss Howard and Miss Conway'.[65] They were not, however, salaried members of the L.C.C. staff, and their names were not included in the staff lists of the period, but they may well have been care committee workers whose names were never officially listed. Between the wars 'care committees', as they were termed, manned mainly by voluntary workers with a core of paid organisers, were an important feature of the education system. 933 such committees attached to London's public elementary schools were in existence in the 1920s, staffed by some 4,500 volunteers. Their duties involved arrangements with regard to medical treatment, home visiting and after-care. The help of care

62. Letter from W. H. Hammond, 30 November 1976.
63. Burt, C. L. *Brit. J. Educ. Psychol.*, XIII, 1943, ftnt. p. 91.
64. Burt, C. L. Test reliability estimated by analysis of variance. *Brit. J. Statist. Psychol.*, VIII, 1955, 103–18.
65. Burt, C. L. Letter to Dr Nichols, 17 March 1964.

committees is specifically referred to by Burt in the letter to Eysenck previously quoted (p. 239). So the most probable conclusion is that Howard and Conway were care committee workers, who assisted Burt in his educational work in the 1920s and 1930s.

This conclusion is strengthened by the fact that the first appearance of Miss Howard was in the joint article on maladjustment in children in 1952.[66] It is stated in this article that Miss Howard was concerned with the analysis of case-histories, and that she carried out the greater part of the calculation. So she may also have had, as Cohen suggests, some mathematical competence; and she may possibly be the Miss M. A. Howard who for a year in 1924 was a member of the British Psychological Society.[67] At that time it was not necessary for members to have qualifications in psychology. We cannot be certain whether Burt was, or was not, in touch with Miss Howard in 1952, as his diary for that year is not extant, and his correspondence incomplete. He was, however, certainly not in touch with her after 1954, though Miss Howard supposedly went on to collaborate with Burt in three further articles (1956, 1957, 1960), and was the sole author of one article (1958) and four book reviews. Her contributions ceased when Burt gave up the editorship of the statistical journal in 1963, and there is no reference in the *Cumulative Author Index to Psychological Abstracts* to any publication other than those contributed to Burt's journal. There is, indeed, very little doubt that Burt was himself the author of Howard's contributions. There is the evidence of content and style; and on 7 April 1962 Burt gave the game away in a diary entry—'chiefly doing Howard's reply to Isaacs'.[68]

Miss Conway, first mentioned in the 1943 article, and again in the 1955 article, burst into print under her own name in 1958, and in the space of four years was responsible for two articles, a note, and three book reviews, all published in the statistical journal. Again, according to *Psychological Abstracts* she contributed to no other journal, and the style and content of her writings are wholly Burtian. As an author, she, like Howard, was no doubt simply an 'alter ego' of Burt.

What is the explanation of these fictions? They would appear to have served multiple purposes. Firstly, they were a sop to Burt's feeling of isolation. Burt always fancied himself as the focus of an

66. Burt, C. L. and Howard, Margaret. The nature and causes of maladjustment among children of school age. *Brit. J. Psychol. (Stats), V*, 1952, 39–59.

67. This was pointed out by R. Rawles of University College. *The Times*, 20 September 1977.

68. This refers to a reply to an article by J. F. Isaacs on 'Frequency curves and the ability of nations' (*Brit. J. Statist. Psychol., XV*, 76–9). The reply, running to 13 pages, is in fact unsigned.

active school of researchers. One of his favourite phrases was 'I and my co-workers'. The truth was rather different. After his retirement he had few, if any, co-workers, apart from Charlotte Banks, who assisted him with a small number of articles. In particular after his exclusion from his old department he was very much alone. It is perhaps, then, more than coincidental that Margaret Howard first appeared on the scene just after he had been ordered to stay clear of the psychology department. Imaginary helpers, we may surmise, were a compensation for the loss of his own research students. Secondly, fictitious contributors were a convenient device whereby Burt could express his views, and call attention to his own achievements, in the statistical journal, without his too obviously monopolising its space. Of the more than forty 'persons' who contributed reviews, notes and letters to the journal during the period of Burt's editorship, well over half are unidentifiable, and judging from the style and content of their contributions were pseudonyms for Burt. Howard and Conway were members of a large family of characters invented to save his face and boost his ego. No doubt this exercise, which other editors are known to have indulged in, tickled Burt's well-developed sense of humour, as well as very often providing him with excuses to expound his own views under his own name by way of reply. Finally, and most important of all, Howard and Conway enabled Burt to maintain the fiction that he was still actively engaged in research and in the collection of material on twins. He was fond of accusing his opponents of basing their criticisms 'not on any fresh evidence or new researches of their own, but chiefly on armchair articles from general principles'.[69] 'My co-workers and I', on the other hand, were engaged in on-going research. It was a powerful argument with which to belabour the environmentalists; but to sustain it there had to be co-workers, and these co-workers had to be currently engaged in data collection. So in 1960 we are told in the statistical journal that 'for a more conclusive answer . . . we must I imagine await the results of Miss Conway and others who are applying tests of various abilities to twins who have been brought up separately from birth'.[70] It was this pretence of on-going research which the evidence from the diaries reveals as a complete fabrication.

What, then, of the data themselves? Were they themselves

69. Burt, C. L. *Brit. J. Psychol.*, *LVII*, 1966, 138.

70. Williams, E. D. The general aesthetic factor. *Brit. J. Statist. Psychol.*, *XIII*, 1960, 89. Miss Elizabeth D. Williams was a real person, who took an M.A. under Burt in 1937. She must have derived this 'information' about Miss Conway from Burt, who as editor was responsible for passing it. It is also possible that Burt himself 'planted' the statement. He was in the habit of making additions and alterations to contributions from others.

fabricated? Above all—to single out the most important set of data—were there ever fifty-three pairs of separated monozygotic twins? It does not necessarily follow if the assistants were ghostly resurrections that the data themselves were simply spoof. The data, too, may have been resurrected, or possibly borrowed,[71] or a mixture of the resurrected, the borrowed and the fabricated. All we know for certain is that no data were collected between 1955 and 1966, when 60 per cent of the MZ twin sample was allegedly obtained, and that some data at least had been collected between 1913 and 1940, and possibly up to as late as 1950.

There are, in fact, strong reasons for thinking that at the time Burt wrote his articles he did not any longer possess the original data, and that he was working mostly from rather sketchy secondary sources. From 1960 onwards he was a good many times asked to supply details, and with two exceptions he always failed to do so. The two exceptions were the supply of kinship data to Erlenmeyer-Kimling in 1963, and the supply of the table of I.Q.s and social classes of the fifty-three MZ twin pairs to Professor Jencks in 1969.[72] Burt took a long time in replying to both these requests, and on both occasions he gave as an explanation that the data were stored at college, and that the college was closed during the vacations and he could not get access to it. This was a mere evasion, as he possessed no material of any significance at college during the 1960s,[73] nor was the college closed apart from a week each at Christmas and Easter and on two Monday public holidays. It took Burt over nine weeks to respond to Erlenmeyer-Kimling's request. Erlenmeyer-Kimling wrote on 27 August 1963; Burt replied on November 4th. The Jencks request was particularly important as it eventually led to the table of I.Q. scores published in Jensen's article. In a letter to Burt, Jencks explained that he wanted data to work out regression differences in I.Q. score on differences in class position within each pair of separated MZ twins, and that Burt's data seemed to provide the only available material. He, therefore, asked for a 'listing of the pairs with I.Q. scores and class positions for each', and that was precisely the full extent of his request. This letter was sent on 2 December 1968. Burt's reply was sent seven weeks later on 25 January 1969. He started his letter, 'I apologise for not replying more promptly; but I was away for the Christmas

71. The reference to Miss Molteno (*Brit. J. Psychol.*, LVII, 1966, ftnt. p. 141) who worked with Cattell in an investigation using twins, suggests this as a possibility. Miss Molteno denies that she ever worked for Burt himself.

72. This table was sent subsequently to Dr Shockley and other inquirers and was published by Jensen (*Behav. Genet.*, IV, 1974, 15).

73. Communication from Miss Gertrude Keir.

vacation, and college (where the data are stored) was closed until the opening of term.' As a matter of fact Burt had not been away for Christmas; his data were not stored at college; and the college had only been closed for a week. So every single particular in his apology was untrue. According to his diary Burt spent the whole of the week from 2 January 1969 onwards 'calculating data on twins for Jencks'. On January 11th he 'finished checking tables for Jencks'. Had the I.Q. scores and social class gradings been available they could have been copied out in half an hour at the most. So quite clearly the table of I.Q. scores and social class gradings was an elaborately constructed piece of work, and we are forced to the conclusion that he simply did not possess detailed data, at any rate for the whole sample of his separated MZ twins.

This conclusion is strengthened by the fact that Burt was never able to respond to other requests for data. On 22 November 1969 Dr W. Shockley, a distinguished American physicist with a strong interest in eugenics, wrote to Burt asking for 'the data for the 95 MZ twins reared together, and the 53 MZ twins reared apart, siblings reared together and siblings reared apart, and finally unrelated children reared together'. Shockley offered to pay for having the data collected and transcribed. Burt replied a month later on December 19th excusing himself this time for the delay on the ground that 'the commercial secretarial office that types my articles for me had some difficulty in finding someone who was able to copy out the figures from my files'. He eventually enclosed the table of separated MZ twins previously sent to Jencks, but that was all. 'It would', he stated, 'be much more difficult to do the same as for MZ twins, whom we have repeatedly interviewed.[74] They are arranged according to schools, not by families; and as we did not intend to use the socio-economic data, the numerical grading would still have to be assigned. As soon as college opens after the vacation, I will look into the matter myself.'[75] He never did, however, and all Shockley ever received was the table for the fifty-three separated MZ twins. Altogether there were at least a dozen further requests for data, some asking for addresses, some to be put in touch with his assistants, some for further information about socio-economic conditions, and some for particulars of dates of visits, and the ages and sex of the twins. All these requests drew blanks, and were

74. One wonders how Burt managed to do this, as according to his letter to Eysenck (27 July 1971) with his later cases he did not bother with addresses! (See p.239.)

75. Burt, C. L. Letter to Dr W. Shockley, 19 December 1969. It is worth noting that Burt never visited college after breaking his ankle in 1960. It is hard to think he ever seriously intended to keep his promise.

evaded by means of one excuse or another. So the suspicion mounts that the data simply did not exist.

Assuming that the data were collected in the first instance, and there seems reasonable grounds for thinking that at least some was, what happened to it? The answer, almost certainly, is that the bulk of it was destroyed during the war. In September 1939 at the outbreak of hostilities the psychology department, together with various other departments of University College, was evacuated to Aberystwyth. Provisional arrangements had been made the previous April with University College, Aberystwyth, to take effect in the event of war, and it had been decided, among other things, that a small amount of psychological apparatus should be taken to Wales. Eventually two filing cabinets and fourteen packing cases and boxes were dispatched, and Philpott, who was organising the operation, suggested that 'if there is room it might be as well to send all the remaining cyclostyled sheets lying on shelves to the right of the store cupboard'.[76] Among the documents taken were files of all past students and notes on the subjects of their possible theses.[77] A large amount of material was necessarily left in London. Burt's own extensive case and research material, however, was not kept at college, where quarters in the old psychology department were extremely cramped. It was kept at his flat in Eton Road. On 18 February 1941 he wrote from Aberystwyth to the college authorities in London as follows:

> As I understand that, with other departments, the department of psychology will remain evacuated from London for the duration of the war, I am arranging to give up my flat in London at the end of the present quarter. It has now proved possible to obtain a remover who will bring my furniture etc. to Aberystwyth. I have, however, at my flat a very large number of documents that I have preserved for research students. These include many files of case-histories of defective, neurotic and delinquent children, rather large collections of children's drawings, compositions etc. systematically gathered while I still had access to London schools. It would be both expensive and unnecessary to transport all this for storage in Aberystwyth, and, on the other hand, it would be a great pity to destroy the material, since it provides an invaluable field of research for students who are taking higher degrees and are interested more particularly in child psychology. I take it

76. Philpott, S. J. F. Letter to E. Tanner, College Secretary, 9 October 1940. There were plans to return to London in the summer of 1940, and then a further evacuation. This letter refers to the second evacuation.

77. Burt, C. L. Letter to Professor Flugel, 1 October 1940.

there would be no objection to my storing it in one of the smaller rooms of the psychological laboratory at Gower Street. I am, therefore, writing to ask whether I could make some arrangement with our office of works for access to the laboratory on some convenient day. If (as I expect) the removal is made during term time it may be difficult for me personally to get to London; but Dr Philpott goes up pretty regularly and my wife would be superintending the general removal from the flat. He, or she, therefore, would be able to arrange with some local remover; but I thought, before going further with the arrangements on our side, it would be well to get in touch with whoever is looking after the buildings at Gower Street.[78]

The College Secretary replied two days later in these terms:

There is, of course, no objection to your using one of the smaller rooms in the Psychological Laboratory at Gower Street for the storage of documents, but I think it might be possible to find somewhere on the ground floor of the college where they would be safer.[79]

And this it seems is what happened. It had been decided earlier that the psychological laboratory on the top floor of the south wing was too vulnerable a place in which to leave documents and apparatus, and in a letter to Burt written in September 1940 Flugel comments on the enormous effort that had been involved in getting things down from the department to the vaults.[80] So it seems more than probable that Burt's documents were added to the rest of the psychological material below ground.

In April 1941, barely a month later, the college was heavily damaged by bombs. The College Annual Report for 1941–42 contains the following passage:

On the night of April 16th 1941 there was another heavy attack on the buildings, in the course of which the departmental libraries (happily empty of books) south of the dome, the Exhibition Room, the General Office, the Provost's and Secretary's rooms, the Council Room, the Botanical Theatre, the Department of

78. Burt, C. L. Letter to E. Tanner, 18 February 1941.
79. Tanner, E. Letter to Burt, 20 February 1941.
80. Flugel, J. C. Letter to Burt, 12 September 1940.

Mathematics above it, and the Records Office, were all burnt out, either partially or completely.[81]

Damage in the psychology department itself was slight, and chiefly the result of water used to put out a couple of incendiaries. We know, however, that Burt lost most, if not all, of the material that had been removed to college. In a letter to Dr (now Professor) Phillip Williams, Burt stated that he could not check on events during his L.C.C. years because 'my diaries for that period perished in the blitz'.[82] In another letter he wrote, 'most of my documents relating to this early period were stored in my lab. at U.C. and were destroyed by fire during the last world war'.[83] It is also known that Burt's entire collection of children's drawings was lost. In this connection Professor Drew writes: 'It is, I think, of interest and possible significance that the papers were destroyed, that Burt mentions that amongst the papers were a large collection of children's drawings. Miss Keir, who was not a member of the college at the time, was also collecting children's drawings and corresponded with Burt about this, and Burt asked to have the opportunity of seeing her collection, because he wished to compare the collection he had made with her somewhat later collection. This, however, was never done, and the implication is that Burt's collection no longer existed.'[84] Miss Keir confirms that Burt's entire collection perished.

We have, therefore, firm evidence that a great deal of Burt's material was lost. It is extremely unlikely that his papers would have been dispersed in separate places, and so the presumption is that everything went. There is no record as to precisely where it had been put, but the most likely place is the College Record Office on the lower ground floor near the corner of the south wing. This possessed suitable storage space, and was geographically the nearest basement area to the psychology department. Everything in the Record Office, apart from some special material in a strong room, was totally destroyed.

We know, however, that some papers were transported from the flat in Eton Road to Aberystwyth. It seems to have been a haphazard selection, and it is impossible to determine precisely what went to

81. University College, *Annual Report*, 1941–42, pp. 27–8. I am indebted to Mr L. J. Gue, Deputy Secretary, for assistance in searching college archives.
82. Burt, C. L. Letter to Dr P. Williams, 16 April 1964.
83. Burt, C. L. Letter to Professor T. H. Wolf, 5 August 1969. The reference to the lab. was probably a mistake on Burt's part.
84. Drew, G. C. Letter to L. J. Gue, 24 January 1978.

Wales. His housekeeper, Miss Archer, in response to enquiries, replied:

> I remember Prof. telling me when someone asked about them that he really did not know what had happened to the test sheets from all the schools after he had extracted the twins from them. It was just before the college evacuated to Aberystwyth. As you know the packing was left to Joyce [Mrs Burt], Erna [domestic] and Miss Bruce [secretary]. And Miss Bruce mentioned they had not enough boxes, and so put a lot into sacks, which were thrown into a damp and dirty coal cellar on arrival at Aberystwyth.[85]

In a subsequent letter Miss Archer amplified this account:

> As far as I remember from remarks made either by himself or his secretary, Miss Bruce, neither of them really knew what went where, and whether some boxes were, or were not, left behind in Eton Road. Several times in my presence Sir Cyril asked Miss Bruce whether certain papers or correspondence were stored at University College, or sent to Aberystwyth, and she was never sure of it. Often she explained to me afterwards that at the time it was all a great muddle. The packing was done by different people in a hurry while she was occupied with Prof's correspondence. Everybody was upset and agitated, and nobody made a note of what went where. I also remember Sir Cyril asking Miss Keir and Charlotte [Banks] whether and where his boxes at college may be, but neither knew anything definite. The suggestions were, either still somewhere around, or thrown out when Professor Russell took over or when the whole department moved into new premises. . . . Whilst at Aberystwyth and then again at University College, Sir Cyril told me he was too busy with lectures, his students and college affairs to miss packed up material. It was only after his retirement, when he revised some of his books and wanted to work on his accumulated material, that he realised that a lot of it had got lost somewhere, and started to ask for it. I think I told you once in which state I found material from Aberystwyth in one of the attic rooms, when I joined the household in 1950, and tried to sort it out and preserve and file somehow the still readable and useable remains of it. Sir Cyril was always very glad afterwards to find something 'useful' upstairs.[86]

85. Archer, G. Letter to Dr Marion Burt, 31 August 1975.
86. Archer, G. Letter to L. S. Hearnshaw, 16 February 1978.

So, for practical purposes, there seems no doubt that the large store of data collected by Burt between 1913 and 1939 must be written off as a casualty of the war.

In the light of this evidence, what are we to make of the successive reports on twins? The first article in 1943 was written when Burt was in Aberystwyth, and must obviously have been based on material available to him there—that is, on data abstracted into note-books, and possibly on documents thrown, it appears quite haphazardly, into sacks. This material, it seems probable, had been collected in the course of 'routine work' in schools. There is no evidence in the 1943 article of any data collected through personal contacts and less formal channels. After his return to London, just prior to the ending of the war, it is probable that Burt, as he informed Eysenck, was able to recruit some additional cases, and that the small increases in the sample sizes of the various twin groups, and the slight changes in correlations between 1943 and 1955, can be accounted for in this way. Although there are no case reports of twins among Burt's papers, some case reports from this period are extant, which at least shows that Burt had access to case material. Thus, in spite of the fact that many of the original records had been lost, Burt can be presumed up to this point of time to have been working with authentic data. The basis of the 1966 article, on the other hand, was quite different. We know that Burt had not collected additional data between 1955 and 1966, yet that he reported big increases in his sample of MZ twins. Where had the additional data come from? It can only have come from three possible sources. It could have involved the reconstruction of data that had been destroyed; it could have been borrowed from other sources; and it could have been simply invented. We cannot rule out the last two hypotheses altogether, but there is reason to think that some at least of the additional cases were based on reconstruction. There is an intriguing entry in Burt's diary for 3 April 1957 which may point to this reconstruction process as having taken place in that year, shortly after the publication of the Burt and Howard article. The entry reads, 'After deciding not to submit two papers for journal felt curiously relieved and calmed'. We do not know definitely to what this refers, but a year later under the name of Conway there was a mention of forty-two pairs of separated MZ twins.[87] It looks as though in 1957 Burt was trying to recruit more material to bolster up the multifactorial theory of inheritance, but felt reservations, which were then set aside under the Conway mask. This additional material may well have included the non-routine cases,

87. Conway, J. The inheritance of intelligence and its social implications. *Brit. J. Statist. Psychol., XI*, 1958, 186.

secured through personal contacts and other informal channels, referred to in several articles. It is possible that Burt attempted to reconstruct these cases from memory after the destruction of the original records. There is circumstantial evidence, in the form of brief histories, scattered in articles and correspondence[88] which suggests that Burt had collected a considerable number of such cases, though it is impossible to establish their exact numbers due to possible overlapping. If this is so, precise numerical data would generally have been lacking. So in the absence of supplementary evidence Burt simply used old correlations again, regardless of changes in sample size; but correlations were changed when there were any scraps of information that seemed to justify it. It is impossible from surviving documents to trace the process in detail, but an explanation along these lines seems best to fit the known facts.

That a man of Burt's standing and reputation should have stooped to these dubious stratagems may, for some, be hard to credit. Only a study of his own psychological make-up can perhaps throw light on the matter. But before we turn to that, we must ask what other areas of Burt's work were similarly doctored. Must all his work be regarded as suspect? We have already provided firm evidence for his falsification of the history of factor analysis, and suspicion naturally attaches to other parts of his work.

V

Two other pieces of work from Burt's later years have been regarded with particular suspicion— his data on parent–child correlations in his article on 'Intelligence and Social Mobility', and his data on declining educational standards published in the *Irish Journal of Education*.[89] In his 1961 article on intelligence and social mobility Burt argued that 'since the correlation between the intelligence of fathers and sons is only about 0·50 it is evident that, when classified according to their occupational status, (i) the mean intelligence of the children belonging to each class will exhibit a marked regression towards the general mean, and (ii) the intelligence of the individual children within each class will vary over a far wider range than that of their fathers. These deductions are fully confirmed by tables compiled to show the actual distributions of

88. Conway, J. *Loc. cit.*; Burt, C. L. Letter to Dr W. Shockley, 14 March 1970.
89. Burt, C. L. Intelligence and social mobility. *Brit. J. Statist. Psychol., XIV*, 1961, 3–24; Intelligence and heredity: some common misconceptions. *Irish J. Educ., III*, 1969, 75–94.

intelligence among adults and children belonging to the various occupational categories. It follows that, if the frequency distribution within the several classes is to remain constant . . . a considerable amount of social mobility must inevitably take place.'[90] This article, like most of Burt's contentious articles, was provoked by arguments with his critics, in this case by the discussions with Floud and Halsey on class differences in intelligence. In 1976 McAskie and Ann Clarke of the University of Hull reviewed the data on parent–offspring resemblances in intelligence in the context of correlation, regression and variance predictions from the polygenic model, and from the environmental model. After examining the evidence from all sources (including Burt's) they concluded that it was impossible to decide whether parent–offspring resemblances in I.Q. were mainly dependent on genetic, or mainly on environmental factors. 'However, the polygenic model does entail certain consequences with respect to variance, for which there appears to be no environmental counterpart. The additive polygenic model predicts that with assortative mating (which for intelligence is appreciable) the offspring variance should exceed the parent variance. However, only Burt with estimated parent I.Q.s was able to fulfil this promise.'[91] This led McAskie and Clarke to look carefully at Burt's data, and they came to the conclusion that not only was his description of the material he had used grossly inadequate, but that there were other anomalies that were hard to account for. As a result of these doubts McAskie carried out a more detailed analysis of Burt's 1961 article and concluded that the data reported were in all probability fraudulent.[92] He documented more fully the deficiencies of Burt's reporting. There is no doubt that these were serious; but, while these deficiencies might well provide a cover, they do not, of course, in themselves establish fraud. The gravamen of McAskie's case, however, lay in his analysis of the internal consistency of the data. He found suspiciously close to normal distributions, so close that very large populations would have been needed to produce them; he found a strange divergence between the within-row distribution characteristics for parents and for children in the tables of intelligence and social class, the parents' rows uniformly deviating from normality, and the children's rows uniformly resembling it; and he found an absence of what he termed 'the social status effect' (i.e. a recently discovered tendency for

90. Burt, C. L. *Brit. J. Statist. Psychol.*, loc. cit., p. 3.

91. McAskie, M. and Clarke, Ann M. Parent–offspring resemblances in intelligence: theories and evidence. *Brit. J. Psychol.*, LXVII, 1976, 243–73.

92. McAskie, M. Burt's 1961 parent–child I.Q. data according to parent occupation: an autopsy (awaiting publication).

there to be more regression to the mean in the children when parents are ordered on the basis of I.Q. alone than when grouped in social status categories). He concluded, 'Whilst perhaps no single piece of evidence from the three lines of inquiry clearly demonstrates fraud, the combined effect of the various anomalies must be regarded as very strong evidence indeed.'

Though the proof of fraud, in the full sense of the word, is much less convincing than in the case of the twin data, there is no doubt that Burt's reporting of his sources and methods was grossly inadequate, and little doubt that the data he possessed had been subjected to a good deal of 'adjustment'. The shaky nature of Burt's assessments of parental I.Q.s has already been noted (see p. 102). In 1968 Professor J. A. Beardmore of the Department of Genetics, University College, Swansea, wrote to Burt asking for raw data on I.Q.s of parents and children classified on social criteria. Burt in his reply claimed to have three sets of data:

1. For parents' intelligence the most reliable set of data I have consists of records of just over 100 fathers who attended L.C.C. schools as children between 1913 and about 1920 and had their I.Q.s assessed. Their own children later attended L.C.C. schools, and also had their I.Q.s assessed. . . .

2. I have a larger group in which each father's I.Q. was roughly assessed as an adult (about 370). The assessments were made by various social workers during their interviews; and the standards of the various interviewers were equated by getting them to apply camouflaged tests— oral questions ostensibly for information, and puzzles embodied in letters the fathers were asked to interpret. . . .

3. In making surveys from time to time of the schools in various boroughs, I again got attendance officers and social visitors to make rough estimates of fathers' I.Q.s and to obtain notes of their occupations. Pooling the whole lot together would yield well over 1000 cases. But the unreliability of the assessments would be very large. Since the errors probably range equally on either side of the true value, the figures are reliable enough for working out class averages.[93]

This letter makes it quite clear that the material Burt dredged up from the past to serve as a basis for his calculations was, from a scientific point of view, mostly rubbish, and his admission that 'for obvious reasons the assessments of adult intelligence were less thorough and reliable' was a misleading understatement.[94] More-

93. Burt, C. L. Letter to Professor J. A. Beardmore, 28 November 1968.
94. Burt, C. L. Brit. J. Statist. Psychol., XIV, 1961, 9.

over he effectively concealed his sample sizes by 'reducing the figures observed to numbers per 1000' (which need not, of course, mean that the actual numbers were *greater* than 1000), and his original assessments of I.Q. by rescaling to the conventional mean of 100 and standard deviation of 15 (which no doubt accounts for the scaling down of the higher professional I.Q. of 153·2 given in the 1943 article to the figure of 139·7).[95] The probability is, once again, that Burt's original data had been destroyed in the blitz. When asked by Professor Beardmore to supply the data under the first of his headings Burt never did so, which suggests that he did not any longer have the original figures, but only summaries of the results. On the other hand, we have no good grounds for thinking that he did not in the first place collect the data. What must be questioned are, firstly, the quality of the data themselves; and secondly, their use for fairly elaborate statistical analysis. It was a dubious exercise, though perhaps 'fraud' is too strong a word to use.

The data on declining educational standards published in the *Irish Journal of Education*[96] were much more open to question. We noted in Chapter Seven that Burt became involved in bitter controversies during the last few years of his life, following the demise of the system of selective secondary education to which he had lent his support, and which he had done much to promote. In the second *Black Paper*[97] he had commented on the decline of educational standards, which he attributed in part to the introduction of comprehensive education and 'progressive' teaching methods. As evidence for this decline he provided in the *Irish Journal of Education* a table of scores for intelligence and school attainments compiled by Miss M. G. O'Connor from various reports over a period of fifty years, from 1914 to 1965. Scores for intelligence, reading (accuracy and comprehension), spelling and arithmetic (mechanical and problems) were given for the years 1914, 1917, 1920, 1930, 1945, 1955 and 1965. The level reached in each of the three 'R's was shown to be well below that for 1914, and intelligence also showed a slight decline. We have seen that these conclusions were greeted with considerable scepticism both by teachers and by educational researchers, since Burt had provided no information either about the tests he had used, or about his methods of sampling,

95. Burt, C. L. *Brit. J. Educ. Psychol.*, XIII, 1943, 84; *Brit. J. Statist. Psychol.*, XIV, 1961, 11.

96. Burt, C. L. Intelligence and heredity: some common misconceptions. *Irish J. Educ.*, III, 1969, 75–94.

97. Burt, C. L. The Mental Differences between Children. In Cox, C. B. and Dyson, A. E. (eds) *Black Paper II*, 1969, pp. 16–25.

which were obviously critical if he was to come to any valid conclusions. And what, too, of the data themselves? How had these results been collected? The years 1917, 1920, 1930 and 1945 present no real problems, as Burt was working in London then, and had access to schools. The 1917 results clearly relate to the surveys carried out for *The Distribution and Relation of Educational Abilities* (1917); the 1920 results to the standardisation of *Mental and Scholastic Tests* (1921). We can also attribute the 1930 results to the work involved in standardising the Stanford Binet Test. In his 1942 article on the factor analysis of the Binet tests Burt spoke of 'a series of inquiries extending over nearly ten years, and with the aid of a small group of teachers and research students nearly 3,000 children attending elementary schools in London were tested'.[98] Similarly the 1945 results were probably linked to the later standardisation of the Terman and Merrill revision commenced by Miss May Davidson in 1938 and completed after the war.[99] The figures for the remaining years, 1914, 1955 and 1965, are not so easy to explain. Burt no doubt had tested a lot of children in 1914 (he mentions about 1400 normal children having been examined personally or with the help of teachers),[100] but at that early stage of his career he had no standardised tests of scholastic attainments. He noted in his report for the year: 'Pedagogical tests are in urgent need of standardisation. The results of examinations as at present conducted are notoriously unscientific. . . . Experiments have been commenced by the psychologist personally with a view to obtaining tests and scales for all school subjects, similar to those devised by Professor Thorndike and others in America, for writing, composition, and arithmetic. Tests of drawing have been carried out upon 1000 children from all departments of a school in Hampstead. Tests of other subjects (reading, arithmetic, writing) have been commenced in the infant's and girl's departments of two schools in St Pancras.'[101] In the light of this contemporary statement it is clear that Burt was not in a position to provide reliable norms for school achievements in 1914. The tests which he was later to use had not at that time been standardised, nor, if they existed, been employed on any but small pilot groups.

The position with regard to the years 1955 and 1965 is even more problematical, because by then Burt had no right of entry to London schools. Following the publication of *Black Paper II* in 1969 Burt

98. Burt, C. L. and John, Enid. A factorial analysis of the Terman–Binet tests. *Brit. J. Educ. Psychol.*, XII, 1942, 117–21, 156–61.

99. *Ibid.*, p. 119.

100. London County Council. Report of the Psychologist, 1915, p. 1.

101. *Ibid.*, p. 4.

was interviewed by a reporter of *The Guardian*, and a statement appeared in its issue for 7 November 1969: 'These tests had been given regularly to a sample of about 200 children, aged 10, in 10 inner London schools between 1914 and 1965. During his long service with the old L.C.C. Sir Cyril supervised these tests. In recent years he had been helped by research students at University College, London and by teachers in the schools concerned. The sample of schools had altered somewhat over the period.' In a letter to Mr G. F. Peaker, Inspector of Schools, who had expressed doubts on the matter of sampling, Burt himself amplified this report. 'We tried to evade the effect of these [social] changes by adopting the method of median sampling described in my early reports. We selected median schools, i.e. those drawing mainly from classes IV and V in my eight-fold scheme . . . and then took a few median pupils from each of the selected schools. How far this device has been successful I am unable to say. . . . I willingly allow that my figures may well be out by 4 or 5 points on a percentage scale.'[102] An investigation of this kind, involving the selection of schools, the cooperation of teachers, and the testing of 200 children on both group and individual tests, could only have been carried out with the consent of the education authority. No such consent was ever given. The Record Keeper of the Greater London Record Office writes as follows:

> Consent to research projects of the type under review were, in the years in question, given or refused by the General Purposes Sub-Committee of the Council's Education Committee, and in the minute books are indexed either under 'Research' or more frequently under 'Use of the School Organization'. We have gone through the minutes over the years 1952 to 1965, but although the Sub-Committee allowed a considerable number of projects of one kind or another, we have not been able to trace any which could be identified with Burt or Miss O'Connor. There was more than one project approved in which the National Foundation for Educational Research was the applicant without the name of their researcher being noted and which centered around progress in reading and arithmetic, but I would hardly think these would be relevant to present consideration.[103]

102. Burt, C. L. Letter to Mr G. F. Peaker, H.M.I., 21 November 1969.

103. Letter from Mr A. R. Neate, Record Keeper, G.L.C., 21 December 1977. I am much indebted to Mr Neate for carrying out this investigation on my behalf. As Mr D. A. Pidgeon of the N.F.E.R. was one of Burt's principal critics on the matter of educational standards it is certain that the Foundation did not sponsor Burt's work.

So it seems improbable in the extreme that any testing programme was carried out under Burt's direction either in 1955 or 1965. There are other difficulties. Burt had no research funds at his disposal, and a programme that involved some hundreds of hours of testing (as at least half the tests had to be given individually) must have been quite expensive to mount. His claim, in a letter to Mr E. Britton of the National Union of Teachers, that these results were obtained in connection with the revision of test standards for the fourth edition of *Mental and Scholastic Tests* (1962) is hard to credit, as in fact no alterations in tests norms were made in any of the four editions of that work. Standards remained unchanged from 1921 (1st edn) to 1962 (4th edn). Finally there is no evidence of any contact or communication with Miss M. G. O'Connor. She never appears to have visited Elsworthy Road, nor to have written to Burt, nor to have met any of Burt's associates. The whole massive operation involved in ascertaining changes in standards of scholastic achievement left not a trace in Burt's detailed diary entries, nor in his carefully filed correspondence. The conclusion seems inescapable: the figures given in Burt's table in the *Irish Journal of Education* were, at least in part, fabricated.

VI

The verdict must be, therefore, that at any rate in three instances, beyond reasonable doubt, Burt was guilty of deception. He falsified the early history of factor analysis (see Chapter Nine); he produced spurious data on MZ twins; and he fabricated figures on declining levels of scholastic achievement. Moreover, other material on kinship correlations is distinctly suspect. It would be tempting to go further and maintain, with Kamin, that all Burt's work from the beginning was scientifically worthless, and to dismiss him, as the Clarkes did, simply as 'a fraudulent scientist', particularly as examples of Burt's devious behaviour in personal relationships would appear to support an all-inclusive condemnation. Nevertheless such a judgment would be one-sided, and less than just. It would fail to account for the esteem in which Burt was held, almost, if not quite, universally in the early stages of his career, and by many up to the time of his death. It would elevate the judgment of persons who knew him slightly, or not at all, over that of those who were intimately associated with him in the days of his prime. It would disregard the assessments of contemporary experts in their appraisal of his work, and it would give insufficient weight to his many scholarly and practical achievements.

There is a great deal of evidence to suggest that the verdict of 'total fraud' is far too simple to accord with the facts. It is, indeed, strange that psychologists so easily seem to succumb to such naive 'black and white' judgments. Burt was in many ways an immensely impressive person; his reputation was not without foundation. On the occasion of his knighthood over a hundred persons wrote to congratulate him with obvious spontaneity, sincerity and warmth. An interesting appreciation was one from Udny Yule, the eminent statistician who had known Burt personally for over thirty years, and who would hardly have been blind to statistical shortcomings: 'My hearty congratulations on your knighthood . . . you have earned it well. But I myself would have been more pleased if the recognition had come from The Royal Society.'[104] Godfrey Thomson, too, another old friend, with a critical mind and a capacity for blunt frankness, wrote: 'I am very pleased indeed, and I am sure that no honour will give such widespread pleasure to so many';[105] while from the public sector came the appreciation of Sir Percy Waterfield of the Civil Service Commission: 'May I begin by offering my very sincere, though belated, congratulations on your recent knighthood, which gave us all in the Commission great pleasure. We know full well how fully it has been merited, and we are delighted that the honour has fallen to one who is our own chosen adviser.'[106] Even psychologists, like William Stephenson, who had clashed on technical questions, wrote to express their 'deep satisfaction that an honour so completely appropriate and merited should have come to you. It is all so completely fitting, so right, so exactly what was obvious.'[107] His old colleagues at the London Institute of Education, who had known him intimately, were equally delighted.[108]

Account must be taken, too, of contemporary appraisals of his major works. A few extracts must suffice.

This long expected book is characterised by the scholarly care and thoroughness which we have learned to look for in everything that Mr Burt produces. (Dr P. B. Ballard, on *Mental and Scholastic Tests*.)[109]

While the writer has written in a popular rather than in a technical

104. Letter from G. Udny Yule, F.R.S., 17 June 1946.
105. Letter from Professor Godfrey Thomson, 13 June 1946.
106. Letter from Sir Percy Waterfield, 1 July 1946.
107. Letter from Dr Wm Stephenson, 20 June 1946.
108. Letter from Professor H. R. Hamley, 14 June 1946.
109. Ballard, P. B. *Brit. J. Psychol.*, XIII, 1922, 92–5.

style he has consistently maintained a scientific viewpoint and restraint in the handling of his subject. (Dr E. N. Ferriss, on *The Young Delinquent*.)[110]

Describes in detail and with the utmost lucidity and interest his attempts to understand it (backwardness) and secondly to recommend measures for dealing with it. (Dr M. D. Vernon, on *The Backward Child*.)[111]

One of the most important contributions to Psychology made during recent years. (Dr R. H. Thouless, on *The Factors of the Mind*.)[112]

In the light of these judgments it is absurd to suggest, as several recent critics have done, that all these persons— experts, colleagues, men of standing in public life, former students and friends— were simply fooled; that Burt, the clever rogue, had just taken them all in, all the time; while they, the critics, often with no personal knowledge of him, could see through the whole sham. The suggestion is not merely absurd; it is arrogant. Indeed it is even more than that— it is to commit the same crime that they accuse Burt himself of committing; it is to fudge the evidence. For it is as reprehensible to push aside historical facts that fail to fit in with simple theories as to fabricate scientific facts.

Burt was a contradictory character. There were several facets to his personality; great strengths, and great weaknesses. He was capable of evoking both rapturous admiration and intense distrust. To some he seemed 'no less than a god', to quote a former student; to others a force of evil. To reconcile these contradictions it is necessary to turn to a fuller analysis of Burt's own psychological make-up. The psychologist must himself be psychologised.

110. Ferriss, E. N. *Amer. J. Psychol.*, XXXVIII, 1926, 611–12.
111. Vernon, M. D. *Brit. J. Psychol.*, XXVIII, 1938, 346–9.
112. Thouless, R. H. *Brit. J. Psychol.*, XXXII, 1941, 287–8.

CHAPTER THIRTEEN

The Man

Burt the man confronts us, then, with startling contradictions. To his oldest friend, Professor Valentine, who knew him as intimately as anyone over a period of more than fifty years, he was not only a great psychologist, 'one of the half dozen greatest psychologists this century has produced',[1] but also a great man, generous and humane. To his critics and enemies, on the contrary, he was both fraudulent as a scientist, and unscrupulous as a person. Nor is it difficult to find evidence on the one hand to support his virtues and achievements, and on the other to confirm his delinquencies. Perhaps, however, this should not wholly surprise us. Even the greatest human beings have displayed their weaknesses. Francis Bacon was convicted of corruptly taking bribes; Newton was paranoically suspicious, and stooped to dishonest devices in his controversies with Bernouilli and Leibniz; Beethoven combined the highest ideals and most sublime visions with sordid and shabby conduct; Tolstoy, the moralist, behaved with intolerable insensitivity to his own family; Bertrand Russell, in spite of the brilliance of his intellect and the depth of his concern for humanity, was callous in his treatment of women. Human beings are not simple; and if Burt, too, had feet of clay, that should not be regarded, even by his admirers, as totally incredible. Before passing judgment, we must seek to understand.

I

Of one thing there is no doubt—Burt was highly intelligent. His intellectual powers were remarkable for their combination of quickness, range and practicality. He could grasp the point of an argument, and spot a logical fallacy in a flash. He was fertile in his suggestions, and imaginative in his proposals. He had an almost unbelievably well-stocked mind, and could call on vast stores of

1. Valentine C. W. Cyril Burt: a Biographical Sketch and Appreciation. In Banks, Charlotte, and Broadhurst, P. L. (eds) *Stephanos: Studies in Psychology presented to Cyril Burt*, 1965.

knowledge—historical, literary and scientific. He could express his ideas with lucidity and style, though, as he realised himself, the facility with which he wrote and the wealth of information at his disposal meant that his written work was often overloaded with detail. He combined academic erudition with a vivid sense of practical realities. He never tried to simplify issues, and was always aware of the complexities of real-life situations. So his advice commended itself not only to his colleagues, but to men of affairs, to whom he appeared eminently endowed with common sense.

No doubt Burt's intellectual gifts were largely innate. He had some distinguished ancestors, including Isaac Barrow, mathematician, classical scholar, theologian, and tutor to Isaac Newton. He early showed signs of unusual capacity. His Canadian uncle thanked him, at the age of 3½ years, for the 'text' in his own handwriting. His parents encouraged his early development, and his father is said to have taught him Latin declensions while Burt was still in his cot. His first term's school report from King's School, Warwick, when he was 9½, placed him first in his form in English, Mathematics and French. Before the year was out he was first in Latin as well. At Christ's Hospital he rose to the top group, the 'Grecians', though never quite the first of the bunch; and at Oxford, too, he just missed the highest distinction. But he more than made up by his intellectual range for what he lacked in specialised excellence.

His verbal abilities were particularly marked. This comes out not only in his literary gifts, but in his facility for acquiring foreign languages. In addition to his command of Latin and Greek, he could speak French, German and Italian fluently, had a smattering of other European languages, including Russian, and an excellent knowledge of Hebrew. A classical education—and Burt's education up to the age of 23 was primarily classical—is, for those who are verbally gifted, a magnificent training in the use of language. The classical scholar is not only required to translate fluently the writers of ancient Greece and Rome, but he has to compose proses and verses in Greek and Latin. He acquires in the process a refined sense of style, a sensitivity to sentence structure and the usage of words, and a mastery of man's most important intellectual tool, language. He also acquires in the course of studying ancient history and literature a large view of human civilisations and the values they enshrine. Such an education, of course, also has its limitations. It pays little attention to the technical and scientific achievements of the modern world; by reason of its exclusiveness it tends to induce feelings of superiority and élitism in those who are classically educated; and in a subtle way it is a training in pretence. This last point requires elucidation. Every week the classical scholar is required to produce pieces of Greek and Latin prose and verse. He is set the task of writing passages in the manner of Demosthenes or Cicero, Euripides or Vergil. The finished product, the 'fair copy', must look in style as like as possible to that of its ancient model—it must, in other words, be, as near as may be, a perfect 'fake'. All the detailed working, the preliminary trials and scratchings out, are thrown away; only the 'fair copy' is presented, and only the 'fair copy' is judged. The best 'fake' achieves the highest marks. For more than ten years of his early life Burt was subjected to this regular discipline.

If Burt's formal education was in some ways narrow, his intellectual curiosity was broad. Throughout his life he was tireless in his search for knowledge. He was driven along by a powerful intellectual urge, not only to extend his knowledge over the widest areas, but to unravel the intricate details and technicalities of what he studied. He was never content with superficial understanding; he strove for mastery, and in a surprising number of fields, both humanistic and scientific, he succeeded in achieving it. Throughout his life he was an avid note-taker, and made detailed summaries of important books he had read. This began at school, where he also made summaries of the sermons he listened to. His boyhood exercise books contain annotations on politics, religion, literature, economics, history, science and philosophy, and his tastes in later life were equally wide. He never stopped studying; and in old age, even when in hospital recovering from an operation, he would amuse himself by improving his knowledge of Hebrew. His idea of relaxation was to switch from one form of intellectual activity to another.

In addition to high general intelligence and intellectual drive, combined with high verbal ability and intensive education, Burt possessed a number of special talents, artistic and mathematical. His artistic talents were encouraged early in life. He could himself draw and paint quite well, and in his schoolboy visits to galleries he acquired an extensive knowledge of the visual arts. In the years when he could travel he was an indefatigable sightseer, and when he could no longer go abroad he still visited London's museums and collections. His real gifts, though, were audile rather than visile, and the art form in which he showed the greatest proficiency was music. He was not merely an erudite musicologist and dabbler in musical composition, but, in his younger days, a chorister, and, until deafness rendered it impossible, a competent performer on both piano and organ. Perhaps his most remarkable special talent, however, was his mathematical talent—remarkable since his formal education in mathematics ceased comparatively early. The pupils at

Christ's Hospital were divided from the age of 14 onwards into two main sections, known as the 'Latin School' and the 'Mathematical School'. The 'Latin School', to which Burt was allocated, studied mainly linguistic subjects—Latin, Greek, French and English, with only a little mathematics, and even this was dropped in the final years. So Burt's formal mathematical training was perfunctory. The proficiency he later attained was self-acquired, and was the result of his natural talents combined with much persistence.

Burt brought, therefore, to the study of psychology powerful intellectual equipment, and this equipment remained in good shape into very advanced years. Burt's verbal and critical powers seemed hardly to decline at all even when he was in his eighties. He could still write with great fluency; he still seemed to be in command of his huge stores of knowledge; and he could still compile erudite and lucid critical reviews of manuscripts submitted to him. In conversation he seemed to be completely in control of his forces. Nevertheless there commonly occurs an intellectual decline in later life, and we have already seen that Burt himself admitted to weakening powers of concentration, to difficulties in following the thread of complex logical arguments, and to a tendency to make careless errors. There is some evidence in the 1960s for a diminution of creative and logical powers. But there was nothing pathological about this, and it can be regarded as the normal and inevitable result of growing old. The blemishes in Burt's later work were not primarily the result of intellectual decline. Even his adversaries respected his intellectual powers. The trouble lay in his personality; and this we must now examine.

II

In many contexts Burt displayed attractive qualities. He was described by one fellow student at Oxford as a 'loveable character'; and that is how he seemed to many who came in contact with him. When he was at ease, as he was with children, women and small groups of students, such as he had at Aberystwyth, he could be lively and entertaining. He had a marvellous way with children, which helped him enormously in his clinical work. He had a great sense of fun and humour, which revealed itself when he was completely relaxed. He was often generous and helpful; generous in giving presents and even financial help from his slender means, and helpful in giving advice lavishly to those who asked for it. Many former students have paid glowing tribute to the help they received from Burt: Sir Alec Clegg, the educationist; Professor

Eysenck, the psychologist; Professor Max Hamilton, the psychiatrist; Mrs Winifred Raphael of the National Institute of Industrial Psychology; Dr W. D. Wall, former Director of the University of London Institute of Education, to name but a few among the eminent; and to them must be added many ordinary students and ordinary folk in trouble.

Yet with this helpfulness there was always a certain reserve. Burt rarely became intimate even with those closest to him. He addressed very few of his friends by their first names. Even very old friends, like Valentine and Pear, whom he had known for fifty years, were called by their surnames. Flugel was almost the only exception among his male associates. To some extent this was, of course, an old-fashioned convention, and there was a large element of old-fashioned courtesy and formality in Burt's demeanour. But in Burt's case there was more to it than that; there was an avoidance, almost a fear of emotional involvements, or any outward display of emotion. Burt was an extremely introverted, extremely private person, who rarely expressed his feelings to others, and, perhaps, did not always admit them to himself. He hardly ever displayed anger, or lost his temper, and he maintained a devastating politeness even when engaged in controversy. He showed what one colleague described as 'benign equanimity'. And this external composure revealed itself not only in social situations, but when confronted with physical danger. When, after his return to London in the autumn of 1944, a rocket fell on Primrose Hill breaking the windows of his flat, Burt displayed no panic, but calmly analysed his feelings introspectively. There was an inwardness about Burt which detached him from close social contacts. He confided in nobody; there was no sharing of his intimate thoughts and feelings. He appreciated an audience to whom he could display his accomplishments—though even this was not perhaps essential to him—but sociability for its own sake meant nothing to him. He disliked and shunned social gatherings. It is said that he had never even entered a public house. The rowdyism of the sporting undergraduates at Oxford had been deeply repellent to him, and he never showed the slightest interest in any form of sport. His wife, who was both sport-loving and social, completely failed to modify his aversions, and they soon found they had almost nothing in common.

Burt was, therefore, in some respects always a very lonely man, who lacked many of the normal interests of the average human being. In some ways this is not a disadvantage for a psychologist. Detachment is not infrequently accompanied by superior powers of observation, and certainly Burt was a superb observer, quick to note significant traits in those he was studying, and perceptive in his descriptions. This came out, as we have seen, even in his schoolboy letters, and was a feature of his case studies in adult life. Detachment from conventional attitudes also helped Burt to sympathise with persons who were somewhat odd or unusual. He could appreciate rather unconventional characters, and could get on with neurotic and difficult people; indeed, he was probably happier with them. His secretary for thirty years, Miss Bruce, was just such a person; highly neurotic, but loyally devoted to him, Burt seemed to understand her, and she was of invaluable assistance to him.

Burt was equally detached from stereotyped political attitudes. The critics, who towards the end of his life regarded him on the basis of his *Black Paper* contributions as a right-wing reactionary, totally misjudged him. Burt was remarkably free from political and social prejudices. 'I don't agree with the views of either political party', he told his sister towards the end of his life,[2] and it is perhaps significant that he never voted at elections. His support for selective education did not imply support for conservative policies as a whole. His inclination had always been to make fun of the 'establishment'. In the 1930s he was critical of Baldwin, and particularly of his 'shabby' treatment of King Edward VIIIth.[3] He enthusiastically welcomed the Beveridge report, which paved the way for the welfare state. And when Russia entered the war in 1941, he commented interestingly as follows:

I do hope the narrow-minded British aristocrats won't get huffy because the Russians are communists. We made an amusing inquiry here in which we asked people to express their belief or disbelief in a number of different doctrines, a large number of them typical communist doctrines. We found that the majority of educated and liberal-minded people accepted the doctrines, although, of course, they would hold up their hands in holy horror at the thought that the doctrines were communistic. However there are a certain number of things in the Bolshevist regime which seem to me to be even more barbarous and medieval than the games played by Hitler's Nazis. But in either case I do not think it quite fair to judge a civilization by the worst events that you can discover within it. After all, if one wanted to be nasty, one could make American civilization sound pretty primitive, simply by emphasising the number of murders carried out by Chicago gangsters, and the horrible bribery and corruption that goes on in the political world. The chief thing in favour of

2. Burt, C. L. Letter to his sister, 11 August 1970.
3. Burt, C. L. Letter to his mother, 22 December 1936.

both Russia and America is that they now seem quite willing to let everybody, in other countries at any rate, live their lives peaceably. Moreover I believe the Russians have lately taken a greater interest in science than even the Germans or Americans.[4]

This was perceptive, realistic and remarkably unprejudiced. If one had to give Burt a political label, the label would be 'liberal'; but his liberalism was tempered by his firm belief in ultimate values, and never degenerated into libertarianism. His attitudes were rooted ultimately in a broadly religious metaphysic. Though not religious, or devout, in the strict and narrow sense, he believed firmly in the divine ordering of the universe.

This explains, no doubt, a certain unworldliness in Burt's make-up. He was utterly disinterested in wealth or place. He never showed any signs of using his many contacts with those in positions of power to enhance his own interests, and he never exploited his own abilities for personal gain. He responded when called on to sit on committees and advisory bodies, but he never sought office, and never pushed himself forward. He was always glad to retreat into the background and get on with his own work. In most of the mundane affairs of life he was dependent on others, his secretaries, housekeepers, and for a time his wife. Even in his professional work he did not mobilise his forces to the last effect. Particularly after his retirement he failed to utilise his time advantageously, showed no interest in obtaining financial support, and made no effort to recruit assistants. He neither expounded his ideas systematically for the benefit of psychologists, nor, apart from occasional broadcasts, popularly for the benefit of the general public; and thereby lost a considerable potential income. In all such matters he seemed totally disinterested, while to make ends meet he slogged away at menial tasks more suited to a struggling junior.

Yet Burt was unquestionably ambitious, and the impulse to dominate was perhaps the driving force of his life—but it was domination on his terms. He sought neither wealth nor power, but intellectual supremacy. There was something egotistical, exalted and grandiose about the resolutions he solemnly wrote down while still an Oxford undergraduate:

My purpose in life concerns primarily myself. It is to produce one perfect being for the universe. The question then for each moment is this: is my present attitude a manifestation of, or conducive to, my perfection. In reforms try 'thorough'. The gradual method lasts no longer. Better a dozen gallops breaking

4. Burt, C. L. Letter to his sister, 23 July 1941.

down in between and starting a fresh horse each time, than a tortoise pace tapering off into a doze. On no philosophical principle can you defend the shirking of the moment's pain or trouble when you have an end in view. Therefore damn your weakness, damn your aches, damn your wanderings, and stick at your task . . . you must rid yourself of your dependence upon the mood of the moment. . . . Anything, work itself may be sacrificed to this. You aim thus at ultimately rendering your adherence to method automatic, and making the machinery of life and work unconscious of agonising, and absorbent of your whole attention and effort.[5]

It took Burt some time before his 'weaknesses' were conquered. At Liverpool he was still struggling with bouts of inertia; then overcoming them and working for fifteen hours a day. He still had moments of cynicism, smothered in their turn by more good resolutions. In the L.C.C. appointment he found the focus and the scope he needed for his energies, and from then on his goal was clear, and the means for reaching it available. He was to become Galton's intellectual heir and realise Galton's dream of creating an individual psychology, based on firm statistical foundations and applied in practice to the solution of human problems. He had already become convinced of the essential rightness of Galton's viewpoint, as his own early papers show. Indeed he believed that in broad outline the whole field of individual psychology had already been mapped out.[6] His former colleague, William Stephenson, described him as 'supremely confident, smoothly superior'.[7] As soon as he had acquired this confidence his task became to propagate the doctrines and findings of individual psychology and to assume the leadership of the movement. To this end he worked assiduously, collecting quantities of data, and gaining a mastery of the techniques—statistical, mathematical and genetic—needed to sustain the role. At the same time he gradually became more and more jealous of any rivals to his own pre-eminence in his chosen field. While Spearman was alive he dared not openly challenge Spearman's leadership, but in lectures and conversation in the 1930s he was already disparaging Spearman's work, and after his death openly strove to overthrow him. He was equally jealous of his American rivals, and in particular of Thurstone. He took Thurstone to task for misrepresenting British work, and ignoring his (Burt's) earlier anticipations of Thurstonian methods. He could not tolerate

5. Burt, C. L. Diary, 1905.
6. Burt, C. L. The mental difference between individuals. *Brit. Ass.*, 1923.
7. Letter from William Stephenson, 1 December 1976.

any challenge from younger contemporaries, including his own brightest students. In seminars and discussions 'he had to win', as one postgraduate student observed. If a former student showed exceptional promise, he fell out of favour with Burt, who attempted to block his progress. This was particularly true in the case of Eysenck, whose promotion and advancement Burt did everything in his power to stop, and to whom he came to show a scarcely veiled hostility. But it applied to others, too, and Burt's correspondence contains disparaging remarks both on former students, and on other distinguished contemporaries. 'There are very few good psychologists in this country at the moment', he informed his friend, Mrs Warde, in 1957,[8] thus dismissing by implication the whole Cambridge school, and its leader, Sir Frederic Bartlett, towards whom his relations had for some time been pretty cool. Even of distinguished foreigners, like Piaget, who had started off his investigations by using his (Burt's) reasoning tests, Burt would speak condescendingly and critically. He seemed to resent the fact that Piaget had not only modified some of his own findings, but had attained such a huge reputation as, perhaps, the world's leading authority on the intellectual development of children. To those who openly challenged his viewpoint and his findings—the sociologists, environmentalists and behaviourists—Burt was even more hostile. He engaged in unceasing warfare with them. Controversy became one of the major activities, and motivated much of the work, of his declining years. It was almost as if he had marked out a certain territory for himself—in this case intellectual territory—within the boundaries of which he was determined to maintain the mastery, lay down the law, and drive off all rivals. To those who presented no challenge—children, women, students of average ability, the maladjusted—he could be both charming and generous. To those who challenged him, directly or indirectly, he presented a very different face—hostile, cantankerous, and, if need be, unscrupulous. Whence came this duality?

III

The profound influence of the early years of life on personality development is now an accepted doctrine among psychologists. It would be inappropriate in this context to provide a detailed documentation of the evidence for this belief. Sluckin in his survey of the recent literature notes that 'what happens early in the individual's life may profoundly influence his psychological devel-

8. Burt, C. L. Letter to Mrs B. Warde, 3 March 1957.

opment . . . there are more and more such findings about the lasting effects of one or another kind of early experience.'[9]

The first nine years of Cyril Burt's life were spent in London, and there are good reasons for thinking that this period played an important part in shaping his development. Burt more or less admitted this himself. He informed Dr Bernstein that he was born a Cockney, and could easily drop his Oxford veneer and talk as a Cockney would talk.[10] He maintained that his early acquaintance with the seamy realities of London life greatly helped him in his later work with delinquents. Unfortunately the records of this very early period of Burt's life are almost non-existent, and his sister, who was eight years his junior, cannot fill in the gaps with her recollections. So we are left with a few bare facts, which have to be supplemented by a good deal of imaginative reconstruction.

Burt's ancestry was a mixed ancestry, part Saxon, part Celtic. His father was of stolid Saxon stock; his mother a more volatile Welsh woman, whose own brother was an unstable artist, constantly in debt. Temperamentally Cyril resembled his mother; but his father provided the admired model. His father was not perhaps a brilliant man, but he was reputed to be a very wise man, and in many ways the ideal family physician. Young Cyril always deeply respected him, and looked with envy on his equable disposition. He regarded him as his greatest friend, and even in later life his sister only had to remark, 'What would your father say to that?' to produce an immediate effect. The home was a cultivated place and provided a favourable and encouraging background for intellectual and artistic development. It was, however, in the London period of Burt's life a very humble one, located in a very seedy environment. The Burts resided in Petty France in the City of Westminster, not much more than a quarter of a mile from the Abbey. Burt's father was a junior house surgeon attached to the Westminster Hospital, supported then wholly by the voluntary contributions of the public. He did not obtain his M.R.C.S. until his son was four years old, paying his way until then by means of a loan from his wife's family. Even after qualifying he was miserably paid. Junior hospital doctors up till quite recent times were described as 'the most under-privileged, underpaid, pushed-about and generally sat-upon section of the profession'.[11] In the 1880s they were barely above the bread line. The only way the Burts could keep afloat was by Burt senior

9. Sluckin, W. (ed) *Early Learning and Early Experience*, Penguin Modern Psychology Readings, 1971, Introduction, p. 9.

10. Burt, C. L. Letter to Dr B. Bernstein, 22 June 1963.

11. Ferris, P. *The Doctors*, 1965, p. 53.

helping with pharmaceutical work, and his wife taking in student lodgers.

In spite of their proximity to the centre of government the surroundings where the Burts lived were squalid. The custom of affording sanctuary to fugitives from the law, not merely in the Abbey precincts, but also in the district north-west of that, resulted in the herding of a most undesirable population in the area. One of the nearby streets was called 'Thieving Lane' well into the nineteenth century. The area was beginning to be opened up and developed by the middle of the century when Victoria Street was constructed. But when the Burts lived there in the late 1880s it was still a very depressed area. It was just at this time that Charles Booth carried out his famous survey of *The Life and Labour of the People of London*,[12] assessing the degree of poverty in each street in central London. He rated the whole region south of St James's Park as having one of the highest poverty levels in London. According to Booth 43·6 per cent of the population of the region round Petty France were living in poverty (and poverty for Booth really meant poverty) compared with 47 per cent for the worst area in London (Bermondsey), 44 per cent for the east end (Bethnal Green) and 30 per cent for central London as a whole. The Burts were living, therefore, in one of the worst parts of the city, in spite of the nearby amenity of the parks. Booth in his survey described it as follows: 'This is the neighbourhood of the Royal Aquarium; very mixed population. Several little bad spots inhabited by beggars and loafers, sandwich men and hawkers, but they are being gradually demolished. Good many offices, and several wealthy mansions let in suites.'[13] This then was the region Burt lived in during the most impressionable years of his boyhood, and it was with children brought up in his poverty-stricken background that he mixed when he went to the local Board School.

The London Board Schools had only recently been established following the passing of the Education Act of 1870, and up till 1890 when the 'New Code' was introduced, were run on regimented lines by teachers who were paid by results. We do not know for certain which school Burt attended, as school registers from the late nineteenth century have not been preserved, but by far the most likely school would be the Buckingham Gate School, situated barely a hundred yards from Petty France. This was a large

12. Booth, C. *The Life and Labour of the People of London*, 2nd edn, 9 vols, 1892–97.

13. The Royal Aquarium stood where the Central Hall now stands. It was demolished in 1902. The wealthy mansions mentioned were those facing St James's Park, and in Queen Anne's Gate.

establishment built in 1882, with a pupil enrolment of 587 in 1891, when Burt would have been there. The inspector's report for that year describes the discipline as excellent, and the teaching as 'full of spirit and intelligence'.[14] Though the discipline in the school was strict, the children themselves must have been an obstreperous crowd of little gamins. Booth described them in these terms: 'To the casual observer street children, especially of the poorer class, proclaim themselves chiefly by their noisiness, their rags and dirt, their tendency to swarm, their occasional pathos, their frequent fun, their general air of squalor and neglect.'[15] They were generally underfed, and their parents often drunkards. We know that these pathetic urchins created a powerful impression on Burt's mother, who used to give informal help at a 'ragged school' (most likely the one which was opposite where Central Hall now stands), and felt a fear that her own son might one day be kidnapped. The young Cyril, sensitive, intelligent, and physically both clumsy and puny, had to mix with this mob, and somehow survive.

But survive he did; and when, three years later in 1895, he was sent back to London to boarding school at Christ's Hospital, he showed no great reluctance to go. So we can be fairly certain that he had learned to hold his own in the gamin culture into which he had been thrown. How did he do this? Certainly not by physical prowess. He must have survived by using his wits, which were far sharper than those of most of his school-fellows. He must have learned, we may presume, to observe them closely, to keep his feelings to himself, to bluff it out, and to outmanoeuvre those who tried to molest him. He had learned the gamin art of survival, and from that time on there was a gamin component to his own personality, which though overlaid by a polite veneer, persisted, much of the time below the surface, for the remainder of his life. Perhaps, too, these early experiences provided at least part of the motivation for his fascination in later life for the problems of delinquency and backwardness, with which he had been confronted in his early years.

It must have been an incredible change to move at the age of nine from this tough environment to the medieval peace of an isolated Warwickshire village, still dominated by the lord of the manor and the church; to leave the milieu of social class V for that of social classes I and II; to reside no longer in a crowded street but in a roomy seventeenth-century house set in three-acre grounds; to be translated from the basic curriculum of a regimented Board School

14. Greater London Record Office. Inspectors' Reports, Buckingham Gate School, January and December, 1891.

15. Booth, C. *Op. cit.*, vol. II, p. 211.

to the classical fare and smaller classes of a centuries-old Grammar School. Burt was quick to adapt himself to his new surroundings, and came to love the country. But he always thought of himself as a Londoner, and at bottom he was a Londoner. The sharp break, which divided his life prior to entering the university precisely in two, was, it may be hypothesised, a major reason for the duality in his own personality, together with a genetic contribution from his mixed stock, part Saxon, part Celtic.

These two sides of Burt's make-up never rested easily together. While at Oxford the diary he intermittently kept suggests that he was a good deal troubled by inner conflict. 'Little sleep during the night', he noted in January 1905, 'Thoughts run incoherently on insanity. Wherein I invent a new theory that it, like death, is falsely bewailed, being a release from excessive responsibility, fallen ambitions, material and old, moral and recent.' He noted again, 'My intermittent apathy and inertness, my anxiety for work and uprightness, and yet perpetual failure, daydreams, affections, temporary insanity.' He was constantly making and noting down good resolutions—in 1904, for example, 'to be scrupulously straightforward and sincere, to make up mind according to conscience quickly and act at once, to be up as soon as awake, to have more moral courage, self-sacrifice wherever possible, no teasing', and 'to clean teeth twice a day'! So it looks as though there were conflicts which went beyond the usual sexual problems of adolescence, and which derived from a deeper duality within his own personality. There are reasons to think, however, that Burt largely surmounted these difficulties when he found his métier, and from 1913 for the next quarter of a century his personality achieved an equilibrium, his creative potential flowered, and his reputation steadily and deservedly mounted.

IV

In the late 1930s things began to go wrong, and over the last thirty years of his life Burt suffered a series of setbacks which gradually upset his inner balance, always somewhat precarious. Outwardly he remained composed, but the tensions showed themselves in other ways.

The first setback was the failure of the marriage he contracted in 1932. We do not know exactly when this ran into difficulties. It is an area of Burt's life veiled in secrecy. Nothing to do with his marriage has been preserved, every scrap of evidence removed from the records. It was something about which Burt himself never wished to talk. When his wife finally left him in 1952 he wanted nothing more to do with her. The difficulties between them arose much earlier. Mrs Burt did not accompany her husband to Aberystwyth in 1939, and this suggests that the rift had begun before the end of the 1930s, which is not surprising as their tastes and temperaments were totally different. At that time Burt was heavily engaged in writing *The Factors of the Mind* and had no leisure for social distractions. So the probability is that the relationship was already strained before the outbreak of the war. There are good reasons to think that this was a heavy blow to Burt's pride. The expert in human nature had failed in the most intimate of human relationships. It was, too, a material blow, as he had hoped that his much younger wife, whose medical training he had helped to finance, would support him in his old age.

The second setback was the destruction of a large part of his papers and research materials in the air raids of April 1941. The details of this loss were described in the previous chapter. It rendered impossible the realisation of the ambitions he had set himself, and was for him a disaster of catastrophic dimensions.

The third setback was the breakdown of his health. Burt had never been physically robust, but he had not been seriously handicapped by illness before developing severe symptoms of Ménière's disease in the summer of 1941. This is a matter which will be discussed fully in the next section. Although the severe outbreaks moderated, to break out again in 1966, Burt had from 1941 onwards to lead a careful and restricted life. He was afraid to travel, never again went abroad, and cut down on his public engagements.

The fourth setback was the breach with his old department following his retirement from the chair. Burt had ardently desired to see the tradition of individual psychology continued at University College. It had been the crown of his life's work to build on the foundations laid by Galton, Sully, Spearman and Pearson. He regarded the University College department as a unique department, and as the centre of a school of psychology adequately represented nowhere else in Britain. Burt failed in his efforts to see someone appointed who would maintain the departmental traditions. He did not even leave behind a body of committed disciples. He made vain attempts to thwart the changes introduced by his successor; and in the end had to be debarred altogether from the department. It was a humiliating defeat.

The fifth setback was Burt's loss of the control over the statistical journal in 1963. For sixteen years, from its inauguration in 1947, this had been the principal vehicle for the exposition of his findings and opinions. After Godfrey Thomson's death he had virtually dictatorial control over its contents, and a large part of his time was devoted to writing contributions under his own and fictitious names, and editing those of other contributors. He fought strenuously to retain control of the journal, but in the end had to bow to the dictates of the British Psychological Society's publication committee, and relinquish the editorship. It was another severe defeat.

The final setback was the gradual erosion of the system of selective secondary education Burt had done so much to promote, the widespread abandonment of the use of intelligence testing at the age of eleven-plus, and the questioning of the whole complex of ideas on which selective education had been based. Up to about 1953 Burt must have felt himself to be in the van of successful progress. But then the tide began to turn. In January 1965 the government's declared objective of ending selection at eleven-plus, and of eliminating separatism in secondary education, was endorsed by the House of Commons. Burt still thought himself right; but more and more he seemed to be engaged in a rearguard defence of a rejected cause, more and more to be surrounded by left-wing critics and by psychologists who had become infected by behaviourist and environmentalist heresies.

How did Burt react to these setbacks? When issues were still undecided he fought strenuously to get his way. He did all he could to influence the committee appointed to select his successor; he engaged in heated arguments with Professor Russell on the running of the department; he fought a protracted battle with the British Psychological Society over the statistical journal; and he devoted immense amounts of time and energy campaigning against the critics of his educational ideas and their psychological foundations. In these fights the gamin component of his personality seemed to surface again, and to his opponents he often appeared quite unscrupulous in the expedients he employed.

When nothing could be done, and the setbacks had taken place, Burt's technique was to maintain a bland composure, and never to loose his cool. He never spoke about his reverses, or confided in others, even to those closest to him. At times it almost seemed that he was refusing to acknowledge them himself. Thus he seemed vainly to hope that somehow or somewhere his lost papers would turn up at college, though references in letters indicate that he was in reality well aware that they had perished. There was, perhaps, something stoical in the way Burt kept his problems to himself, but it meant that even those nearest to him misjudged him and failed to

understand him, and there was nobody to support him or sympathise with him in his difficulties.

So, a lonely figure, he fought when he could; then masked his
defeats. But at a more basic level his reactions to setbacks were
psychosomatic and psychological. It is to the examination of these
that we must now turn.

V

There was in all probability an innate instability in Burt's psychosomatic make-up. His sister, herself a medical practitioner, writes:

> I would like it to be emphasised that throughout his whole life
> Cyril was handicapped by poor health. His physiological mis-
> functions were no doubt innate, some being inherited. He had to
> take constant precautions against being incapacitated or under
> par for his engagements, and except in his home circle he was
> understandably secretive about this lest he should be judged
> 'neurotic'. . . . And his unreliable health contributed to nervous
> tension before examinations or public occasions. And it is singular
> that his intimate friends were men with permanent physical or
> physiological drawbacks, which gave rise to mutual sympathy.[16]

Again Dr Marion Burt reports:

> He was a late talker and an even later walker; and from his early
> history I think his semi-circular canals were not innately very
> efficient. Examples leading me to this theory are: more than
> normal difficulty in learning to cycle and to dance; great difficulty,
> according to Mother, to get him to jump even from a couple of
> steps; also virtual horror of the school gymnasium, as you can see
> in his letters from Christ's Hospital, pathetically begging his
> father to get him excused from it.[17]

He had, too, always been afraid of heights for fear of losing his
balance. As a boy Burt was delicate and underweight. He was
shortsighted, flat-footed, and liable to petty illnesses. On the
outbreak of the First World War, when he was just over thirty years
of age, his medical disabilities had not been overcome. He was
three times rejected for military service, by the Liverpool, London

16. Letter from Dr Marion Burt, 19 June 1973.
17. Communication from Dr Marion Burt, 14 January 1977.

and Warwickshire Medical Boards because of 'disordered action of the heart', flat feet and myopia.

Such a constitution was not well-adapted to cope with setbacks; so it is not altogether surprising that he reacted to them psychosomatically. A detailed medical history of Burt's ailments is not available for the 1920s and 1930s, but from 1940 onwards the documentation is ample.

There is reason to think that his more serious symptoms first began to come into prominence in the late 1930s about the time his setbacks commenced. Before the college was evacuated to Aberystwyth he is reported to have experienced the vertiginous attacks which later developed into Ménière's disease. By the summer of 1941 the attacks had become violent, and in December 1941 Dr Seymour Jones, a Birmingham specialist who had retired to Machynlleth, diagnosed Ménière's disorder.

This disease was first given a full clinical description and linked with a disturbance of the semicircular canals, by the French physician, Prosper Ménière, in 1861. The Ménière syndrome is described by Professor R. Hinchcliffe, Professor of Audiological Medicine in the University of London,[18] as 'a syndrome of paroxysmal attacks of vertigo in association with tinnitus and a gradually developing sensoneural hearing loss'.[19] In the Proceedings of the Symposium on Ménière's Syndrome held in the Netherlands in 1970 one speaker spoke of 'attacks of vertigo that seize the healthy patient, take away his forces, make him vomit, and strike him down, until, after a period of sleep, he rises again but for a slight deafness'.[20] Such attacks of vertigo were known in the time of Galen, but not recognised as a clinical entity or associated with the semicircular canals.

Burt's severe Ménière attacks in the summer of 1941, which had been preceded by a certain amount of nausea during the previous year, were of an extremely incapacitating nature. Sometimes he was prostrated for hours. On one occasion he was caught on the stairs of his Aberystwyth lodgings, and 'too giddy to get either up or down'.[21] He was stuck there, and got so cold that he developed a chill. While the attacks lasted, he said, 'even thinking is out of the question'. At that time there was no effective pharmacological treatment for Ménière's disease, and Burt had to learn as best he

18. I am much indebted to Professor R. Hinchcliffe for his advice on Ménière's Disease, and for guidance on the relevant bibliography.

19. Hinchcliffe, R. Ménière's Syndrome. In *Recent Advances in Otolaryngology*, 1973, p. 127.

20. Report of the Symposium. *Acta Otolaryngologica*, Supp. 305, 1972.

21. Burt, C. L. Letter to his sister, 22 February 1942.

could to cope with his disability. He was advised to cut down his smoking from the twenty cigarettes a day to which he was accustomed, and to be careful with his diet. But none of these expedients helped much, and Burt

> found it a good rule to keep absolutely still where one is, and particularly to avoid moving the head about from the very outset. One is tempted to rush off to a bedroom and collect basins and towels round one. Then when the world begins to go round it seems pretty effective steadily to fixate a given spot with the eyes. This has to be kept up with little intermittence for three-quarters of an hour or more, and so ultimately gets very tiring. But if one does that and avoids even the tiniest movement of the head one seems to be able to prevent the actual giddy feeling, and I think . . . that the sickness is caused by the giddy feeling. It usually comes ten minutes after these experiences of giddiness. They, of course, are very violent. The tiniest movement of the head is apt to make one feel as though the bed had rapidly shifted its position and angle by many yards and by many degrees. Also the world will spin round with amazing rapidity when the nystagmus begins—that is if one lets the nystagmus have its way.[22]

As a result of these attacks Burt was forced to adopt a much more careful regime. He travelled as little as possible; he dieted; he led as quiet a life as he could. Fresh air, gentle exercise, and keeping fit, he found, were the best preventives. He cut down smoking from twenty to five or six cigarettes a day. And with these precautions the attacks eased off, though he was always liable to them. There was, however, a permanent loss of hearing in the left ear.

In the spring of 1966 the disease attacked the right ear, accompanied by severe giddiness and vomiting. The attacks had been preceded about a year before by a sudden access of deafness in the right ear, without tinnitus or vomiting, however. His hearing was now very seriously impaired, so much so that he was incapable any longer of enjoying music. But a remedy was now available and the attacks could to some extent be controlled pharmacologically. Burt reported that 'the Stermetil has acted like magic. I've had no rotatory spells and no vomiting or colic. Instead only short spells of instability (20 mins) which feel like a threatened attack that doesn't mature. So I can get on fairly well with my work if I don't

22. Burt, C. L. Letter to his sister, 22 February 1942.

sit long at a desk, but scribble most of the time on the bed.'[23] For the remainder of his life Burt was prone to Ménière attacks and had to be extremely careful. His hearing loss was permanent and disabling.

It is now believed by some, though by no means all, physicians that Ménière's disease is a psychosomatic disorder, brought about, in persons with a constitutional disposition, as a result of emotional stress. Clinicians were slow to recognise this, Hinchcliffe suggests,[24] because they regarded the psychological disturbances as secondary to the vestibular disorders. A great deal of evidence now goes to show that the psychological disturbances are primary. This was first pointed out by Fowler and Zeckel in 1952.[25] It has been confirmed by other workers in Great Britain (Hinchcliffe, Stephens), Italy (Ceroni and Franzoni), Finland (Siirala *et al.*) and Poland (Czubalski, Bochenek and Zawisza).[26]

Among the essential features of psychosomatic disorders as listed by Halliday[27] are the presence of emotional disturbances as precipitating factors, and association with a particular type of personality. Both of these have been confirmed in the case of Ménière's disease. Ceroni and Franzoni (1963) were able to observe a relation between emotional stress and the onset of Ménière symptoms in 44 per cent of their cases. Hinchcliffe (1967a) observed emotional factors related to the onset of the symptoms in 64 per cent of Ménière cases compared with only 10 per cent of a control group of otosclerotics. Siirala (1970) noted that 42 per cent of his Ménière cases had been exposed to stress. Czubalski, Bochenek and Zawisza (1975) report that in 76·6 per cent of the cases the onset of Ménière attacks coincided with psychic conflict. There is, therefore, plenty of

23. Burt, C. L. Letter to his sister, 1 April 1960. Stermetil is a prochlorperazine preparation with sedative properties, and is used in psychiatric work.

24. Hinchcliffe, R. Ménière's Syndrome. In *Recent Advances in Otolaryngology*, 1973.

25. Fowler, E. P. and Zeckel, A. Psychosomatic aspects in Ménière's disease. *J. Amer. Med. Ass., CXLVIII*, 1952, 1265–1268.

26. Hinchcliffe, R. Emotion as a precipitating factor in Ménière's disease. *J. Laryngol. & Otol, LXXXI*, 1967a, 471–5; Personality profile in Ménière's disease. *Ibid.*, 1967b, 477–81; Stephens, S. D. G. Personality tests in Ménière's disorder. *J. Laryngol. & Otol., LXXXIX*, 1975, 479–90; Ceroni, T. and Franzoni, M. Aspetti psicosmatici della malatia di Ménière. *Ann. Laring. (Torino), IV*, 1963, 306; Siirala, U., Siltola, P. and Lumio, J. S. Psychological aspects of Ménière's disease. *Acta Otolaryng., LIX*, 1959, 350–7; Siirala, U. and Gelher, K. Further studies on the relationship between Ménière, psychosomatic constitution and stress. *Acta Otolaryng., LXX*, 1970, 142–7; Czubalski, K., Bochenek, W. and Zawisza, E. Psychological stress and personality in Ménière's disorder. *J. Psychosomat. Res., XX*, 1976, 187–91.

27. Halliday, J. L. Concept of a psychosomatic affliction. *Lancet, II*, 1943, 692–6.

evidence to support the association of the onset of Ménière's disease with emotional factors.

There is also supporting evidence for the linkage between Ménière's disease and personality characteristics. Fowler and Zeckel[28] using a number of personality tests noted a preponderance of obsessional—compulsive types among Ménière patients. Fowler and Appell[29] using a control group of otosclerotics to compare with Ménière cases found that those in the Ménière group tended to have mesomorphic body-build and to display perfectionist traits. Hinchcliffe (1967b) revealed an increased prevalence of psychosomatic personality profiles in a group of Ménière patients, again using otosclerotics as controls. Stephens (1975), evaluating personality by means of the Eysenck Personality Inventory and the Middlesex Hospital Questionnaire, stated that 'the most notable finding was an elevated obsessionality score in the patients with Ménière's disorder as compared with other groups'. Brightwell and Abramson[30] observe that 'clinicians have frequently observed apparent peculiar personality characteristics in patients with vertigo, such as aggressive dependency, emotional lability, and over-reactivity'. A fairly clear picture, therefore, seems to emerge from these findings, showing the typical Ménière patient to have obsessional, perfectionist, characteristics and marked psychosomatic lability.

All this evidence fits the known facts of the Burt case extremely well. Burt certainly seemed to have a constitutional weakness in his balancing organ going back to his boyhood, but the actual appearance of Ménière symptoms coincided with the earliest setbacks described in the previous section, in particular, in the case of the first series of severe Ménière attacks, with the difficulties in his marriage and the loss of his research material. Siirala et al. (1959, 1970) specifically mention as prominent among the stresses precipitating Ménière's disease, marital difficulties and the loss of valued objects. It is highly likely that the final causative agent was the destruction of his papers. The timing seems to support this view, though it cannot prove it conclusively. The fatal raid took place on 16 April 1941. After suffering from Ménière symptoms for some months Burt was finally put in touch with the retired specialist in Maccynlleth, and it was he who diagnosed Ménière's disease in December 1941. Burt was certainly concerned about the papers he

28. Fowler, E. P. and Zeckel, A. Psychosomatic aspects in Ménière's disease. *J. Amer. Med. Ass.*, CXLVIII, 1952, 1265–8.

29. Fowler, E. P. and Appell, W. Psychological and constitutional factors in otosclerosis and Ménière's disorder. *Acta Otolaryng.*, XLVI, 1956, 194–206.

30. Brightwell, D. R. and Abramson, M. Personality characteristics in patients with vertigo. *Arch. Otolaryng.*, CI, 1975, 364–6.

had left in London—after all they represented the fruits of more than a quarter of a century's work—and he had expressed his anxiety as to their safety at the time of the Battle of France.[31] His gradual realisation during the summer of 1941 of their almost certain loss in the air raid on the college was just the sort of stress situation that various investigators have pointed to as Ménière-producing.

The second set of Ménière attacks began in the spring of 1966. What, it may be asked, were the stresses to which Burt was subjected at that time? The most probable answer, and once again we cannot be completely certain, is that they had something to do with the now notorious article on monozygotic twins which was published in the summer of that year. We noted that in his diary for 3 April 1957 Burt had recorded, 'After deciding not to submit two papers for journal felt curiously relieved and calmed.' So it is not far-fetched to suppose that when he did finally submit a paper that certainly contained spurious material he felt just the opposite. The twin paper may not have been the first paper to contain such material; but it was the first paper which was on a topic of wide public interest and where the risk of exposure was considerable. Burt finally sent the revised version of the paper to Professor Summerfield, the editor of the *British Journal of Psychology*, on 7 September 1965. His bouts of nausea began in January 1966, finally developing into full-blown Ménière attacks on March 27th. These attacks lasted on and off until the end of July. The proofs of the article were read on 19 April 1966, and the journal (the May issue) was published rather late, on 15 July 1966. There seems to be some concordance in time between the various stages in the processing of the twin article and the outbreak of Ménière symptoms, which perhaps points to Burt's understandable anxieties about its reception. If these hypotheses are right, Burt's Ménière attacks are useful pointers to the stresses which he was undergoing.

They are equally valuable as pointers to aspects of his personality, his perfectionism, his obsessionality and his psychosomatic lability. There is, indeed, satisfactory evidence for all of these characteristics in Burt. The young man who proclaimed his life's purpose to be 'to produce one perfect being for the universe' certainly had a perfectionist streak in his make-up. If this drive became less exalted and more realistic as he grew up, it continued to show itself in his tireless striving for omniscience. Though Burt was not an obsessional character in the incapacitating sense of the word, there was something obsessionally-compulsive about this striving, something anancastic in his disposition. He rarely relaxed, even on holidays. He had an obsessional concern for detail, and his published writings

31. Burt, C. L. Letter to his sister, 23 May 1940.

are overloaded with footnotes. When he took up his pen he found it difficult to stop. All through his life he was a meticulous note-taker. There were other marks, too, of the obsessional syndrome in Burt's character. There were the repressed aggressive impulses, which Freud in his early classic paper[32] noted as a feature of the obsessional character, and which in Burt, so studiously polite, manifested themselves in his eager controversialism. And there was the marked tendency in Burt's communications to complicate and obfuscate, which Salzman has noted as one of the features of the obsessional. 'The communicative process of the obsessional', writes Salzman, 'tends more towards obfuscation and confusion rather than clarification. The insistent tendency towards distraction also interferes with making a particular point, and the exchanges with the obsessional seem like a never-ending series of waves in which each new idea sets off a multitude of ripples which go on ad infinitum.'[33] This is precisely what many of those who got into controversy with Burt experienced in their interchanges with him. So Burt's personality type accords well with that of the typical Ménière patient.

Even more marked in Burt was that other feature of Ménière cases, psychosomatic lability. As we have seen, this lability went back to early days, and, indeed, there was almost certainly a genetic component involved, as both his father and his sister manifested similar symptoms. But whereas in the case of his sister the psychosomatic lability stabilised in middle age, in the case of Burt it continued to the end of his life, and, as a result of the setbacks he experienced, even increased in intensity. 'Any unfamiliar function gives me tachycardia,' he noted in 1949 and again in 1965.[34] This was followed by a compensatory slowing, a very low pulse rate and sleepiness. His pulse was highly unstable, rising to over 100 during the tachycardic incidents, when he felt nervy, breathless and Ménière-ish, and falling to 50 or even 45, which made him cold and sleepy. In this connection he noted, 'my lifelong eagerness to keep warm by piles of clothing'.[35] He also had an uncomfortable tendency to profuse sweating ('I get soaking suddenly and unexpectedly'), and constant trouble with micturition. He was eternally fussing about his symptoms; would count his pulse beats, take his temperature, and measure his fluid input and output. He suffered

32. Freud, S. Notes upon a Case of Obsessional Neurosis, 1909, *Collected Papers*, vol. III.

33. Salzman, L. Obsessions. In Krauss, S. (ed.) *Encyclopaedic Handbook of Medical Psychology*, 1976, pp. 345–9.

34. Burt, C. L. Letters to his sister, 21 April 1949 and 8 October 1965.

35. Burt, C. L. Letter to his sister, 4 February 1952.

from chronic indigestion, and any change of diet, or mode of cooking, would be liable to upset him. He was highly suggestible, and even attributed changes in his autonomic balance to changes in barometric pressure. He noted, too, the curious fact that 'I get no symptoms leaving London for Malvern (where he went to stay with his sister), but nearly always do on leaving Malvern for London— pulse up, temperature up, and a drenching sweat attack'[36]— an indication, no doubt, as to where the problems lay.

There can be no question, then, that beneath his composed, polite, exterior Burt showed many of the marks of an anxious, disturbed character. The unconcern towards his setbacks which he pretended to show masked tensions which revealed themselves psychosomatically in the form of Ménière's disease and a whole spectrum of other symptoms. But, over and above this, there were also regressive changes in his personality, and a recrudescence of earlier patterns of behaviour, which began to obtrude both in his personal relationships and in his published work.

VI

These personality changes seem to date from about the same time as the first reported vertigo symptoms, that is in the late 1930s, and seem to have marked the exaggeratedly egotistical and somewhat devious behaviour which became more and more prominent as the years went by. In recounting Burt's contributions to factor analysis we noted (p. 170) that in an article in the *British Journal of Educational Psychology* in 1937 he made egotistical claims to priority, which were immediately withdrawn when challenged by Spearman. That did not stop him, however, from dropping hints against Spearman in his lectures, and after Spearman's death Burt's campaign against him steadily mounted, eventually becoming obsessive in its repetitiveness. The first example of his devious behaviour also comes from the late 1930s; it had to do with a review article by Eysenck, who writes as follows:

I also remembered the rather unscrupulous way in which he dealt with an earlier offer he had made, when I was still a student, I think, in my first year at University College in his department. Thurstone's monograph on 'Primary Abilities' had just come out, and he suggested to me that we would jointly review it; he would write the text, and I would reanalyse the huge table of intercorrelations, using his group factor method. Of course, I

36. Burt, C. L. Letter to his sister, 1 July 1969.

agreed, and nearly went blind doing all this work on a simple handcrank machine. Burt then showed me the paper he had written under our joint names, and I thought it was very good. I was rather surprised when it finally appeared in the *British Journal of Educational Psychology* in 1939[37] with only my name at the top, and with many changes in the text praising Cyril Burt.[38]

This high-handed practice of altering material supplied by others and slanting it to enhance his own achievements and reputation became, of course, almost standard practice with Burt, carried out brazenly and without compunction. I have, however, come across no authenticated example of such conduct prior to the incident recounted by Eysenck.

It is tempting to assert, as several critics have asserted, that Burt was always a bad character, and that his work must be regarded as suspect from the beginning. I find no firm evidence to support this view, and several reasons for thinking it unacceptable. Burt came from a good home; he had had a good education; and there was a genuinely idealistic element in his make-up. His adolescent 'anxiety for uprightness', and his desire 'to be scrupulously straightforward and sincere', were genuine impulses, even if they were not the only impulses in his nature, and he did attempt to put them into practice. The admiration he attracted in the early stages of his career was not undeserved. Those who knew him in the 1920s and early 1930s had a high regard for him, and any suggestion that his work was not entirely above board was regarded by them as unbelievable. Dr Thouless of Cambridge, who had known Burt from the 1920s, writes, 'I find it quite unthinkable that he knowingly fudged his results.'[39] Professor R. B. Cattell, who studied under him at the London Day Training College, says 'If I had to base a judgment of Burt purely on my own interactions with him over the years 1924 (when I first heard him lecture) to his death, the fact is that it would record many instances of generosity, no instances of "cheating", and many benefits of intellectual interactions more valuable to me than those of any contemporary psychologist (after Spearman's retirement at any rate).'[40] An even older acquaintance, Dr R. R. Rusk of Glasgow, the eminent Scottish educationalist, whose contacts with Burt went back to the 1910–14 period, spoke just before his death at the age of 93, of the 'strong sympathy' between

37. Eysenck, H. J. Primary mental abilities. *Brit. J. Educ. Psychol.*, IX, 1939, 270–6.
38. Letter from H. J. Eysenck, 16 November 1977.
39. Letter from Dr R. H. Thouless, 12 November 1976.
40. Letter from Professor R. B. Cattell, 17 February 1978.

himself and Burt.[41] The testimony of those who knew Burt in his early days must outweigh the unsupported suspicions of those who did not. The community of psychologists in the 1920s and 1930s was a small and fairly intimate one. The meetings of the British Psychological Society, as I myself can testify, were rarely attended by more than a few dozen members. In this close-knit band of pioneers no totally fraudulent character could have escaped suspicion for long. Up to the late 1930s I see no reason to regard Burt's work as other than basically sound, and his conduct as other than acceptable. If there were weaknesses, such as a certain vanity, some overconfidence in his pronouncements, and the inadequate reporting of evidence in early articles, these are venial failings, and such as anyone might have been guilty of. Had Burt died at the age of 60 his reputation would have been unblemished, and his standing as a psychologist generally acclaimed, even by those who differed from him in viewpoint.

It is much more plausible to suggest that the egotistical and devious behaviour was a reaction to the setbacks he began to suffer in the late 1930s, and that as the setbacks accumulated, so the changes in his personality became more pronounced. There was, it would seem, a regression to, and a surfacing of, the primitive 'gamin' element in his make-up, together with the development of paranoic characteristics, self-aggrandising, suspicious, cantankerous and devious. These characteristics began to intrude into his personal relationships and to infect his published work just before the beginning of the Second World War, and became prominent in Aberystwyth. The relentless onslaught on Philpott and his researches, recounted in Chapter Eight (p. 142), was certainly pathological in its intensity. It is explicable only in terms of the intense jealousy Burt must have felt towards a member of his staff, who had been wise enough to transport all his research data to Aberystwyth, while he himself, who had collected so much more material, had lost most of it in the blitz. To this loss he reacted by trying to assemble what was left, and by extracting conclusions which were hardly justified by the evidence. As pointed out in Chapter Eight, 'Ability and Income'[42] marked a watershed in Burt's career. It was provocative in content, and suspect in its procedures.

After his return to London Burt's unscrupulousness became obvious in the course of University business, and alienated both well-disposed colleagues, like D. W. Harding (see p. 147), and postgraduate students, like the Clarkes (see p. 148). The whisperings against Spearman that were just audible in the late 1930s swelled into a strident campaign of belittlement, which grew until

41. Letter from Dr. R. R. Rusk, 7 December 1971.
42. Burt, C. L. *Brit. J. Educ. Psychol.*, XIII, 1943, 83–98.

Burt arrogated to himself the whole of Spearman's fame (see p. 176). Indeed, Burt seemed to be becoming increasingly obsessed with questions of priority, and increasingly touchy and egotistical. After his retirement he still seemed to regard it as his prerogative to dictate the policy of the department, so much so that he had to be forcibly ejected from it. He was equally self-centred in connection with the journal he controlled. As editor Burt took liberties, and displayed a high-handedness which frequently passed the bounds of propriety. He altered texts without their authors' consent; he replied to criticisms of his own contributions using false names for the replies, obviously with the aim of providing supposedly external support for his views; on occasion he found excuses for not giving authors an opportunity of correcting their own proofs or approving changes he himself had made. For example, in 1960 in the controversy with C. E. M. Hansel concerning Soal's experiments on telepathy in children, Burt as editor altered Hansel's reply to his review: Hansel restored his original version in the proof, which was finally altered again by Burt. The published version, therefore, did not represent Hansel's intention, but Hansel was dissuaded by the British Psychological Society from taking the matter further.[43]

Many similar examples could be quoted: one more must suffice. In January 1958 Mr D. F. Vincent of the National Institute of Industrial Psychology wrote to Dr C. Wrigley in connection with the history of factor analysis: 'I have been trying to get some documentary evidence of who was the first to use values less than unity in the diagonal cells. You say in your footnote on page 88[44] that it "seems to have been Burt". Can you give me a reference that supports this view?'[45] To this Dr Wrigley replied:

While the other footnotes in the paper were my own, that one was added by Cyril Burt on his own initiative. . . . Let me explain how it came about that Burt will add a footnote to my paper on a matter on which I myself am not qualified to express an opinion. He was my tutor when I was working for my Ph.D. at U.C.L. and he seems to have continued in his tutorial role by making more changes in terms of wording, footnotes etc. in my manuscripts submitted to his journal than an editor would generally be expected to do. Mostly I don't mind it. He does not ever change the main arguments, and most of the incidental changes he introduces do seem to me to improve the paper. . . .

43. Letter from C. E. M. Hansel, 20 April 1978.
44. Wrigley, C. F. The distinction between common and specific variants in factor theory. *Brit. J. Statist. Psychol.*, X, 1957, 81–98.
45. Letter from D. F. Vincent to C. Wrigley, 7 January 1958.

The greater part [of the changes] are Burt's, introduced after I
had submitted the revision to him. I did not see the paper again
after that; galley-proof was read in England.[46]

To which Vincent commented after comparing the published
version with the original text, which Wrigley sent him:

You say that Burt does not ever change your main arguments. It
seems to me that your main arguments are the only things he has
not changed; not only has he made extensive revisions, but he has
re-worded a great deal of your text, often with changes of
emphasis. Personally I should mind very much, but I can
understand that the situation is rather different; Burt is not my
former tutor. Your remark 'more changes in terms of wording,
footnotes etc. . . . than an editor would generally be expected to
do' seems to me the record understatement of the century.[47]

If Burt was high-handed as an editor, he was no less exasperating
as a controversialist. From 1950 onwards he was increasingly
involved in, and increasingly seemed to relish, controversy. This
had not previously been a feature of his writings, or of his personal
relationships. In fact the first publication essentially controversial in
character was the joint article with Stephenson in 1939, in which
they set out their divergent views on correlations between persons.[48]
From 1950 onwards, however, Burt was clearly on the defensive,
and controversy came to occupy a good part of his energies. Even
his research reports were, as we have seen, at bottom replies to
critics rather than reports in the proper sense. He appeared to go
out of his way to invite scraps; delighted to confuse and misrepresent
his opponents; shifted his ground, dazzled them with erudition, and
made claims which it was hard for anyone to verify. In these
controversies it was clear that he was out to win at all costs, and he
was, as we have already seen (p. 206), quite unscrupulous in the
means he was prepared to use.

What accounts for these tendencies that developed in Burt? Why
this exaggerated egotism, this cantankerousness and this unscrupulousness? There was possibly an element of sheer mischievousness
in it, for there was certainly a love of mischief in his nature. He
enjoyed teasing and outwitting. But more fundamentally it was

46. Letter from C. Wrigley to D. F. Vincent, 23 September 1958.
47. Letter from D. F. Vincent to C. Wrigley, 23 October 1958.
48. Burt, C. L. and Stephenson, Wm. Alternative views on correlations between
persons. *Psychometrika, IV*, 1939, 269–82.

because he felt threatened; because the exalted aims he had set himself—his dream of intellectual mastery in the footsteps of Galton—were in danger of collapse. His whole world was insecure. His home had broken up; his research data had perished; his health was precarious; his old department had defected; he had been robbed of his journal; new modes of thinking and younger rivals were ousting him from the centre of the stage; the doctrines he believed in were being rejected. The changes in his personality from the late 1930s onwards were responses to these threats, and as the threats grew, so the changes became more marked. Burt could no longer respond creatively by going out and doing more research. He had neither the physical fitness, nor the assistants, nor the resources to make this possible. Instead he had recourse to the well-established mechanisms of defence, compensation and regression; on the one hand, inflated claims as to his own achievements, and on the other a regression to earlier ways of coping with threats—ways he had learned we must suppose in the tough Board School playground of his early boyhood, where survival involved out-smarting his opponents. There was in Burt's reactions, beneath the bland exterior, a compulsive, almost phrenetic, quality, which suggests such a deep motivational origin. He was a lonely man, who had few close friends, and who did not communicate his anxieties to others. He attempted to fight his battles single-handed, and in doing so became distinctly paranoic.

Paranoia in its fully developed form is generally classed as a delusional psychosis. The delusional system is commonly a circumscribed one, leaving the personality otherwise intact, and in many respects capable of perfectly normal functioning. Moreover it often occurs in the milder form of a marginal psychical abnormality, in which the delusional element is fairly inconspicuous. Characteristic features of such marginal forms are self-aggrandisement and inflated egocentricity, oversensitiveness and suspiciousness, querulousness, secretiveness, compulsive drive ('a temperament which never allows itself to flag') and hypochondria.[49] Such a condition is regarded by Jaspers as reactive, that is primed by external events, usually of a repeated nature, in a personality with some basic peculiarity or weakness.[50] It is also perhaps significant that paranoid conditions are not infrequently associated with hearing loss.[51] The

49. Leonhard, K. Paranoia and Related States. In Krauss, S. (ed.) *Encyclopaedic Handbook of Medical Psychology*, 1976, pp. 361–3. I have largely followed Leonhard in describing the symptoms of paranoia.

50. Jaspers, K. *General Psychopathology*, Eng. trans. 1963, p. 389.

51. Roth, M. *et al*. Hearing loss in paranoid and affective psychoses of the elderly. *Lancet, II*, 1974, 851–4.

picture is concordant with the known facts about Burt. Self-aggrandisement and inflated egocentricity were certainly a marked feature of his later behaviour, and accounted for many of the devices to which he had recourse—the alterations, for example, in contributors' articles, and the distortions of factor-analytic history. Burt, too, was oversensitive to criticism. He was sharply on the look-out for anyone who challenged his views, and wrote 'out of the blue' to upbraid and correct them. He was deeply suspicious of rivals, particularly his own most able students, like Cattell and Eysenck. Others, who in fact admired him and supported many of his views, he disparaged and sometimes alienated because they did not wholly accept his authority. Finally Burt was most surely secretive, hypochondrical, and compulsively motivated. He shows then all the essential marks of a marginally paranoid personality. Whether actual delusions were involved is harder to determine. Was Burt himself deceived by his own deceptions? Did he really come to believe, for example, that he himself, not Spearman, was the first psychologist to employ factor analysis: that his twin data were somewhere around in college, and might yet turn up? As Jaspers notes, 'once the game of fancy has started, it frequently leads to self-deception'.[52] Some of Burt's deceptions were so transparent (the complete contradiction, for instance, between the first and the unpublished revisions for the second edition of *Factors of the Mind*) that it is hard to think that he could have perpetuated them had he not first deceived himself. But of this we cannot be certain. What is certain is that as his paranoic condition developed his veracity diminished, and he became very careless of the truth. Kamin noted that in his published papers there were contradictory statements which could not all be true.[53] There are even more contradictions when his letters are compared among themselves and with his published articles, and, as we have seen (p. 247), he was quite capable of making statements which were demonstrably untrue in every particular. There was an element of 'pseudologica phantastica' in this lack of veracity, which naturally makes a great deal of his later work suspect.

It would seem, then, that we are justified in concluding that Burt suffered, in the final phase of his life, from a marginally paranoid condition; that this condition was a reaction to the setbacks which he experienced from the late 1930s onwards; and that it led to a regressive reactivation of behaviour patterns he had acquired in the London period of his boyhood, and from the 'gamin' sub-culture in which he had been immersed. This, we suggest, is the basic

52. Jaspers, K. *Op. cit.*, p. 329.
53. Kamin, L. *The Science and Politics of I.Q.*, 1974, pp. 35–47.

explanation of the deceptions and subterfuges which marred his work in its later stages. In the end he chose to cheat rather than see his opponents triumph. To trace the origins of these defections from probity to childhood experiences would seem to receive support not only from the findings of psychology, but from the deeper intuitions of humanity:

> In ancient shadows and twilights
> Where childhood has strayed
> The world's great sorrows were born
> And its heroes were made.
> In the lost boyhood of Judas
> Christ was betrayed.[54]

So, in the lost boyhood of Cyril Burt psychology was betrayed—yet, not totally; for there still remains something of splendid achievement. If Burt, the man, had his weaknesses; Burt, the psychologist, also had his strengths.

54. A. E. (G. W. Russell). Germinal, *Collected Poems*, 1913.

CHAPTER FOURTEEN

The Psychologist

I

What, then, were Burt's essential contributions to psychology? How are we to assess and evaluate his work as a whole? Less than ten years after his death no final answers can be given to these questions; nevertheless an attempt must be made to do so provisionally.

To the main stream of academic psychology, that is to say general experimental psychology, Burt contributed almost nothing, though he lectured in this field, and was responsible for conducting a scholarly, though rather old-fashioned, elementary course in experimental psychology, with a good deal of emphasis on sensations and psychophysics. His contributions were concentrated in two main areas: theoretical psychology and individual psychology. He sketched the framework of a theoretical psychology, or philosophy of mind; and he worked out in detail the structure, technology, methodology and applications of individual, or differential, psychology. It is with the second of these areas that Burt's name is mainly associated among psychologists and among the general public. His theoretical contributions have been largely ignored, perhaps for two reasons. Firstly, Burt never expounded his theories systematically, nor developed them in detail. They are scattered in a variety of journals, some of them obscure. Secondly, they ran counter to the prevailing behaviouristic trends of the time, and thus tended to be disregarded.

The main influences shaping Burt's psychological outlook were examined in Chapter Two. They were the theoretical psychology of Ward and Stout, with its rejection of mosaicism and emphasis on mental unity; the biology of Darwin and Galton, with its emphasis on inheritance and individual differences; and the psychology of McDougall. Throughout his life Burt remained loyal to the doctrines of his early teachers, and faithful to what he regarded as the central core of British psychology. He had no sympathy at all with behaviourism, which ran completely counter to everything he had learned, and which seemed to him to be crudely American.

Behaviourism rejected the concept of mind; it discounted the influence of heredity; and it reintroduced all the fallacies of the associationism that Ward and Stout had disposed of. None of this was acceptable to Burt, and he deplored the growing hold of behaviouristic ideas on many younger British psychologists in the 1950s and 1960s. Burt regarded the behaviourists' conception of scientific method as absurdly dogmatic and antiquated, and the philosophical theories of the logical positivists, used to buttress behaviourism, as simply 'untenable'.[1] However, the tide of behaviourism has been ebbing since the end of the 1950s and there has been, to use a phrase of Koch's, 'a massive return of the repressed',[2] a revival in psychology of many of the topics outlawed by the behaviourists, such as conscious experience, imagery, intentions and inner structures. Burt's theoretical psychology, which seemed to many old-fashioned when he first propounded it, now appears far from unacceptable. Indeed, for reasons that will be set out later, it deserves, in spite of certain weaknesses, quite serious consideration.

II

There were four main components, or layers, in Burt's theoretical psychology—dualism, evolutionism, holism, and probabalism. We must examine these four in turn.

1. *Dualism*. Burt's dualism, the belief that mind and matter, consciousness and brain, the subjective and the objective, were irreducible to each other, was no doubt derived from his principal teachers, all of whom were dualists. Ward made a sharp distinction between the subject of experience and the object of experience; Stout held that there was a gulf fixed between the physical and the psychical; and McDougall defended 'animism', the doctrine that an animating principle distinct from the body was necessary to account for the behaviour at least of human organisms.[3] The origin of dualistic theories of this kind is commonly attributed to Descartes, but Popper has recently argued that in fact they go back to the beginning of European thought.[4] So Burt no doubt absorbed them from more sources than his immediate teachers in psychology, for

1. Burt, C. L. Logical positivism and the concept of consciousness. *Brit. J. Statist. Psychol., XIII*, 1960, 55–77.
2. Koch, S. Psychology and Emerging Conceptions of Knowledge as Unitary. In Wann T. W. (ed.) *Behaviorism and Phenomenology*, 1964, p. 19.
3. McDougall, W. *Body and Mind*, 1911.
4. Popper, K. R. and Eccles, J. C. *The Self and its Brain*, 1977, p. 5.

his classical education had given him a first-hand acquaintance with the development of European thought from its origins. Dualism, according to Burt, entailed three main consequences: firstly, it was necessary for psychologists to adopt concepts based on *private* observation (concepts such as consciousness and its specifically mental contents and processes); secondly, it was possible by means of systematic introspection to derive generalisations and to formulate laws; and thirdly, it was essential to postulate some kind of entity 'which has a capacity for consciousness, and may therefore conveniently be referred to as "mind".' So in two of his most important theoretical articles Burt pleaded for 'the reinstatement of consciousness as a useful and necessary concept', the rehabilitation of 'introspection as a valid scientific procedure', and the 'reintroduction into psychology of the concept of mind'.[5] To deny these propositions seemed to Burt a symptom of the 'obsessive psychophobia' from which behaviourists suffered. To the majority of behaviouristically inclined psychologists, however, Burt's views were regarded as 'the last kicks of an outdated culture, which had great value in its time, but has now outlived its usefulness'.[6] It is, I think, to Burt's credit that he never just swam with the tide.

Consciousness, then, for Burt was an essential ingredient in the subject matter of psychology. It cannot be defined; 'it is one of those primitive facts which we can only indicate by citing witnesses'.[7] 'When I assert that I am conscious . . . the distinctive element in the situation is the inscrutable but undeniable fact of simple awareness.'[8] Consciousness is necessarily private, but that is not, as the behaviourists suppose, an objection to its employment in psychology for 'every first-hand observation is necessarily private'.[9] In a telling example Burt compared the observation of a point of light by an astronomer and by a psychologist:

> Whether certain observations are treated as 'public' turns not on their specific or intrinsic nature, but merely on the context. X is asked: can he, or can he not, detect a faint point of light somewhere near the centre of a dark field. He answers 'Yes'. If the field is the field of a 4-inch telescope, and the faint point of light is presumed to be one of Jupiter's smaller satellites, then what is observed is said to be 'public'. If the field is the far end of

5. Burt, C. L. The structure of the mind. *Brit. J. Statist. Psychol., XIV*, 1961, 145–70; The concept of consciousness. *Brit. J. Psychol., LIII*, 1962, 229–42.
6. Broadbent, D. E. *In Defence of Empirical Psychology*, 1973, p. 9.
7. Burt, C. L. The concept of mind. *J. Psychol. Res. (India), II*, 1960, 1–11.
8. Burt, C. L. *Psychology and Psychical Research*, 1968, p. 11.
9. Burt, C. L. The concept of consciousness. *Loc. cit.*, p. 231.

a psychologist's dark-room, and the experiment is intended to determine the subject's threshold for visual sensation then what is observed is said to be 'private'. Nevertheless when astronomers are permitted to accept such observations at their face value, why should psychologists be forbidden to do so?[10]

In practice the attempt to eliminate terminology derived from conscious experience merely leads to the creation of impossibly clumsy circumlocutions.

The consciousness, however, that Burt directly experienced could not be analysed into bits in the manner of the old-fashioned introspectionists of the Titchenerian kind. It was essentially a 'continuum', as Ward had pointed out; 'a vast and variegated continuum, fading away at the edges, but peculiarly vivid at the centre'.[11] Because of these gradations in sensory clearness it was perfectly acceptable to postulate subconscious and unconscious regions of the mind. Nevertheless consciousness possessed 'a peculiar kind of unity which would be quite inexplicable were it merely the effect of a miscellaneous aggregate of simultaneous and successive processes going on in a number of separate cells or synapses within the central nervous system. It presents both a simultaneous and a successive continuity.'[12] Such a conscious continuum was best regarded, Burt maintained, not as a substance in the Cartesian manner, but as a 'field', a term borrowed from electro-magnetism and theoretical physics.[13] In fact it was necessary, Burt thought, to postulate two fields of consciousness, the field of passive consciousness and the field of active consciousness. The former was concerned with sense-data, images and ideas, merged no doubt with 'feelings of pleasure or pain, beliefs, memories, wishes and desires',[14] but basically having the status of experienced objects. The latter, the field of active consciousness, on the contrary was concerned with acts of experiencing, volitions, decisions, and implied the existence of an active self, which Burt conceived of as an elementary entity, a kind of Leibnizian monad which he termed a 'psychon'.[15] This distinction of Burt's seems an old-fashioned one; indeed it goes back at least to Aristotle. The evidence suggests

10. Burt, C. L. The concept of consciousness. *Loc. cit.*, p. 231.

11. Burt, C. L. *Psychology and Psychical Research*, 1968, p. 16.

12. Burt, C. L. The structure of the mind. *Loc. cit.*, p. 153.

13. Burt, C. L. Field theories and statistical psychology. *Brit. J. Statist. Psychol.*, XII, 1959, 153–64; The field concept in psychology. *Bull. B.P.S.*, XXII, 1969, 267–71.

14. Burt, C. L. Logical positivism and the concept of consciousness. *Brit. J. Statist. Psychol.*, XIII, 1960, 73.

15. Burt, C. L. *Psychology and Psychical Research*, 1968, p. 47.

rather that sensation and perception are always active processes. As Gregory puts it, 'the perceived object is a hypothesis, suggested and tested by sensory data . . . perceiving and thinking are not independent.'[16] Even in simple sensation activity is involved. 'The brain's problem is to "decide" whether neural activity is representing outside events, or whether it is mere "noise" which should be ignored.'[17] As Hayek had earlier pointed out, even the most simple sensory event involves interpretation and categorisation.[18]

In spite of his belief in passive consciousness Burt held a realistic view of perception. 'Under normal conditions perception does give us some direct acquaintance with the existence and nature of physical objects.'[19] 'Objective reference is implicit from the start; it is part of the very nature of cognition to transcend itself.'[20] In fact Burt went so far as to maintain that all perception had the character of clairvoyance, and that the function of the brain was 'to confine the mind's clairvoyant powers to those features of the ever-changing environment which are of vital importance for the survival of the individual organism'.[21] The obverse of this inhibiting function of the brain was its selecting or detective function. Most influences from the external world were inhibited, a few selected and detected. The brain was not a generator of experience, but its detector, involving 'an interaction, probably at the quantum level, between the material brain and an immaterial agent'.[22] In particular the brain could be influenced by the volition of the active psychic principle, or 'psychon', a view which Burt perhaps derived from, and which certainly had the support of the neurophysiologist, Eccles.[23] Burt's own acquaintance with the findings of neurophysiological research was extensive, and he expounded his views on brain–consciousness relations in a number of articles and reviews.[24]

16. Gregory, R. L. Eye and Brain, 1966, p. 12.
17. Ibid., p. 81.
18. Hayek, F. A. The Sensory Order, 1952.
19. Burt, C. L. The sense datum theory. Brit. J. Statist. Psychol., XV, 1962, 187.
20. Ibid., p. 189.
21. Burt, C. L. Psychology and Psychical Research, 1968, p. 43. A similar theory was advocated and ably expounded by M. M. Moncrieff in The Clairvoyant Theory of Perception, 1951; the idea that brain did not generate consciousness, but rather confined its working within certain limits appears first to have been mooted by the Oxford philosopher F. C. S. Schiller. See Burt, C. L. The structure of the mind. Loc. cit., p. 157.
22. Burt, C. L. Psychology and Psychical Research, 1968, p. 39.
23. Eccles, J. C. The Neurophysiological Basis of Mind, 1953.
24. Burt, C. L. Factor analysis and its neurological basis. Brit. J. Statist. Psychol., XIV, 1961, 53–71; Working models of the brain. Ibid., XV, 1962, 199–215; Consciousness and space perception. Ibid., XVII, 1964, 77–85; Brain and consciousness. Brit. J. Psychol., LIX, 1968, 55–69; Brain and consciousness. Bull. B.P.S., XXII, 1969, 29–36.

Consciousness, then, was no mere epiphenomenon. It influenced the workings of the brain and it had a function to perform. Developing a theory of Thorpe's,[25] itself derived from William James, Burt held that consciousness was 'an organ added for the sake of steering a nervous system grown too complex to regulate itself'.[26] It was the central focus of the individual's 'mind', and from the point of view of the practical psychologist Burt regarded a sympathetic rapport with the conscious processes of the child or adult he was studying as an essential component in the psychologist's procedures.[27]

Burt never ceased to use the term 'mind' long after it had been tacitly dropped by the majority of psychologists. His popular broadcast talks given in 1933 were entitled *How the Mind Works*; his Heath Clark lectures *The Subnormal Mind*. Mind, for Burt, was 'a convenient label to designate the hypothetical basis of consciousness',[28] or as he expressed it more fully, 'A mind is a particular continuant which is capable of entering into conscious relations, namely relations of cognition, affection and conation. In entering into these relations it manifests certain dispositional properties and a certain structure, which it is the business of the psychologist to investigate.'[29] To the objection that to postulate 'mind' was to postulate something unobservable, and that psychology should confine itself to observable behaviour, Burt quite properly retorted that the most advanced sciences had no hesitation in postulating unobservables.[30] The value of the concept of mind was that of a provisional working model, and such a model was needed to explain a number of observed facts, in particular, the unity and permanence of conscious experience. 'This unity and continuity strongly suggest that the constituent events are related to some permanent and central entity of a special non-material kind, in short, a personal self, who, so to speak, owns these events, and refers to them as my conscious experience or states, and describes himself by the proper name of "I".'[31] Theories of mind as process, and epiphenominalistic theories cannot explain these facts, and fly in the face of common sense. Mind is a continuant, and that means

25. Thorpe, W. H. *Science, Man and Morals*, 1965.

26. Burt, C. L. Brain and consciousness. *Brit. J. Psychol.*, LIX, 1968, 61.

27. Burt, C. L. Logical positivism and the concept of consciousness. *Brit. J. Statist. Psychol.*, XIII, 1960, 68.

28. Burt, C. L. The structure of the mind. *Brit. J. Statist. Psychol.*, XIV, 1961, 145–70.

29. Burt, C. L. The concept of mind. *J. Psychol. Res. (India)*, II, 1960, 1–11.

30. Burt, C. L. The structure of the mind. *Loc. cit.*

31. *Ibid.*, p. 154.

something comparable to substance rather than to process. According to Burt, 'We can regard the mind as a kind of field existing in the neighbourhood of an individual brain, much as the physicist conceives of an electromagnetic field existing in the neighbourhood of a set of electric currents.'[32] Such a field is primordial; it is not something that 'emerges'. As we shall see when we look at Burt's evolutionism, he rejected emergence theories as explaining nothing. Minds have dispositional properties; they possess complexity and structure; and they have histories. In discussing these properties Burt largely accepted the classical scheme of cognitive, affective and conative dispositions, the details of which he believed could be mapped in by using factor-analytic techniques.[33] The dispositional properties of the mind like those of other substances are manifested in its interactions and among these interactions Burt assumed 'at least the possibility of inter-psychical reactions'.[34] Indeed, 'the main advantage [of postulating an immaterial mind] as compared with the purely physiological interpretations favoured by the materialists, physicalists and behaviourists, springs from the fact that it does not from the very outset preclude investigations concerned with conscious processes as such or with the alleged paranormal phenomena studied in psychical research; and it forms a far more convenient framework for describing the conscious processes of everyday life, and consequently for the various branches of applied psychology.'[35]

2. *Evolutionism.* Evolutionism is the second main ingredient of Burt's psychology, and because it provided the essential foundation for that branch of psychology, individual or differential psychology, on which his attention was principally concentrated, it was an indispensable ingredient. Yet it was not easy to reconcile with dualism; for Darwin's theory of evolution was materialistic in complexion. Mind, for Darwin, was something biological; a piece of equipment that had evolved with the rest of the organism's machinery in the struggle for survival by a process of natural selection—and this process was a blind, mechanistic one. As a modern exponent puts it: 'It necessarily follows that chance *alone* is at the source of every innovation, of all creation in the biosphere. Pure chance, absolutely free, but blind, at the very root of the

32. Burt, C. L. The structure of the mind. *Loc. cit.*, p. 167.

33. Burt, C. L. The structure of the mind: a review of the results of factor analysis. *Brit. J. Educ. Psychol., XIX*, 1949, 100–11, 176–99; The Factorial Study of the Emotions. In Reymert, M. L. (ed.) *Feelings and Emotions*, 1950, pp. 531–51; The Factorial Study of the Mind. In *Essays in Psychology dedicated to David Katz*, 1951, pp. 18–47.

34. Burt, C. L. The structure of the mind. *Loc. cit.*, 1961, p. 166.

35. *Ibid.*, p. 170.

stupendous edifice of evolution: this central concept of modern biology is no longer one among other possible or even conceivable hypotheses. It is to-day the *sole* conceivable hypothesis, the only one compatible with observed and tested fact.'[36]

Burt accepted the doctrine of evolution. He believed that the psychology of the characteristically British school to which he belonged was at bottom a biological psychology, derived from the work of Darwin, Spencer and Galton. He held that 'the primary explanation of men's mental processes was to be sought in their biological utility'.[37] From the doctrine of evolution he derived not only his belief in the importance of individual variability and of genetic influences, but his belief in the all-pervading presence of hierarchical structure, in the concept of development, and in the central importance of conative drives on the one hand and intelligence on the other. So evolution was in a sense the keystone of his system.

How then did he reconcile it with his dualism? He reconciled it by following his master, McDougall, and denying that evolution was a wholly mechanistic process, and that mind itself had evolved from matter.[38] McDougall believed that intelligence and purpose had played a part in the process of evolution from the beginning, that it was not a wholly blind process; and he held that the theories of the emergent evolutionists (Lloyd Morgan, Bergson, Alexander and others) who had proposed that somehow mind had 'emerged' from matter were incapable of accounting for the peculiar characteristics of mental processes. Burt expounded his own rather similar views on evolution in his review of Sir Alister Hardy's Gifford Lectures, *The Living Stream* (1965). There was, he maintained, 'a strong presumption against any completely mechanistic hypothesis of the origin of life'.[39] Following Schrödinger he regarded the chances of the emergence of living cells with their complicated structures from a purely random concurrence of atoms and molecules as too improbable to happen within the limits of available time. This pointed to 'some internal principle of organization, embodying something very like a controlling aim or purpose'. Selection was not merely an external selection by the environment; there was also an internal process of selection, and it was primarily these internal factors which made for increasing complexity of

36. Monod, J. *Chance and Necessity*, Eng. trans. 1972, p. 110.
37. Burt, C. L. *The Subnormal Mind*, 1935, p. 6.
38. McDougall, W. *Modern Materialism and Emergent Evolution*, 1929.
39. Burt, C. L. Reviews of Sir Alister Hardy's Gifford Lectures. *J. Soc. Psychical Res.*, XLIII (1966) and XLIV (1967), reprinted as Evolution and Parapsychology. *E.S.P. and Psychology*, 1975 (ed. Anita Gregory).

organisation. 'So in the study of living organisms the biologist is
obliged to introduce new categories and principles unknown to
any of the physical sciences; and most of these innovations, it will
be noted, centre on the concept of purpose or function— on activities
expressly directed towards the attainment of an end or goal.' As
Hardy himself stressed, animals themselves select environments
which are appropriate; so behaviour itself becomes a major selective
force. Burt ends his review by stating that 'the main conclusion to
be drawn is the supreme importance of consciousness in deciding
the direction and furthering the progress of animal evolution'.[40]

There was nothing profoundly original in these views of Burt,
which were derived from his fairly extensive reading in biology.
He was influenced, for example, by the views of Darlington,
Elasser, L. L. Whyte, Quastler and Thorpe, as well as by those of
Hardy himself. Many of his points would be quite widely accepted
today. Thus the Medawars unashamedly revert to teleology.[41] The
distinguished French biologist Jacob, in his history of the biological
sciences, notes that 'the notion that evolution results exclusively
from a succession of micro-events, from mutation, each occurring
at random is denied both by time and by arithmetic . . . evolution
has become possible only because genetic systems have themselves
evolved.'[42] And again, 'At each level of organization, novelties
appear in both properties and logic.'[43] Even Monod has to admit
that 'in a very real sense the organism effectively transcends physical
laws— even while obeying them.'[44] Once novelties are admitted—
as they must be— there are only two possible ways of explaining
them: the novelties were either there implicitly from the beginning,
or they were created and 'emerged'. Monod adheres to the first
theory. 'The necessary information was present, but unexpressed,
in the constituents. The epigenetic building of a structure is not a
creation, it is a revelation.'[45] In effect, too, Burt, though he did not
say so explicitly, favoured this theory. It would for one thing be
too improbable for minds to evolve in precise parallelism with
brains at every stage of the evolutionary process, if minds are quite
independent of brains. So the powers of the mind must have been
there from the beginning, and must have been progressively
unfolded as the brain's detecting capacities evolved. The alternative
'emergent' hypothesis Burt, following McDougall, decisively

40. *E.S.P. and Psychology*, p. 95.
41. Medawar, P. B. and Medawar, J. S. *The Life Science*, 1977, p. 11.
42. Jacob, F. *The Logic of Living Systems*, Eng. trans. 1974, p. 308.
43. *Ibid.*, p. 306.
44. Monod, J. *Op. cit.*, p. 81.
45. *Ibid.*, p. 87.

rejected. 'To stop with the blissful word "emergence" is not in itself an explanation.'[46] It is hard not to feel that Burt was mistaken in his curt rejection of the emergence principle. Not only does it accord far more closely with the hierarchical schemata he was so fond of, but it is by far the more probable theory. For in our own experience we are directly acquainted with creativity; while any kind of preformation seems an entirely gratuitous assumption. Emergence may not in itself be an explanation; but it is a fact, which one day perhaps may receive explanation, possibly within the framework Wolman has termed 'Monistic Transitionism'.[47]

3. *Holism*. Holism, a term coined by J. C. Smuts[48] to designate the theory that whole entities have specific characteristics which differ from those of their constituent parts, perhaps best describes that combination of ideas derived from Gestalt psychology, field theory and structuralism which marks the third component in Burt's psychology. The teachings of Ward, Stout, and McDougall early disposed Burt to holistic ideas, and he eagerly welcomed the findings of the Gestalt psychologists from 1912 onwards. He considered their work as 'the most significant area of experimental psychology'[49] and he was especially attracted by their reintroduction of the concept of the 'field' into psychology. This concept had, for Burt, two main merits:[50] firstly, it was an accurate description of the observable facts, the phenomenal continuum of Ward; and secondly, it lent itself to mathematical treatment, since a field is a region within which points can be quantified in terms of scalar quantities, vectors, matrices, sets, or even more complex mathematical elements.[51] A mathematical treatment of psychic fields had been proposed in 1881 by the economist, F. Y. Edgeworth,[52] who derived provisional equations to describe such fields from Clerk Maxwell's *Treatise on Electricity and Magnetism* (1873). Field concepts had for this reason, Burt maintained, an advantage over the qualitative term 'disposition' employed by Stout, McDougall and others. Problems of psychodynamics could up to a point be described in terms of field change and transformations, and the

46. Burt, C. L. The structure of the mind. *Brit. J. Statist. Psychol., XIV*, 1961, 145–70.
47. Wolman, B. B. Principles of Monistic Transitionism. In Wolman, B. B. and Nagel, E. (eds) *Scientific Psychology*, 1965.
48. Smuts, J. C. *Holism and Evolution*, 1926.
49. Burt, C. L. Psychology and the future. *The Listener*, 21 December 1950.
50. Burt, C. L. The field concept in psychology. *Bull. B.P.S., XXII*, 1969, 267.
51. Burt, C. L. Field theories and statistical psychology. *Brit. J. Statist. Psychol., XII*, 1959, 155.
52. Edgeworth, F. Y. *Mathematical Psychics*, 1881.

theory also lent itself to a possible, if somewhat specialised, explanation of paranormal phenomena, an explanation which the mathematician, G. D. Wasserman, had suggested some years before Burt himself put it forward (see p. 223).

Holistic ideas are closely allied to the concept of structure. The Gestalt psychologists had insisted that fields were organised, both phenomenally and behaviourally, and organisation implies structuralisation or articulation. Burt accepted this proposition; he always asserted that the mind had a structure, and that the behaviourists' doctrine of the 'empty organism' was quite unacceptable. Indeed he regarded it as one of the psychologist's primary tasks to elucidate this structure, and he devoted much time to it, developing the methods of factor analysis specifically to this end. In his historical note on faculty psychology appended to the Spens Report[53] Burt explained his point of view.

The reaction against faculty psychology may have gone a little too far. Granting that the mind is not an aggregate of mental powers, it is not a homogeneous unity, but an organization. Valuable distinctions, noted and perhaps over-emphasised by the earlier classifications, are now in some danger of being lost; and the later notion of the mind as a simple mechanism for linking up elements by association, much as subscribers are linked up by the switchboard at a central telephone exchange, is not only a gross over-simplification of the facts, but fails to explain the peculiar individual differences observable between individual pupils . . . These peculiarities, which have been studied statistically, have given rise to the description of specific mental 'factors' operating over and above 'general intelligence'.

In his scheme of mental structure Burt took over from classical psychology the major distinction between the cognitive and conative aspects of mind, and from the evolutionary theories of Herbert Spencer the concept of hierarchical levels, a concept previously adopted by Hughlings Jackson and by McDougall.[54] The details Burt attempted to fill in factorially. Though he admitted that the concept of hierarchy was based in the first place on non-mathematical considerations, he believed it was something that could be

53. *Report on Secondary Education* (Spens Report). H.M.S.O., 1938, App. IV.
54. See Moursey, E. M. K. The hierarchical organization of cognitive levels. *Brit. J. Statist. Psychol.*, V, 1952, 151–80. Based on a Ph.D thesis supervised by Burt, University of London, 1952.

submitted to statistical tests.[55] Nevertheless it must be admitted that as a whole Burt's structural scheme fails to carry conviction, and his claim that 'probably all the more important broad group factors have now been approximately identified'[56] seems recklessly premature. The factors of general intelligence and general emotionality, together with the group factors of verbal and spatial ability on the one hand, and of sthenic and asthenic emotions on the other, may have something to be said in their favour; the rest of Burt's scheme, very little. The hierarchical idea as such, on the contrary, has much to recommend it. It is deeply rooted in biology. 'From virus to men, from cell to species, biology is interested in systems whose complexity is constantly increased by the successive integration of lower level systems.'[57] But factor analysis, with its top-heavy mathematical apparatus, is a blunt tool for laying bare the details of the hierarchy; and Burt's reliance on physical models for his analysis of fields and structures gave insufficient weight to the immense importance of historical and developmental processes in the generation of psychical structures in man. The point was made by Piaget in his criticism of the Gestalt psychologists;[58] the weight they accorded to the analogy between physical and psychological fields led them to minimise the importance of functional and psychogenetic influences. 'The basic epistomological alternatives', wrote Piaget,[59] 'are predestination or some sort of constructivism.' Burt, fascinated like the Gestaltists by physics, inclined to the former, and it coloured all his views.

4. *Probabalism*. The mesh of predestination in Burt's system was not, however, completely rigid. The laws of nature were not laws of strict causality, but laws of probability. Probabalism was the fourth major component of his theoretical system. Here again its seeds were sown early in Burt's development. Karl Pearson in his *Grammar of Science* (1892) had put forward the view that a logic based on probability and the new statistical techniques he himself had devised would give the biological and human sciences the same exactitude that had been attained in the physical sciences. In fact he maintained that probability, not strict causality, was the basis of all science. As Burt noted, this famous book 'had a profound influence

55. Burt, C. L. *Factors of the Mind*, 1940, ch. XIV: Tests of Significance and of Hierarchical Tendency.

56. Burt, C. L. The structure of the mind. *Brit. J. Educ. Psychol.*, *XIX*, 1942, 199.

57. Jacob F. *The Logic of Living Systems*, Eng. trans. 1974, p. 266.

58. Piaget. J. *Structuralism*. Eng. Trans. 1971, p. 54.

59. *Ibid.*, p. 141.

on British psychologists at the beginning of the present century'.[60]
It certainly influenced Burt; and with this belief in probability
rather than strict causality it became easy for him to hold that
'human beings really are choosers between possibilities'.[61]

The formulation of quantum theory by Planck at the beginning
of the century, and the development of quantum mechanics by
Born, Dirac, Heisenberg, Schrödinger and others in the 1920s,
seemed to Burt to confirm Pearson's probabalism. By the middle
of the 1920s, as Heisenberg notes, 'it became clear that quantum
theory forces us to formulate these laws precisely as statistical laws
and to depart radically from determinism'.[62] In spite of Burt's lack
of mathematical and scientific training he became absorbingly
interested in quantum mechanics, and by the middle 1930s he had
acquired, for someone not trained in the physical sciences, a
remarkable understanding of the subject—an understanding which
few psychologists could match.[63] He suggested as early as 1936 that
'psychologists might find much that is fruitful in the new mathematical methods used for example by contemporary physicists'[64]—
in particular the use of matrices and linear operators in problems of
probability as expounded by Weyl in his *Theory of Groups and
Quantum Mechanics* (1931). Burt developed this suggestion in a
number of later articles, particularly in 'Quantum Theory and the
Principle of Indeterminacy',[65] and 'Scientific Method in Psychology, II'.[66] He believed that there were close parallels between the
study of quantum phenomena in physics and the study of psychological phenomena, as the physicist Niels Bohr had noted. 'The
mathematical methods employed in both branches of science display
many striking analogies.' Burt attached a mathematical appendix to
his article on quantum theory dealing with those aspects of wave
mechanics and probability functions of particular relevance to the
psychologist.[67] He likened the multi-dimensional analysis of space
developed by the mathematician Hilbert to the determination of the

60. Burt, C. L. Logical positivism and the concept of consciousness. *Brit. J.
Statist. Psychol.*, XIII, 1960, 58.

61. Burt, C. L. Psychologists and moral judgments. *J. & Newsletter, Assoc.
Educ. Psychol.*, I, 1966.

62. Heisenberg, W. *The Physicist's Conception of Nature*, 1958, p. 39.

63. Dr Wasserman has pointed to some misunderstandings of quantum mechanics
on Burt's part, but has, I think, failed to do justice to Burt's very real achievements
in this area. See Burt–Wasserman correspondence, Burt Archives, University of
Liverpool.

64. Hartog, P., Rhodes, E. C. and Burt, C. L. *The Marks of Examiners*, 1936, p.
313.

65. Burt, C. L. *Brit. J. Statist. Psychol.*, XI, 1958, 77–93.

66. Burt, C. L. *Brit. J. Statist. Psychol.*, XI, 1958, 105–28.

67. Burt, C. L. *Loc. cit.*, pp. 85–93.

latent roots and latent vectors of the matrices analysed by the psychological factorist. The conceptual models adopted by the quantum theorist and by the psychologist possessed four crucial characteristics in common:[68] in quantum theory and in modern psychology (i) 'processes are treated as indivisible wholes'; (ii) the observer can no longer be excluded from the data of observation; (iii) beneath the apparent continuity of what is observed there are unexpected discontinuities (e.g. the all-or-nothing discharges that underlie the stream of consciousness); and (iv) the principle of indeterminacy rules out mechanical causation.

Advances in neurophysiology, with which he kept closely in touch, further confirmed Burt in his probabalism. He was much influenced by D. A. Sholl's *The Organization of the Cerebral Cortex* (1956), in which Sholl argued on the basis of histological and neurological research that the brain acted on a probability basis; and he frequently quoted Sholl's work, together with later developments by Beurle, Uttley, Pask and others. Burt's review of F. H. George's *The Brain as a Computer*[69] revealed a knowledge of neurophysiology at least as extensive as his knowledge of quantum mechanics. But the real value of probabalism for Burt was that it opened the way, not only for a measure of human freedom, but for the whole range of human experience, 'the world of art, poetry and music as well as the world of fact, the dictates of morality, the visions of the mystic, the beliefs and rituals of the priest and the saint'[70]—all of which, Burt believed, the psychologist must take into account.

If we must give Burt's theoretical psychology a label, the label must obviously be 'humanistic'.

III

The basic postulates of humanistic psychology have been linked by J. F. T. Bugental, first president of the American Association for Humanistic Psychology, as follows:

1. Man, as man, supersedes the sum of his parts. He must be recognized as something other than the additive product of various part functions;
2. Man has his being in a human context. The unique nature of

68. Burt, C. L. Scientific method in psychology. *Brit. J. Statist. Psychol.*, *XI*, 1958, 117–21.

69. Burt, C. L. Working models of the brain. *Brit. J. Statist. Psychol.*, *XV*, 1962, 199–215.

70. Burt, C. L. *Psychology and Psychical Research*, 1968, p. 68.

man is expressed through his always being in relationship to
his fellows;

3. Man is aware. All aspects of his experience are not equally
available to man, but awareness is an essential part of man's
being;

4. Man has choice. When man is aware, he is aware that his
choice makes a difference, that he is not a bystander but a
participant in experience;

5. Man is intentional. Man intends through having purpose,
through valuing, and through creating and recognising meaning. Man's intentionality is the basis on which he builds his
identity, and it distinguishes him from other species.[71]

Burt would have accepted all these propositions, even the second
relating to the essentially social nature of man, as his Hobhouse
lecture makes clear. He is entitled, therefore, to be called a
humanistic psychologist. That does not mean, however, that he
would altogether have sympathised with some of the manifestations
of contemporary humanistic psychology, because some humanists
display a deeply anti-scientific attitude, of which Burt would have
strongly disapproved.

The roots of humanistic psychology go back at least as far as
Kant's distinction between the noumenal and phenomenal worlds,
and his restriction of scientific knowledge to phenomena. This left
the way open for understanding (*Verstand*), a different sort of
intuitive awareness, of the transcendental realm, and for the proposal
of Dilthey towards the end of the nineteenth century that there
were in fact two sorts of psychology, scientific (*naturwissenschaf-
tlich*) and humanistic (*geisteswissenschaftlich*), employing different
methods and concepts. Buttressed by the revived Aristotelianism of
Brentano and his stress on the essential intentionality of mind, this
led on the continent to a growing band of phenomenological and
existentialist psychologists, and in America from the 1920s onwards
to a school of personality theorists, of whom G. W. Allport was
the best known representative. Since the late 1950s these movements
have coalesced into a somewhat heterogeneous 'third force' in
psychology, which can broadly be termed humanistic. This third
force is often marked by its conspicuously anti-scientific approach
to psychology. Shotter, a leading British representative, for example, wants to replace the 'natural science of behaviour' completely

71. Bugental, J. F. T. The third force in psychology. *J. Human. Psychol., IV*,
1964, 19–26. Quoted in Sargent, S. S. The Humanistic Approach to Personality,
ch. XL in *Handbook of General Psychology*, ed. Wolman, B. B., 1973.

with 'a moral science of action', and the methods of natural science with 'conceptual analysis'.[72]

Two features of this anti-scientific brand of humanistic psychology are profoundly unsatisfactory—its radical dualism, and its methodological flabbiness. It altogether cuts off the human mind from its biological roots, and it totally differentiates man from the rest of the animal kingdom.[73] Man becomes a 'self-defining' entity who escapes the limitations of his biological past (if he ever had such a past), and psychology ceases to retain any methodological links with the natural sciences. Such a psychology develops its own methods of hermeneutic and conceptual analysis, and its own non-quantitative logic. Burt would have rejected both the radical dualism and the methodological anti-scientism of the more extreme humanists; for although he was a dualist, he always held that psychology was a biologically-rooted science; and he always believed that scientific method in its accepted form was the foundation of psychology, however necessary it was to supplement it with intuitive understanding. Nevertheless it is still appropriate to label Burt a humanistic psychologist, because he accepted the basic humanistic propositions about human nature. He was, however, a humanist with a difference—a humanist who believed that the special characteristics of human nature could be studied scientifically with the usual methods of science. And this is precisely why Burt is important as a theorist. He attempted to combine the vision of the humanists, their intuitive grasp of 'The Further Reaches of Human Nature', to use Maslow's phrase,[74] with the methodological toughness of the empirical psychologists—and there have been very few psychologists who have made this attempt. Perhaps the German psychologist, William Stern, whose achievements in many ways show a remarkable parallel to those of Burt,[75] is the other most conspicuous example from the first half of the century. Whether Burt succeeded in his attempt is another matter; his importance lies in the very fact that he made the attempt, that he believed in principle in bringing to bear on the problems of a humanistic psychology the full rigours of the logic of science and of quantitative method. Popper has argued convincingly that 'all theoretical or generalizing sciences make use of the same method, whether they

72. Shotter, J. *Images of Man in Psychological Research*, 1975, pp. 23, 35.

73. *Ibid.*, p. 132.

74. Maslow, A. H. *The Further Reaches of Human Nature*, 1971.

75. William Stern (1871–1938) was one of the founders of *Differentielle Psychologie* (1911). Director of the Hamburg Institute, he was distinguished as an experimental, child and applied psychologist (he was the inventor of the I.Q. index), and also a leading 'personalist' theorist.

are natural sciences or social sciences',[76] and Holt has devastatingly exposed the special claims of 'verstehende Psychologie'.[77] In the long and difficult task of creating a science of human nature the way forward is not to abandon the methods of science because some of the problems faced by the psychologist are peculiar to psychology, but to adapt these methods to the special problems encountered. And this is what Burt in principle attempted to do.

Burt was well equipped for this task by reason of his extensive knowledge of philosophy, logic and scientific method on the one hand, and his self-acquired competence in mathematics and physical theory on the other. He developed his views most fully in the two erudite articles on scientific method in psychology which he published in 1958.[78] But there are also many references to methodology in *Factors of the Mind*, and Burt provided his students with a full set of notes on scientific method in psychology, in which he went in great detail into the history and logic of scientific method and its application to the special problems of psychology, particularly differential psychology. It is regrettable that these learned notes were never written up in book form.

'Since the human sciences are far more complex than the physical, the methodological problems are far more difficult. Yet the writer on human problems seems scarcely aware that their discussion needs a technical approach quite as much as mechanics and chemistry.'[79] So Burt commenced his lectures on scientific method in psychology. Burt adhered completely to the Popperian view of the methodological comparability of all the sciences. 'The logical structure of every empirical science must', he insisted, 'be in all essential features the same.'[80] In sketching the model for a scientific discipline Burt had recourse to dynamics, 'partly because it is at once the simplest and the most complete example of a science and consequently the one that comes nearest to a finished model or ideal, and partly because what may be called the dynamical aspects of psychology are the most neglected and the least developed'.[81] At the basis of Burt's model was not only a thorough grasp of logic, both Aristotelian and modern, but also an extensive acquaintance with

76. Popper, K. R. *The Poverty of Historicism*, 1957, p. 130.

77. Holt, R. R. Individuality and generalization in the psychology of personality. *J. Pers.*, XXX, 1962, 377–404.

78. Burt, C. L. Definition and scientific method in psychology. *Brit. J. Statist. Psychol.*, XI, 1958, 31–69; Scientific method in psychology II. *Ibid.*, 105–28.

79. Burt, C. L. Notes on Scientific Method in Psychology, p. 1, Burt Archives, University of Liverpool.

80. Burt, C. L. Definition and scientific method in psychology. *Loc. cit.*, p. 37.

81. Burt, C. L. Definition and scientific method in psychology. *Brit. J. Statist. Psychol.*, XI, 1958, 37.

the writings of German and Austrian writers on the methodology of the physical sciences, particularly Hilbert, Cassirer, Weyl, Kraft, Planck and Carnap. In the first of his articles Burt outlines the essential features of simple scientific systems, including the assumption of primary propositions and concepts, derivative concepts, the formulation and testing of hypotheses, followed by an account of the special problems encountered at more complex levels. It is at these levels that the scientist searches for unifying concepts, such as the concept of energy, which 'becomes a kind of common denominator linking together practically all the processes with which the physical sciences deal into one comprehensive quantitative scheme'.[82] And he goes on, 'Plainly this is just the type of concept which the psychological factorist, by methods that in many ways are formally analogous to those of the physicist, has endeavoured to supply.'[83] This being so, it was obvious, Burt claimed, that mathematical models and formal definitions were essential in psychology. Nor was there any reason why the psychologist should not follow the physical scientist in simplifying complex situations in the search for underlying regularities. Thermodynamics and statistical mechanics both offer 'instructive models for the analysis of the behaviour of human aggregates'.[84] The model of the physical sciences suggests that the finished scheme 'should exhibit a hierarchical structure in which levels of increasing generality lie one on top of the other, like courses of overlapping bricks . . . thus forming (in Bacon's picturesque phrase) "a soaring pyramid of knowledge". But it is a pyramid of knowledge resting on a platform of abstractions.'[85] Burt deplored the tendency of recent textbooks of psychology, particularly those published in America, to abandon all attempts 'to integrate the facts and theories they describe into anything like a coherent scheme'.[86] Burt, therefore, clearly envisaged the idea of a systematic, general psychology founded on the accepted principles of the logic of science.

The remainder of the first article, and all of his second article, were devoted by Burt to rebutting common objections to the kind of system he had expounded. He replied in the first article to 'the prior objection that the problems of the psychologist are from their very nature unsuited to investigation by the methods of science'; to the doctrinaire adherence to operational definition; and to misunderstandings of the nature of the 'hypothetico–deductive method'.

82. Burt, C. L. Definition and scientific method in psychology. *Brit. J. Statist. Psychol.*, XI, 1958, p. 49.
83. *Ibid.*, p. 49.
84. *Ibid.*, p. 51.
85. *Ibid.*, p. 53.
86. *Ibid.*, p. 55.

And in the second article he dealt with the fallacious dichotomy between Aristotelian and Galilean methods, with the outdated demand for strictly causal laws, and again with the hypothetico-deductive requirement.

The combination of a high-powered grasp of scientific methodology with humanistic insight makes Burt's theoretical psychology important, and indeed almost unique. It was well in advance of its times, and also, it must be admitted, far beyond Burt's capacity to realise in practice. It is as hopeless for the present-day psychologist to follow a system such as that outlined by Burt, as it would have been for a medieval alchemist to have adopted prematurely the mathematics of quantum mechanics, had they then been available in the abstract. The basic empirical work had simply not been done. Nor has the psychologist today made more than very modest inroads into the empirical nature of his subject matter. It is only fair to add that a few years later Burt himself came to realise this. For he stated in 'The Concept of Consciousness':

> In my view the attempt to construct a comprehensive and coherent axiomatic system, derived from a minimum list of concepts and postulates is something that can be reasonably undertaken only when the science in question has, like mathematics or mechanics, arrived at a highly developed stage. Otherwise it almost inevitably leaves out too much. The general trend of modern research, even in sciences which like astronomy and physics, were once thought to be ripe for systematic formulation of this kind, has been to reveal an unexpected richness and variety in the universe; and surely the study of human life is likely to be the most complex of all scientific disciplines.[87]

All the same Burt's earlier vision was important, because it highlighted the essential task of the psychologist—to marry his humanistic insight with the logic and methodology of the sciences. Too many psychologists have opted for one or other alternative—to retain the insights and sacrifice the methodology, or to retain the methodology and sacrifice the insights. Burt insisted that both should play a part in psychology. He failed, as was inevitable, to produce a psychology exemplifying these proposals, but it was a worthy ideal to have put forward, and deserves wider recognition than it has received.

87. Burt, C. L. The concept of consciousness. *Brit. J. Psychol., LIII*, 1962, 234.

IV

In the field of individual, or differential, psychology Burt was one of the pioneers, and as a pioneer his place in history is assured, whatever judgments are passed on the validity of his theories, or on the integrity of some of his work. Though the existence of individual differences had been recognised in Greek times by philosophers like Plato and characterologists like Theophrastus, and they later played a part in various typologies and pseudo-scientific systems like phrenology, it was the work of Galton, derived from the evolutionary theory of his cousin, Charles Darwin, that laid the foundations of differential psychology. Galton, however, was an unsystematic thinker: he sowed the seeds, leaving others to tend the plants. Binet and Henri in France; Stern in Germany; Spearman and Burt in England; J. M. Cattell and Terman in America, were the principal second founders of the subject. Binet and Henri in their famous article of 1895 set out the programme of individual psychology with remarkable clarity, advocated 'the method of mental tests', and suggested that to be practically useful the individual psychologist must deal straightaway with 'superior psychic faculties'.[88] Just over a quarter of a century later Burt, in his presidential address to the psychology section of the British Association, commented on 'the rapid development of what threatens to become a new and separate branch of science, the study of individual differences in mind', and even went on to claim that 'the whole territory of individual psychology has . . . been completely covered in the large'.[89] To these advances Burt himself had made a substantial contribution. In the face of opposition and neglect from many general psychologists he asserted the right of the individual psychologist to exist; he went some way to elucidate the major variables of ability and personality; he investigated the origins of individual differences, and he studied in depth the problems of special groups, the subnormal, the delinquent, neurotic and gifted. In doing all this Burt was not only incontestably among the pioneers of the subject, he was also, in spite of certain limitations and weaknesses, arguably in broad terms mainly right in what he upheld.

Burt was certainly right to stress that individual differences were as important in psychology as in biology. The fact of individual variations is, as Darwin saw, fundamental to the whole of the

88. Binet, A. and Henri, V. La psychologie individuelle. *L'Année Psychol.*, II, 1895, 411–65.

89. Burt, C. L. The Mental Differences between Individuals. *British Association, Annual Report*, 1923.

evolutionary process. Recent advances in genetics and biochemistry have confirmed the ubiquity of such variations. They extend from the molar to the molecular level, and are all-pervading. A psychologist who ignores them is ignoring a vital component in his subject matter. Burt, too, was absolutely right in insisting that the study of individual differences was not only of practical importance to the psychologist, but of great theoretical importance, also. These differences are, as a recent writer has put it, 'a crucible of theory construction'.[90] It is worth noting that a large part of chemistry is derived from a study of the different properties of different materials; and genetics, the key biological science, from a study of the variations obtaining between members of a species. In a subject like psychology, where the experimental manipulation of variables is necessarily restricted by moral considerations, the examination of naturally occurring differences between individuals and between groups is one of the most promising lines of enquiry. Burt clearly saw this. He had no use for the facile distinction between the nomothetic and the ideographic, which would set general and differential psychology in two different camps. He regarded the study of individuality as one of the foundation stones of a general psychology of human nature. This is a point of view that has not been widely recognised among psychologists. From the time of Wundt onwards experimental psychologists have tended in their search for general laws to ignore individual differences. In 1957 Cronbach could still talk of 'the two disciplines of psychology' (general and differential),[91] and even today the divide has not been bridged. Burt will deservedly be remembered for his consistent advocacy of the central theoretical importance of differential psychology.

He will be remembered, too, for his sturdy belief in the use of quantitative methods in psychology, not to supplant, but to supplement qualitative and introspective assessment. In this belief Burt diverged radically from F. C. Bartlett, who had been his pupil in Cambridge in 1913–14 and from many members of the Cambridge school of psychologists, who went out of their way to decry statistics. No doubt quantitative methods can be abused, and no doubt Burt himself can sometimes be justly accused of erecting top-heavy statistical edifices on unsure foundations. Nevertheless the steady development of statistical and mathematical psychology in the last quarter of a century makes it increasingly certain that Burt

90. Underwood, B. J. Individual differences as a crucible in theory construction. *Amer. Psychol., XXX*, 1975, 28–34.

91. Cronbach, L. J. The two disciplines of scientific psychology. *Amer. Psychol., XII*, 1957, 671–84.

was basically right in his belief. Quantitative methods can be employed fruitfully in psychology over a wide range of problems, as advances in scaling methods, mathematical models, the analysis of qualitative data, and multivariate analysis, to mention a few of the main areas, quite clearly show. In the quantification of psychology Burt was among the leaders.

Burt's particular contributions to individual psychology have been discussed in earlier chapters of this book, and need not be detailed again here. Among the more important were his theory of intelligence as 'innate, general, cognitive ability'; his work on the development of mental and scholastic tests; his factorial approach to the study of personality; his early adumbration of the methods of behaviour therapy; his magisterial studies of special groups, in particular of delinquent and backward children; and his applications of the methods and findings of differential psychology to child guidance, educational selection, vocational guidance and military problems. These were significant contributions in their day, and to disparage them is to fudge the historical record. Nor should it be forgotten that Burt was a first-rate clinician endowed with perceptive diagnostic skills. In the field of differential psychology Burt has a secure place in history. This does not mean that he was invariably right, or that his work has not been to some extent superseded. Priority, not finality, is the hallmark of a pioneer. And, if not the first, Burt was among the first in the development of differential psychology. His shortcomings, to which we must now turn, derived partly from the exigencies of circumstances, partly from limitations in his intellectual frames of reference, and partly from the psychopathic component in his own personality.

V

Burt had the vision to grasp the potentialities and to map the ground-plan of individual psychology; he never had the resources to implement his vision in a scientifically satisfactory manner. His data were mostly collected while he was employed as an educational psychologist by the London County Council. He was employed only half-time; he was grossly over-worked; he had no paid assistants, and most of the help he got was from half-trained teachers and social workers; he had no special research grants, and research aims had to be subordinated to the practical requirements of his main job. As an employee of the Council Burt was not in a position to enlist outside financial support, or to organise research teams. In any case, unlike Bartlett, he had few talents in this direction, and when he gained his independence on his appointment to University College, other tasks occupied his attention. In these circumstances it is hardly surprising that Burt's research data left much to be desired. In the strictly educational field he did good work, and with small manageable groups, such as his two hundred delinquents, Burt's clinical skills and psychological expertise enabled him to produce brilliant results. But he was never in a position to collect adequate material to serve as a basis for a whole system of differential psychology with far-reaching social implications. His data were 'dirty data', collected for a variety of *ad hoc* purposes, by a variety of uncoordinated techniques, frequently administered by semi-trained assistants, and often 'adjusted' in the interests of immediate practical requirements. As research material the data were at times, for example in the case of parental I.Q.s,[92] simply rubbish. Yet Burt attempted to use these data, or such fragments as had survived, and by adroit statistical manipulation to squeeze conclusions out of them. The attempt ought never to have been made. Burt should have applied for funds, recruited a team of trained assistants, and undertaken properly planned research. He could have done this any time after 1932, but he never even tried to do so. Instead he dredged up material from the past, made disingenuous reservations about its approximate nature, and on the basis of these unsound foundations was prepared to publish conclusions highly charged in their social implications. It was an irresponsible and unscrupulous thing to have done. Burt's own overconfidence in his statistical wizardry does not exonerate him. From 1943 onwards Burt's research reports must be regarded as suspect.

Burt's system of individual psychology was, however, flawed by more than these empirical shortcomings; it was marked by certain intellectual limitations. In the first place Burt was deeply imbued with preformist modes of thinking, which imply that development is essentially the unfolding of innate potentialities. At Oxford he was indoctrinated by his philosophy teacher, H. W. B. Joseph, with Aristotelian logic, and it is obvious from the frequent references to Aristotle in Burt's writings that this had a lasting effect on him. His fourfold scheme of factors, for example, was based on the fourfold Aristotelian scheme of predicables; and it seems probable that his preformism was at any rate in part derived from the Aristotelian concept of potentiality. These Aristotelian ideas were reinforced by his psychology teacher, McDougall. According to McDougall, 'underlying and determining the main lines and limits of the mental activity of any creature is a complex organization

92. See pages 102 and 255.

which we conveniently call its mental structure'.[93] This structure, in the case of human nature, McDougall described as consisting of 'the innate propensities and abilities of men'. These propensities and abilities, though to some extent plastic, determine the whole course of mental life, and the main task of the psychologist is, therefore, McDougall maintained, to provide a 'valid, adequate and useful account of the structure of the human mind'.

These ideas that he imbibed at Oxford had a permanent and decisive effect on Burt's outlook and on the direction of his own work. They led him to focus his attention on mental structure, and to pay little attention to developmental processes, and they resulted in his sharply distinguishing the innate features of the mind from the acquired. When he wrote on child development it was in terms of maturation rather than in terms of learning or socialisation.[94] He conceived growth in quantitative rather than in qualitative terms, and was more interested in measuring outcomes than in tracing stages. He stressed continuity, constancy and predictability.

For a variety of reasons these preformist conceptions carry much less weight today either among biologists or among psychologists. Biologists no longer regard it necessary to choose between preformism and the rival theory of epigenesis. Development rather is guided by instructions within the DNA of the cell nucleus, but the implementation of these instructions depends on the right sequence of stimuli from without. It is a matter neither of preformation, nor of epigenesis, but of interaction. Likewise in psychology Piaget's studies of cognitive growth, which lay stress on the twofold processes of accommodation and assimilation, point to the interactionist nature of psychological development. There is now a mass of information relating to the permanent influence of early learning both in animal and in human psychological growth.[95] It is impossible to regard this growth as mainly depending on the maturation of innate potentials. The task of the psychologist becomes that of understanding how psychological growth takes place, what factors block and what stimulate it—becomes, in other words, a study of processes, interactions and qualitative change, rather than merely the measurement of maturation and the determination of norms. Innate factors may still be important, and measurement may still have a part to play, but they are seen in a different context to the rather rigid one in which Burt employed them. His conception of individual psychology, therefore, has a distinctly dated look today.

93. McDougall, W. *The Energies of Men*, Preface to 3rd edn 1935.
94. See Burt's appendices to the various Hadow reports.
95. Hunt, J. McV. *Intelligence and Experience*, 1961; Sluckin, W. (ed.) *Early Learning and Early Experience*, 1971.

Preformism, however, was not the only limitation of Burt's individual psychology; it was also essentially non-sociological. Burt always regarded psychology as a biological science, and, as we have seen (Chapter Two), he had something of a blind spot with regard to sociology. He grew up at a time when sociology was very poorly developed in Great Britain, and he never showed more than a perfunctory acquaintance with the classics of nineteenth and twentieth century sociological literature. As a result, though Burt was, of course, aware that environment influenced human development, he thought in terms of biological models, not in terms of the bio-social models more appropriate to man. Thus society was regarded by Burt as merely part of the individual's environment, on a level with other environmental variables; it was not conceived as an integral part of the human personality itself. This is, of course, what the sociological thinkers— Comte, Marx, Durkheim, Weber, G. H. Mead, Sorokin and others— had argued was the case. Human personality is the result of an internalisation of socio-cultural norms, values and influences. Society cannot be categorised as merely part of the environment, because it is in some degree internalised within the personality. This is what Burt never grasped. In *The Young Delinquent*, for example, he devoted two chapters to environmental conditions. He spoke of poverty, family relationships, companionships, leisure facilities, and even dropped a hint that the 'complicated tangle of habits and attitudes' within the family might have a bearing on delinquency. But all this was something external to the individual. The important thing, in the last resort, was 'the personal reaction to the situation, not the situation itself',[96] which shows quite clearly that Burt was distinguishing sharply between the person and the situation, that he conceived the person as standing apart from the situation and capable of reacting independently of it. In this view Burt was essentially mistaken. This does not imply that human beings can never transcend their social environment; in special circumstances they may occasionally be able to do so. But that certainly does not apply to the average, immature child growing up in a narrow, restricted family and community setting. Burt simply did not comprehend the kind of relationship that obtains between the average individual and his culture.

The limitations of Burt's viewpoint, and his inability to appreciate the sociological component in human nature, had important consequences when he came to apply the Fisher multifactorial model of inheritance to the analysis of human intelligence. The basic aim of Fisher's method, as we have seen (p. 59), was to partition the variability observed in the characteristics of the members of a

96. Burt, C. L. *The Young Delinquent*, 1925, p. 188.

species between different components, genetic and environmental, subdividing these in their turn into additive and dominant genetic sub-components, special and general environmental sub-components, and a genetic–environmental interaction component. The scheme has proved highly successful in assessing the heritability of various characters, physical and behavioural, of domestic and laboratory animals, and of physical characters in human populations. Its application to human psychological characteristics rests on the assumption that these characteristics can be treated wholly in biological terms. If this is not the case, if human beings are bio-social, if culture cannot be regarded solely as an environmental variable, then the Fisher model becomes inappropriate.

Burt, of course, would have denied this, and would have argued that the concordance between the variances predicted by the Fisher model were so close to those established from his empirical data that the model is clearly appropriate. There are two objections to this rejoinder. Firstly, it involves a circularity; the assumptions employed in the model have been based on empirical findings, and the empirical data to be tested have been adjusted to fit the model. And secondly, even if data and model were found to reveal a close fit, this concordance does not finally establish the model's appropriateness. Newtonian models in physics were eventually superseded in spite of many precise confirmations.

Medawar in his discussion of the posthumous Burt controversy expressed the essence of the matter succinctly: 'Human beings owe their biological supremacy to the possession of a form of inheritance quite unlike that of other animals; exogenetic or exosomatic heredity. . . . This differentiates our characteristically human heredity absolutely from ordinary biological heredity. . . . The pattern of inheritance of intellectual differences in human beings is indeed different from the inheritance of other character differences in other animals.'[97] Burt's attempt to apply the Fisherian model of multifactorial inheritance to human psychological characteristics was, therefore, misguided, and was the result of his lack of appreciation of the sociological component in human nature.

Much recent work in psychology has begun to provide evidence for the importance of this component; for example, the work of Vygotsky and Luria in Russia;[98] the researches of Cole and his

97. Medawar, P. B. Unnatural Science. *The New York Review of Books*, 3 February 1977. See also Medawar, P. B. and Medawar, J. S. *The Life Science*, 1977, ch. vi.

98. Vygotsky, L. S. *Thought and Language*, Eng. trans. 1962; Luria, A. R. *Cognitive Development; Its Cultural and Social Foundations*, Eng. trans. 1976.

associates on the cultural context of learning and thinking;[99] and the investigations of Philip Vernon on intelligence and cultural environment.[100] Moreover— and this in the long run may be of even greater significance— Popper's theory of the Third World, first clearly stated in published form in his book *Objective Knowledge* (1972), furnishes a theoretical framework in which the empirical findings can be fitted, as Medawar, too, has appreciated.[101] The replacement of the traditional two-tier, body-mind, model of psychology by the three-tier model of Popper may eventually have revolutionary consequences for psychology. Popper himself, in association with the physiologist Eccles, has begun to sketch out these consequences.[102] It is the kind of framework in which a good many of Burt's insights might well have found a logical resting place, and in which some of his mistakes might have been corrected. Unfortunately the Popper model was not available to Burt before his death, and in any case he might have been too set in his ways of thinking to appreciate its importance. It is worth observing that Burt's German counterpart, William Stern, had propounded a comparable three-tier system a generation previously, which Burt, like most other psychologists, had disregarded.[103]

So Burt's individual psychology was flawed in more ways than one. Nevertheless it represents an important phase in the development of the subject, incorporates many advances in techniques, and contains many elements of value.

VI

It will be a pity if posterity fixes exclusively on the limitations and deceptions in Burt's work, gloats over his downfall, and simply points to him as a warning. The charges of fraud no doubt brought Burt far greater public attention after his death than his achievements ever brought him during his lifetime. The evidence reviewed earlier in this book has shown beyond reasonable doubt that these charges were true: Burt did deceive the scientific community on matters of moment, and even after the utilisation of his data by others to substantiate conclusions of social significance, he never issued disclaimers. He committed a grave offence against the tacitly

99. Cole, M., Gay, J., Glick, J. A. and Sharp, D. W. *The Cultural Context of Learning and Thinking*, 1971.
100. Vernon, P. E. *Intelligence and Cultural Environment*, 1969.
101. Medawar, P. B. and Medawar, J. S. *The Life Science*, 1977, p. 55.
102. Popper, K. R. and Eccles, J. C. *The Self and its Brain*, 1977.
103. Stern, W. *General Psychology from the Personalistic Standpoint*, Eng. trans. 1938, ch. iv.

accepted codes of scientific ethics. Such lapses may be more common than we care to admit,[104] but in a man of Burt's standing they were scandalous and hard to forgive. We must, however, keep two points in mind: firstly, there were mitigating circumstances in the psychological disturbances from which he suffered; and secondly, his positive achievements, and they were many, are not automatically invalidated by his malpractices. His various achievements must be judged on their merits.

What these merits are, is likely to be a matter of contention for some time. Burt was a specialist, rather than a generalist, in psychology, and the evaluation of his work will depend in part on the evaluation of the importance of the areas in which he specialised. He contributed almost nothing to general experimental psychology, nor to those areas which might be regarded as central to a biologically-based psychology—physiological and comparative psychology. Burt's main achievements were in the field of individual, or differential, psychology; in some branches of mathematical psychology; and in a theoretical psychology of a humanistic type— all areas about whose status psychologists have as yet reached no consensus. Burt's doctrines are unlikely to be accepted in the form in which he propounded them. They belong to the past, and are marked by the limitations of past frameworks of thought. Nevertheless the future may well vindicate the central core of Burt's insights—his stress on individuality, and the importance of some genetic contribution to it; his faith in quantification; his hierarchical reconciliation of unity and diversity; and his blending of humanism and methodology.

It would be totally unfair for a final judgment on Burt to focus on his deceptions to the exclusion of all his positive achievements. He was not, perhaps, either by training or by temperament a scientist. He was too impatient to reach, and too confident of having reached, firm conclusions which became for him very early in his career articles of almost religious faith, to be defended at all costs. Yet he brought to psychology many conspicuous gifts— intelligence, erudition of the most varied kinds, a powerful and synthetic imagination, sharp powers of observation and immense application, together with outstanding verbal and mathematical skills. Few psychologists can stand comparison with him in the richness of his intellectual equipment. When political controversies have lost their stridency, and when psychologists have evolved more adequate and comprehensive models, it may be possible to

104. St James-Roberts, I. Are researchers trustworthy? *New Scientist*, 2 September 1976, pp. 481–3; Cheating in science. *New Scientist*, 25 November 1976, pp. 466–9.

look more dispassionately on Burt's achievements and to evaluate them more impartially. In spite of the tragic flaws in his character Burt may yet be accorded a place in history as one of psychology's imaginative pioneers.

List of Publications by Cyril Burt

Two earlier bibliographies of Burt's writings have been published. The first, edited by Hannah Steinberg, covered the years up to 1950, and appeared in the *British Journal of Educational Psychology, XXXI*, 1951, pp. 53–62; the second, in *Stephanos: Studies in Psychology presented to Cyril Burt*, (1965), edited by Charlotte Banks and P. L. Broadhurst, covered the years up to 1965. Both were based entirely on information provided by Burt, and contained a considerable number of errors. I have been assisted in compiling the present bibliography by the list prepared by Stephen Sharp of Newnham College, Cambridge, for the years 1909–1940, and by the list prepared by Miss Archer, Burt's former secretary, for the years 1965–1971. I have included a number of the more important Critical Notices and Reviews written by Burt, as he often used them as a vehicle for expressing his views. I have not included newspaper articles, prefaces to books written by others, nor the L.C.C. reports listed in earlier bibliographies, which appear never to have been published, and of which there is no trace in the Greater London Council Archives.

1909
Experimental Tests of General Intelligence. *Brit. J. Psychol., III*, pp. 94–177.

1910
Experimental Tests of General Intelligence. *Rep. Brit. Ass. Adv. Sci., LXXIX*, p. 804.

1911
The Experimental Study of General Intelligence. *Child Study, IV*, pp. 33–45, 92–101.
Experimental Tests of Higher Mental Processes and their Relation to General Intelligence. *J. Exp. Ped., I*, pp. 93–112.

1912
The Inheritance of Mental Characteristics. *Eugen. Rev., IV*, pp. 168–200.
The Mental Differences between the Sexes. (With R. C. Moore) *J. Exp. Ped., I*, pp. 273–84, 355–88.
Experimental Investigation of Formal Training. *Rep. L.C.C. Ann. Conf. Teachers*. London: King & Son.

1913
The Mental Differences between the Sexes. *Rep. Brit. Ass. Adv. Sci., LXXXII*, pp. 750–1.

The Relation of Attention to Instinct and Interests. *Rep. L.C.C. Ann. Conf. Teachers*. London: King & Son.

1914

Mental Tests (lecture given at a Conference in the Provincial Training College, Edinburgh). Edinburgh: Andrew Brown, pp. 1–11. (Reprinted in *Child Study*, VIII, 1915, pp. 8–13.)

The Measurement of Intelligence by the Binet Tests. *Eugen. Rev.*, VI, pp. 36–50, 140–52.

1915

The General and Specific Factors underlying the Primary Emotions. *Rep. Brit. Ass. Adv. Sci., LXXXIV*, pp. 694–6.

Report by the Council's Psychologist as to the work of the Psychologist from 10 May 1913 to 31 October 1914, pp. 1–5. London: King & Son.

Appeal for Cooperation in Research. *Child Study*, VIII, pp. 92–3.

1916

Report of a Committee on Mental and Physical Factors in Education. (With C. S. Myers, J. A. Green *et al.*) *Rep. Brit. Ass. Adv. Sci., LXXXV*, pp. 307–25.

Some Results of Mental and Scholastic Tests. (With M. Bickersteth) *Rep. IVth Ann. Conf. Educ. Assoc.*, pp. 30–7.

Psychology and the Emotions. *School Hygiene*, VII, pp. 57–69.

1917

The Distribution and Relations of Educational Abilities. London: King & Son.

The Unstable Child. *Child Study*, X, pp. 61–79.

1918

Report on Provision for Backward Children. *L.C.C. Development Memorandum No. 1*, pp. 1–4. London: King & Son.

1919

Facial Expression as an Index of Mentality in Children. *Child Study*, XII, pp. 1–3.

The Development of Reasoning in School Children. *J. Exp. Ped.*, V, pp. 68–77, 121–7.

Moral Conflicts and Juvenile Crime. *Child Study*, XII, pp. 22–5.

1920

Vocational Diagnosis in Industry and at School. *Lectures on Industrial Administration* (ed. B. Muscio), pp. 79–120. London: Pitman & Sons.

The Definition and Diagnosis of Mental Deficiency. *Studies in Mental Inefficiency*, I, pp. 49–54, 69–78.

Children's Dreams. *Child Study*, XIII, pp. 29–30.

1921

Mental and Scholastic Tests. London: King & Son; 4th edn 1962, Staples Press.

The Dreams and Daydreams of a Delinquent Girl. *J. Exp. Ped.*, *VI*, pp. 1–11, 66–74, 142–54, 212–23.

Report of an Investigation upon Backward Children in Birmingham. City of Birmingham Education Committee.

1922

The Mental After-Effects of Sleeping Sickness in School Children. *Brit. J. Med. Psychol.*, *II*, pp. 237–8.

Tests for Clerical Occupations. *J. Nat. Inst. Indust. Psychol.*, *I*, pp. 23–7, 79–81.

The Causes and Treatment of Juvenile Delinquency. *Psyche*, *II*, pp. 339–51, 385–403; ibid., *III*, pp. 1–24.

A Comparison of Judgments in the Evaluation of Cloths. (With H. Binns) *J. Nat. Inst. Indust. Psychol.*, *I*, pp. 93–8.

1923

The Neurotic School Child. *Studies in Mental Inefficiency*, *IV*, pp. 7–12.

Handbook of Tests for Use in Schools. London: King & Son; 2nd edn 1948, Staples Press.

The National Institute Group Test of Intelligence, No. 33. London: National Institute of Industrial Psychology.

The Mental Differences between Individuals. *Rep. Brit. Ass. Adv. Sci.*, *XCII*, pp. 215–39. (Presidential Address to Section J, Psychology.)

Preface to 'On the Relation between Home Conditions and the Intelligence of School Children' by L. Isserlis. Medical Research Council Report. London: H.M.S.O.

The Causal Factors of Juvenile Crime. *Brit. J. Med. Psychol.*, *III*, pp. 1–33.

Delinquency and Mental Defect. *Brit. J. Med. Psychol.*, *III*, pp. 168–78.

1924

The Principles of Vocational Guidance. *Brit. J. Psychol.*, *XIV*, pp. 336–52.

History of the Development of Psychological Tests. Chapter I of Board of Education's *Report on Psychological Tests of Educable Capacity*. H.M.S.O., pp. 1–61; also Appendices on Tests, Statistical Procedure, and Bibliography.

1925

The Young Delinquent. London: University of London Press; New York: Appleton. Translated into Danish 1937, into Swedish 1941; 4th edn 1957.

The Northumberland Standardized Tests: Test I, Arithmetic; Test II, English; Test III, Intelligence; Manual of Instructions. London: University of London Press.

The Standardization of the Definitions of Mental Deficiency and its Different Degrees. *Ier Cong. gén. de l'Enfant (Génève)*, Sect. II.

Psychological Tests for Scholarship and Promotion. *The School (Toronto)*, *XIII*, pp. 734–43.

1926

A Study in Vocational Guidance. (With M. Smith *et al*.) London:
H.M.S.O. *Industrial Fatigue Research Board, Report No. 33. Medical
Research Council.*

The Contribution of Psychology to Social Hygiene. *Brit. J. Soc.
Hygiene*, I, pp. 14–37.

The Causes of Sex Delinquency in Girls. *Brit. J. Soc. Hygiene*, pp. 251–
71.

The Definition and Diagnosis of Moral Imbecility. *Brit. J. Med. Psychol.*,
VI, pp. 10–46.

Local Distribution of Juvenile Delinquency in London. Appendix II,
Report of L.C.C. Education Committee, Juvenile Delinquency in London.

1927

Die Verteilung der Schulfähigkeiten und ihre gegenseitigen Beziehungen
(Trans. W. Betz). Langensalza: J. Beltz.

The Measurement of Mental Capacities. The Henderson Trust
Lectures— *VIII*. London: Oliver & Boyd.

1929

The Psychology of the Bad Child. *The Listener*, 6 February.

Chapters on 'The Nature of Mental Defect' and 'The Classifications of
Mental Defectives', and Appendix on 'Mental and Educational Tests'.
*Report of Joint Committee of Board of Education and Board of Control on
Mental Deficiency.* London: H.M.S.O.

Formal Training: the Psychological Aspect. *Rep. Brit. Ass. Adv. Sci.*,
XCVIII, pp. 302–5.

1930

The Study of the Mind. *The Listener*. (1) 'The Observation of Others'
30 April; (2) 'Educational Tests' 7 May; (3) 'Intelligence Tests' 14
May; (4) 'Mental Development' 21 May; (5) 'Temperament' 28 May;
(6) 'Observation of Oneself' 4 June; (7) 'Experiments' 11 June; (8)
'Errors and Illusions' 18 June; (9) 'Measurements in Psychology' 25
June; (10) 'Attention' 2 July; (11) 'Psychology of Animals' 9 July;
(12) 'Psychology of the Sexes' 16 July.

The Mind of the Child. *The Listener*. (1) 'Growth of Intelligence' 1
October; (2) 'The Backward Child' 8 October; (3) 'The Growth of
Character' 15 October; (4) 'Criminals in the Making' 22 October;
(5) 'The Nervous Child' 29 October; (6) 'The Difficulties of Youth'
5 November.

1931

The Mental Development of Children from Seven to Fourteen.
Appendix to the *Board of Education's Report of the Consultative
Committee on the Primary School* (Hadow Report). London: H.M.S.O.

1932

How the Mind Works. *The Listener*. (1) 'Studying the Minds of

Others' 16 November; (2) 'Studying One's Own Mind' 23
November; (3) 'Reason and Emotion' 28 December.

1933

How the Mind Works (With W. Moodie, E. Miller and E. Jones; ed. C.
Burt). London: Allen & Unwin, 1933; 2nd edn 1945, 3rd edn 1948.
Translated into Arabic and Swedish, 1950.
The Backward Child. *The New Era in Home and School*, *XIV*, pp. 89–93.

1934

In Trouble. *The Listener*. (1) 'Causes of Crime' 2 May; (2) 'How
Society Treats the Offender' 18 July; (3) 'Is My Child Normal?' 24
October.
Emotional Development of Children up to the Age of Seven Plus.'
(With Susan Isaacs) *Board of Education's Report of the Consultative
Report on Infant and Nursery Schools* (Hadow Report). Appendix *III*
244–51. London: H.M.S.O.

1935

The Subnormal Mind. London: Oxford University Press. Translated into
Dutch, 1936. 3rd edn with new Preface, 1955; 4th edn with Preface by
H. J. Eysenck, 1977.

1936

The Analysis of Examination Marks: A Review of the Methods of Factor
Analysis in Psychology. Memorandum in *The Marks of Examiners* by
P. Hartog, E. C. Rhodes and C. Burt. London: Macmillan, pp. 245–
314. (Also reprinted as a separate pamphlet.)

1937

The Backward Child. London: University of London Press Ltd, 5th edn,
1961.
Methods of Factor-Analysis with and without Successive
Approximation. *Brit. J. Educ. Psychol.*, *VII*, pp. 172–95.
Correlations between Persons. *Brit. J. Psychol.* (Gen. Sec.), *XXVIII*,
pp. 59–96.
How Speech Began. *The Listener*, 16 June.

1938

Historical Note on Faculty Psychology. Board of Education's *Report of
Consultative Committee on Secondary Education with Special Reference to
Grammar Schools and Technical High Schools* (Spens Report). London:
H.M.S.O., Appendix IV, pp. 429–38.
The Analysis of Temperament. *Brit. J. Med. Psychol.*, *XVII*, pp. 158–88.
The Latest Revision of the Binet Tests. *Eugen. Rev.*, *XXX*, pp. 255–60.
Factor Analysis by Submatrices. *Journ. Psychol.*, *VI*, pp. 339–75.
The Changing Functions of the Teacher. *Jubilee Book of London Head
Teachers' Association*. University of London Press, pp. 96–110.
The Terman-Merrill Revision of the Binet Scale. *Mind*, *XLVII*, pp.
101–3.

Recent Developments of Statistical Method in Psychology. *Occup. Psychol., XII*, pp. 169–77.

Recent Developments in Statistical Method. *Proc. Roy. Soc., B, CXXV*, pp. 419–20.

The Unit Hierarchy and its Properties. *Psychometrika, III*, pp. 151–68.

1939

William McDougall: An Appreciation. *Brit. J. Educ. Psychol., IX*, pp. 1–7.

The Relations of Educational Abilities. *Brit. J. Educ. Psychol., IX*, pp. 45–71.

The Factorial Analysis of Ability. *Brit. J. Psychol.* (Gen. Sec.), *XXX*, pp. 84–93.

The Factorial Analysis of Emotional Traits. *Char. and Pers., VII*, pp. 238–54, 285–99.

A Judgment Test for Measuring Intelligence. *Mental Welfare, XX*, pp. 45–8.

Alternative Views on Correlations between Persons. (With Wm. Stephenson) *Psychometrika, IV*, pp. 269–81.

Formal Training. *School Science Review, LXXXI*, pp. 653–66.

1940

The Factors of the Mind. London: University of London Press.

The Incidence of Neurotic Symptoms among Evacuated Children. *Brit. J. Educ. Psychol., X*, pp. 9–15.

An Analysis of Performance Test Scores of a Representative Group of Scottish Children. (Critical notice) *Brit. J. Educ. Psychol., X*, pp. 238–44.

1941

The Billeting of Evacuated Children. *Brit. J. Educ. Psychol., XI*, pp. 85–98.

Is the Doctrine of Instincts Dead? A Symposium. I. The Case for Human Instincts. *Brit. J. Educ. Psychol., XI*, pp. 155–72.

Juvenile Delinquency: A Comparative Study of the Position in Liverpool and England and Wales. (Critical notice) *Brit. J. Educ. Psychol., XI*, pp. 138–42.

The Psychology of the Interview: A Critical Review. *Occup. Psychol., XV*, pp. 153–9.

1942

The Evacuation of Children under Five. In *Under-Fives in Total War.* London: British Psychological Society.

A Factorial Analysis of the Terman-Binet Tests. (With Enid John) *Brit. J. Educ. Psychol., XII*, pp. 117–21, 156–61.

Backwardness in the Basic Subjects. (Critical notice) *Brit. J. Educ. Psychol., XII*, pp. 172–5.

Psychology of Early Childhood. (Review) *Brit. J. Educ. Psychol., XII*, pp. 176–81.

The Psychology of the Interview. (Review) *Occup. Psychol.*, *XVI*, pp. 38–41.

The Value of Statistics in Vocational Psychology. *Occup. Psychol.*, *XVI*.

Psychology in War: The Military Work of American and German Psychologists. (Presidential Address, British Psychological Society) *Occup. Psychol.*, *XVI*, pp. 95–111.

Juvenile Crime. (Review) *Nature*, *CLI*, pp. 291–2.

1943

Ability and Income. *Brit. J. Educ. Psychol.*, *XIII*, pp. 83–98.

The Education of the Young Adolescent: The Psychological Implications of the Norwood Report. *Brit. J. Educ. Psychol.*, *XIII*, pp. 126–40.

Validating Tests for Personnel Selection. *Brit. J. Psychol.* (Gen. Sec.), *XXXIV*, pp. 1–19.

Delinquency in Peace and War. *Health Educ. Journ.*, *I*, pp. 165–72.

Young Offenders. *Nature*, *CLI*, pp. 291–2.

A Factorial Analysis of Physical Growth. *Nature*, *CLII*, p. 75.

Selection for Secondary Education. *Occup. Psychol.*, *XVII*, pp. 42–5.

An Inquiry into Public Opinion on Educational Reforms I. *Occup. Psychol.*, *XVII*, pp. 157–67.

The Revision of the Stanford-Binet Scale. *Occup. Psychol.*, *XVII*, pp. 204–6.

1944

An Inquiry into Public Opinion on Educational Reforms II. *Occup. Psychol.*, *XVIII*, pp. 13–23.

Mental Abilities and Mental Factors. *Brit. J. Educ. Psychol.*, *XIV*, pp. 85–94.

The Factorial Study of Physical Types. *Man*, *XLIV*, pp. 82–6.

Race and Crime. (Review) *Nature*, *CLIII*, p. 48.

Statistical Problems in the Evaluation of Army Tests. *Psychometrika*, *IX*, pp. 219–35.

Psycho-analysis and Crime. Preface, pp. 2–11, *English Studies in Criminal Science: Pamphlet Series.* Toronto: Canadian Bar Association.

1945

The Education of Illiterate Adults. *Brit. J. Educ. Psychol.*, *XV*, pp. 20–7.

The Reliability of Teachers' Assessments. *Brit. J. Educ. Psychol.*, *XV*, pp. 80–92.

The Assessment of Personality. (Part I of 'Personality—A Symposium.') *Brit. J. Educ. Psychol.*, *XV*, pp. 107–21.

British Psychology in Wartime. *Educ. Forum*, *IX*, pp. 139–48.

The Psychology of Laughter. *Health Educ. Journ.*, *III*, pp. 101–5.

Defective Colour Vision in Relation to Pigmentation of Eyes and Hair. *Man*, *XLV*, pp. 103–6.

The Use of Stereographic Projection for Statistical Problems. *Nature*, *CLVI*, pp. 338–9.

1946

Intelligence and Fertility. (Eugenics Society— Occasional Papers No. 2.)
London: Hamish Hamilton; 2nd edn 1952, Cassell.

Teaching Backward Readers. (With R. B. Lewis) *Brit. J. Educ. Psychol.,*
XVI, pp. 116–32. Appendix on 'The Application of Analysis of
Variance to Educational Problems'.

The Assessment of Personality. *Egypt. J. Psychol., II*, pp. 65–85.

The Relation between Eye-Colour and Defective Colour Vision. *Eugen.*
Rev., XXXVII, pp. 149–56.

Studying the Minds of Others. *The Listener*, 31 October; Studying
One's Own Mind, *ibid.*, 14 November.

The Work of Charles Edward Spearman. (With C. S. Myers) *Psychol.*
Rev., LIII, pp. 67–71.

L'étude factorielle des types physiques. *Biotypologie, VIII*, pp. 42–5.

1947

A Factor Analysis of Body Measurements for Adult British Males.
(With C. Banks) *Ann. Eugen., XIII*, pp. 238–56.

L'analyse factorielle dans la psychologie anglaise. *Biotypologie, IX*, pp. 7–
44.

Reply to Criticisms, and Conclusions (Part V of 'Personality— A
Symposium'). *Brit. J. Educ. Psychol., XVII*, pp. 6–19.

Recent Work in Factor Analysis. *Brit. J. Educ. Psychol., XVII*, pp. 40–8.

Symposium on the Selection of Pupils for Different Types of Secondary
Schools. I. A. General Survey. *Brit. J. Educ. Psychol., XVII*, pp. 57–
71.

Multiple Factor Analysis. (Critical notice) *Brit. J. Educ. Psychol., XVII*,
pp. 163–9.

A Comparison of Factor Analysis and Analysis of Variance. *Brit. J.*
Psychol. (Stat. Sec.), *I*, pp. 3–26.

Intelligence and the Birthrate: A Reply to Dr Woolf's Criticism. *Brit.*
Med. Bull., 1947–8, *V*, pp. 228–30.

Factor Analysis in Psychological Medicine. *Brit. Med. Bull., V*, pp. 375–
6.

The Subnormal Child. *Journ. Educ., LXXIX*, pp. 597–8.

Statistical Methods in the Selection of Army Personnel (Discussion).
J. Roy. Stat. Soc., VIII, pp. 148–9.

Multivariate Analysis (Discussion). *J. Roy. Stat. Soc., VIII*, pp. 321–3.

Is the Level of National Intelligence Declining? *The Listener*, 8 May.

The Happy Life. *The Listener*, 17 July.

Factor Analysis: Its Aims and Results. *Miscellanea Psychologica, Albert*
Michotte, pp. 49–75. Louvain: Institut Supérieur de Philosophie.

Charles Samuel Myers. (Obituary notice) *Occup. Psychol., XXI*, pp. 1–
5.

Psychology in the Forces. *Occup. Psychol., XXI*, pp. 141–6.

Family Size, Intelligence and Social Class. *Population Studies, I*, pp. 177–
86.

Morphological Level of Personality. *Proc. Roy. Soc. Med., XL*, pp. 307–8.

Factor Analysis and Physical Types. *Psychometrika, XII*, pp. 171–88.

The Transfer of Training. *Universities Quarterly, I*, pp. 281–90.

1948

Factor Analysis and Canonical Correlations. *Brit. J. Psychol.* (Stat. Sect.), *I*, pp. 95–106.

The Description and Measurement of Personality. *Brit. J. Psychol.*, (Stat. Sect.), *I*, pp. 134–6.

The Factorial Study of Temperamental Traits. *Brit. J. Psychol.* (Stat. Sect.), *I*, pp. 179–203.

Factor Analysis in Psychological Medicine. *Brit. Med. Bull., V*, pp. 375–6.

1949

Psychology. *Britannica Book of the Year*, pp. 541–2.

The Structure of the Mind: A Review of the Results of Factor Analysis. *Brit. J. Educ. Psychol., XIX*, pp. 100–11, 176–99.

Recent Discussions on Juvenile Delinquency. *Brit. J. Educ. Psychol., XIX*, pp. 32–43.

Subdivided Factors. *Brit. J. Psychol.*, (Stat. Sect.), *II*, pp. 41–63.

Pearson's Method Modified to Allow for Specific Factors. *Brit. J. Psychol.* (Stat. Sect.), pp. 65–6.

Alternative Methods of Factor Analysis and their relation to Pearson's Method of 'Principal Axes'. *Brit. J. Psychol.* (Stat. Sect.), *II*, pp. 98–121.

The Two Factor Theory. *Brit. J. Psychol.* (Stat. Sect.), *II*, pp. 151–79.

Educational Psychology: Its Implications for Mental Health. *Brit. Med. Bull., VI*, pp. 11–15.

Eugenics, Intelligence and Genius. *Brit. Med. Bull., VI*, pp. 78–9.

An Autobiographical Sketch. *Occup. Psychol., XXIII*, pp. 9–20.

1950

Psychology. *Britannica Book of the Year*, pp. 531–2.

Symposium on the Selection of Pupils for Different Types of Secondary Schools: IX—Conclusion. *Brit. J. Educ. Psychol., XX*, pp. 1–10.

The Trend of Scottish Intelligence. (Critical notice) *Brit. J. Educ. Psychol., XX*, pp. 55–61.

Human Ability. (Critical notice) *Brit. J. Educ. Psychol., XX*, pp. 192–9.

Group Factor Analysis. *Brit. J. Psychol.* (Stat. Sect.), *III*, pp. 40–75.

The Influence of Differential Weighting. *Brit. J. Psychol.* (Stat. Sect.), *III*, pp. 105–25.

A Reply to Sir Godfrey Thomson's Note. *Brit. J. Psychol.* (Stat. Sect.), *III*, pp. 126–8.

Maximum Likelihood Loadings Obtained from Single Factor Correlations. *Brit. J. Psychol.* (Stat. Sect.), *III*, pp. 161–5.

The Factorial Analysis of Qualitative Data. *Brit. J. Psychol.* (Stat. Sect.), *III*, pp. 165–84.

Experimental Design in Psychological Research. *Brit. J. Psychol.* (Stat. Sect.), *III*, pp. 193–4.

The Trend of National Intelligence. (Review Article). *Brit. J. of Sociology*, *I*, pp. 154–68.

The Study of the Mind. *The Listener*: (1) 'What is Psychology?' 2 November; (2) 'Observation of Self and Others' 9 November; (3) 'Testing Intelligence' 16 November; (4) 'Temperament and Character' 23 November; (5) 'The Psychology of Crime' 30 November; (6) 'Can our Memory be Improved?' 7 December; (7) 'Which is Real, Body or Mind?' 14 December; (8) 'Psychology and the Future' 21 December.

Factorial Study of the Emotions. In Reymert, M. L. (ed.) *Feelings and Emotions*, pp. 531–51. New York: McGraw-Hill Book Co.

1951

Autobiography. *History of Psychology in Autobiography*, *IV*, pp. 53–73, ed. Boring, E. G. and Langfeld, H. S., Worcester, Mass.: Clark University Press.

The Factorial Study of the Mind. *Essays in Honour of David Katz*, pp. 18–47. Uppsala: Almquist & Wiksells.

General Psychology. *A Century of Science* (ed. H. Dingle), pp. 272–86. London: Hutchinson.

Psychology. *Scientific Thought in the Twentieth Cetuty* (ed. A. E. Heath), pp. 299–327. London: Watts & Co.

The Aims and Methods of Factorial Analysis. *L'Année Psychologique*, *LI*, pp. 39–59.

The Structure of Human Abilities. (Critical notice) *Brit. J. Educ. Psychol.*, *XXI*, pp. 63–8.

Psychology of Intelligence. (Critical notice) *Brit. J. Educ. Psychol.*, *XXI*, pp. 230–4.

The Numerical Solution of Linear Equations. *Brit. J. Psychol.* (Stat. Sect.), *IV*, pp. 31–55.

Test-Construction and the Scaling of Items. *Brit. J. Psychol.* (Stat. Sect.), pp. 95–129.

Factor Analysis of Assessments for a Single Person (With H. Watson) *Brit. J. Psychol.* (Stat. Sect.), pp. 179–91.

1952

The Nature and Causes of Maladjustment among Children of School Age (With Margaret Howard) *Brit. J. Psychol.* (Stat. Sect.), *V*, pp. 39–58.

Tests of Significance in Factor Analysis. *Brit. J. Psychol.* (Stat. Sect.), *V*, pp. 109–33.

The Explanation of Human Behaviour. (Critical notice) *Brit. J. Educ. Psychol.*, *XXII*, pp. 212–21.

The Causes and Treatment of Backwardness. (The Convocation Lecture of the National Children's Home.) London: National Children's Home and University of London Press, 4th edn 1957.

Une Étude Expérimentale des Méthodes Factorielles. *Biotypologie, XIII*, pp. 6–19.

Dr William Brown. (Obituary notice.) *Brit. J. Psychol.* (Stat. Sect.), *V*, pp. 137–8.

Bipolar Factors as a Cause of Cyclic Overlap. *Brit. J. Psychol.* (Stat. Sect.), *V*, pp. 198–202.

1953

Scale Analysis and Factor Analysis. *Brit. J. Statist. Psychol., VI*, pp. 5–24.

The Relative Merits of Ranks and Paired Comparisons. *Brit. J. Statist. Psychol., VI*, pp. 112–19.

Symposium on Psychologists and Psychiatrists in the Child Guidance Service: Conclusion. *Brit. J. Educ. Psychol., XXIII*, pp. 8–28.

Personality Tests and Assessments. (Critical notice) *Brit. J. Educ. Psychol., XXIII*, pp. 200–2.

Contributions of Psychology to Social Problems (Hobhouse Lecture). London: Oxford University Press.

Statistical Analysis in Educational Psychology. (With C. Banks) *Current Trends in British Psychology*, pp. 152–71. London: Methuen.

1954

The Sign Pattern of Factor-Matrices. *Brit. J. Statist. Psychol., VII*, pp. 15–29.

The Identification of Factors from Different Experiments. (With J. A. Barlow) *Brit. J. Statist. Psychol., VII*, pp. 52–6.

A Reliability Coefficient based on Analysis of Variance. *Brit. J. Statist. Psychol., VII*, p. 61.

The Reduced Correlation Matrix. (With C. Banks) *Brit. J. Statist. Psychol., VII*, pp. 107–17.

Early Researches on General and Special Abilities. (With P. Durant) *Brit. J. Statist. Psychol., VII*, pp. 119–24.

The Deprived and the Privileged. (Critical notice) *Brit. J. Educ. Psychol., XXIV*, pp. 46–8.

The Differentiation of Intellectual Ability. *Brit. J. Educ. Psychol., XXIV*, pp. 76–90.

Age, Ability and Aptitude. *Studies in Education*, pp. 1–31. London: Evans Bros.

The Effects of Coaching on Tests of Intelligence. *Educational Review, VI*, pp. 126–32.

The Assessment of Personality (26th Maudsley Lecture). *J. Mental Science, C*, pp. 1–28.

Les Tendances Actuelles de la Psycho-Pédagogie en Grande-Bretagne. *La Revue Internationale de Psycho-Pédagogie, II*, pp. 77–84.

1955

The Historical Development of the Guidance Movement in Education. *Year Book of Education*, pp. 80–99.

Sir Godfrey Thomson. (Obituary notice) *Brit. J. Statist. Psychol., VIII*, pp. 1–2.

A Psychological Study of Typography. (With W. F. Cooper and J. L. Martin) *Brit. J. Statist. Psychol., VIII*, pp. 29–57.

Test Reliability Estimated by Analysis of Variance. *Brit. J. Statist. Psychol., VIII*, pp. 103–18.

The Permanent Contribution of McDougall to Psychology. *Brit. J. Educ. Psychol., XXV*, pp. 10–22.

The Evidence of the Concept of Intelligence. *Brit. J. Educ. Psychol., XXV*, pp. 158–77.

The Meaning and Assessment of Intelligence (Galton Lecture). *Eugen. Review, XLVII*, pp. 81–91.

Psychology: Review of Recent Publications. *Britannica Book of the Year*.

L'Analyse Factorielle: Méthodes et Résultats. Collôques Internationaux du Centre National de la Recherche Scientific. Paris, pp. 79–92.

Digital Computing Machines. (Review) *Brit. J. Statist. Psychol., VIII*, pp. 59–64.

1956

L. L. Thurstone. (Obituary notice) *Brit. J. Statist. Psychol., IX*, pp. 1–4.

The Statistical Analysis of the Learning Process. (With E. Foley) *Brit. J. Statist. Psychol., IX*, pp. 49–62.

Weighted Summation applied to Paired Comparisons. *Brit. J. Statist. Psychol., IX*, pp. 63–5.

The Multifactorial Theory of Inheritance and its Application to Intelligence. (With Margaret Howard) *Brit. J. Statist. Psychol., IX*, pp. 95–131.

The Contributions of C. W. Valentine to Psychology. *Brit. J. Educ. Psychol., XXVI*, pp. 8–14.

The Psychological Basis of Education. (Critical notice) *Brit. J. Educ. Psychol., XXVI*, pp. 218–22.

Les Contributions de Alfred Binet. *L'Année Psychologique, LVI*, pp. 363–75.

The Scientific Study of the Backward Child. *Forward Trends, I*, pp. 4–9.

British Psychology during the Past Fifty Years. *Rivista di Psicologia, L*, Fascicolo Giubilare, pp. 59–71.

1957

Heredity and Intelligence: A Reply to Criticisms. (With Margaret Howard) *Brit. J. Statist. Psychol., X*, pp. 33–63.

The Relative Influence of Heredity and Environment on Assessments of Intelligence. (With Margaret Howard) *Brit. J. Statist. Psychol., X*, pp. 99–104.

The Distribution of Intelligence. *Brit. J. Psychol., XLVIII*, pp. 161–75.

The Inheritance of Mental Ability. *Eugen. Review, XLIX*, pp. 137–41.

The Application of Mathematics to Psychology. (Godfrey Thomson Lecture.)

Instinct in Man. *Medical World, LXXXVII*, pp. 305–9.

L'hérédité de l'intelligence. *Biotypologie, XVIII*, pp. 55–71.

Apports de Binet aux Tests d'Intelligence et Développement Ultérieur de cette Technique. *Revue de Psychologie Appliquée, VII*, pp. 231–48.

The Impact of Psychology upon Education. *Year Book of Education*, pp. 163–80.

1958

Definition and Scientific Method in Psychology. *Brit. J. Statist. Psychol.*, XI, pp. 31–69.

Quantum Theory and the Principle of Indeterminacy. *Brit. J. Statist. Psychol.*, XI, pp. 77–93.

Scientific Method in Psychology: II. (With W. L. Gregory) *Brit. J. Statist. Psychol.*, XI, pp. 105–28.

A Note on the Theory of Intelligence. *Brit. J. Educ. Psychol.*, XXVIII, pp. 281–8.

The Psychology of Learning. *Educational Review*, X, pp. 117–39.

The Inheritance of Mental Ability. Bingham Lecture, 1957. *American Psychologist*, XIII, pp. 1–15.

1959

Class Differences in Intelligence: III. *Brit. J. Statist. Psychol.*, XII, pp. 15–33.

Experiments on Telepathy in Children. *Brit. J. Statist. Psychol.*, XII, pp. 55–99.

Field Theories and Statistical Psychology. *Brit. J. Statist. Psychol.*, XII, pp. 153–64.

The Accomplishment Quotient: A Reply. *Brit. J. Educ. Psychol.*, XXIX, pp. 259–60.

The Examination at Eleven Plus. *Brit. J. Educ., Studies*, VII, pp. 99–117.

General Ability and Special Aptitudes. *Educ. Research, I*, pp. 3–16.

Mental Deficiency. *Medical World*, XC, pp. 263–9.

A Psychological Study of Typography. Cambridge University Press.

The Meaning and Assessment of Intelligence. Ap. *Readings in General Psychology*, ed. Halmos, P. and Iliffe, A., pp. 65–84. London: Routledge & Kegan Paul.

Television and the Child. (Critical notice) *Brit. J. Educ. Psychol.*, XXIX, pp. 173–5.

1960

Gustav Theodor Fechner: Elemente der Psychophysik, 1860. *Brit. J. Statist. Psychol.*, XIII, pp. 1–10.

Logical Positivism and the Concept of Consciousness. (Critical notice) *Brit. J. Statist. Psychol.*, XIII, pp. 55–77.

Factor Analysis of the Wechsler Scale. *Brit. J. Statist. Psychol.*, XIII, pp. 82–7.

The General Aesthetic Factor (Reply). *Brit. J. Statist. Psychol.*, XIII, pp. 90–2.

Statistical Psychology and Physical Laws (Reply). *Brit. J. Statist. Psychol.*, XIII, pp. 95–103.

Experiments on Telepathy in Children: Reply to Mr. Hansel. *Brit. J. Statist. Psychol.*, XIII, pp. 179–88.

Hebrew Psychology and Current Psychological Concepts. *Brit. J. Statist. Psychol.*, *XIII*, pp. 193–203.

The Crowther and Albemarle Reports. (Critical notice) *Brit. J. Educ. Psychol.*, *XXX*, pp. 277–82.

The Transfer of Training. *Educ. Review, XII*, pp. 77–93.

The Typography of Children's Books. *Year Book of Education*, pp. 242–56.

The Concept of Mind. *Indian J. Psychol. Researches, II*, pp. 1–11.

The Readability of Type. *The New Scientist, VII*, pp. 277–9.

Individual Differences and their Bearing on Education. Paris: Unesco.

Discrepancies in the Variances of Test Results. (With Margaret Howard) *Brit. J. Statist. Psychol.*, *XIII*, pp. 173–4.

1961

Galton's Contribution to Psychology. *Bull. Brit. Psychol. Soc., XLV*, pp. 10–21.

Intelligence and Social Mobility. *Brit. J. Statist. Psychol.*, *XIV*, pp. 3–24.

Factor Analysis and it Neurological Basis. *Brit. J. Statist. Psychol.*, *XIV*, pp. 53–71.

The General Aesthetic Factor. (Reply with E. D. Williams) *Brit. J. Statist. Psychol.*, *XIV*, pp. 75–7.

The Gifted Child. *Brit. J. Statist. Psychol.*, *XIV*, pp. 123–39.

The Structure of the Mind: A Reply. *Brit. J. Statist. Psychol.*, *XIV*, pp. 145–70.

The Psychology of Perception. (Critical notice) *Brit. J. Statist. Psychol.*, *XIV*, pp. 173–80.

The Evidence for Paranormal Phenomena. *Internat. J. Parapsychol., III*, pp. 77–87.

Physicality and Psi: A Symposium and Forum Discussion. *J. Parapsychol., XXV*, pp. 27–31.

Theories of Mind. *J. Soc. Psychic. Res., XLI*, pp. 55–60.

Mathematical Studies in the Psychology of War. *Nature*, p. 427.

Gifted Children. *Eugen. Review, LIII*, pp. 17–20.

Psychological Research on Mental Deficiency. *Nursing Times*, pp. 893–5.

1962

Francis Galton and his Contribution to Psychology. *Brit. J. Statist. Psychol.*, *XV*, pp. 1–49.

Frequency Curves and the Ability of Nations. II. *Brit. J. Statist. Psychol.*, *XV*, pp. 80–92.

The Three Dimensions of Factor Analysis. (A reply with E. D. Williams) *Brit. J. Statist. Psychol.*, *XV*, pp. 93–4.

Truman Lee Kelly. (Obituary notice) *Brit. J. Statist. Psychol.*, *XV*, pp. 95–6.

The Influence of Motivation on the Results of Intelligence Tests. (With E. L. Williams) *Brit. J. Statist. Psychol.*, *XV*, pp. 129–36.

The Sense Datum Theory: A Reply. *Brit. J. Statist. Psychol.*, *XV*, pp. 170–97.

Sir Ronald Fisher. (Obituary notice) *Brit. J. Statist. Psychol.*, *XV*, pp. 197–8.

Working Models of the Brain. (Critical notice) *Brit. J. Statist. Psychol.*, *XV*, pp. 199–215.

The Psychology of Creative Ability. (Critical notice) *Brit. J. Educ. Psychol.*, *XXXII*, pp. 292–8.

Mind and Consciousness. *The Scientist Speculates*, ed. by I. J. Good, pp. 78–89. London: William Heinemann.

The Gifted Child. *Year Book of Education*, pp. 1–58.

The Concept of Consciousness. *Brit. J. Psychol.*, *LIII*, pp. 229–42.

Psychological Research on Mental Deficiency. *Proceedings of the London Conference on the Scientific Study of Mental Deficiency*, *II*, pp. 604–16. Dagenham: May & Baker Ltd.

Encyclopaedia Britannica, XVIth edn. Articles on Consciousness, History of Psychology, Psychological Tests and Measurements, Binet, Brentano, Havelock Ellis, Hartley, Janet, McDougall, Rank, Ribot, Rivers, Spearman, Stout.

1963

The Psychology of Value: A Reply. *Brit. J. Statist. Psychol.*, *XVI*, pp. 59–104.

Ability and Attainment: II. *Brit. J. Statist. Psychol.*, *XVI*, pp. 106–12.

The Use of Electronic Computers in Psychological Research. (Critical notice) *Brit. J. Statist. Psychol.*, *XVI*, pp. 118–25.

Is Intelligence Distributed Normally? *Brit. J. Statist. Psychol.*, *XVI*, pp. 175–90.

The Cause and Treatment of Backwardness. *Australian J. Educ. of Back. Child.*, *IX*, pp. 145–50.

Jung's Account of his Paranormal Experiences. *J. Soc. Psychic. Res.*, *XLII*, pp. 163–80.

Psychology and the Science of Education: Selected Writings of Edward L. Thorndike. (Critical notice) *Hist. Educ. Quarterly*, *III*, pp. 169–71.

1964

Consciousness and Space Perception. *Brit. J. Statist. Psychol.*, *XVII*, pp. 77–85.

The Stability of Factors. *Brit. J. Statist. Psychol.*, *LXVII*, pp. 177–80.

Consciousness and Behaviourism. (A reply) *Brit. J. Psychol.*, *LV*, pp. 93–6.

Obituary: Charles Wilfred Valentine. *Brit. J. Psychol.*, *LV*, pp. 385–90.

Baudouin on Jung. *Brit. J. Psychol.*, *LV*, pp. 477–84.

Obituary: Charles Wilfred Valentine. *Brit. J. Educ. Psychol.*, *XXXIV*, pp. 219–22.

Personality Assessment. (Critical notice) *J. Child Psychol. Psychiat.*, *V*, pp. 151–5.

Message from Sir Cyril Burt. *Newsletter, Assoc. Educ. Psychol.*, *I*, 1, p. 1.

Educational Psychology at the Crossroads. *Newsletter, Assoc. Educ. Psychol.*, *I*, 2, pp. 3–5.

1965

Education and Environment. (Critical notice) *Brit. J. Educ. Psychol.*, *XXXV*, pp. 98–9.

The Home and the School: A Study of Ability and Attainment in the Primary Schools. (Critical notice) *Brit. J. Educ. Psychol.*, *XXXV*, pp. 200–6.

Factorial Studies of Personality and their Bearing on the Work of the Teacher. *Brit. J. Educ. Psychol.*, *XXXV*, pp. 368–78.

Child Prodigies. *New Scientist*, *XXVII*, 14 October, pp. 122–4.

1966

The Early History of Multivariate Techniques in Psychological Research. *Multivariate Behav. Res.*, *I*, pp. 24–42.

The Appropriate Use of Factor Analysis and Analysis of Variance. In Cattell, R. B. (ed.) *Handbook of Multivariate Experimental Psychology.* Chicago: Rand McNally & Co.

The Genetic Determination of Differences in Intelligence: A Study of Monozygotic Twins Reared Together and Apart. *Brit. J. Psychol.*, *LVII*, pp. 137–53.

The Human Perspective. In *Perspectives in Biology and Medicine*, *IX*, pp. 317–32. University of Chicago Press.

Parapsychology and Its Implications. *Int. J. Neuropsychiat.*, *II*, pp. 363–77.

Evolution and Parapsychology. *J. Soc. Psychical Res.*, *XLIII*, pp. 391–422.

The Soul in 1966. Oxford: *Common Factor Monographs*, *IV*, pp. 14–23.

Information Theory and Aesthetic Education. *J. Aesthet. Educ.*, *I*, pp. 55–69.

Counterblast to Dyslexia. *Newsletter, Assoc. Educ. Psychol.*, *I*, 5, pp. 2–5.

Psychologists and Moral Judgements. *Newsletter, Assoc. Educ. Psychol.*, *I*, 6, pp. 5–12; 7, pp. 3–6.

1967

The Genetic Determination of Intelligence: A Reply. *Brit. J. Psychol.*, *LVIII*, pp. 153–62.

The Education of the Gifted. (Critical notice) *Brit. J. Educ. Psychol.*, *XXXVII*, pp. 143–9.

Psychology and Parapsychology. In Smythies, J. R. (ed.) *Science and E.S.P.*, pp. 61–141. London: Routledge & Kegan Paul; New York: Humanities Press.

The Implications of Parapsychology for General Psychology. *J. Parapsychol.*, *XXXI*, pp. 1–18.

The Divine Flame. (Review) *J. Soc. Psychical Res.*, *XLIV*, pp. 189–93.

Evaluation. *Initial Teaching Alphabet Symposium.* London: National Foundation for Educational Research.

The Psychological Aspects of Aesthetic Education. *Art Education*, *XX*, 3, pp. 26–8.

There were giants in those days. *Newsletter, Assoc. Educ. Psychol.*, *I*, 8, pp. 2–6.

The Initial Teaching Alphabet. *Newsletter, Assoc. Educ. Psychol.*, *I*, 9, pp. 2–5.

1968

Brain and Consciousness. *Brit. J. Psychol.*, *LIX*, pp. 55–69.
The Analysis of Cognitive Abilities. (Review) *Contemp. Psychol.*, *XIII*, pp. 545–7.
Statistical Methods in Psychiatric Research. *Int. J. Psychiat.*, *VI*, pp. 118–26.
Psychology and Psychical Research. XVIIth F. W. H. Myers Memorial Lecture. London: Society for Psychical Research.
Education by Discovery. (Essay review) *J. Aesthet. Educ.*, *II*, pp. 117–26.
Mensa's President discusses some pertinent Topics. *Intelligence: The Mensa Journal*, *CVII*, January 1968, pp. 1 and 8.
Mental Capacity and its Critics. *Bull. Brit. Psychol. Soc.*, *XXI*, pp. 11–18.
Transfer of Training. *J. & Newsletter, Assoc. Educ. Psychol.*, *II*, 1, pp. 1–7.
Creativity in the Classroom. *J. & Newsletter, Assoc. Educ. Psychol.*, *II*, 2, pp. 3–8.

1969

Intelligence and Heredity: Some Common Misconceptions. *Irish J. Educ.*, *III*, pp. 75–94.
Recent Studies of Abilities and Attainments. *J. & Newsletter, Assoc. Educ. Psychol.*, *II*, 4.
Personal Knowledge, Art and the Humanities. *J. Aesthet. Educ.*, *III*, pp. 29–46.
The Genetics of Intelligence. In Toronto Symposium *On Intelligence*, ed. W. B. Dockrell, pp. 15–28. Toronto: Ontario Institute for Studies in Education; London: Methuen, 1970.
What is Intelligence? (Critical notice) *Brit. J. Educ. Psychol.*, *XXXIX*, pp. 198–201.
Psychologists in the Education Service. *Bull. Brit. Psychol. Soc.*, *XXII*, pp. 1–11.
Brain and Consciousness: A Reply. *Bull. Brit. Psychol. Soc.*, *XXII*, pp. 29–36.
The Field Concept in Psychology. *Bull. Brit. Psychol. Soc.*, *XXII*, pp. 267–71.
The Mental Differences between Children. In Cox, C. B. and Dyson, A. E. (eds) *Black Paper II*, pp. 16–25. London: The Critical Quarterly Society.
Intelligence and Heredity. *New Scientist*, *XLII*, 1 May, pp. 226–8.
The Psychology of the Public School Boy. *J. & Newsletter, Assoc. Educ. Psychol.*, *II*, 3. pp. 2–7.
Recent Studies of Abilities and Attainment. *J. & Newsletter, Assoc. Educ. Psychol.*, *II*, 4, pp. 4–9.

1970

History of the Concept of Intelligence. *J. & Newsletter, Assoc. Educ. Psychol.*, *II*, 5, pp. 16–38.

The Organization of Schools. In Cox, C. W. and Dyson, A. E. (eds)
  Black Paper III, pp. 14–25. London: The Critical Quarterly Society.
Urgent Issues in Educational Psychology. *Symposium on The State of
  Health of the Education Service*. Brit. Psychol. Soc. Annual General
  Conference, 1970.
Forward Trends in Educational Psychology. *Forward Trends, XIV*, 1, pp.
  3–6.
Maladjustment and Misconduct. *J. & Newsletter, Assoc. Educ. Psychol.*,
  II, 6, pp. 3–8.

1971

Quantitative Genetics in Psychology. *Brit. J. Math. Statist. Psychol.*,
  XXIV, pp. 1–21.
Intelligence and Heredity: Some Common Misconceptions. *Question*,
  London: Pemberton Publishing Co.
Heredity and Environment. *Bull. Brit. Psychol. Soc., XXIV*, pp. 9–15.
Religious Education. *J. & Newsletter, Assoc. Educ. Psychol., II*, 8, pp. 3–
  10.
Religious Education: A Reply. *J. & Newsletter, Assoc. Educ. Psychol., II*,
  9, pp. 4–6.
The Development and Training of Reasoning. *J. & Newsletter, Assoc.
  Educ. Psychol., II*, 10, pp. 4–8.
Forward be Our Watchword. *Forward Trends, XV*, 10.

1972

The Inheritance of Mental Differences. In Szamuely, T. (ed.) *Education,
  Equality and Society*, London: Allen & Unwin.
The Inheritance of General Intelligence. *Amer. Psychol., XXVII*, pp.
  175–90.
Comments on Arthur R. Jensen's 'Do Schools Cheat Minority
  Children?' *Educ. Res., XIV*, pp. 87–92.
The Reciprocity Principle. In Brown, S. R. and Brenner, D. J. (eds)
  Science, Psychology and Communication, pp. 39–56. New York:
  Teachers College Press.
General Ability and Special Aptitudes. In Dreger, R. M. (ed.)
  Multivariate Personality Research . Baton Rouge: Claitor's Publishing
  Division.

1974

The Gifted Child. In Pringle, M. L. K. and Varma, V. P. (eds)
  Advances in Educational Psychology, II, pp. 150–65. London:
  University of London Press.

1975

The Gifted Child, London: Hodder & Stoughton.
  E.S.P. and Psychology, ed. Anita Gregory. London: Weidenfeld and
  Nicolson.

Theses Presented by Burt's Students

List A

List of psychological theses awarded the degrees of M.A. in Education and Ph.D. by students at the London Day Training College (from October 1932 onwards renamed the University of London Institute of Education) between 1924 and 1934. This list has been abstracted from the full list given in *Studies and Impressions, 1902–1952* published by the Institute of Education.

List B

Complete list of theses awarded the degrees of M.A., M.Sc, and Ph.D. in Psychology by students registered at University College, London, during the years 1931–1951, together with theses which Burt was still responsible for supervising between 1951 and 1954. Not all the theses submitted between 1931 and 1951 were supervised personally by Burt. In general, those in experimental psychology (particularly those concerned with work curves and fluctuations of output) were supervised by Dr S. J. F. Philpott, and those in social and abnormal psychology by Professor J. C. Flugel. In the late 1940s some students working at the Maudsley Hospital were officially registered at University College. Older theses are kept by the University of London Library in a store at Woolwich, and several days' notice needs to be given by those wishing to inspect them.

List A

London Day Training College (Institute of Education)

M.A. IN EDUCATION

1925
Bloor, Constance. The psychological doctrine of temperament.

1926

Hume, E. G. A study of backwardness in reading among London elementary school children.

1927

Weeks, E. J. Some tests of disposition.

Wheeler, E. C. An investigation into backwardness in arithmetic among London elementary school children.

1929

Culshaw, J. E. The development of the free place system and its effect on the secondary school system.

1930

Foulger, T. R. The psychological approach to religious education.

Thomas, F. C. On the standardisation of group tests of intelligence and the interpretation of their results.

1931

Jones, E. W. Psychological problems in the teaching of geography.

Simmonds, H. A. T. Vocational guidance in secondary schools.

1932

Cattell, R. B. Perseveration tests of temperament. An assessment of teaching ability.

Staynor, Eryx V. The psychology of reasoning with special reference to educational problems.

1933

Scrivens, A. G. An objective study of the factors underlying ability in verbal expression.

1934

Potts, E. W. M. Prognostic tests of ability in school geometry.

Williams, Emily M. The geometrical concepts of children from 5 to 8 years of age.

Ph.D.

1925

Slocombe, C. S. The construction of mental tests.

Strasheim, J. J. Some aspects of developing intelligence.

1928

Hughes, A. G. An investigation into the comparative intelligence and attainments of Jewish and non-Jewish school children.

1929

Wilson, J. H. A critical evaluation of certain intelligence scales with special reference to the effects of coaching and practice.

1930

Shendarkar, D. D. An experimental investigation in teaching to solve problems in arithmetic and the light it throws on the doctrine of formal training.

1931

Schonell, F. J. An investigation into disability in spelling.

Sleight, G. F. The diagnosis and treatment of the dull and backward child.

1932

Entwistle, W. H. Some aspects of mental work.

1933

Field, H. E. Rebuilding character in delinquent youth: a study of the English Borstal system and the responses of individuals to its method of treatment.

Murdoch, J. H. An analysis of reasoning ability in school children, with a view to determining the nature and extent of any group factor involved.

List B

University College, London

M.A. and M.Sc.

1934

McDonnell, Eileen. An analysis of perseveration tests with special reference to schizophrenic conditions.

1935

Clapham, J. H. The ability to arrange concepts in order, and the relation of this ability to reasoning.

Highfield, H. Some psychological characteristics of retarded children.

Tsao, D. F. A comparative study of drawing ability in English children by the Goodenough scale.

Wallace, R. N. R. Fluctuation of attention and the perception of meaning.

1936

Hines, H. J. Oscillation of attention: an inquiry into the effect on the degree of oscillation of ambiguous figures of different degrees of meaning.

1937

Ahmed, M. K. The moral reasoning of the child and its relation to mental age.

Cohen, I. An analytic and experimental study of relation and correlate finding.

Good, C. W. The influence of the form of a question upon the answers of children.

Harwood, Mary K. B. The curve of output during a combined series of tasks varying in nature.

Hu, P. C. A study of the intelligence of Anglo-Chinese children.

Orde, Faye. The psychological conditions in two representative factories.

Williams, Elizabeth D. A standardised test of literary appreciation.

1938

Dave, K. J. The effect of practice on intelligence tests.

Davis, Margaret M. A study of individual preferences with olfactory stimuli.

Warburton, F. W. The influence of short rest pauses on fluctuations of mental output.

1939

Adinarayaniah, S. P. The psychology of colour prejudice.

Blackwell, Anne M. A comparative investigation into factors in the mathematical ability of boys and girls (aged 13½–15 years).

Cast, Beatrice. An investigation into methods of marking compositions.

Chen, Z. T. Fluctuations of attention at and near the threshold.

Corea, J. C. A. Fluctuations of meaning in binocular rivalry.

Fontaine, B. L. S. Human problems of organization in industry.

Gibbs, J. M. A contribution to the standardisation of the Terman–Merrill intelligence test.

Glüksohn, Naomi. A contribution to the standardisation of the new Stanford-Binet tests (4–6 years).

Peterson, J. L. Adolescence: a study of elementary school leavers and public school boys of the same age.

Spinks, A. G. S. A psychological study of some aspects of the religious consciousness of XVIIth century England considered with particular reference to the psychological factors involved in the development of English 'dissent'.

Stephen, Jane L. Occupational interests in relation to intelligence.

Wagner, Gertrude. Psychological factors in saving and spending.

Ward, D. F. Correlation between increase in amplitude and decrement in work curves.

1940

de Alwis, E. H. The effect of change of meaning in periodicity in the perception of ambiguous figures.

1941

Hammond, W. H. Factorial analysis in the study of types.

John, Enid M. A study of evacuees of pre-school age.

Schonell, Florence. An experimental study of diagnostic tests in English.

1943

Denton, Eva R. Individual differences in fluctuations of attention.

Hindmarsh, Nora. The psychology of advertising in war.

1944

Stevenson, Margaret S. The predictive value of certain vocational tests with special reference to personnel selection in the Army.

1945

Williams, Jessie. An experimental and theoretical study of humour in children.

1948

Cunningham, M. A. A comparison of methods in assessing personality in children.

Reeve, E. G. Some problems in the selection of service personnel.

Trouton, D. S. A critical study of some aspects of psychoanalytic characterology.

1949

Sinha, C. P. Relation between I.Q. and curves of output.

1950

Bradshaw, J. A psychological study of the development of religious beliefs among children and young people.

Chattopadhay, A. K. A study of the methods of work of operatives engaged in certain laundry processes.

Sinha, Una. A study of the reliability and validity of the Progressive Matrices Test.

1951

Manley, D. R. An experiment in the standardisation of a general information test.

Pickard, Phyllis. A study of the more important traits assessed by the Rorschach group test.

Strizower, Schefra. Personality traits and motivational factors in religious behaviour.

1952

Carlile, Jane S. H. A comparison of a thematic apperception test as applied to neurotic and non-neurotic children.

Palmer, F. C. The influence of unconscious factors as revealed in experiments on telepathy and mental testing in the same group of individuals.

Scott, Diana. A study of the relations between children's behaviour and their preference for different types of entertainment.

Sofer, Louise. Psychological abnormality, intelligence and suggestibility— their relation to one another.

1953

Bucher, Sheila. A study of the Thematic Apperception Tests applied to a group of girls aged 11–13.

Walters, Clare A. A study of the Rorschach Test and other projective tests as indicators of anxiety in children.

1954

Thomas, M. H. A study of factors in juvenile delinquency.

Ph.D.

1931

Drake, R. M. Tests of musical talent.

Griffiths, Ruth. A study of imagination in children of five years.

1932

Alton, Ellen. An experimental contribution to the study of imagery.

Purushottam, T. A. A study of individual differences in fluctuation of attention.

1933

Chen, L. Oscillation at the threshold and in mental work.

Grewal, D. K. Fluctuation of attention during short periods of work.

Pachauri, A. R. A study of gestalt problems concerning completed and uncompleted test items.

Rama-Rao, K. O. R. The comparative value of certain verbal and non-verbal (principally perceptual) tests and their relation to tests of mechanical ability.

Wedeck, J. Ability to estimate character.

1934

El Koussi, A. A. H. An investigation into the factors in tests involving the visual perception of space.

Sivaprakasam, K. Oscillation of attention.

1935

Forbes, J. M. A study of emotion by means of free association in conjunction with the PGR.

Lewis, M. M. The development of language in children—a study of infant speech.

Shepherd, Flora. Responses of infants in feeding situations and in periods antecedent to the feeding situation.

1936

Seymour, A. H. The effects of different conditions of temperature and ventilation on the mental output and mental fatigue of school children.

1937

Clarke, Grace. The range and nature of factors in perceptual tests.

Desai, M. M. A study of surprise.

Dewar, Heather. Tests of artistic appreciation.

McElwain, D. W. A psychological study of ownership in children.

Maund, D. H. Tests of aesthetic appreciation.

1938

Bramchari, S. Moral attitudes in relation to upbringing, personal adjustment and social opinion.

Ghosh, R. An experimental study of humour.

Kerr, Madelaine. Emotional fluctuations in women.

Mukhopadhyay, N. Oscillation at threshold in relation to other mental functions.

Pillai, R. B. A study of the threshold in relation to subliminal impressions and allied phenomena.

1939

Anthony, Helen S. The development of the concept of death.

Marshall, A. J. The changes in visual acuity during the course of dark adaptation.

Philips, R. L. Individual differences in dark adaptation.

Unmack, Emily. A comparative study of speech development and motor coordination in children of 24–40 months by means of specially devised tests.

1940

Cohen, I. A statistical study of physical and mental types.

Crocket, Helen E. An investigation of social attitudes in school children.

Eysenck, H. J. An experimental and statistical investigation of some factors influencing aesthetic judgment.

Parry, J. B. The role of attention in aesthetic experience.

1941

Chaterjee, P. H. Studies of labour wastage and sickness absence.

Wing, H. D. Musical ability and appreciation.

1943

Harwood, Mary K. B. An illustrative study of examination marks by the methods of factor analysis and the analysis of variance.

1945

Adler, Manassa. An experimental investigation into cognitive development in infants of 1–2 years.

Banks, Edith K. C. Factor analysis applied to current psychological problems with special reference to data from H.M. Forces.

Warburton, F. W. The influence of rest pauses on fluctuations of mental output.

1948

Ramzy, I. An experiment in assessing personality.

Saleh, A. M. Z. Individual differences in fluctuations in output of mental work.

Wheller, D. K. Factors in mechanical ability among adults.

1949

Akil, F. H. Curves of output produced by one individual.

Anstey, E. The construction and item analysis of aptitude tests.

Ghosh, Suhari. The temporal arrangement of errors or failures in perceptual work.

McKellar, T. P. H. A psychological study of human aggressiveness.

Sanai, M. An investigation of social and political attitudes: an experimental and statistical study.

Sen, Amya. A study of the Rorschach test.

Wilkie, J. S. A biologist's approach to the mind-body problem.

1950

Al-Bassam, A. A. I. A study of character traits in school children.

Barakat, M. K. Factors underlying the mathematical abilities of grammar school pupils at age 14.

Bhandari, L. C. The personality background in pulmonary tuberculosis.

Clarke, A. D. B. The measurement of emotional instability by means of objective tests.

Crane, Sybile. An experimental investigation of the general factor in aesthetic judgment.

Crawford, Agnes. An investigation of colour blindness with special reference to its relation to eye colour.

Gravely, Ann. An investigation of perceptual tests as measures of temperament.

Hamilton, M. The personality of dyspeptics with special reference to gastric and duodenal ulcer. (M.D. Psych. Med.)

Robertson, J. P. S. The group word-association test— an investigation of its diagnostic capacity in abnormal psychology.

Shields, R. W. A psychological study of the effects of contemporary nonconformist revivals.

Wrigley, C. F. A psychological study of methods of predicting success in flying training.

1951

Bennet, Ivy V. P. A comparative study of delinquent and neurotic children.

Ganguly, D. The influence of change of task on the curve of mental work.

Granger, G. W. An experimental study of colour preferences.

Jilani, G. The relation between Philpott's theoretical curve of fluctuations of attention and empirical curves.

Loos, F. M. A study of the interrelations of sense of humour with other personality variables.

Lubin, A. Some contributions to the testing of psychological hypotheses by means of statistical multivariate analysis.

Meadows, A. W. An investigation of the Rorschach and Behn tests.

Small, J. S. A contribution to the study of mental work curves.

1952

Bradley, N. C. A study of the conditioned development of sexual attraction.

Callagan, J. E. The effect of electro-convulsive therapy on the test performance of hospitalised depressed patients.

Cole, Raymonde. The standardisation of group intelligence tests for English children, aged 7–11.

De Monchaux, Cecily. The effect on memory of completed and uncompleted tasks.

Dunsdon, Marjorie. An application of the Myers–Gifford response pattern scoring scheme to the Terman-Merrill records of children.

Freeman, F. E. An experimental study of discrimination among normal, neurotic and psychotic subjects by means of a new projective test.

Howe, E. S. An investigation of conditioned galvanic skin response in normals, anxiety states and functional schizophrenics.

Jones, L. C. T. The effects of frustration on learning in human subjects.

Makdhum, M. A. A comparative study of Freudian and Jungian methods of analysis.

Moursi, E. M. K. M. A factorial investigation of the hierarchical organisation of cognitive levels.

Newbigging, P. L. Individual differences in the effects of subjective and objective organising factors on perception.

1953

Abi-Rafi, A. Y. The effect of psychological abnormality on curves of mental output.

Ainsworth, L. H. A study of rigidity.

Bannatyne, A. D. An experimental study of introversion–extraversion by means of projective techniques.

Brengelmann, J. C. The effect of repeated electrical stimulation on the capacity of depressed patients to learn visual patterns.

Norton, W. A. The construction and standardisation of a group test of general knowledge for junior school children.

Srinivasiah, T. V. The factorial analysis of the psychological and material environments of a group of children referred to a child guidance clinic.

1954

Cankardas, Aydin. A comparative study of tests of aesthetic appreciation.

Petrie, Asenath. A study of experimental methods of assessing personality: group differences in degree of neuroticism and extraversion.

The Burt Archives

Burt's surviving papers and other material relating to Burt have been lodged in the Archives Department of the University of Liverpool, and may be consulted by applying to:

> The Archivist,
> Senate House,
> University of Liverpool,
> P.O. Box 147,
> LIVERPOOL, L69 3BX

quoting reference D.191.

The papers may be broadly classified under five main headings:

1. Biographical Material

Juvenilia
Early letters, drawings, etc.
School reports.
Letters from school.
Notes on books read.

Correspondence
Letters to his family, in particular an extensive correspondence with
  his sister, Dr Marion Burt, 1940–71.
Letters from Oxford, Würzburg and Liverpool.
Correspondence (incomplete), 1925–60.
Correspondence (complete), 1961–71.
Correspondence with Mrs Beatrice Warde, 1954–69.

Diaries
Incomplete diaries for the years 1900, 1902, 1903, 1904, 1905, 1909,
  1910, and 1912.
Diary of Easter holiday, 1936.
Engagement diaries (mostly complete), 1953–71.

Photographs

Reading
Notes on books read, 1960–70.

2. Material Relating to Organisations

Association of Educational Psychologists
Correspondence and journal contributions.

Board of Education
Particularly material relating to the Consultative Committee in the 1920s
and 1930s.

British Broadcasting Corporation
Various talks, 1930–69.

British Psychological Society
Working parties on maladjusted children, mental deficiency, and
secondary school selection.
Publications committee papers.
Statistical journal—correspondence and discussions.

Child Guidance Council
Various papers from 1927 onwards.

Cinema Commission of Enquiry
Psychological research sub-committee, papers, 1920–22.

Civil Service Commission
Research Unit, progress report, 1947.

London County Council
Letters and reports, 1912–15.

Mensa
Correspondence, etc.

Publishers
Reports on manuscripts for Allen & Unwin, University of London Press
and Penguin Books.

T.V. Research Unit (Leeds)
Correspondence.

University College, London
Appointment of Burt's successor in the Chair of Psychology, 1949–50.

War Research Committee (British Association for the Advancement of
Science, 1916)
Report of first meeting.
Minutes and questionnaire.

3. Material on Various Topics

Cutaneous Sensations
46-page manuscript.

Factor Analysis
Spearman–Burt correspondence, 1909–39.
Correspondence relating to the Paris Colloquium, 1955.
Revisions for the second edition of *Factors of the Mind*.

Initial Teaching Alphabet
Correspondence, reports, and other material.

Intelligence
Influence of home conditions on intelligence, 1921.
Various reports and correspondence relating to intelligence and the
  birthrate, and decline of national intelligence, 1947.

Parapsychology
Correspondence with The Society for Psychical Research.
Myers Memorial Lecture, 1968.
Correspondence with Psychophysical Research Unit (Oxford).

Physiognomy
Large collection of material, apparently for a projected book.

Reports (various)
Difference in arithmetic of boys and girls, 1915.
Transition from school to industry (Royal Commission on Population).
Recent developments in statistical method (Royal Society).
Some problems of education in London (no date).
Daydreams.
Sample case reports.

Test material and problems

Typography
Papers and reviews.

4. Offprints and Notes

Offprints of published articles (incomplete), 1909–72.

Lecture Notes (unpublished)
Notes on Factor Analysis and Scientific Method, 1945–46.
Note on Factor Analysis (revised), 1948.
Lectures on Elementary General Psychology.

First Year Practical Course.

Extension Lecture Outlines
The Mind and its Workings.
The Human Mind.
Psychology and its Application to Social Problems.
The Psychology of Everyday Life.

5. Hearnshaw Papers

Material collected in the course of preparation of the present biography. Correspondence with Dr Marion Burt, Miss Archer, and others.

Other Archive Material

There are three other principal sources of Archive material relating to Burt:

1. *The Greater London Record Office*
   County Hall, London, S.E. 1.

Reports to Teachers' Annual Conference, 1912, 1913.
Appointment of the Council's Psychologist.
Report of the Psychologist, 1913–14.
Report of the Psychologist, 1915.
Various communications from Burt.
Burt's resignation, April 1932.

2. *University College, London: Records Office*
   Gower Street, London, W.C. 1.

Burt's appointment, 1931–32.
Memoranda and letters dealing with staffing, grants and other matters
   connected with the department of Psychology.
Storing of Burt's research papers.
Communications from Aberystwyth.
Matters connected with Burt's pension.

3. *The British Psychological Society Archives*
   St Andrews House, 48 Princess Road East, Leicester.
Council Minutes.
Minutes of the Publications Committee.
Material relating to Working Parties.

Copies of Spearman-Burt correspondence.
Spearman's papers.

Addendum

At the time of publication certain papers, offprints and manuscripts of
Burt have been retained by his former secretary, Miss G. Archer. Under
the terms of her will these will eventually be transferred to Liverpool
University Archives. In the meantime they can be consulted by writing
to:

> Miss G. Archer,
> 7 Holmesdale Court,
> Holmesdale Gardens,
> Hastings, Sussex.

APPENDIX FOUR

General Bibliography*

Anstey, E. *Psychological Tests*. London: Methuen, 1966.

Banks, Charlotte and Broadhurst, P. L. (eds) *Stephanos: Studies in Psychology presented to Cyril Burt*. London: University of London Press, 1965.

Bartlett, M. S. Internal and external factor analysis. *Brit. J. Psychol. (Stat. Sect.), I*, 1948, 73–81.

Beloff, J. R. *The Existence of Mind*. London: MacGibbon & Kee, 1962.

Binet, A. and Henri, V. La psychologie individuelle. *L'Année Psychologique, II*, 1895, 411–65.

Birch, L. B. C. L. Burt: Obituary. *Brit. J. Educ. Psychol., XLII*, 1972, 1–2.

Black, N. and Dworkin, G. (eds) *The I.Q. Controversy*. New York: Pantheon Books, Random House, 1976.

Blackburn, J. M. *Psychology and the Social Pattern*. London: Kegan Paul, 1945.

Blackwell, A. M. List of researches in educational psychology and teaching method. *Brit. J. Educ. Psychol., XIII-XV*, 1943–45.

Board of Education. *Psychological Tests of Educable Capacity*. London: H.M.S.O., 1924.

Board of Education: Consultative Committee Report. *The Education of the Adolescent* (Hadow Report). London: H.M.S.O., 1926.

Board of Education: Consultative Committee Report. *The Primary School* (Hadow Report). London: H.M.S.O., 1931.

Board of Education: Consultative Committee Report. *Infant and Nursery Schools* (Hadow Report). London: H.M.S.O., 1933.

Board of Education: Consultative Committee Report. *Secondary Education with special reference to Grammar Schools and Technical High Schools* (Spens Report). London: H.M.S.O., 1938.

Broadhurst, P. L. New light on behavioural inheritance. *Bull. Brit. Psychol. Soc., XXIV*, 1971, 1–8.

Broady, E. B. and Broady, N. *Intelligence: Nature, Determinants and Consequences*. New York: Academic Press, 1976.

* The works listed in this bibliography either contain references to Burt, or relate to major topics with which he was concerned. It does not include works only incidentally referred to in the text.

Brown, W. and Thomson, G. *The Essentials of Mental Measurement.* Cambridge: University Press, 1925.

Butcher, H. J. *Human Intelligence: its Nature and Assessment.* London: Methuen, 1968.

Butcher, H. J. and Lomax, D. E. (eds) *Readings in Human Intelligence.* London: Methuen, 1972.

Cancro, R. (ed.) *Intelligence: Genetic and Environmental Influences.* New York: Grune & Stratton, 1971.

Cattell, R. B. *The Scientific Analysis of Personality.* Harmondsworth: Penguin Books, 1965.

Cattell, R. B. The multiple abstract variance analysis for nature-nurture research. *Psychol. Rev., LXVII*, 1960, 353–72.

Central Advisory Council for Education. *Children and Their Primary Schools* (Plowden Report). London: H.M.S.O., 1967.

Chambers, E. K. Statistical psychology and the limitations of the test method. *Brit. J. Psychol., XXXIII*, 1943, 189–99.

Clarke, A. D. B. Predicting human development: Problems, evidence and implications. *Bull. Brit. Psychol. Soc., XXXI*, July 1978, 250–8.

Clarke, A. D. B. and Clarke, Ann M. *Mental Deficiency*, 3rd edn. London: Methuen, 1974.

Cohen, J. The Detractors. *Encounter*, March 1977, 86–90.

Committee on Higher Education. *Higher Education* (Robbins Report). London: H.M.S.O., 1963.

Conway, J. The inheritance of intelligence and its social implications. *Brit. J. Statist. Psychol., XI*, 1958, 171–90.

Conway, J. Class difference in general intelligence. *Brit. J. Statist. Psychol., XII*, 1959, 5–14.

Conway, J. A note on the intelligence of twins. *Brit. J. Statist. Psychol., XIII*, 1960, 104.

Cox, C. B. and Dyson, A. E. (eds) *Black Papers, I*, 1969; *II*, 1969; *III*, 1970. London: Critical Quarterly Society.

Darlington, C. D. and Mather, K. *The Elements of Genetics.* London: Allen & Unwin, 1949.

Dockrell, B. (ed.) *On Intelligence.* London: Methuen, 1970.

Douglas, J. W. B. *The Home and the School.* London: MacGibbon & Kee, 1964.

Eaves, L. J. Testing models for variation in intelligence. *Heredity, XXXIV*, 1975, 132–6.

Erlenmeyer-Kimling, L. and Jarvik, L. F. Genetics and intelligence: a review. *Science, CXLII*, 1963, 1477–9.

Eysenck, H. J. *The Scientific Study of Personality.* London: Routledge & Kegan Paul, 1952.

Eysenck, H. J. Obituary: Sir Cyril Burt. *Brit. J. Math. Statist. Psychol.*, *XXV*, i–iv, 1972.

Eysenck, H. J. *Race, Intelligence and Education*. London: Temple Smith, 1971.

Eysenck, H. J. *The Inequality of Man*. London: Temple Smith, 1973.

Eysenck, H. J. *The Measurement of Intelligence*. Lancaster: Medical & Technical Publishing Co., 1973.

Eysenck, H. J. The Case of Sir Cyril Burt. *Encounter*, January 1977, 19–24.

Falconer, D. S. *Introduction to Quantitative Genetics*, 1st edn. Edinburgh: Oliver & Boyd, 1960; reprinted, London: Longman, 1975.

Fisher, R. A. The correlation between relatives on the supposition of Mendelian inheritance. *Trans. Roy. Soc. Edin.*, *LII*, 1918, 399–433.

Fisher, R. A. *Statistical Methods for Research Workers*. Edinburgh: Oliver & Boyd, 1934.

Fleming, C. M. *Adolescence: its Social Psychology*. London: Kegan Paul, 1947.

Floud, J. E., Halsey, A. H. and Martin, J. M. *Social Class and Educational Opportunity*. London: Heinemann, 1956.

Flugel, J. C. A hundred years or so of psychology at University College, London. *Bull. Brit. Psychol. Soc.*, *XXIII*, 1954, 21–31.

Fraser, E. *Home Environment and School*. Scottish Council for Research in Education, 1959; 3rd imp. London: University of London Press, 1973.

Galton, F. *Hereditary Genius*. London: Macmillan, 1869.

Galton, F. *Natural Inheritance*. London: Macmillan, 1881.

Gaw, F. *Performance Tests of Intelligence*. Industrial Fatigue Research Board, Report No. 31. London: H.M.S.O., 1927.

Gillie, O. Crucial Data was faked by eminent psychologist. London: *Sunday Times*, 24 October 1976.

Ginsberg, H. and Koslowski, B. Cognitive development. *Ann. Rev. Psychol.*, *XXVII*, 1976, 29–61.

Glass, D. V. *Social Mobility in Britain*. London: Longmans & Green, 1954.

Goldberger, A. S. *Models and Methods in the I.Q. Debate: Part I. Revised*. Social Studies Research Institute. University of Wisconsin-Madison, February 1978.

Guilford, J. P. The structure of the intellect. *Psychol. Bull.*, *LIII*, 1956, 267–93.

Guilford, J. P. *The Nature of Human Intelligence*. New York: McGraw-Hill, 1967.

Guilford, J. P. and Hoepfner, R. *The Analysis of Intelligence*. New York: McGraw-Hill, 1971.

Halsey, A. H. and Gardner, L. Selection for secondary education. *Brit. J. Sociol., IV*, 1953, 60–75.

Halsey, A. H. Genetics, social structure and intelligence. *Brit. J. Sociol., IX*, 1958, 15-28.

Halsey, A. H. Class differences in intelligence. *Brit. J. Statist. Psychol., XII*, 1959, 1–4.

Halsey, A. H. (ed.) *Heredity and Environment*. London: Methuen, 1977.

Harmon, H. H. *Modern Factor Analysis*, 2nd edn. Chicago: University of Chicago Press, 1967.

Harte, N. and North, J. *The World of University College, London, 1828–1978*. Portsmouth: Grosvenor Press, 1978.

Hearnshaw, L. S. *A Short History of British Psychology, 1840–1940*. London: Methuen, 1964.

Hearnshaw, L. S. Obituary: Sir Cyril Burt. *Bull. Brit. Psychol. Soc., XXV*, 1972, 86.

Hearnshaw, L. S. Cyril Ludowic Burt, 1883–1971. *Proc. Brit. Acad., LVIII*, 1972, 475–92.

Hearnshaw, L. S. Sir Cyril Burt and the N.I.I.P. *Occup. Psychol., XLVI*, 1972, 35–7.

Hearnshaw, L. S. Sherrington, Burt and the beginnings of psychology in Liverpool. *Bull. Brit. Psychol. Soc., XXVII*, 1974, 9–14.

Hearnshaw, L. S. British Psychologists at the University of Würzburg at the Beginning of the Century. In Kuhn, O. (ed.) *Grossbritannien und Deutschland*, pp. 661–71. Munich: W. Goldman Verlag, 1974.

Hearnshaw, L. S. Structuralism and intelligence. *Int. Rev. Appl. Psychol., XXIV*, 1975, 85–90.

Heim, A. *The Appraisal of Intelligence*. London: Methuen, 1954.

Heywood, R. *The Infinite Hive: A personal record of extra-sensory experiences, with an introduction by Cyril Burt*. London: Chatto & Windus, 1964.

Heywood, R. Professor Sir Cyril Burt: Obituary. *Proc. Soc. Psychical Res., XLVI*, 1972, 70–7.

Howard, M. The conversion of scores to a uniform scale. *Brit. J. Statist. Psychol., XI*, 1958, 199–207.

Hudson, L. *Contrary Imaginations*. London: Methuen, 1966.

Hunt, J. McV. *Intelligence and Experience*. New York: Ronald Press, 1961.

Hunt, J. McV. (ed.) *Human Intelligence*. New Brunswick: Transaction Books, 1972.

Hunt, J. McV. Heredity, Environment and Class or Ethnic Differences. In *Proc. 1972 Invitational Conference on Testing Problems*. Princeton: Educ. Testing Service, 1973.

Husén, T. *Talent, Equality and Meritocracy*. Amsterdam: European, 1974.

Institute of Education, University of London. *Studies and Impressions, 1902–1952*. London: Evans Bros, 1952.

James, C., Pidgeon, D. A., Graham, C., and Vernon, P. E. Modern concepts of intelligence. *J. & Newsletter Ass. Educ. Psychol., II,* 5, 1970, 1–64.

Jencks, C. *Inequality.* New York: Basic Books, 1972.

Jensen, A. R. How much can we boost I.Q. and scholastic achievement? *Harvard Educ. Rev., XXXIX,* 1969, 1–123.

Jensen, A. R. Obituary: Sir Cyril Burt. *Psychometrika, XXXVII,* 1972, 115–17.

Jensen, A. R. *Educability and Group Differences.* London: Methuen, 1973.

Jensen, A. R. Kinship correlations reported by Sir Cyril Burt. *Behav. Genet., IV,* 1974, 1–28.

Jensen, A. R. Burt in perspective. *Amer. Psychol., XXXIII,* 1978, 499–503.

Jensen, A. R. The current state of the I.Q. controversy. *Australian Psychologist, XIII,* 1978, 7–27.

Jinks, J. L. and Eaves, L. J. I.Q. and Inequality. *Nature,* 22 March 1974.

Jinks, J. L. and Fulker, D. W. Comparison of the biometrical, genetical, MAVA and classical approaches to the analysis of human behaviour. *Psychol. Bull., LXIII,* 1970, 311–49.

Kamin, L. J. Heredity, Intelligence, Politics and Psychology. Paper presented to the *13th Int. Congress of Genetics,* 1973.

Kamin, L. J. *The Science and Politics of I.Q.* Potomac, Md: Lawrence Erlbaum, 1974.

Kamin, L. J. The Hole in Heredity. *New Society,* 2 December 1976.

Kamin, L. J. Burt's I.Q. data. *Science, CXCV,* 1977, 246–8.

Keehn, J. D. Consciousness and behaviourism. *Brit. J. Psychol., LV,* 1964, 89–91.

Kendal, M. G. Factor analysis as a statistical technique. *J. Roy. Statist. Soc., XII,* 1950, 60–94.

Koestler, A. *The Act of Creation.* Foreword by Cyril Burt. London: Hutchinson, 1964.

Lafitte, J. Spearman's form of criterion analysis. *Brit. J. Statist. Psychol., VII,* 1954, 57–61.

Lawley, D. N. and Maxwell, A. E. *Factor Analysis as a Statistical Method.* London: Butterworth, 1963.

Lewis, D. G. The normal distribution of intelligence: a critique. *Brit. J. Psychol., XLVIII,* 1957, 98–104.

Lewis, D. G. Commentary on 'The Genetic Determination of Differences in Intelligence' by Cyril Burt. *Brit. J. Psychol., LVII,* 1966, 431–3.

Lewontin, R. C. Genetic aspects of intelligence. *Ann. Rev. Genet.,* 1975, 387–403.

Luria, A. R. *Cognitive Development.* Cambridge, Mass.: Harvard University Press, 1977.

Maberley, A., Allport, G. W. and Thomson, G. Personality—a symposium. *Brit. J. Educ. Psychol., XVI*, 1946.

McAskie, M. Burt's 1961 parent-child I.Q. data according to parent occupation: an autopsy. (Awaiting publication.)

McAskie, M. Carelessness or fraud in Burt's kinship data? *Amer. Psychol., XXXIII*, 1978, 496–8.

McAskie, M. and Clarke, Ann M. Parent-offspring resemblances in intelligence: theories and evidence. *Brit. J. Psychol., LXVII*, 1976, 243–73.

McDougall, W. *Body and Mind.* London: Methuen, 1911.

McLeish, J. *The Science of Behaviour.* London: Barrie & Rockliff, 1963.

Maddox, H. Nature-nurture balance sheets. *Brit. J. Educ. Psychol., XXVII*, 1957, 166–75.

Mather, K. *Biochemical Genetics: the Study of Continuous Variations.* London: Methuen, 1949.

Meade, J. E. The inheritance of inequalities: some biological, demographic, social and economic factors. *Proc. Brit. Acad., LIX*, 1973, 355–81.

Meade, J. E. and Parkes, A. S. (eds) *Genetic and Environmental Factors in Human Ability.* Edinburgh: Oliver & Boyd, 1966.

Medawar, P. B. Unnatural Science. *New York Review of Books*, 3 February 1977.

Medawar, P. B. and Medawar, J. S. *The Life Science: Current Ideas of Biology.* London: Wildwood House, 1977.

Moursey, R. M. The hierarchical organization of cognitive levels. *Brit. J. Statist. Psychol., V*, 1952, 151–80.

Newman, H. H., Freeman, F. N. and Holzinger, K. J. *Twins: A study of Heredity and Environment.* Chicago: Chicago University Press, 1937.

Norton, B. Metaphysics and population genetics: Karl Pearson and the background to Fisher's multi-factorial theory of inheritance. *Annals of Science, XXXII*, 1975, 537–53.

Pear, T. H. Sir Cyril Burt: a tribute. *J. & Newsletter Assoc. Educ. Psychol., III*, 1972, 3.

Pearson, K. On the systematic fitting of curves to observations and measurements. *Biometrika, I*, 1901, 265–303.

Pearson, K. The lines of closest fit to a system of points. *Phil. Mag., II*, 1901, 559–72.

Pearson, K. On the inheritance of mental and moral characteristics in man. *Biometrika, IV*, 1904, 131.

Pearson, K. Critical notice: On the Relation between Home Conditions and the Intelligence of School Children, by L. Isserlis. *Biometrika, XV*, 1923, 161–72.

Popper, K. R. and Eccles, J. C. *The Self and its Brain.* Berlin: Springer, 1977.

Raven, J. C. Note on Burt's 'The Distribution of Intelligence'. *Brit. J. Psychol., L*, 1959, 70–1.

Richmond, W. K. Educational measurement: its scope and limitations. *Brit. J. Psychol., XLIV*, 1953, 221–31.

Rimland, B. and Munsinger, H. Burt's I.Q. data. *Science, CXCV*, 1977, 248.

Rowe, D. and Plomin, R. The Burt controversy: a comparison of Burt's data on I.Q. with data from other studies. *Behav. Genet., VIII*, 1978, 81–3.

Scarr-Salapatek, S. Race, social class and I.Q. *Science, CLXXVII*, 1971, 1285–95.

Schonell, F. J. The development of educational research in Great Britain, Parts I–VI. *Brit. J. Educ. Psychol., XVII–XIX*, 1947–49.

Schwartz, J. After Burt, what's left? *New Scientist*, 11 November 1976, 331–2.

Serebriakoff, V. *I.Q. A Mensa Analysis and History*. London: Mensa, 1966.

Shields, J. *Monozygotic Twins: brought up apart and brought up together*. London: Oxford University Press, 1962.

Sholl, D. A. *The Organization of the Cerebral Cortex*. London: Methuen, 1956.

Silver, H. (ed.) *Equal Opportunity in Education; A Reader in Social Class and Educational Opportunity*. London: Methuen, 1973.

Simon, B. *Intelligence Testing and the Comprehensive School*. London: Lawrence & Wishart, 1953.

Sluckin, W. (ed.) *Early Learning and Early Experience*. Penguin Modern Psychology Readings. Harmondsworth: Penguin Books, 1971.

Spearman, C. E. General intelligence objectively measured and determined. *Amer. J. Psychol., XV*, 1904, 201–99.

Spearman, C. E. *The Abilities of Man*. London: Macmillan, 1927.

Spearman, C. E. and Wynn Jones, L. *Human Ability*. London: Macmillan, 1950.

Stephenson, Wm. The inverted factor technique. *Brit. J. Psychol., XXVI*, 1936, 344–61.

Stephenson, Wm. *The Study of Behaviour: Q-technique and its Methodology*. Chicago: Chicago University Press, 1953.

Stott, D. H. Commentary on 'The genetic determination of differences in intelligence: a study of monozygotic twins reared together and apart', by Cyril Burt. Congenital influences on the development of twins. *Brit. J. Psychol., LVII*, 1967, 423–9.

Thomson, G. H. *The Factorial Analysis of Human Ability*. London: University of London Press, 1939.

Thomson, G. H., Spearman, C. E., Burt, C. L. and Stephenson, Wm. The factorial analysis of ability. *Brit. J. Psychol., XXX*, 1939, 71–108.

Thurstone, L. L. *The Vectors of the Mind*. Chicago: Chicago University Press, 1935.

Thurstone, L. L. Primary Mental Abilities. *Psychomet. Monogr. I*, 1938.

Thurstone, L. L. *Multiple Factor Analysis*. Chicago: Chicago University Press, 1947.

Tizard, J. The Burt affair. *Univ. of London Bull., XLI*, May 1977, 4–7.

Tobias, P. V. I.Q. and the nature-nurture controversy. *J. Behav. Sci., II*, 1974, 5–24.

Valentine, C. W. *The Experimental Psychology of Beauty*. London: Methuen, 1962.

Vandenburg, S. G. Contributions of twin research to psychology. *Psychol. Bull., LXVI*, 1966, 327–52.

Vandenberg, S. G. The Nature and Nurture of Intelligence. In Glass, D. V. (ed.) *Genetics*, pp. 3–58. New York: Rockefeller University Press & Russell Sage Foundation, 1968.

Van der Eyken, W. (ed.) *Education, the Child and Society: A Documentary History, 1900–1973*. Harmondsworth: Penguin Books, 1973.

Vernon, P. E., Thorndike, E. L., Drever, J., Pear, T. H. and Myers, C. S. Is the doctrine of instincts dead? A symposium. *Brit. J. Educ. Psychol., XII*, 1942.

Vernon, P. E. *The Structure of Human Abilities*. London: Methuen, 1950.

Vernon, P. E. (ed.) *Secondary School Selection*. London: Methuen, 1957.

Vernon, P. E. *Intelligence and Cultural Environment*. London: Methuen, 1969.

Vernon, P. E. *Cyril Lodowic Burt: a Biographical Memoir*. Stanford, California: National Academy of Education, 1972.

Wade, N. I.Q. and heredity: suspicion of fraud beclouds classic experiment. *Science, CXCIV*, 26 November 1976, 916–19.

Wiseman, S. *Education and Environment*. Manchester: Manchester University Press, 1964.

Wiseman, S. (ed.) *Intelligence and Ability*. Penguin Modern Psychology Readings. Harmondsworth: Penguin Books, 1967.

Young, M. *The Rise of the Meritocracy*. London: Thames & Hudson, 1958.

Young, M. and Gibson, J. In search of an explanation of social mobility. *Brit. J. Statist. Psychol., XVI*, 1963, 27–35.

Zapan, M. L. The conceptual development of quantification in experimental psychology. *J. Hist. Behav. Sci., XII*, 1976, 145–58.

Index of Names

Aberdeen University Press, 193
Adams, J., 43, 94
Aitkin, A. C., 157
Alexander, S., 30, 299
Alexander, W. P., 156, 157
Allen and Unwin Ltd, 185
Anstey, E., 94, 108, 136
Archer, Gretl, ix, 182, 209, 238, 251, 321,
    348, 352
Aristotle, 11, 47, 50, 296, 314
Arnold, M., 8
Audley, R. J., 195, 241
Aveling, F. A. P., 34
Ayer, A. J., 134, 206

Bacon, F., 262, 309
Balerno, Lord, 106
Ballard, P. B., 34, 91, 94, 260
Banks, Charlotte, 146, 167, 199, 209, 245,
    251, 321
Bartlett, F. C., 22, 41, 44, 45, 109, 150, 270,
    312
Bartlett, M. S., 157
Bateson, W., 20
Beardmore, J. A., 255
Beazley, J., 4
Beethoven, L. v., 208, 262
Bell, E. T., 67
Bentham, J., 46
Bergson, H., 299
Berrill, R., 84–5
Bevin, E., 107
Binet, A., 16, 47, 87, 311
Blackwell, A. M., 96
Blair, R., 34, 36, 127
Bohr, N., 304
Booth, C., 39, 272
Bradley, F. H., 11
Brentano, F., 306
Britton, E., 259
Broad, C. D., 41, 50
Broadbent, D. E., 56, 294
Broadhurst, P. L., 321
Brown, W., 11, 34, 54, 66, 175
Bruce, Gladys, 133, 182, 251, 267

Bruner, J. S., 60
Bryce, J., 32, 112
Bugental, J. F. T., 305
Bühler, K., 14
Bulley, Margaret, 215–16
Burns, C. L. C., 98
Buros, O. K., 203
Burt, C. C. B., 2, 3, 271
Burt, C. L., see Index of Topics
Burt, G. E., 1
Burt, Lady (née Joyce Woods), 43, 131,
    140, 145, 149, 182, 251, 266, 275
Burt, Marion, vii, ix, x, 2, 199–200, 277
Butcher, H. J., 176
Butler, R. A., 116

Campagnac, E. T., 26, 31
Cancardas, Aydin, 219
Cattell, J. McK., 87, 311
Cattell, R. B., 43, 54, 80, 99, 151, 158, 178,
    181, 215, 229, 237, 285, 290
Chambers, E. G., 109
Charlesworth, W. R., 56
Chesterton, G. K., 12
Churchill, W. S., 40
Cicero, M. T., 47
Clarke, A. D. B., 65, 148, 234, 237, 259,
    286
Clarke, Ann M., 234, 237, 254, 259, 286
Clegg, A. B., 265
Cohen, J. I., 136, 236
Cole, M., 60, 317
Comte, A., 316
Conway, J., 230, 231, 235, 236, 240, 242–4,
    245, 252
Corelli, Marie, 7
Cox, C. B., 120, 123–6, 189, 228, 256
Cox, J. G., 100
Crawford, Agnes, 136, 140, 171
Cronbach, L. J., 312
Crosland, C. A. R., 119
Cunningham, M., 56

Darlington, C. D., 300
Darwin, C., 19, 20, 57, 292, 298, 299, 311

Davidson, May, 141, 257
de Monchaux, Cecily, 136, 146
Desai, M., 136
Dilthey, W., 306
Dingle, H., 134
Douglas, J. W. B., 62, 64, 119, 241
Downing, J., 190
Drever, J., jnr, 194
Drever, J., snr, 104
Drew, G. C., 250
Durkheim, E., 21, 316
Dyson, A. E., 120, 123–6, 189, 228, 256

Ebbinghaus, H., 87
Eccles, J. C., 225, 293, 296, 318
Edgeworth, F. Y., 171, 175, 301
Einstein, A., 19
Ellis, H., 28, 77
English, H. B., 27
Erlenmeyer-Kimling, L., 246
Evans, I., 152
Evans, Martha, 2
Eyken, W. van der, 111
Eysenck, H. J., 64, 80, 127, 136, 148, 151,
     181, 216, 218, 237, 239, 247, 266, 270,
     284, 290

Falconer, D. S., 59
Ferguson, G. A., 50, 108
Ferriss, E. N., 261
Field, H. E., 43
Fisher, R. A., 20, 46, 58, 134, 167, 316
Floud, J. E., 68, 119, 241, 254
Flugel, J. C., 11, 13, 14, 27, 133, 135, 139,
     145, 149, 249, 266
Forsdyke, J., 4
Foster, H. S., 185
Fox, C., 4
Fraser, Elizabeth D., 62
Fraser Roberts, J. A., 188, 229
Freud, S., 16, 79, 80, 281
Frey, M. v., 14
Frisby, C. B., 180, 229
Fulker, D. W., 60

Galton, F., 3, 8, 19, 20, 23, 27, 46, 48, 53,
     57, 65, 82, 87, 96, 122, 128, 171, 174,
     269, 292, 298, 311
Gardiner, P., 8
Garnett, J. C. M., 157
Gaw, Frances, 101
George, F. H., 305
Gibbs, W., 19
Gillie, O., viii, 235, 236
Ginsberg, M., 22
Glass, D. V., 69
Graham, C., 63
Green, J. A., 91

Green, T. H., 11, 17
Gregory, Anita, 224
Gregory, R. L., 296
Gregson, R. A. M., 219
Griffiths, Ruth, 136
Gue, L. J., 250
Guilford, J. P., 54, 55, 155, 157
Guntrip, H. J. S., 204

Hadow, H., 94, 111, 115
Haldane, J. B. S., 134
Halliday, J. L., 280
Halsey, A. H., 68, 119, 120, 228, 241, 254
Hamilton, M., 136, 146, 266
Hamilton, W., 47
Hamley, H. R., 42, 260
Hammond, W. H., 139, 243
Hansel, C. E. M., 223, 224, 287
Harding, D. W., 147, 148, 286
Hardy, A. C., 225, 299
Harper, F. N., 178
Hartog, P., 93, 162
Hayek, F. A., 296
Heim, Alice, 51, 55, 66, 67, 228, 241
Heisenberg, W., 304
Henri, V., 47, 311
Heron, D., 27, 29
Heywood, Rosalind, 203
Hinchcliffe, R., 278, 280, 281
Hobbes, T., 50
Hobhouse, L. T., 22
Hogben, L., 229
Holt, R. R., 308
Honzinck, M. P., 64
Hopkins, P., 133
Hotteling, H., 157, 163, 179, 180, 209
Howard, Margaret, 56, 57, 79, 190, 235,
     236, 240, 242–4, 245
Hudson, L., 86, 205–6, 238
Hughes, A. G., 43
Humphries, L., 240
Hunt, J. McV., 60, 64, 315
Huxley, J. S., 146, 203

Isaacs, Susan, 53, 96, 111

Jackson, J. H., 19, 302
Jacob, F., 300, 303
James, W., 16, 297
Jaspers, K., 289, 290
Jencks, C., 65, 69, 121, 239, 246
Jensen, A. R., 59, 64, 68, 121, 209, 228,
     231, 232, 234, 237, 242, 246
Jinks, J. L., 60
John, Enid, 141
Jonckheere, A. R., 136
Joseph, H. W. B., 11, 51, 314

Kamin, L. J., viii, 61, 232–4, 237, 259, 290
Kant, I., 306
Keatinge, M. W., 12, 96
Keir, Gertrude, 38, 137, 146, 250, 251
Kelley, T. L., 156, 157
Kenrick, K. L., 9
Kimmins, C. W., 34, 35, 36, 39
Kerr, J., 210
Knight, R., 151, 193
Koch, S., 293
Koestler, A., 203, 224
Kogan, M., 112
Koussy, El, 136, 156
Külpe, O., 13–14, 214

Labov, W., 60
Lafitte, J., 178
Lankester, R., 16
Laski, Marghanita, 203
Lawley, D. N., 157, 158, 179
Leonhard, K., 289
Lewis, A. J., 98, 147
Lewis, D. G., 66
Lewis, M. M., 136
Lewontin, R. C., 60
Li, C. C., 68
Line, W., 150
Lombroso, C., 77
Lubin, A., 136
Luria, A. R., 60, 317

MacCunn, J., 26, 30
Macmillan, Margaret, 33
Macmurray, J., 44, 134
Mair, A., 26
Marquis, F. (Lord Woolton), 29, 31, 146
Marshall, A. J., 136
Martin, J. M., 68, 119
Marx, K., 316
Maslow, A. H., 307
Mather, K., 58
Maxwell, A. E., 158, 179
Maxwell, J. C., 301
Mays, J. B., 79
McAskie, M., 242, 254
McDougall, W., 11, 12, 18, 22, 23, 24, 27,
    44, 46, 47, 50, 73, 79, 80, 128, 168,
    170, 177, 221, 292, 293, 299, 300, 301,
    302, 314
McElwain, D. W., 136
McKellar, T. P. H., 136
McLeish, J., 55, 205, 228, 241
Mead, G. H., 316
Medawar, P. B., 203, 300, 317, 318
Mendel, J. G., 20, 57, 181
Meumann, E., 13, 28, 47, 53
Michotte, A., 13
Miller, E., 97

Moles, A., 220
Molteno, E. V., 229, 246
Moncrieff, M. M., 225
Monod, J., 298–9, 300
Moodie, W., 97, 98
Moore, G. E., 17
Moore, R. C., 28, 29, 159
Morant, R., 32
Morgan, C. Lloyd, 19, 299
Morison, S., 212
Mottram, V. H., 31
Moursey, E. M. K., 302
Muir, R., 30
Münsterberg, H., 99
Muscio, W. R., 41
Myers, C. S., 41, 94, 100, 104
Myers, F. W. H., 188, 224

Neate, A. R., 258
Neisser, U., 56
Newell, A., 56
Newman, G., 33
Newman, H. H., 232
Newton, I., 262
Norwood, C., 94, 116
Nunn, P., 42, 43, 111

O'Connor, M. G., 125, 256, 258, 259

Pareto, V., 21
Parry, J. B., 104, 135–6, 216, 218
Peaker, G. F., 126, 258
Pear, T. H., 13, 45, 150, 266
Pearson, E., 134, 153
Pearson, K., 12, 17, 20, 23, 29, 30, 46, 66,
    93, 128, 134, 156, 157, 159, 161, 163,
    171–9, 303
Pelling, V. G., 40, 133, 216
Penguin Books Ltd, 186, 196
Penrose, L. S., 29, 134, 229
Percy, Lord E., 114
Philpott, S. J. F., 104, 132, 133, 135, 139,
    142–4, 147, 248, 286
Piaget, J., 51, 53, 89, 124, 270, 303, 315
Pidgeon, D. A., 64, 66, 258
Planck, M. C. E. L., 19, 304
Plato, 51, 311
Popper, K. R., 50, 206, 293, 307, 318
Prince of Wales (Edward VII), 5
Proctor, Margaret, 76
Punnett, Margaret, 43

Quetelet, L. A. J., 65

Raper, J. T., 134
Raphael, Winifred (née Spielman), 102,
    260
Rawles, R., 244

Rawlings, Grace, 137, 146
Reid, R. S., 190
Reid, T., 47
Rhine, J. B., 222
Richmond, W. K., 66
Rivers, W. H. R., 41, 46
Rodger, A., 150
Romanes, G. J., 19
Ross, W. D., 11
Roth, M., 289
Roxby, P. M., 31
Rusk, R. R., 285
Russell, B., 17, 41, 206, 262
Russell, G. W. ('A.E.'), 291
Russell, R. W., 152, 153, 276
Ryle, G., 50, 206

St James-Roberts, I., 319
Salzman, L., 283
Scarr-Salapatek, Sandra, 231
Schonell, Florence, 136
Schonell, F. J., 43, 96
Serebriakoff, V., 85–6, 205
Seth, G., 96
Sharp, S., 321
Sheppard, W. F., 163
Sherrington, C. S., 16, 25–6, 30, 31, 55, 146, 168
Shields, J., 232, 241
Shockley, W., 246, 247, 253
Sholl, D. A., 305
Shotter, J., 306–7
Shrubsall, F. C., 34, 98
Simmins, Constance, 133, 137
Simon, B., 57, 109, 118, 227, 228, 241
Simon, H. A., 56
Skinner, B. F., 50
Slade, I. M., 141
Slater, P., 177
Sleight, W. G., 34
Slocombe, C. S., 43
Sluckin, W., 270, 271
Smith, May, 11, 41
Smith, W. G., 26
Smuts, J. C., 301
Soal, S. G., 222
Sorokin, P., 316
Spearman, C. E., 12, 16, 27, 31, 40, 46, 47, 53–4, 66, 94, 104, 108, 128, 129, 130, 154, 155, 158, 159, 162, 163, 165, 167–79, 269, 284, 286, 311
Spencer, H., 19, 48, 168, 298, 302
Spens, W., 111, 115
Spielman, Winifred, see Raphael
Stapledon, O., 31
Steinberg, Hannah, 321
Stephens, S. D. G., 280, 281
Stephenson, W., 133, 156, 260, 269

Stern, W., 47, 164, 307, 311, 318
Stevens, S. S., 67
Stott, D. H., 55, 228
Stout, G. F., 11, 18, 45, 51, 292, 293, 301
Strachey, St Loe (Mrs), 97
Studman, Grace, 133
Sully, J., 19, 46, 128
Summerfield, A., 98, 99, 137–8, 282

Tawney, R. H., 113
Taylor & Francis Ltd, 194
Terman, L. M., 90, 311
Theophrastus, 311
Thomson, G. H., 54, 55, 89, 95, 155, 156, 164, 167, 174, 180, 191–2, 260
Thomson, H. W., 10
Thorndike, E. L., 54, 66, 257
Thorpe, W. H., 297, 300
Thouless, R. H., 151, 222, 223, 261, 285
Thurstone, L. L., 54, 156, 161, 172, 173, 174, 269, 284
Tizard, J., 236, 237
Trevelyan, G. O., 7

Underwood, B. J., 312
University of London Press, 185–6, 192, 196

Valentine, C. W., 13, 14, 105, 191, 209, 214–17, 262, 266
Vandenberg, S. C., 63
Vernon, M. D., 261
Vernon, P. E., 60, 64, 89, 104, 119, 318
Vincent, D. F., 177, 180, 287
Vries, H. de, 20
Vygotsky, L. S., 317

Wade, N., 237
Wall, W. D., 266
Warburton, F. W., 136, 204
Ward, J., 4, 18, 27, 292, 293, 295, 301
Warde, Beatrice, 188, 194, 200–3, 212, 27(
Ware, L. L., 84
Wason, P. C., 204
Wassermann, G. D., 223, 302, 304
Waterfield, P., 260
Watkins, S. H., 34
Watson, J. B., 50
Watt, H. J., 13, 26
Webb, E., 79, 158
Webb, S., 32
Weber, M., 21, 316
Weismann, A., 20
Weyl, H., 304
Whitfield, J. W., 146, 194
Whyte, L. L., 300
Wilde, H., 11, 12, 17
Wilkie, J. S., 139

Wilkinson, Ellen, 146
Williams, Elizabeth D., 245
Williams, P., 250
Wilson, J. Cook, 11
Winch, W. A., 34, 91
Wiseman, S., 62
Wittgenstein, L., 206
Wolman, B. B., 301
Wolters, A. W., 146

Woods, Joyce, *see* Burt, Lady
Woodworth, R. S., 26
Wrigley, C. F., 136, 181, 287

Young, J. Z., 134
Young, M., 204, 238
Yule, G. Udny, 21, 41, 92, 161, 260

Zangwill, O. L., 109, 151

Index of Topics

Aberystwyth, 104, 131, 138–44, 248, 251–2, 278

Ability, concept of, 50

Abstractions, 51

Admiralty, 105

Aesthetics, 13, 213–21

Air Force, 105, 106

Analogies Test, 89

Anthropology, 22

Applied Psychology Unit, Cambridge, 109

Archives, Burt, 348–52

Armed Services, 93, 103–7

Army, 104–6

Artistic education, 221

Association of Educational Psychologists, 190

Astronomy, 207, 294

Attention, 56

Backwardness, educational, 37, 74–7

Behaviourism, 18, 292–4

Behaviour therapy, 78, 81

Beveridge Report, 116

Bilingualism, 141

Binet Scale, 37, 47, 90, 167, 257

Biology, 19, 298–301

Black Papers, 120, 123–6, 189, 228, 256

Body measurements, 167

Bradford Educational Authority, 89, 95

British Abilities Scale, 90

British Academy, vii, 146

British Association for the Advancement of Science
  Anthropometric committee, 12, 27, 47, 87
  Burt's presidential address to Section J, 50, 88, 104, 311
  Printing of school books, 211
  Psychological war research committee, 40

British Child Study Association, 94

British Journal of Statistical Psychology, 167, 172, 180, 191–5, 275–6, 287
  Spurious contributors to, 178, 192, 245

British Psychological Society, 191, 276, 286
  Archives, 351

Committee on Research in Education, 96

Publications Committee, 193

Report on Secondary School Selection, 123

Symposium on Child Guidance, 98

Working Party on Maladjusted Children, 80, 189

Working Party on Mental Deficiency, 190

Burt, C. L. (Sir Cyril)
  Ancestry, 1, 271
  Articles
    Experimental Tests of General Intelligence (1909), 49, 57, 129, 158, 170; Ability and Income (1943), 58, 69, 141, 230, 252, 286; Intelligence and Fertility (1946), 58; Evidence for the Concept of Intelligence (1955), 49, 228, 230; Multifactorial Theory of Inheritance (with Howard) (1956), 56, 59, 60, 230, 252; Intelligence and Social Mobility (1961), 69, 253–6; Psychology of Value (1963), 219–20; Genetic Determination of Intelligence; MZ twins (1966), 231, 241, 252, 282; Intelligence and Heredity (1969), 19, 125, 189, 228, 256–9
  Artistic gifts, 214, 264
  Assistants (see also Conway, Howard and O'Connor), 36; co-workers, 245; secretarial assistants, 132
  Birth, 2
  Books
    Distribution and Relations of Educational Abilities (1917), 36, 66, 160, 257; Mental and Scholastic Tests (1921), 37, 38, 52, 63, 91–2, 126, 161–2, 196, 215, 257, 259, 260; Young Delinquent (1925), 38, 44, 62, 72, 77–8, 97, 147, 261, 316; How the Mind Works (1933), 22, 196, 216–17; Subnormal Mind (1935), 39, 72, 79; Marks of Examiners (1936), 158, 162, 163, 165, 169; Backward Child (1937), 38, 58, 62, 63, 75–6, 261; Factors of the Mind (1940),

55, 138, 154, 164–7, 169, revisions for
2nd edition, 55, 167, 179, 196, 290;
Gifted Child (1975), 64, 82–4, 196,
197, 210; revisions, 196; unfulfilled
plans, 196–7
Broadcasts, 44, 189, 216
Character, 10, 137, 138, 142, 147–8, 152–
3, 169–78, 204–6, 261, 262–91;
ambitious, 268; carelessness, 197, 233,
234, 242; delusions, 177, 289–90;
deviousness, 147, 148, 283–8;
egocentricity, 153, 288, 290; insularity,
21; intelligence, 262; intellectual
limitations, 314–18; introversion, 268;
kindness, 265; mathematical talent,
264; obsessionality, 282; paranoia, 289;
pathological aspects, 274;
perfectionism, 282; psychosomatic
lability, 277, 283–4; regressive changes,
284, 286, 289; verbal ability, 263
Childhood, 2–3, 270–3
Clinical work, 38, 39, 73–4
Controversies, 121, 125–7, 270, 288
Data, 36, 61, 70, 131, 239, 246, 248–52,
255, 275, 313–14
Death, 210
Examining, 184
Fabrications, 160, 179–80, 235, 241, 242,
245, 252–3, 259, 311
Finances, 10, 183–4
Health, 140, 146, 207, 275, 277–83 (*see
also* Ménière's Disease); declining
powers, 197, 265; exemption from
military service, 40, 277–8
Holidays, 30, 210
Honours
    John Locke Scholarship, 12; F.B.A.,
    146; Honorary degrees, 146; Hon.
    Fellow, Jesus College, Oxford, 146;
    Knighthood, 127, 146, 260; Thorndike
    Award, 227
Journalistic demands, 189
Lectures
    extra-mural, 30; Institute of Education,
    189; London Day Training College,
    43; London School of Economics, 189;
    University College, 135; Bingham
    Lecture, 188, 231; Godfrey Thomson
    Lecture, 244; Galton Lecture, 188;
    Hobhouse Lecture, 22, 187, 306;
    Maudsley Lecture, 188; F. W. H.
    Myers Lecture, 188, 224; National
    Children's Home Lecture, 188;
    Thorndike Lecture, 210
Marriage, 131, 274–5, *see also* Burt, Lady
Memorial Service, vii, 229
Ministry of Munitions, 40
Musical interests, 208, 214

Papers, disposal of, 238, *see also* 248–50
Pension, 45, 183–4
Political attitudes, 61, 126–7, 267–8
Posts held
    University of Liverpool, 15, 25–31;
    London County Council, 31–41;
    University of Cambridge, 41; National
    Institute of Industrial Psychology, 41,
    100–3; London Day Training College,
    41–4; University College, London, 44–
    5, 128–53, retirement from, 149,
    appointment of a successor, 149–52,
    exclusion from college, 153
Reading, 206–7
Research funds, 239
Religious beliefs, 200, 207–8
Residences
    Petty France, 2, 271–2; Park House,
    Snitterfield, 2, 7, 273; University
    Settlement, Liverpool, 29, 31; The
    Settlement, Tavistock Place, London,
    39; 4a, Eton Road, London N.W.3,
    132, 248; 9, Elsworthy Road, London
    N.W.3, 145
Schools
    London Board School, 2, 122, 272,
    289; Dame's School, Jersey, 2; King's
    School, Warwick, 3, 263; Christ's
    Hospital, 3–7, 122, 263, 265, 273
Setbacks, 274–7, 281
Social contacts, 199, 266, 268
Teachers Diploma, 12
Universities
    St John's College, Cambridge, 7; Jesus
    College, Oxford, 7, 8–12, 146;
    Würzburg, 12–14, 213
Views on education, 122–7
Visits to museums and galleries, 4, 209
Work for publishers, 185–7

Canonical analysis, 168, 173
Care Committees, 33, 243
Case History Schedule, 72, 100
Child Guidance, 38, 44, 96–8
    Child Guidance Council, 97
Children Act, 1908: 77
Child Study Association, 95–6
Civil Service, 93, 107
Clairvoyance, 296
Classics, 4, 8, 9–11, 263–4
Clerical tests, 101
College of Preceptors, 184
Communication theory, 212
Cognitive powers, 51
Comprehensive schools, 115, 118
Conation, 18
Consciousness, 223, 294–7
Correlating persons, 158, 164

Creativity, 101, 124, 301

Delian Society, 12, 159, 213
Delinquency, 31, 38, 77–9, 190
Departmental Committee on the Treatment of Young Offenders, 79, 190
Development, 114, 315
Diploma in Psychology, University of London, 99, 137
Directorate for the Selection of Personnel, 104
Dispositions, 50, 298
Drawings, children's, 215
Dualism, 24, 293

Early Leaving, 119
Education, 32, 95–9, 111–27, 256–9
Education Acts
   1870: 112
   1902: 32, 112, 113
   1944: 96, 108, 112, 113, 116
Education, Board of, 27, 32, 44, 111
Educational Priority Areas, 120
Educational psychology, 35, 95–9
Educational Reconstruction, White Paper on, 116, 118
Educational research, 96
Educational standards, 124, 125, 256–9
Egalitarianism, 67, 83, 86, 121
Elementary School Code, 1904: 32
Eleven-plus selection, 114, 115, 117, 118, 119, 123
Elitism, 83, 86
Emergence, 299–301
Emotions, 159, 174
Emotionality, 80, 160, 303
Environment, 39, 52, 59, 62, 73, 76, 78, 114, 316
Eton College, 184
Eugenics, 12, 20, 29, 46, 48, 70
Evacuation, wartime, 105, 141
Evolutionism, 298–301
Examinations, 93, 162
Experimental pedagogy, 95

Factor analysis, 53–4, 154–81, 302, 303
   Burt's contribution to, 181
   Centroid method, 161, 173
   Four-factor theorem, 165
   History of, 169–80, 287
   Of school marks, 160
   Paris Symposium on, 161, 178
   Of personality, 158
   Principal Axes, 172, 173, 176, 179
   Two-factor theory, 84, see also General factor, Group factors
Faculty Psychology, 111, 116, 302
Faking, 225, 264, 319

First-cousin marriages, 63
Fields, 295, 298, 301

General Educational Ability, 37, 161
General factor, 'g', 28, 47, 53–6, 123, 155, 158, 303
Genetics, 20, 28–9, 58–60, 231–2, 316–17
Gestalt Psychology, 301–2
Gifted children, 82–4
Group factors, 37, 49, 53–6, 156, 161, 162
Group Test 33, 89, 101
Growth curves, 64
Guild of Teachers of Backward Children, 76, 190

Hadow Reports, 94, 95, 111–15
Harvard Pre-School Study, 62
Hebrew, 208
Hierarchy, 24, 168, 302–3, 309
Holism, 301–3

Income, 69
Individual differences, 23, 47, 311–12
Individual Psychology, see Psychology, Differential
Industrial Fatigue Research Board, 41, 101
Information theory, 218, 220
Inheritance, see Genetics
Initial Teaching Alphabet, 190, 204
International Congresses of Psychology
   Oxford (1923), 103
   Edinburgh (1948), 109
International Association of Psychotechnics, 100
Institute for the Scientific Treatment of Delinquency, 79
Institute of Education, University of London (formerly London Day Training College), 42, 184, 187, 260
Intelligence, 18, 27, 46–71, 94, 114, 155
   Artificial, 56
   Decline of, 69
   Generality, 53–6
   Innate, general cognitive ability, 49–71
   Innateness, 56–63
   Normal distribution, 65–7
   Psychometric approach to, 71
   The term, 47–8
Intelligence Quotient (I.Q.), 47
   Constancy of, 63–5, 94
Intelligence tests, 27, 47
International Institute Examinations Enquiry, 162
Introspection, 294
Item analysis, 92

Job analysis, 101

Kinship data, 246

Left-handedness, 76
Local Education Authorities, 32, 33
Logical Positivism, 293
London County Council, 31–45, 313
  Appointment of a psychologist, 34
  Reports to, 321
London Day Training College, 42–5, 134

Maladjustment, 79–82
Mathematics, 23, 264
Matrix algebra, 163
Medical inspection of children, 33
Medical profession, 34, 97–8
Ménière's Disease, 140, 142, 278–84
  Relation to personality, 281
Mensa, 84–6, 190
Mental Deficiency Act, 1913: 33, 74, 77
Meritocratic principle, 32
Methodology, 308–10, 312–13
Mind, 294, 297–8
Modern Schools, 114, 115
Monistic transitionism, 301
Multivariate techniques, 167
Music, 208, 214, 264

National Association of Labour Teachers,
  118
National Child Development Study, 62
National Foundation for Educational
  Research, 96, 258
National Institute of Industrial Psychology,
  41, 100
Neurology, 54
Neurophysiology, 305
Neuroses, 79
Northumberland Tests, 89
Norwood Report, 116–18, 123

Paranoia, 289–90
Parents–children correlations, 29, 102, 253–6
Perception, 295
Performance tests, 101
Personality, 52, 158
Philosophy, 11, 206
Phrenology, 311
Physical deterioration, 33
Physics, 19, 304, 309
Plowden Report, 83, 112, 120, 124
Preformation, 300–1, 303, 314, 315
Primrose Hill, 183, 209
Probabalism, 303–5
Prodigies, child, 83
Progressive education, 124, 256
Progressive League, 127
Pseudologica phantastica, 290
Psychical research, 221–6

Psychoanalysis, 81
Psychogalvanic reflex, 28
Psychological Tests of Educable Capacity, 44,
  94, 111
Psychology
  In the first decade of the 20th century,
    16–19
  In the University of Liverpool, 26
Psychology
  Applied, 72, 87–110; weaknesses in, 108–
    9
  Clinical, 108
  Differential, 46, 311–18, 319
  Experimental, 109, 292
  Humanistic, 305–10
  Military, 103–7
  Theoretical, 292–310
  See also Educational psychology, Faculty
    Psychology, Gestalt Psychology, Social
    psychology
Psychometrics, 71, 122
Psychon, 224, 295–6
Punishment, 81

Quantum Theory, 19, 304

Races, 30
Reading, 91, 190
Reasoning tests, 28, 53, 89
Reciprocity principle, 164
Robbins Report, 120, 241
Royal Commission on Mental Defect, 33
Royal Commission on Population, 70

Scholarships, 82, 113
Scientific American, 202
Secondary education, 32
Selection for secondary schools, 94, 95, 109,
  114–15, 123, 124, 227, 276
Self, 297
Sex differences, 28
Sleep, 39
Sir Cyril Burt School, 227
Social class, 27, 29, 68, 83, 121, 122
Social mobility, 69
Social psychology, 22
Sociology, 21–2, 67–71, 109, 316–18
Special school and classes, 76, 83
Speech defects, 76
Spelling, 39
Spens Report, 111, 115, 302
Statistics, 23, 37, 106, 312–13
Stephanos, 204
Sthenic-asthenic, 80, 160, 303
Streaming, 37
Structure, 50, 302, 315
Structure of the mind, 166, 168
Subnormality, 74–7

Summerfield Report, 98, 99, 137–8
Sunday Times, 125, 228, 235, 236

Telepathy, 221, 223
Tests, 37, 38, 73, 87–94
  Adjustments to scores, 52, 90
  Test construction, 53, 91, 93, 108
  Test technology, 92–3, 106
Tetrad difference equation, 155, 170
Theology, 200, 207–8
Theses, 136
  List of, 339–47
The Times, 88, 256
Treatment, 76, 78, 81–2
Trisomy, 63
Twin studies, 39, 229–37, 239–53

Typography, 39, 201–2, 211–13, 220

Underwood Committee, 80, 98, 189
University College, London, 44, 128–53,
  275
  Bombing of, 249

Values, 218
Vocational guidance, 31, 41, 99–103, 215

Work curves, 142–3
World War I, 103–4
World War II, 104–7, 138–45

Year Book of Education, 84

About the Author

Leslie S. Hearnshaw, Emeritus Professor of Psychology at the University of Liverpool, delivered the Memorial Address following Burt's death. He was subsequently invited to write Burt's official biography, and was afforded full cooperation by those closest to Burt. This cooperation was not withdrawn when events caused the nature of the biography to change.

VINTAGE WORKS OF SCIENCE AND PSYCHOLOGY

V-286 **ARIES, PHILIPPE** / Centuries of Childhood

V-292 **BATES, MARSTON** / The Forest and The Sea

V-267 **BATES, MARSTON** / Gluttons and Libertines

V-994 **BERGER, PETER & BRIGITTE AND HANSFRIED KELLNER** / The Homeless Mind: Modernization & Consciousness

V-129 **BEVERIDGE, W. I. B.** / The Art of Scientific Investigation

V-837 **BIELER, HENRY G., M. D.** / Food Is Your Best Medicine

V-414 **BOTTOMORE, T. B.** / Classes in Modern Society

V-742 **BOTTOMORE, T. B.** / Sociology: A Guide to Problems & Literature

V-168 **BRONOWSKI, J.** / The Common Sense of Science

V-419 **BROWN, NORMAN O.** / Love's Body

V-877 **COHEN, DOROTHY** / The Learning Child: Guideline for Parents and Teachers

V-972 **COHEN, STANLEY AND LAURIE TAYLOR** / Psychological Survival: The Experience of Long-Term Imprisonment

V-233 **COOPER, DAVID** / The Death of the Family

V-43 **COOPER, D. G. AND R. D. LAING** / Reason and Violence

V-918 **DAUM, SUSAN M. AND JEANNE M. STELLMAN** / Work is Dangerous to Your Health: A Handbook of Health Hazards in the Workplace & What You Can Do About Them

V-638 **DENNISON, GEORGE** / The Lives of Children

V-671 **DOMHOFF, G. WILLIAM** / The Higher Circles

V-942 **DOUGLAS, MARY** / Natural Symbols

V-157 **EISELEY, LOREN** / The Immense Journey

V-874 **ELLUL, JACQUES** / Propaganda: The Formation of Men's Attitudes

V-390 **ELLUL, JACQUES** / The Technological Society

V-802 **FALK, RICHARD A.** / This Endangered Planet: Prospects & Proposals for Human Survival

V-906 **FARAGO, PETER AND JOHN LAGNADO** / Life in Action: Biochemistry Explained

V-97 **FOUCAULT, MICHEL** / Birth of the Clinic: An Archaeology of Medical Perception

V-914 **FOUCAULT, MICHEL** / Madness & Civilization: A History of Insanity in the Age of Reason

V-935 **FOUCAULT, MICHEL** / The Order of Things: An Archaeology of the Human Sciences

V-821 **FRANK, ARTHUR, & STUART** / The People's Handbook of Medical Care

V-866 **FRANKL, VIKTOR D.** / The Doctor & The Soul: From Psychotherapy to Logotherapy

V-132 **FREUD, SIGMUND** / Leonardo da Vinci: A Study in Psychosexuality

V-14 **FREUD, SIGMUND** / Moses and Monotheism

V-124 **FREUD, SIGMUND** / Totem and Taboo

V-491 **GANS, HERBERT J.** / The Levittowners

V-938 **GARDNER, HOWARD** / The Quest for Mind: Piaget, Levi-Strauss, & The Structuralist Movement

V-152 **GRAHAM, LOREN R.** / Science & Philosophy in the Soviet Union

V-221 **GRIBBIN, JOHN AND STEPHEN PLAGEMANN** / The Jupiter Effect: The Planets as Triggers of Devastating Earthquakes (Revised)

V-602 **HARKINS, ARTHUR AND MAGORAH MARUYAMA (eds.)** / Cultures Beyond The Earth

V-372 **HARRIS, MARVIN** / Cows, Pigs, Wars, and Witches: The Riddles of Culture

V-453 **HEALTH POLICY ADVISORY COMMITTEE** / The American Health Empire

V-283 **HENRY, JULES** / Culture Against Man

V-73 **HENRY, JULES & ZUNIA** / Doll Play of the Pilaga Indian Children

V-970 **HENRY, JULES** / On Sham, Vulnerability & Other Forms of Self-Destruction

V-882 **HENRY, JULES** / Pathways to Madness

V-663 **HERRIGEL, EUGEN** / Zen in the Art of Archery

V-879 **HERSKOVITS, MELVILLE J.** / Cultural Relativism

V-566   **HURLEY, RODGER** / Poverty and Mental Retardation: A Causal Relationship

V-953   **HYMES, DELL (ed.)** / Reinventing Anthropology

V-2017   **JUDSON, HORACE FREEDLAND** / Heroin Addiction: What Americans Can Learn from the English Experience

V-268   **JUNG, C. G.** / Memories, Dreams, Reflections

V-994   **KELLNER, HANSFRIED AND PETER & BRIGITTE BERGER** / The Homeless Mind: Modernization & Consciousness

V-210   **KENYATTA, JOMO** / Facing Mount Kenya

V-823   **KOESTLER, ARTHUR** / The Case of the Midwife Toad

V-934   **KOESTLER, ARTHUR** / The Roots of Coincidence

V-361   **KOMAROVSKY, MIRRA** / Blue-Collar Marriage

V-144   **KRUEGER, STARRY** / The Whole Works: The Autobiography of a Young American Couple

V-906   **LAGNADO, JOHN AND PETER FARAGO** / Life in Action: Biochemistry Explained

V-776   **LAING, R. D.** / Knots

V-809   **LAING, R. D.** / The Politics of the Family & Other Essays

V-43   **LAING, R. D. AND D. G. COOPER** / Reason and Violence

V-280   **LEWIS, OSCAR** / The Children of Sánchez

V-634   **LEWIS, OSCAR** / A Death in the Sánchez Family

V-421   **LEWIS, OSCAR** / La Vida: A Puerto Rican Family in the Culture of Poverty —San Juan and New York

V-370   **LEWIS, OSCAR** / Pedro Martinez

V-727   **MANN, FELIX, M. D.** / Acupuncture (rev.)

V-602   **MARUYAMA, MAGORAH AND ARTHUR HARKINS (eds.)** / Cultures Beyond the Earth

V-816   **MEDVEDEV, ZHORES & ROY** / A Question of Madness

V-427   **MENDELSON, MARY ADELAIDE** / Tender Loving Greed

V-442   **MITCHELL, JULIET** / Psychoanalysis and Feminism

V-672   **OUSPENSKY, P. D.** / The Fourth Way

V-524   **OUSPENSKY, P. D.** / A New Model of The Universe

V-943   **OUSPENSKY, P. D.** / The Psychology of Man's Possible Evolution

V-639   **OUSPENSKY, P. D.** / Tertium Organum

V-558   **PERLS, F. S.** / Ego, Hunger and Aggression: Beginning of Gestalt Therapy

V-462   **PIAGET, JEAN** / Six Psychological Studies

V-221   **PLAGEMANN, STEPHEN AND JOHN GRIBBIN** / The Jupiter Effect (Revised)

V-6   **POLSTER, ERVING & MIRIAM** / Gestalt Therapy Integrated: Contours of Theory & Practice

V-70   **RANK, OTTO** / The Myth of the Birth of the Hero and Other Essays

V-214   **ROSENFELD, ALBERT** / The Second Genesis: The Coming Control of Life

V-301   **ROSS, NANCY WILSON (ed.)** / The World of Zen

V-441   **RUDHYAR, DANE** / The Astrology of America's Destiny

V-464   **SARTRE, JEAN-PAUL** / Search for a Method

V-806   **SHERFEY, MARY JANE, M. D.** / The Nature & Evolution of Female Sexuality

V-918   **STELLMAN, JEANNE M. AND SUSAN M. DAUM** / Work is Dangerous to Your Health

V-440   **STONER, CAROL HUPPING** / Producing Your Own Power: How to Make Nature's Energy Sources Work for You

V-972   **TAYLOR, LAURIE AND STANLEY COHEN** / Psychological Survival

V-289   **THOMAS, ELIZABETH MARSHALL** / The Harmless People

V-800   **THOMAS, ELIZABETH MARSHALL** / Warrior Herdsmen

V-310   **THORP, EDWARD O.** / Beat the Dealer

V-588   **TIGER, LIONEL** / Men in Groups

V-810   **TITMUSS, RICHARD M.** / The Gift Relationship From Human Blood to Social Policy

V-761   **WATTS, ALAN** / Behold the Spirit

V-923   **WATTS, ALAN** / Beyond Theology: The Art of Godsmanship

V-853	**WATTS, ALAN** /	The Book: On the Taboo Against Knowing Who You Are
V-999	**WATTS, ALAN** /	Cloud-Hidden, Whereabouts Unknown
V-665	**WATTS, ALAN** /	Does It Matter?
V-299	**WATTS, ALAN** /	The Joyous Cosmology
V-592	**WATTS, ALAN** /	Nature, Man, and Woman
V-609	**WATTS, ALAN** /	Psychotherapy East and West
V-835	**WATTS, ALAN** /	The Supreme Identity
V-904	**WATTS, ALAN** /	This Is It
V-298	**WATTS, ALAN** /	The Way of Zen
V-468	**WATTS, ALAN** /	The Wisdom of Insecurity
V-813	**WILSON, COLIN** /	The Occult
V-313	**WILSON, EDMUND** /	Apologies to the Iroquois
V-197	**WILSON, PETER J.** /	Oscar: An Inquiry into the Nature of Sanity
V-893	**ZAEHNER, R. C.** /	Zen, Drugs & Mysticism

VINTAGE BIOGRAPHY AND AUTOBIOGRAPHY

V-2024   **CARO, ROBERT A.** / The Power Broker: Robert Moses and the Fall of New York

V-608   **CARR, JOHN DICKSON** / The Life of Sir Arthur Conan Doyle

V-888   **CLARKE, JOHN HENRIK (ed.)** / Marcus Garvey and the Vision of Africa

V-261   **COHEN, STEPHEN F.** / Bukharin and the Bolshevik Revolution: A Political Biography

V-746   **DEUTSCHER, ISAAC** / The Prophet Armed

V-748   **DEUTSCHER, ISAAC** / The Prophet Outcast

V-617   **DEVLIN, BERNADETTE** / The Price of My Soul

V-2023   **FEST, JOACHIM C.** / Hitler

V-225   **FISCHER, LOUIS (ed.)** / The Essential Gandhi

V-132   **FREUD, SIGMUND** / Leonardo Da Vinci

V-969   **GENDZIER, IRENE L.** / Franz Fanon

V-979   **HERZEN, ALEXANDER** / My Past and Thoughts (Abridged by Dwight Macdonald)

V-268   **JUNG, C. G.** / Memories, Dreams, Reflections

V-728   **KLYUCHEVSKY, V.** / Peter the Great

V-280   **LEWIS, OSCAR** / Children of Sanchez

V-634   **LEWIS, OSCAR** / A Death in the Sanchez Family

V-92   **MATTINGLY, GARRETT** / Catherine of Aragon

V-151   **MOFFAT, MARY JANE AND CHARLOTTE PAINTER (eds.)** / Revelations: Diaries of Women

V-151   **PAINTER, CHARLOTTE AND MARY JANE MOFFAT (eds.)** / Revelations: Diaries of Women

V-677   **RODINSON, MAXINE** / Mohammed

V-847   **SNOW, EDGAR** / Journey to the Beginning

V-411   **SPENCE, JONATHAN** / Emperor of China: Self-Portrait of K'ang-hsi

V-133   **STEIN, GERTRUDE** / The Autobiography of Alice B. Toklas

V-826   **STEIN, GERTRUDE** / Everybody's Autobiography

V-100   **SULLIVAN, J. W. N.** / Beethoven: His Spiritual Development

V-287   **TAYLOR, A. J. P.** / Bismarck: The Man and the Statesman

V-275   **TOKLAS, ALICE B. AND EDWARD BURNS (ed.)** / Staying on Alone: Letters of Alice B. Toklas

V-951   **WATTS, ALAN** / In My Own Way: An Autobiography

V-327   **WINSTON, RICHARD AND CLARA** / Letters of Thomas Mann 1899-1955

VINTAGE POLITICAL SCIENCE AND SOCIAL CRITICISM

V-568 **ALINSKY, SAUL D.** / Reveille for Radicals
V-736 **ALINSKY, SAUL D.** / Rules for Radicals
V-286 **ARIES, PHILIPPE** / Centuries of Childhood
V-604 **BAILYN, BERNARD** / Origins of American Politics
V-334 **BALTZELL, E. DIGBY** / The Protestant Establishment
V-571 **BARTH, ALAN** / Prophets With Honor: Great Dissents and Great Dissenters in the Supreme Court
V-60 **BECKER, CARL L.** / The Declaration of Independence
V-513 **BOORSTIN, DANIEL J.** / The Americans: The Colonial Experience
V-358 **BOORSTIN, DANIEL J.** / The Americans: The National Experience
V-11 **BOORSTIN, DANIEL J.** / The Americans: The Democratic Experience
V-501 **BOORSTIN, DANIEL J.** / Democracy and Its Discontents: Reflections on Everyday America
V-414 **BOTTOMORE, T. B.** / Classes in Modern Society
V-305 **BREINES, SIMON AND WILLIAM J. DEAN** / The Pedestrian Revolution: Streets Without Cars
V-44 **BRINTON, CRANE** / The Anatomy of Revolution
V-30 **CAMUS, ALBERT** / The Rebel
V-33 **CARMICHAEL, STOKELY AND CHARLES HAMILTON** / Black Power
V-2024 **CARO, ROBERT A.** / The Power Broker: Robert Moses and the Fall of New York
V-98 **CASH, W. J.** / The Mind of the South
V-555 **CHOMSKY, NOAM** / American Power and the New Mandarins
V-248 **CHOMSKY, NOAM** / Peace in the Middle East: Reflections on Justice and Nationhood
V-743 **CLOWARD, RICHARD A. AND FRANCES FOX PIVEN** / Regulating the Poor: The Functions of Public Welfare
V-383 **CLOWARD, RICHARD A. AND FRANCES FOX PIVEN** / The Politics of Turmoil: Essays on Poverty, Race, and the Urban Crisis
V-940 **COBB, JONATHAN AND RICHARD SENNETT** / The Hidden Injuries of Class
V-311 **CREMIN, LAWRENCE A.** / The Genius of American Education
V-2019 **CUOMO, MARIO** / Forest Hills Diary: The Crisis of Low-Income Housing
V-305 **DEAN, WILLIAM J. AND SIMON BRIENES** / The Pedestrian Revolution: Streets Without Cars
V-638 **DENNISON, GEORGE** / The Lives of Children
V-746 **DEUTSCHER, ISAAC** / The Prophet Armed
V-748 **DEUTSCHER, ISAAC** / The Prophet Outcast
V-617 **DEVLIN, BERNADETTE** / The Price of My Soul
V-671 **DOMHOFF, G. WILLIAM** / The Higher Circles
V-812 **ELLUL, JACQUES** / The Political Illusion
V-390 **ELLUL, JACQUES** / The Technological Society
V-998 **EPSTEIN, EDWARD JAY** / News From Nowhere: Television and the News
V-2023 **FEST, JOACHIM C.** / Hitler
V-927 **FITZGERALD, FRANCES** / Fire in the Lake
V-316 **FREEMAN, S. DAVID** / Energy: The New Era
V-368 **FRIEDENBERG, EDGAR Z.** / Coming of Age in America
V-378 **FULBRIGHT, J. WILLIAM** / The Arrogance of Power
V-846 **FULBRIGHT, J. WILLIAM** / The Crippled Giant.
V-167 **GANS, HERBERT** / More Equality
V-2018 **GAYLIN, WILLARD** / Partial Justice: A Study of Bias in Sentencing
V-174 **GOODMAN, PAUL AND PERCIVAL** / Communitas
V-325 **GOODMAN, PAUL** / Compulsory Mis-education and The Community of Scholars
V-32 **GOODMAN, PAUL** / Growing Up Absurd
V-457 **GREENE, FELIX** / The Enemy: Some Notes on the Nature of Contemporary Imperialism
V-453 **HEALTH/PAC** / The American Health Empire

V-635 **HEILBRONER, ROBERT L.** / Between Capitalism and Socialism
V-283 **HENRY, JULES** / Culture Against Man
V-882 **HENRY, JULES** / Pathways to Madness
V-465 **HINTON, WILLIAM** / Fanshen
V-95 **HOFSTADTER, RICHARD** / The Age of Reform: From Bryan to F. D. R.
V-795 **HOFSTADTER, RICHARD** / America at 1750: A Social Portrait
V-9 **HOFSTADTER, RICHARD** / The American Political Tradition
V-317 **HOFSTADTER, RICHARD** / Anti-Intellectualism in American Life
V-686 **HOFSTADTER, RICHARD AND MICHAEL WALLACE (eds.)** / American Violence
V-540 **HOFSTADTER, RICHARD AND CLARENCE VER STEEG** / Great Issues in American History, From Settlement to Revolution, 1584-1776
V-541 **HOFSTADTER, RICHARD (ed.)** / Great Issues in American History, From the Revolution to the Civil War, 1765-1865
V-542 **HOFSTADTER, RICHARD (ed.)** / Great Issues in American History, From Reconstruction to the Present Day, 1864-1964
V-385 **HOFSTADTER, RICHARD** / The Paranoid Style in American Politics and Other Essays
V-591 **HOFSTADTER, RICHARD** / The Progressive Historians
V-201 **HUGHES, H. STUART** / Consciousness and Society
V-241 **JACOBS, JANE** / Death & Life of Great American Cities
V-584 **JACOBS, JANE** / The Economy of Cities
V-433 **JACOBS, PAUL** / Prelude to Riot
V-459 **JACOBS, RAUL AND SAUL LANDAU WITH EVE PELL** / To Serve the Devil: Natives & Slaves Vol. I
V-460 **JACOBS, RAUL AND SAUL LANDAU WITH EVE PELL** / To Serve the Devil: Colonial & Sojourner Vol. II
V-2017 **JUDSON, HORACE FREEDLAND** / Heroin Addiction: What Americans Can Learn from the English Experience
V-790 **KAPLAN, CAROL AND LAWRENCE (eds.)** / Revolutions: A Comparative Study
V-361 **KOMAROVSKY, MIRRA** / Blue-Collar Marriage
V-675 **KOVEL, JOEL** / White Racism
V-367 **LASCH, CHRISTOPHER** / The New Radicalism in America
V-560 **LASCH, CHRISTOPHER** / The Agony of the American Left
V-280 **LEWIS, OSCAR** / The Children of Sanchez
V-421 **LEWIS, OSCAR** / La Vida
V-634 **LEWIS, OSCAR** / A Death in the Sanchez Family
V-533 **LOCKWOOK, LEE** / Castro's Cuba, Cuba's Fidel
V-406 **MARCUS, STEVEN** / Engels, Manchester, and the Working Class
V-480 **MARCUSE, HERBERT** / Soviet Marxism
V-2001 **MARX, KARL AND NICOLOUS, MARTIN (trans.)** / The Grundrisse: Foundations of the Critque of Political Economy
V-2002 **MARX, KARL AND FERNBACH, DAVID (ed.)** / Political Writings, Vol. I: The Revolution of 1848
V-2003 **MARX, KARL AND FERNBACH, DAVID (ed.)** / Political Writings, Vol. II: Surveys from Exile
V-2004 **MARX, KARL AND FERNBACH, DAVID (ed.)** / Political Writings, Vol. III: The First International and After
V-619 **McCONNELL, GRANT** / Private Power and American Democracy
V-386 **McPHERSON, JAMES** / The Negro's Civil War
V-928 **MEDVEDEV, ROY A.** / Let History Judge: The Origins and Consequences of Stalinism
V-816 **MEDVEDEV, ZHORES AND ROY** / A Question of Madness
V-112 **MEDVEDEV, ZHORES** / Ten Years After Ivan Denisovich
V-614 **MERMELSTEIN, DAVID (ed.)** / The Economic Crisis Reader
V-971 **MILTON, DAVID AND NANCY, SCHURMANN, FRANZ (eds.)** / The China Reader IV: Peoples China
V-93 **MITFORD, JESSICA** / Kind and Usual Punishment: The Prison Business
V-539 **MORGAN, ROBIN (ed.)** / Sisterhood is Powerful

V-389 **MOYNIHAN, DANIEL P.** / Coping: On the Practice of Government
V-107 **MYRDAL, GUNNAR** / Against the Stream: Critical Essays on Economics
V-730 **MYRDAL, GUNNAR** / Asian Drama: An Inquiry into the Poverty of Nations
V-170 **MYRDAL, GUNNAR** / The Challenge of World Poverty
V-793 **MYRDAL, JAN** / Report From a Chinese Village
V-708 **MYRDAL, JAN AND GUN KESSLE** / China: The Revolution Continued
V-337 **NIETZSCHE, FRIEDRICH** Beyond Good and Evil, Walter Kaufmann (trans.)
V-369 **NIETZSCHE, FRIEDRICH** / The Birth of Tragedy & The Case of Wagner, Walter Kaufmann (trans.)
V-401 **NIETZSCHE, FRIEDRICH** / On the Genealogy of Morals and Ecce Homo, Walter Kaufmann (ed.)
V-437 **NIETZSCHE, FRIEDRICH** / The Will to Power
V-985 **NIETZSCHE, FRIEDRICH** / The Gay Science
V-383 **PIVEN, FRANCES FOX AND RICHARD A. CLOWARD** / The Politics of Turmoil
V-743 **PIVEN, FRANCES FOX AND RICHARD A. CLOWARD** / Regulating the Poor
V-128 **PLATO** / The Republic
V-719 **REED, JOHN** / Ten Days That Shook the World
V-159 **REISCHAUER, EDWIN O.** / Toward the 21st Century: Education for a Changing World
V-622 **ROAZEN, PAUL** / Freud: Political and Social Thought
V-204 **ROTHSCHILD, EMMA** / Paradise Lost: The Decline of the Auto-Industrial Age
V-965 **SALE, KIRKPATRICK** / SDS
V-2067 **SAKHAROV, ANDREI D.** / My Country and the World
V-738 **SCHNEIR, MIRIAM (ed.)** / Feminism
V-971 **SCHURMANN, FRANZ AND DAVID AND NANCY MILTON (eds.)** / The China Reader IV: Peoples China
V-375 **SCHURMANN, FRANZ AND O. SCHELL (eds.)** / The China Reader I: Imperial China
V-376 **SCHURMANN, FRANZ AND O. SCHELL (eds.)** / The China Reader II: Republican China
V-377 **SCHURMANN, FRANZ AND O. SCHELL (eds.)** / The China Reader III: Communist China
V-940 **SENNETT, RICHARD AND JONATHAN COBB** / The Hidden Injuries of Class
V-405 **SERVICE, JOHN S. AND JOSEPH ESHERICK, (ed.)** / Lost Chance in China: The World War II Despatches of John S. Service
V-279 **SILBERMAN, CHARLES E.** / Crisis in Black and White
V-353 **SILBERMAN, CHARLES E.** / Crisis in the Classroom
V-850 **SILBERMAN, CHARLES E.** / The Open Classroom Reader
V-681 **SNOW, EDGAR** / Red China Today: The Other Side of the River
V-930 **SNOW, EDGAR** / The Long Revolution
V-388 **STAMPP, KENNETH** / The Era of Reconstruction 1865-1877
V-253 **STAMPP, KENNETH** / The Peculiar Institution
V-959 **STERN, PHILIP M.** / The Rape of the Taxpayer
V-908 **STONE, I. F.** / The Truman Era
V-231 **TANNENBAUM, FRANK** / Slave & Citizen: The Negro in the Americas
V-312 **TANNENBAUM, FRANK** / Ten Keys to Latin America
V-686 **WALLACE, MICHAEL AND RICHARD HOFSTADTER (eds.)** / American Violence: A Documentary History
V-483 **ZINN, HOWARD** / Disobedience and Democracy